THE CLASSIC THEATRE

Volume Two

THE CLASSIC THEATRE, Volume I, contains the following six Italian plays:

The Mandrake	Niccolò Machiavelli
Ruzzante Returns From The Wars	Angelo Beolco
The Three Cuckolds	Anonymous
The Servant Of Two Masters	Carlo Goldoni
Mirandolina	Carlo Goldoni
The King Stag	Carlo Gozzi

THE CLASSIC THEATRE, Volume III, contains the following six Spanish plays:

Celestina	Fernando de Rojas
The Siege of Numantia	Miguel de Cervantes
Fuente Ovejuna	Lope de Vega
The Trickster of Seville	Tirso de Molina
Love After Death	Calderón de la Barca
Life Is a Dream	Calderón de la Barca

THE CLASSIC THEATRE, Volume IV, contains the following six French plays:

The Cid	Pierre Corneille
The Misanthrope	Molière
Phaedra	Jean Racine
Turcaret	Alain-René Lesage
The False Confessions	Pierre de Marivaux
Figaro's Marriage	Beaumarchais

THE MODERN THEATRE, Volumes I, II, III, IV, V, and VI, edited by Eric Bentley, are also available in the Anchor series.

THE
CLASSIC THEATRE

Volume Two

FIVE GERMAN PLAYS

Edited by Eric Bentley

DOUBLEDAY ANCHOR BOOKS
DOUBLEDAY & COMPANY, INC.
GARDEN CITY, NEW YORK

Cover design by Leonard Baskin. Portraits of Goethe and Schiller on the cover are by Tischbein and Jagemann respectively, courtesy of the Bettmann Archive. Typography by Edward Gorey.

•

Library of Congress Catalog Card Number 58–12033

CONTENTS

CONTENTS

EGMONT

A TRAGEDY

Johann Wolfgang von Goethe

(1788)

English Version by Michael Hamburger

CHARACTERS

MARGARET OF PARMA, *daughter of Charles V and Regent of the Netherlands*

COUNT EGMONT, *Prince of Gavre*

WILLIAM OF ORANGE

DUKE OF ALBA

FERDINAND, *his natural son*

MACHIAVELLI, *in the Regent's service*

RICHARD, *Egmont's private secretary*

SILVA
GOMEZ } *in Alba's service*

CLARE, *Egmont's mistress*

HER MOTHER

BRACKENBURG, *a burgess*

SOEST, *grocer*
JETTER, *tailor*
CARPENTER } *citizens of Brussels*
SOAPBOILER

BUYCK, *soldier under Egmont*

RUYSUM, *invalid and deaf*

VANSEN, *a clerk*

People, attendants, guards, etc.

The scene is Brussels.
The year is 1568.

ACT I

Crossbow Target Shooting

SOLDIERS *and* CITIZENS *with crossbows*

JETTER, *citizen of Brussels, a tailor, steps forward and prepares to shoot.*

SOEST, *citizen of Brussels, a grocer.*

SOEST. Well, go ahead and shoot so there'll be an end to it. You won't beat me, anyway. Three in the black is more than you ever got in all your life. That means I'm champion for the year.

JETTER. Champion, indeed, and king as well. Who would begrudge you the honour? But you'll have to pay for two rounds; you'll have to pay for your skill as every champion does.

BUYCK, *a Dutchman, soldier serving under* EGMONT.

BUYCK. Jetter, I'll buy those shots off you, share the prize, pay for the gentlemen's drinks: I've been here so very long and feel indebted to them for so much courtesy. If I miss, the turn shall count as yours.

SOEST. I should really protest, for your bargain makes *me* the loser. But never mind, Buyck, shoot ahead.

BUYCK *shoots.* Well, here goes— One, two, three, four.

SOEST. What, four in the black? You're the winner, then.

ALL. Three cheers for the king. Hip, hip, hurray, hurray, hurray.

BUYCK. Thank you, gentlemen. But even "Champion" would be too much. Thank you for the honour.

JETTER. You've yourself to thank for it.

RUYSUM, *a Frisian, invalid and deaf.*

RUYSUM. Let me tell you!

SOEST. Tell us what, old man?

RUYSUM. Let me tell you: he shoots like his master, like Egmont.

BUYCK. Compared to him I'm only a poor bungler. You should see him on the musket range; he hits the mark like no one else in the world. I don't mean when he's lucky or in the right mood. No: every time, he's no sooner taken aim than he's got the bull's-eye. It's he who taught me. I'd like to see the fellow who's served with him and not learnt anything from him! But I haven't forgotten, gentlemen. A king looks after his people; so let's have some wine, at the king's expense.

JETTER. It was agreed between us that each of us——

BUYCK. I'm a stranger here, and king, and I pay no attention to your laws and customs.

JETTER. Why, you're worse than the Spaniards; they've had to leave our laws and customs alone, till now, anyway.

RUYSUM. What do you say?

SOEST, *loudly.* He wants to stand all the drinks; he doesn't want us to put our money together and let the king only pay double.

RUYSUM. Let him, then. But no offence. That's his master's way too—to be lavish and never leave money to burn a hole in his pocket.

They bring wine.

ALL. Good health, your Majesty, and a prosperous life!

JETTER, *to* BUYCK. That's right: your Majesty. You deserve the honour.

BUYCK. Well, if it must be, thank you with all my heart.

SOEST. It must be; for no true citizen of the Low Countries will easily drink the health of our Spanish Majesty—not with all his heart.

RUYSUM. Whose health, did you say?

SOEST, *loudly.* Philip the Second, King of Spain.

RUYSUM. Our most gracious King and Lord! May God grant him a long reign.

SOEST. Didn't you prefer his father of blessèd memory, Charles the Fifth?

RUYSUM. God have mercy on his soul. He was a great gentleman. He had the whole earth to take care of, but he was a
father and brother to us all. And if he met you in the street,
he greeted you as one neighbour greets another, and if that
gave you a start, he was gracious enough to—— Don't misunderstand me. I mean: he went out, rode out just as the
fancy took him, with only a few men. There wasn't a dry
eye to be seen when he abdicated and made his son governor of these parts. Don't misunderstand me, I say. But
Philip's different, you'll admit; more majestic, if you like.

JETTER. No man ever saw him, when he was here, but in
royal pomp and ceremony. He doesn't talk much, people
say.

SOEST. He's not the man for us of the Low Countries. Our
princes must be light-hearted like ourselves, live and let live.
We won't be despised or pressed, good-natured fools though
we are.

JETTER. The King would be gracious enough, I think, if only
he had better advisers.

SOEST. No. Never. He doesn't take to our sort, he has no
sympathy for us, he doesn't love us. How, then, can we love
him in our turn? Why is every single one of us so fond of
Count Egmont? Why would we gladly carry him about on
our hands? Because you can see that he wishes us well; because you can read his cheerfulness, the free life he lives,
the good opinion he has of us, in his eyes; because he
hasn't a single possession that he wouldn't give away to a
needy man, even to a man who didn't need it. Let's drink to
Count Egmont! Buyck, it's your privilege to propose the first
toast. Propose the health of your master!

BUYCK. With the greatest pleasure: Count Egmont.

RUYSUM. Victor at St. Quentin!

BUYCK. To the hero of Gravelingen!

ALL. To his health!

RUYSUM. St. Quentin was my last battle. I could hardly move
another inch, hardly drag my heavy musket any further.
And yet! I gave the Frenchman one last thing to remember

me by, and got something too, though it only grazed my right leg.

BUYCK. But Gravelingen, friends, that was a pretty lively affair. There victory was ours alone. Hadn't those French dogs been burning and laying waste the whole length and breadth of Flanders? But, there's no doubt about it, we gave them what they deserved. Their old, tried soldiers held out for a long time, but we pressed and shot and slashed at them till they pulled faces and their lines began to give way. Then Egmont's horse was shot away from under him, and there was a long uncertain struggle, man to man, horse against horse, troop against troop, on the broad flat sand of the seashore. Then suddenly it came as if down from heaven, from the river mouth—the "bow, bow" of the big cannons firing right into the midst of the French. It was the English, who just happened to be passing on their way from Dunkirk under Admiral Malin. They didn't help us much, it's true; they could only get in with their smallest ships, and not close enough at that; and sometimes they shot at us by mistake. But it did us good, all the same. It broke the Frenchmen's spirit and gave us new courage. So now we made short work of them. Killed the whole lot or drove them into the water. And those fellows drowned as soon as they tasted water. As for us Dutchmen, we went in after them. Amphibians that we are, we didn't feel happy till we were in the water, like frogs, and we just went on fighting the enemy in the river, shot them down as if they were ducks. The few that got away after that—well, the peasant women saw to them: beat them down as they ran with pitchforks and pickaxes. So his French Majesty had no choice but to come to heel and make peace. So it's to us you owe that peace, to our great Egmont!

ALL. To our great Egmont! And again! And again! And yet again!

JETTER. If only he'd been appointed our Regent in Margaret of Parma's place!

SOEST. No, that's going too far. Honour where honour is due. I won't hear Margaret's name abused. Now it's my turn. Long live our gracious lady!

ALL. Long live Margaret!

SOEST. It's true, there's no denying the excellence of the women in the ruling house. Long live the Regent!

JETTER. She's clever and moderate in everything she does. If only she didn't stick to the parsons through thick and thin. It's partly her fault that we have those fourteen new bishoprics in our country. What can they be for? Only to push a lot of strangers into the best positions, where they used to put abbots elected by the chapter. And they want us to believe it's all for religion's sake. That's the root of the trouble. Three bishops were enough for us; honesty and decency were the rule in those days. Now everyone has to pretend that they're really necessary, and so there's no end to the trouble and bickering. And the more you look into the thing, the more murky it seems.

They drink.

SOEST. That was simply the King's will; she can do nothing about it either way.

JETTER. And now they tell us we mustn't sing those new psalms. And yet they're beautifully versified, and their tunes couldn't be more uplifting. We mustn't sing those, but as many profane and scurrilous ditties as we please. Why, do you think? They say those psalms contain heresies and goodness knows what else. And yet I've sung them before now and I couldn't see anything bad in them. It's a new idea.

BUYCK. I shouldn't dream of asking their permission. In our province we sing what we like. That's because Count Egmont is our governor; he doesn't interfere with things of that kind—in Ghent, in Ypres, in the whole of Flanders, whoever wants to, sings them.

Loudly.

Surely there's nothing more innocent than a spiritual song? Isn't that so, Father?

RUYSUM. Indeed. For it's a form of devotion and it purifies the heart.

JETTER. But they say it doesn't do so in the right way—not in *their* way. And it's always dangerous, so one leaves it alone. The servants of the Inquisition creep and snoop about everywhere. Many an honest man has come to grief already. To suppress our freedom of conscience—that was the last straw. If I can't do what I please, they might at least let me think and sing what I please.

SOEST. The Inquisition won't get the better of us. We're not like the Spaniards and will never let anyone tyrannize over our conscience. And the nobility too will have to start resisting it soon.

JETTER. We're in a very awkward position. If those fine people take it into their heads to come rushing into my house, and I'm sitting down, doing my work, and just happen to be humming a French psalm, without a thought in my head, whether virtuous or wicked, but I simply hum it because the tune is there inside me—well, that makes me a heretic, and they put me in jail. Or I'm out for a walk and stop when I see a crowd of people listening to some new preacher —one of those who've come from Germany—that makes me a rebel, no less, and they'll chop off my head as likely as not. Have you ever heard one of them preach?

SOEST. Very fine preachers, if you ask me. The other day I heard one speak to thousands and thousands of people. That was a different kettle of fish—not like ours, always beating about the bush, stuffing Latin tags down the people's throats. That one made no bones about it. He told us straight how they've been leading us by the nose till now, keeping us ignorant, and how we could have more light for the asking. And he proved it all from the Bible.

JETTER. I'm sure there is something in that. I've often said so myself and pondered on those matters. It's been troubling my head for a long time.

BUYCK. I suppose that's why they're so popular.

SOEST. And no wonder. Who wouldn't go to hear something that's good and new?

JETTER. What's the matter, then? Why can't any man be allowed to preach in his own way?

BUYCK. Drink up, gentlemen. All this chatter is making you forget your wine—and William of Orange too.

JETTER. Oh, we mustn't forget him. He's a real tower of strength: you've only to think of him to feel that you can hide behind him, and the devil himself wouldn't be able to get you out. To William of Orange, then!

ALL. To his health!

SOEST. Now, old man, propose your own health too!

RUYSUM. Old soldiers! All soldiers! Long live war!

BUYCK. Well said, old man. All soldiers! Long live war!

JETTER. War, war! Do you know what you're saying? That word comes to you easily enough, and I suppose that's natural, but I can't tell you how wretched it sounds to those of my kind. To hear nothing but drumbeats the whole year round; and hear nothing but one troop marching in here, another there; how they came over a hill and stopped by a windmill, how many were left there, how many in another place, and how they fight, and how one wins, the other loses, though for the life of me I can't understand who's won anything, who's lost. How a town is captured, the citizens murdered, and what becomes of the poor women, the innocent children. Affliction and terror, that's what it means to us, and every moment one thinks: "Look, they're coming! And they'll do the same to us."

SOEST. That's why a citizen too should always be trained to use arms.

JETTER. Yes, whoever has a wife and children learns to defend them. But I'd still rather hear about soldiers than see them.

BUYCK. I should take offence at that remark.

JETTER. It isn't aimed at you, friend. We were all relieved when we'd got rid of the Spanish occupation forces.

SOEST. Yes, indeed. You found those most irksome of all, didn't you?

JETTER. Don't try to make a fool of me.

SOEST. They were sorry to leave your house.

JETTER. Shut your mouth.

SOEST. They'd driven him out of his kitchen, his cellar, his sitting-room—and his bed.

Laughter.

JETTER. You're a fool.

BUYCK. Peace, gentlemen! Do you need a soldier to make peace between you? Well, since you don't want to have anything to do with our sort, you'd better propose a toast to yourselves, a civil toast.

JETTER. That we'll do gladly. Security and quiet!

SOEST. Order and freedom!

BUYCK. Bravo! That suits us too.

They chink glasses and cheerfully repeat these words, but in such a way that each calls out a different word and a kind of canon results. The old man listens and finally joins in also.

ALL. Security and quiet! Order and freedom!

The Regent's Palace

MARGARET OF PARMA *in hunting attire. Courtiers. Pages. Servants*

REGENT. You will cancel the hunt; I shall not ride today. Tell Machiavelli to come to me.

Exeunt all.

The thought of these terrible happenings gives me no peace. Nothing pleases me, nothing distracts me; always these misgivings, these cares torment me. The King will say that these are the fruits of my kindness, my consideration; and yet my conscience tells me that at every moment I did what was most advisable, that my only purpose was to do the right thing at the right time. Should I, then, have fanned these flames even sooner and made them spread, by exposing them to a tempest of wrath? It was my hope to set limits to their progress and stifle them by driving them back upon themselves. I know that this is the truth and by reminding myself of it I can absolve myself from all self-reproach. But how will my brother receive the news? For there is no denying it: the insolence of the new preachers has been growing daily. They have blasphemed against our most sacred tenets, subverted the dull minds of the common people, and released the spirit of confusion in their midst. Arrant rogues have joined the ranks of the insurgents and caused dreadful atrocities to be committed. Only to think of them makes me shudder, and now I must report them one by one to the Court, one by one and speedily, so that the general rumour will not forestall our account, so that the King will not suspect us of trying to conceal the rest. I can see no means, whether stern or gentle, of opposing this evil. Oh, what are the great, we the crests on the surge of humanity? We think that we rule its fury, but it bears us up and down, to and fro.

Enter MACHIAVELLI.

REGENT. Have those letters to the King been drafted?

MACHIAVELLI. They will be ready for your signature in an hour's time.

REGENT. Have you made the report sufficiently detailed?

MACHIAVELLI. Detailed and elaborate, as the King likes them to be. I recount how the iconoclastic fury first broke out at St. Omer. How a raging mob, furnished with staves, axes, hammers, ladders, and ropes, accompanied by a few armed men, began by attacking chapels, churches, and monasteries, driving out the worshippers, breaking open the doors, throwing everything into disorder, tearing down the altars, breaking the statues of saints, destroying every painting, shattering, ripping up, stamping to pieces every consecrated and holy thing they could lay hands upon. How this rabble grew in numbers as it proceeded, how the inhabitants of Ypres opened the gates to them. How they laid waste the cathedral there with incredible speed, how they burnt the bishop's library. How a great mob of common folk, seized with the same frenzy, poured into Menin, Comines, Verwich, Lille, encountered no resistance anywhere, and how, in the twinkling of an eye, the conspiracy declared itself and struck almost throughout the whole of Flanders.

REGENT. Oh, the repetition of it renews my pain. And now there is the added fear that the evil will only grow and grow. Tell me what you think, Machiavelli?

MACHIAVELLI. Forgive me, your Highness, if my thoughts are more like whims; and though you have always been satisfied with my services, you have rarely chosen to take my advice. Often you have said in jest: "You're too farsighted, Machiavelli! You should be a historian: the man who acts should keep his eyes on what is nearest to him." And yet, didn't I predict this whole story? Did I not foresee it all?

REGENT. I too foresee a great deal without having the power to forestall it.

MACHIAVELLI. Briefly, then, and to the point: you will not suppress the new doctrine. Let them have their way but separate them from the orthodox. Give them churches, integrate them in the framework of society, restrict their influence: then you will have silenced the rebels at a single stroke. Every other measure will be in vain, and you will lay waste the country.

REGENT. Have you forgotten with what repugnance my brother condemned the very suggestion that the new doctrine might be tolerated? Don't you know how in every letter he reminds me most emphatically of my duty to maintain the true faith? That he will not hear of a peace and a unity established at the expense of religion? Even in the Provinces does he not keep spies unknown to us, so as to observe who is likely to go over to the new creed? Did he not amaze us by naming more than one person close to us who has become guilty of heresy, though in secret? Does he not command us to practise severity and ruthless justice? And you want me to be merciful? To make proposals to him that call on him to be considerate and tolerant? Should I not lose all his confidence, all his trust?

MACHIAVELLI. Well I know it; the King gives orders, he lets you know his intentions. You are to establish peace and quiet once more by a measure that will only increase the general embitterment, that will inevitably fan the fires of war from every direction. Consider what you are doing. The most powerful merchants have been infected, the nobility, the people, the soldiers. What is the use of adhering to his ideas, when everything around us is changing? If only some benevolent spirit would make it clear to Philip that it is more fitting for a king to rule citizens of two different creeds than to incite one party against the other.

REGENT. I forbid you to speak in that way. I know very well that in politics one can rarely keep faith or troth, but must ban frankness, kindness, and indulgence from one's heart. In worldly affairs that is only too true, but are we to toy with God, as we toy with one another? Are we to be indifferent to our proven doctrine, for which so many have offered up their lives? Should we yield even that to an upstart, uncertain, and self-contradictory fad?

MACHIAVELLI. Please don't think ill of me on that account.

REGENT. I know you to be a loyal servant, and I know that a man can be honest and prudent even though he has missed the nearest, straightest way to his soul's salvation. You are not the only one, Machiavelli, not the only man whom I must both respect and reproach.

MACHIAVELLI. To whom are you alluding?

REGENT. I will confess to you that Egmont aroused my deep and acute displeasure today.

MACHIAVELLI. By what kind of conduct?

REGENT. By his usual conduct, by his nonchalance and recklessness. I received the terrible news just as I was coming out of church in his and many others' company. I could not contain my grief, voiced my complaint and, turning to him, cried out: "Look what is happening in your province! And you put up with it, Count, you of whom the King expected so much?"

MACHIAVELLI. And what did he reply?

REGENT. As if it were nothing, a mere irrelevance, he retorted: "If only the people of the Netherlands were assured that the Constitution is safe, the rest could easily be settled."

MACHIAVELLI. Perhaps he spoke with more truth than prudence or piety. How can confidence be established and preserved when the people of the Netherlands see that we are more concerned with their possessions than with their wellbeing or the good of their souls? Have the new bishops saved more souls than they've swallowed rich benefices, and are not most of them foreigners? Still all the town governorships are held by Netherlanders: do the Spaniards trouble to conceal their irresistible covetousness for these places? Does not a people prefer to be ruled by its own kind, in its own fashion, rather than by strangers who begin by endeavouring to acquire property in the country at everyone's expense, who apply strange standards, and who rule harshly and without sympathy?

REGENT. You are placing yourself on the opposing side.

MACHIAVELLI. Not in my heart, certainly, and I wish that my head could be wholly on ours.

REGENT. If that is your view, it would be necessary for me to abdicate from the Regency; for Egmont and Orange once lived in high hopes of occupying that place. At that time they were rivals; now they are in league against me and have become friends, inseparable friends.

MACHIAVELLI. A dangerous couple!

REGENT. To be frank, I fear Orange, and I fear for Egmont. Orange is up to no good, his thoughts reach out to the distant future, he is secretive, seems to accept everything, never contradicts, and with the deepest reverence, with the greatest caution, he does what he pleases.

MACHIAVELLI. Quite the contrary of Egmont, who walks about as freely as if the world belonged to him.

REGENT. He wears his head as high as if the hand of Majesty were not suspended over it.

MACHIAVELLI. The people's eyes are all fixed on him, and all their hearts.

REGENT. He has never troubled about appearances—as if there were no one to call him to account. Still he bears the name of Egmont; is glad to hear himself called "Count Egmont," as if loath to forget that his ancestors were the lords of Gelden. Why doesn't he call himself Prince of Gavre, as he is entitled to? Why does he do it? Does he want to re-establish obsolete rights?

MACHIAVELLI. I look upon him as a loyal servant of the King.

REGENT. If he only wanted to, what indispensable services he could render the Government, instead of causing us endless annoyance without any profit to himself, as he's already done! His receptions, banquets, and carousals have done more to unify the nobility than the most dangerous secret conferences. From his toasts the guests have drawn a lasting intoxication, a chronic giddiness. How often his jests and jibes have stirred up the people's minds, and how the populace gaped at his new liveries, at the foolish badges of his servants!

MACHIAVELLI. I'm sure this was not his intention.

REGENT. So much the worse for us all. As I was saying: he harms us and does himself no good. He turns serious things into a joke, and we, so as not to appear idle and careless, must take his jokes seriously. So one worries the other, and what we try to avert is all the more certain to occur. He is more dangerous than the declared head of a conspiracy, and I should be very much surprised if at Court they don't keep a record of all his misdeeds. There's no denying it: hardly a week passes without his causing me grave discomfort, the very gravest discomfort.

MACHIAVELLI. It seems to me that in all things he acts according to his conscience.

REGENT. His conscience has a flattering mirror; his conduct is often offensive. Often he looks as if he were firmly convinced that he is really our master, though out of kindness he's obliging enough not to make us feel it, to refrain from simply driving us out of the country—with the assumption that we'll go in any case, all in good time.

MACHIAVELLI. I beg of you, don't put such a dangerous construction upon his frankness, his happy disposition, that takes important things lightly. You will only harm him and yourself.

REGENT. I put no construction on anything. I am merely speaking of the inevitable consequences and I know him well. His Netherlandish nobility and the Order of the Golden Fleece strengthen his confidence, his boldness. Both can guard him against the King's sudden, arbitrary displeasure. Just examine the matter precisely and you must agree that he alone is responsible for all the misfortunes that have descended on Flanders. He was the first to tolerate the new teachers, easy-going as he is, and perhaps secretly pleased that they gave us something to reckon with. No, don't interrupt me: I am taking the opportunity to tell you all that is on my mind. And I don't wish to discharge my arrows in vain; I know where he is vulnerable. Yes, Egmont too is vulnerable.

MACHIAVELLI. Have you summoned the Council? Is Orange coming too?

REGENT. I've sent to Antwerp for him. I propose to move the burden of responsibility very close to them; they must join me in seriously resisting the evil or else declare themselves rebels. Lose no time in finishing the letters and bring them to me for signature! Then quickly send off the experienced Vasca to Madrid—he is indefatigable and loyal—so that he shall be the first to convey the news to my brother, so that the rumour will not precede him. I will speak to him myself before he leaves.

MACHIAVELLI. Your commands will be executed both speedily and exactly.

Citizen's House

CLARE, CLARE'S MOTHER, BRACKENBURG

CLARE. Won't you hold the thread for me, Brackenburg?

BRACKENBURG. I beg you to spare me, my dear.

CLARE. What's the matter with you to-night? Why do you refuse me this little attention?

BRACKENBURG. Your thread keeps me so spell-bound that I can't avoid your eyes.

CLARE. Nonsense! Come and hold it!

MOTHER, *knitting in her arm-chair*. Why don't you sing? Brackenburg makes such a good second. You used to be so cheerful, both of you, and I never stopped laughing at your pranks.

BRACKENBURG. We used to be.

CLARE. Let's sing, then.

BRACKENBURG. Whatever you wish.

CLARE. Well, then, sing up; and make it lively. It's a military song and my favourite.

She winds the thread and sings with BRACKENBURG.

> Strike up! To your drumming!
> And blow the fife loud.
> My sweetheart in armour
> Commands the whole crowd.
> His lance held aloft rules
> Their going and coming.
> Now faster my blood flows
> My heart goes pit-pat.
> O, would I wore doublet
> And breeches and hat!
>
> Then marching I'd follow
> Him out through the gate
> And roam with him fighting
> Through province and state.
> Our enemy's fleeing.
> We shoot them as they run!
> There's nothing like being
> A man with a gun!

As they sing BRACKENBURG *looks at* CLARE *repeatedly; at the end his voice fails him, tears come into his eyes, he drops the thread, and goes to the window.* CLARE *finishes the song by herself, her mother signals to her half-angrily,* CLARE *rises, takes a few steps towards him, turns back irresolutely, and sits down.*

MOTHER. What's going on outside, Brackenburg? I hear the sound of marching.

BRACKENBURG. It's the Regent's Life Guards.

CLARE. At this hour? What's the meaning of that?

She gets up and goes to the window with BRACKENBURG.

That's not the ordinary guard, there are many more of them, nearly the whole regiment. Oh, Brackenburg, do go and find out what's happening. It must be something special. Please go, my dear. Do me this favour!

BRACKENBURG. I'm going. I shall be with you again in a moment.

He holds out his hand to her as he leaves; she clasps it.

MOTHER. There you go again, sending him off!

CLARE. I'm curious; and besides—don't be angry with me—his presence pains me. I never know how to behave towards him. I'm in the wrong where he's concerned, and it grieves me to see him suffer so much because of it. When there's nothing I can do about it.

MOTHER. He's such a loyal fellow.

CLARE. That's why I can't help being kind to him. Often my hand seems to close of its own accord when his hand touches me in that tender, loving way. I reproach myself for deceiving him, for keeping a vain hope alive in his heart. I'm in a terrible quandary. God knows I'm not deceiving him. I don't want him to hope and yet I can't let him despair.

MOTHER. That's not right of you.

CLARE. I used to be fond of him and still wish him well with all my soul. I could have married him, and yet I think I was never in love with him.

MOTHER. But you would have been happy with him if you had.

CLARE. I'd have been well provided for and led a quiet life.

MOTHER. And you've lost all that through your own fault.

CLARE. I'm in a very strange position. When I ask myself how it came about, I know the answer and I don't know it. And then I've only to look at Egmont again to understand everything that's happened—and *more* than what's happened. What a man! All the Provinces idolize him; so how could I help being the happiest creature in the world when he holds me in his arms?

MOTHER. But what will become of us? What of the future?

CLARE. Oh, all I ask is whether he loves me; and would you call that a question?

MOTHER. Distress and anxiety, that's all one gets from one's children. How will it end, I ask you? Worry and grief all the time. No good will come of it. You've made yourself unhappy and made me unhappy.

CLARE, *nonchalantly.* You raised no objection at first.

MOTHER. Unfortunately not. I was too kind, too easy-going. I always am.

CLARE. When Egmont rode past and I went to the window, did you tell me off? Didn't you go to the window too? When he looked up, smiled, nodded, and called to me: did you mind? Didn't you feel that he honoured you by honouring your daughter?

MOTHER. Now you're reproaching me!

CLARE, *moved.* And then when he came more often to our street and it was clear to us that he came this way because of me, weren't you pleased in secret? Did you call me away when I stood behind the panes, waiting for him?

MOTHER. Could I know that it would go so far?

CLARE, *in a halting voice, restraining her tears.* And when he surprised us in the evening, wrapped in his cloak, and we were working by lamplight, who was it that hurried to receive him, since I remained seated, amazed, and glued to the chair?

MOTHER. And had I any reason to fear that this unhappy love would knock my clever little Clare off her feet and so quickly too? Now I have to accept the fact that my daughter——

CLARE, *breaking into tears.* Mother! There's no need to put it like that. Anyone would think you enjoy frightening me.

MOTHER, *weeping.* Yes, go on and cry on top of everything! Make me even more miserable by being sad! Isn't it bad enough that my only daughter is a fallen creature?

CLARE, *rising coldly.* Fallen? Egmont's mistress a fallen creature? There isn't a duchess who wouldn't envy little Clare her place in his heart. Oh, Mother, you've never used such words till now. Be patient with me, dear. . . . Leave other people to think *that* of me, leave the neighbours to whisper what they please. This room, this little house have been heaven to me since Egmont's love first crossed the threshold.

MOTHER. Well, it's true one can't help liking him. He's always so amiable and frank and easy.

CLARE. There's no strain of falsehood in him at all. And yet, Mother, he's the great Egmont. And when he comes to see me, he's all kindness and goodness. Why he even does his best to conceal his rank and his courage, he's so concerned about me. Here he's simply a man, a friend, and my dearest love.

MOTHER. Do you think he will come to-day?

CLARE. Didn't you notice how often I've been to the window? Didn't you notice how I listen when there's a noise at the door? Though I know that he won't come before nightfall, I still expect him every moment from the instant I get up in the morning. If only I were a boy and could go about with him all the time, to Court and everywhere! If only I could carry his standard for him in battle!

MOTHER. You've always been a sort of tomboy, even when you were a small child, now wild, now pensive. Don't you think you should put on something a little better?

CLARE. Maybe, Mother—if I feel bored. You know, yesterday some of his men passed by, singing songs in his praise. At least his name was part of the songs; I couldn't catch the rest. I could feel my heartbeats right up in my throat. I should have liked to call them back, if I hadn't been afraid of drawing attention to myself.

MOTHER. You be careful! Or your impulsive nature will spoil everything. You'll give yourself away. Just as you did the other day at your cousin's, when you found that woodcut and the inscription and exclaimed with a cry: "Count Egmont!" I turned crimson with shame.

CLARE. How could I not cry out? It was the battle of Gravelingen, and I found the letter C at the top of the picture, so I looked for C in the description. There I read: "Count Egmont, when his horse was shot dead under him." I felt my blood rise—and later I had to laugh at the woodcut Egmont, who was as tall as the tower of Gravelingen just next to him and the English ships on one side. What a strange idea I used to have of what a battle is like and what Count Egmont himself is like, when I was a girl, when they told stories about him, and of every Count and Duke—and how different they all seem now!

Re-enter BRACKENBURG.

CLARE. What's happening?

BRACKENBURG. No one is sure. They say that a new riot has broken out in Flanders, that the Regent is afraid it may spread to our parts. The Palace Guard has been strongly reinforced, there are crowds of citizens at the gates, the streets are full of people. . . . I think I should call on my old father.

As if about to leave.

CLARE. Shall we see you to-morrow? I'm just going to dress. We're expecting my cousin, and I look too slovenly for words. Will you help me, Mother? Take that book, Brackenburg, and bring me another of those histories!

MOTHER. Good-bye.

BRACKENBURG, *holding out his hand.* Won't you give me your hand?

CLARE, *refusing the hand.* When you come again.

Exeunt mother and daughter.

BRACKENBURG, *alone.* I had intended to leave at once, and now that she accepts the gesture and lets me go, I can hardly bear it. Oh, what a wretch I am! Not even moved by the fate of my country, the growing unrest. My own kind or the Spaniards, it's all the same to me, who's in power and who's in the right. How very different I was when I was a schoolboy! When they set us a piece called "Brutus's Speech on Liberty, an Exercise in Oratory," it was always Fritz who came first, and the headmaster said: "If only it were more tidy, not such a jumble of enthusiasms." I was all drive and ferment then! Now I drag myself along, hanging on that girl's eyes. Since I can't leave her alone, and she can't love me. Oh, she can't have rejected me entirely—can't have, yes or no, but half her love is no love. I'll not put up with it a moment longer! . . . Could it be true, then, what a friend whispered in my ear the other day? That she secretly receives a man at night, since she always drives me out so respectably before the evening? No, it's not true, it's a lie, a shameful, slanderous lie! Clare is as innocent as I'm unhappy. She's rejected me, cast me out of her heart. And can I go on like that? I'll not put up with it. . . . Already my country is divided against itself—more violently each day— and I simply languish away in the midst of all that turmoil!

No, I'll not put up with it. When the bugle sounds, when a shot rings out it pierces me to the marrow. Yet it doesn't provoke me, doesn't challenge me to enter the fray, to save and dare with the rest. . . . Oh, wretched, despicable state. Better to put an end to it once and for all. Already once I threw myself into the water and sank—but my terrified nature was stronger. I felt that I could swim and reluctantly saved myself. . . . If only I could forget the time when she loved me or seemed to love me! . . . Why did that happiness pervade every bone of my body? Why have these hopes deprived me of all pleasure in life by showing me a paradise from afar? And that first kiss, the only one! Here

Resting his head on the table.

at this very place we were alone together—she had always been kind and pleasant to me—then she seemed to soften, she looked at me, all my senses were in a whirl, and I felt her lips on mine. And now? There's only death. Why do I hesitate?

He takes a small bottle out of his pocket.

This time it must not be in vain; not in vain that I stole this poison out of my brother's medicine chest. It shall rid me once and for all of this anguish, this uncertainty, this fever worse than death.

ACT II

Square in Brussels

JETTER *and a* CARPENTER *meet.*

CARPENTER. Didn't I predict it? Only a week ago, at the Guild meeting, I said there would be serious clashes.

JETTER. Is it true, then, that they've robbed the churches in Flanders?

CARPENTER. Plundered them, ruined them completely, both churches and chapels. Left nothing but the four bare walls. A lot of hooligans, every one of them. And that put a bad face on our good cause. We should rather have pleaded our just cause to the Regent in an orderly and firm manner and insisted on it. If we make speeches now or meet, they accuse us of joining the rebels.

JETTER. Yes. And so everyone thinks: why should I stick out my face—since my neck is all too close to it?

CARPENTER. I feel very uncomfortable, now that this turmoil has taken possession of the mob, the people who have nothing to lose. They make a mere pretext of what we too profess and will plunge our country into misfortune.

SOEST *joins them.*

SOEST. Good morning, gentlemen. What's the news? Is it true that the iconoclasts are on their way here?

CARPENTER. They'd better keep their hands off here.

SOEST. A soldier came into my shop to buy tobacco. I questioned him. The Regent, clever, brave woman though she remains, has lost her head this time. Things must be very bad for her to hide like this behind her Guard. The Palace Guard has been heavily reinforced. It's even rumoured that she intends to flee from the town.

CARPENTER. She mustn't leave. Her presence protects us, and we shall give her more security than her clipped beards.

And if she maintains our rights and liberties, we shall chair her.

SOAPBOILER *joins them.*

SOAPBOILER. A nasty, filthy roughhouse! There's more and more trouble, and it will come to a bad end. . . . Be careful, now, and keep quiet, so that they won't take you for rebel agents.

SOEST. Look! There are the seven sages from Greece!

SOAPBOILER. I know there are many who secretly support the Calvinists, slander the bishops, and have no respect for the King. But a loyal subject, a true Catholic——

One by one various people join them, listening. VANSEN *joins them.*

VANSEN. Greetings, gentlemen! What's been happening?

CARPENTER. Have nothing to do with that one. He's a scoundrel.

JETTER. Isn't he Dr. Wiet's clerk?

CARPENTER. He's had a good many masters. First he was a clerk and, when one employer after another had kicked him out for his knaveries, he began to botch the briefs of solicitors and barristers, and he's too fond of the brandy bottle.

More and more people gather and stand about in groups.

VANSEN. Why, you've got quite a crowd collected here and, what's more, you're putting your heads together. Quite an interesting occasion.

SOEST. I think so too.

VANSEN. Now, if one or the other of you had the heart, and one or the other had the head as well, we could break the Spanish chains with one blow.

SOEST. Sir, you must not speak like that! We have sworn loyalty to the King.

VANSEN. And the King to us! Don't forget that!

JETTER. Very true! Tell us your views!

SOME OTHERS. Listen to him! He knows what he's talking about.

VANSEN. I had an old employer once, who owned documents and letters about the most ancient decrees, contracts, and laws. He collected the rarest books. In one of them our whole constitution was set out: how we Netherlanders were ruled at first by single princes, all according to traditional rights, privileges, and customs; how our ancestors had every kind of respect for their Prince, as long as he ruled them as he must; and how they sat up as soon as he looked like being too big for his boots. Our deputies were after him at once; for every Province, however small, had its parliament and deputies.

CARPENTER. Shut your mouth! We've known all that for a long time. Every decent citizen knows as much about the constitution as he needs to know.

JETTER. Let him speak; there's always something new to be learnt.

SOEST. He's quite right.

SEVERAL OTHERS. Go on, tell us more. We don't hear that kind of thing every day.

VANSEN. That's what you're like, citizens. You just drift along from day to day and, just as you took over your trades from your parents, you let the government rule you as it pleases. You ask no questions about tradition, about history, about the rights of a Regent; and because you have failed in that, the Spaniards have pulled tight the net right over your heads.

SOEST. Who worries about that? If only a man has enough to eat.

JETTER. Damnation! Why didn't somebody get up in time and tell us these things?

VANSEN. I'm telling you now. The King in Spain, who happens to own all our provinces, has no right, all the same, to rule them any differently from the little princes who once owned them separately. Do you understand that?

JETTER. Explain it to us.

VANSEN. It's as clear as daylight. Should you not be judged according to the laws of your country? How could it be otherwise?

A CITIZEN. True enough!

VANSEN. Hasn't the citizen of Brussels other laws than the citizen of Antwerp? And the citizen of Antwerp than the citizen of Ghent? How could it be otherwise?

OTHER CITIZENS. By God, it's true.

VANSEN. But if you let things go on as they are, they'll soon show you a very different picture. Shame on it! What Charles the Bold, Frederick the Warrior, Charles V could not do, Philip does through a woman!

SOEST. Indeed. The old princes too tried to get away with it.

VANSEN. Naturally. . . . Our ancestors were on their guard. When they had a grudge against one of their masters, they would capture his son and heir, keep him prisoner, and only release him when all their conditions had been met—or something of that kind. Our ancestors were real men! They knew what was good for them. They knew how to get hold of things and keep them. Real men, I say. And that's why our privileges are so clearly outlined, our liberties so securely guarded.

SOAPBOILER. What's that you're saying about our liberties?

THE CROWD. Yes, our liberties, our privileges! Tell us more about our privileges!

VANSEN. We men of Brabant especially, though all Provinces have their advantages, we have the most splendid rights. I've read about them all.

SOEST. Tell us what they are.

JETTER. Let's have them all.

A CITIZEN. I beg you.

VANSEN. Firstly, it is written: The Duke of Brabant shall be a good and loyal master to us.

SOEST. Good, was that the word? Is that what it says?

JETTER. Loyal? Is that so?

VANSEN. That's what I'm telling you. He's bound to us by oath, as we are to him. Secondly: he must not impose on us, make felt, or propose to apply to us any power or expression of his will in whatever manner.

JETTER. Excellent. Must not impose on us.

SOEST. Not make felt.

ANOTHER. And propose to apply. That's the crux of it. Apply to no one, in whatever manner.

VANSEN. Most emphatically.

JETTER. Bring in the book.

A CITIZEN. Yes, we must see it.

OTHERS. The book, the book!

ANOTHER. Let's go to the Regent and show her the book.

ANOTHER. And you, Doctor, shall be our spokesman.

SOAPBOILER. Oh, the poor fools!

OTHERS. Give us another extract from the book.

SOAPBOILER. Another word out of him, and I'll make him swallow his teeth!

THE CROWD. Just let anyone try to do that! Tell us more about the privileges! Haven't we any more privileges?

VANSEN. Quite a number, friends, and very good and wholesome ones they are. It is written there too: The ruler must neither improve nor increase the status of the clergy without the consent of the nobles and the commons. Mark that, my friends! Nor alter the constitution of the Province in any way.

SOEST. Is that so?

VANSEN. I'll show it to you in writing, as set down two, three centuries ago.

CITIZENS. And we put up with the new bishops? The nobles must protect us, we must make trouble at once.

OTHERS. And we allow the Inquisition to terrorize us?

VANSEN. That's your fault.

THE PEOPLE. We still have Egmont! And Orange! They will see to it.

VANSEN. Your brothers in Flanders have begun the good work.

SOAPBOILER. You rat!

He hits him.

OTHERS *resist and cry out*. Are you a Spaniard too?

ANOTHER. What? Strike that honourable gentleman?

ANOTHER. Strike a man of such erudition?

They fall upon SOAPBOILER.

CARPENTER. For heaven's sake, stop it.

Others join in the brawl.

Citizens! Are you out of your senses?

Boys whistle, throw stones, incite dogs to attack. Citizens stand and gape, new people arrive, others walk about calmly, others again play all sorts of clownish tricks, shriek, and cheer.

OTHERS. Freedom and privileges! Privileges and freedom!

Enter EGMONT with retinue.

EGMONT. Steady, steady now, all of you. What's going on? Silence! Separate them!

CARPENTER. Your lordship, you come like an angel from heaven. Quiet, all of you! Can't you see it's Count Egmont? Pay your respects to Count Egmont!

EGMONT. You here too? What do you think you are doing? Citizen against citizen. Doesn't even the proximity of our royal Regent restrain you from this folly? Disperse, all of you. Go back to your work. It's a bad sign when you start celebrating on working days. What was it all about?

The tumult dies down gradually, they all surround EGMONT.

CARPENTER. They're brawling for their privileges.

EGMONT. Which they will recklessly destroy in the end. And who are you? You seem honest people to me.

CARPENTER. That is our endeavour.

EGMONT. Your trades?

CARPENTER. Carpenter, and master of the Guild.

EGMONT. And you?

SOEST. Grocer.

EGMONT. You?

JETTER. Tailor.

EGMONT. I remember, you worked at the liveries of my men. Your name is Jetter.

JETTER. It is gracious of you to recall it.

EGMONT. I don't easily forget anyone I have seen and spoken to. . . . Now do what you can to restore order, all of you, and to maintain it. Your position is awkward enough as it is. Do not provoke the King even more, for it is he who is in power, and will show it too. A decent citizen, who earns an honest and industrious living will always have as much freedom as he needs.

CARPENTER. Very true, sir. And that's the rub. The pickpockets, the drunkards, the idlers, by your lordship's leave, those are the ones who make trouble out of boredom and root for privileges out of hunger, and tell lies to the inquisitive and credulous, and start brawls for the sake of a tankard of beer that someone will stand them, though many thousands will suffer because of it. That's just what they want. We keep our houses and cupboards too well locked, so they'd like to drive us out with fire-brands.

EGMONT. You can rely on every kind of help. Measures have been taken to resist this evil in the most effective way. Stand fast against the alien doctrine, and never think that privileges can be secured by riots. Stay at home. Do not allow them to create disturbances in the streets. A few sensible people can do much.

Meanwhile the great crowd has dispersed.

CARPENTER. Thank you, Your Excellency, thank you for your good opinion of us. We shall do all we can.

Exit EGMONT.

A gracious gentleman! A true Netherlander! Nothing Spanish about him.

JETTER. If only he were our Regent! It would be a pleasure to obey him.

SOEST. The King takes good care to prevent that. He always puts one of his people in that place.

JETTER. Did you notice his dress? It was in the latest fashion, the Spanish cut.

CARPENTER. A handsome gentleman.

JETTER. His neck would be a real feast to the executioner.

SOEST. Are you mad? What's got into your head?

JETTER. Yes, it's silly enough, the things that get into one's head. It's just what I happen to feel. When I see a fine, long neck, I can't help thinking at once: that's a good one for the axe. . . . All these cursed executions! One can't get them out of one's mind. When the young fellows go swimming and I see a bare back, at once I remember dozens that I've seen lashed by the cat-o'-nine-tails. If I meet a really fat paunch I can already see it roast on the stake. At night in my dreams I feel pinches in all my limbs. It's simply that one can't be carefree for one hour. Every sort of pleasure or jollity is soon forgotten; but the horrible apparitions might be branded on my forehead, they never leave me alone.

Egmont's House

SECRETARY *at a table covered with papers; he rises restlessly.*

SECRETARY. He still doesn't come, and I've been waiting these two hours pen in hand, papers in front of me; and it's the very day when I want to leave early. My feet itch to be gone; I can hardly bear the delay. "Be there on the stroke of the clock," he commanded before he went out. And now he doesn't come. There's so much to be done, I shan't be finished before midnight. True, he's quite capable of closing an eye. But I should still prefer him to be strict and then let me go at the proper time. One could arrange things in that case. It's two whole hours since he left the Regent; I wonder who it is he's button-holed on the way.

Enter EGMONT.

EGMONT. Well, how is it?

SECRETARY. I am ready, and three messengers are waiting.

EGMONT. It seems I was out too long for your liking—to judge by the face you're making.

SECRETARY. I have been waiting for some considerable time to execute your orders. Here are the papers!

EGMONT. Donna Elvira will be angry with me when she hears that I've kept you.

SECRETARY. You are joking.

EGMONT. No, my dear fellow. There's no need to feel ashamed. You have shown the best taste. She's pretty enough, and I'm very glad that you have a lady friend in the Palace. What do the dispatches say?

SECRETARY. All kinds of things, but little that is pleasing.

EGMONT. In that case it's a good thing that we have no lack of pleasantness in our own house and needn't wait for it to come to us from outside. Are there many letters?

SECRETARY. Quite enough, and three messengers are waiting.

EGMONT. Tell me, then! Only what's essential.

SECRETARY. It's all essential.

EGMONT. One thing after another, then, but be quick about it.

SECRETARY. Captain Breda sends a report on the latest occurrences in Ghent and the surrounding district. Things are more quiet there, on the whole.

EGMONT. I suppose he mentions certain isolated cases of insolence and insubordination?

SECRETARY. Yes, there are incidents of that sort.

EGMONT. Well, spare me the particulars.

SECRETARY. They've arrested six more persons who tore down the statue of Our Lady at Verwich. He asks whether they are to be hanged like the others.

EGMONT. I'm tired of hangings. Let them be soundly whipped and released.

SECRETARY. There are two women among them. Are they to be whipped as well?

EGMONT. As for them, he is to let them off with a warning.

SECRETARY. Brink, of Breda's company, wants to marry. The captain hopes you will forbid it. There are so many women hanging around the regiment, he writes, that when we're on the march it looks less like a body of soldiers than a troop of gipsies.

EGMONT. Let it pass in Brink's case. He's a fine young fellow. He begged me most urgently before I left. But after him no one is to receive permission, much as it grieves me to refuse the poor devils their best amusement—and they've troubles enough as it is.

SECRETARY. Two of your men, Seter and Hart, have behaved abominably towards a girl, an innkeeper's daughter. They caught her when she was alone, and the girl had no means of defending herself.

EGMONT. If she's an honest girl, and they used force, they are to be birched for three days in succession, and if they have any possessions, Captain Breda is to confiscate enough of them to make provision for the girl.

SECRETARY. One of the foreign preachers entered Comines in secret, and was apprehended. He swears that he was on his way to France. According to orders he is to be beheaded.

EGMONT. They are to take him to the frontier quietly and assure him that he won't get away with it a second time.

SECRETARY. A dispatch from your Receiver-General. He writes that too little money is coming in, that he can hardly send the required sum within a week, that the disturbances have thrown everything into the greatest disorder.

EGMONT. The money must be sent. Let him find it how and where he can.

SECRETARY. He says he will do his best and will at last take action against Raymond, who has been your debtor for so long, and have him arrested.

EGMONT. But Raymond has promised to repay the money.

SECRETARY. Last time he gave himself a fortnight to do so.

EGMONT. Well, let him have another fortnight; after that they may go ahead and sue him.

SECRETARY. You are right. It's not incapacity, but ill will on his part. He will certainly take notice as soon as he sees that you're in earnest. . . . The Receiver-General goes on to say that he proposes to withhold half a month's pay from the old soldiers, widows, and some others to whom you have granted pensions. That would give him time to make arrangements, and they would have to manage as best they can.

EGMONT. How does he think they will manage? Those people need the money more than I do. He will refrain from withholding the pensions.

SECRETARY. What are your orders then? Where is he to obtain the funds?

EGMONT. That's his business, and I told him so in my previous dispatch.

SECRETARY. That's why he makes these proposals.

EGMONT. They are not good enough. He must think of other measures. He is to make other proposals, acceptable ones, and above all, he must find the money.

SECRETARY. I have left Count Olivat's letter here for you once more. Forgive me for drawing your attention to it again. More than anyone, the old gentleman deserves a full reply. It was your wish to write to him in person. Without doubt, he loves you like a father.

EGMONT. I haven't the time. And of all odious things, writing is the most odious to me. You're so good at imitating my handwriting, write it in my name. I'm expecting Orange. I haven't the time—and I would like his doubts to be answered by something truly comforting.

SECRETARY. Only tell me roughly what you think; I can then draft the reply and submit it to you. It shall be penned in such a way that it could pass for your handwriting in a court of law.

EGMONT. Give me the letter.

After glancing at it.

The dear, honest old man! I wonder were you as cautious as that when you were young? Did you never climb a fortress wall? In battle, did you remain at the back, as prudence demands? The loyal, solicitous old man! He wants me to live and be happy and does not feel that to live for safety's sake is to be dead already. Tell him not to be anxious; I shall act as I must and shall know how to protect myself. Let him use his influence at Court in my favour and be assured of my wholehearted gratitude.

SECRETARY. Is that all? He expects a great deal more.

EGMONT. What more should I say? If you want to be more long-winded, be so by all means. The crux is always the same: they want me to live in a way that is not my way. It's my good fortune to be cheerful, to take life easy, to travel light and fast, and I will not exchange these for the security of a tomb. It happens that I haven't a drop of blood in my veins that accords with the Spanish way of life; nor any desire to adapt my gait to the measured courtly cadence. Do I live only to take thought for my life? Should I forbid myself to enjoy the present moment, so as to be certain of the next? And consume the next moment too with cares and apprehensions?

SECRETARY. I beg you, sir, don't be so hard on the good gentleman. You are kind to everyone else. Only tell me a few agreeable words that will calm your noble friend. You see how careful he is, how delicately he touches you.

EGMONT. And yet he always touches this same string. He has long known how I hate these incessant admonitions. They serve only to unnerve me, never to help. And if I were a sleepwalker, balanced on the knife-edge of a roof top, would it be a friendly act to call out my name to warn me, wake me, and kill me? Let every man go his own way and look after himself.

SECRETARY. It is fitting for you not to be worried. But someone who knows and loves you——

EGMONT, *reading the letter*. There he goes again, repeating the old tales of what we did and said one evening in the easy expansiveness of sociability and wine! And of all the consequences and proofs drawn and dragged from them the whole length and breadth of the kingdom. Very well, we had cap and bells embroidered on the arms of our servants, and later had this badge of folly changed to a sheaf of arrows—an even more dangerous symbol to all those who looked for significance where there was none. There was this folly and that, conceived and born within a single moment of merriment; we were responsible for sending off a most noble band, furnished with beggars' scrips and a self-chosen sobriquet to remind the King of his duty with mock humility; are responsible for—— What else? Is a carnival charade to be accounted high treason? Are we to be grudged the small coloured rags which our youthful exuberance, our excited imagination may wrap around the wretched bareness of our lives? If you take life too seriously, what is it worth? If the mornings do not rouse us to new pleasures, if the evenings leave us without the comfort of hope, is it worth while to dress and undress at all? Does the sun shine for me to-day so that I may ponder on what happened yesterday? So that I may fathom and link that which is not to be fathomed or linked—the destiny of a future day? Spare me these considerations, leave them to scholars and courtiers. Let these reflect and make plans, creep and crawl, arrive where they may, creep their way into what positions they can. If any of this is of any use to you, without turning your epistle into a book, you are welcome to it. The dear old man takes everything too seriously. His letter makes me think of a friend who has long held my hand in his and presses it once more before releasing it.

SECRETARY. Forgive me, but it makes a pedestrian dizzy to watch a traveller rush past him with such speed.

EGMONT. Enough, my dear fellow! Not another word! As though whipped by invisible spirits, the horses of the sun, Time's horses, run away with the light chariot of our destinies; and we have no choice but to grip the reins with resolute courage and, now to the right, now to the left, avert the wheels from a stone here, a precipice there. As for the end of the journey, who knows what it is? When we hardly remember where it began.

SECRETARY. Oh, sir!

EGMONT. I stand in a high and prominent place and must rise still higher. I have hope, courage, and strength. I have not yet attained the crest of my growth and when I *have* attained the highest point, I shall stand there unwavering, without fear. If I must fall, let a thunderbolt, a gale, even a false step hurl me down into the depths; I shall not be alone there but with thousands of good men. I have never disdained to stake my all in war for the slightest gain, like any decent soldier; and do you expect me to turn niggard when the prize is nothing less than the entire worth of a free life?

SECRETARY. Oh, sir! You do not know what you are saying. May God preserve you!

EGMONT. Collect your papers now. Orange is coming. Complete whatever is most urgent, so that the couriers can leave before the gates are shut. Other things can wait. Leave the letter to the Count till to-morrow. Don't fail to visit Elvira and give her my regards. Find out how the Regent is keeping; they say that she's not well, though she conceals it.

Exit SECRETARY.

Enter ORANGE.

EGMONT. Welcome, Orange. You seem somewhat constrained.

ORANGE. What do you say to our conversation with the Regent?

EGMONT. I saw nothing extraordinary in her manner of receiving us. It wasn't the first time I have seen her in that state. I had the impression that she was unwell.

ORANGE. Didn't you observe that she was more reticent? At first, she wanted to be calm and express her approval of our conduct during the new uprising of the mob. Later, she hinted that this could easily appear in a false light, then diverted the conversation to her usual topic: that her amiable, benevolent disposition, her friendship for us Netherlanders have never been duly appreciated, that we have taken it too much for granted, that none of her efforts seemed to lead to the desired results, that she might well grow weary in the end and the King resort to very different measures. Did you note all this?

EGMONT. No, not all of it; I was thinking of something different at the time. She is a woman, dear Orange, and women always wish that everyone will meekly creep under their gentle yoke, that every Hercules will doff his lion's skin and join their knitting group; that, because they desire peace, the ferment that seizes a people, the tempest that mighty rivals raise among themselves, can be soothed by a kind word, and that the most hostile elements will lie down together at their feet in gentle concord. That is the case with her also. And since she cannot bring about this state, she has no alternative but to become ill-tempered, to complain of ingratitude and lack of wisdom, to threaten us with terrible consequences and to threaten—that she will leave us!

ORANGE. And don't you believe that this time she will carry out her threat?

EGMONT. Never! How often I've seen her in her travelling clothes! Where could she go? Here she is Governor, Queen. Do you suppose that she relishes the thought of going into insignificant retirement at her brother's court? Or of going to Italy and burdening herself with the old family matters?

ORANGE. People think her incapable of such a decision because they have seen her hesitate and withdraw. And yet she has it in her; new circumstances drive her to the long-delayed resolution. What if she did go? And the King sent someone else?

EGMONT. Well, he would come, and would find plenty of things to occupy him. He would come with great plans, projects, and ideas of how to arrange, control, and hold together all things; and would be struggling with this trifle to-day, that trifle to-morrow, would come up against this obstruction the day after, spend a month on preparations and schemes, another on being disappointed with undertakings that have failed, half a year on the troubles caused by a single Province. For him too time would pass, his head would grow giddy, and one thing follow another as before, so that he would have cause to thank God if he succeeded in keeping his ship off the rocks instead of navigating great oceans along a charted course.

ORANGE. But what if someone advised the King to make an experiment?

EGMONT. And what might that be?

ORANGE. To see what the torso would do without a head.

EGMONT. What do you mean?

ORANGE. Egmont, for many years now I have been deeply concerned with all our affairs, my head always bent over them as over a chessboard, and I do not regard any move on the other side as insignificant. And just as idle persons enquire with the greatest care into the secrets of nature, so I consider it the duty, the vocation, of a prince to know the views and strategy of all parties. I have cause to fear an eruption. The King has long acted according to certain principles; he sees that these are inadequate; what can be more likely than that he will try other means?

EGMONT. That's not my opinion. When one grows old and has tried so many things and the world still refuses to become a tidy place, surely one puts up with it in the end.

ORANGE. There's one thing he hasn't tried.

EGMONT. Well?

ORANGE. To spare the people and destroy the princes.

EGMONT. An old fear, and widespread. It's not worth worrying about.

ORANGE. Once it was a worry; gradually it became a probability to me; finally, it's become a certainty.

EGMONT. And has the King any subjects more loyal than ourselves?

ORANGE. We serve him in our fashion; and we can admit to each other that we know well how to balance the King's rights against ours.

EGMONT. Who wouldn't? We are his subjects and pay him such tribute as is due to him.

ORANGE. But what if he claimed *more,* and called disloyalty what we call insisting on our rights?

EGMONT. We shall be able to defend ourselves. Let him convoke the Knights of the Golden Fleece; we shall submit to their judgement.

ORANGE. And what if the verdict precedes the trial, the punishment precedes the verdict?

EGMONT. That would be an injustice of which Philip could never be guilty, and an act of folly of which, in my view, both he and his counsellors are incapable——

ORANGE. And what if they did prove to be unjust and foolish?

EGMONT. No, Orange, it's impossible. Who would dare to lay hands on us? . . . To arrest us would be a vain and useless act. No, they do not dare to raise the banner of tyranny so high. The gust of wind that would bear this news across the country would fan an enormous blaze. And what would be the point of it? It is not the King alone who has the right to judge and condemn. And would they destroy us in secret, like a band of vulgar assassins? They cannot even think of such a thing. A terrible pact would unite the whole people at once. Undying hatred and eternal separation from the Spanish name would violently declare themselves.

ORANGE. In that case the fire would rage over our graves, and the blood of our enemies would flow as an idle expiatory offering. Let us take thought to prevent it, Egmont.

EGMONT. But how can we?

ORANGE. Alba is on his way.

EGMONT. I don't believe it.

ORANGE. I know it.

EGMONT. The Regent would not hear of it.

ORANGE. Another reason for my conviction. The Regent will yield her place to him. I know his murderous disposition, and he will bring an army with him.

EGMONT. To harass the Provinces once more? The people will grow most unruly.

ORANGE. They will take care of the people's heads.

EGMONT. No, no, I say.

ORANGE. Let us leave, each for his Province. There we shall reinforce ourselves. He will not begin with a show of brute force.

EGMONT. Must we not be there to welcome him when he comes?

ORANGE. We shall procrastinate.

EGMONT. And if he demands our presence at his arrival, in the King's name?

ORANGE. We shall look for evasions.

EGMONT. And if he presses us?

ORANGE. We shall excuse ourselves.

EGMONT. And if he insists on it?

ORANGE. We shall refuse all the more firmly.

EGMONT. And war will have been declared, and we shall be the rebels. Orange, don't let your cleverness mislead you; I know that it isn't fear that moves you to retreat. Consider the implications of this step.

ORANGE. I have considered them.

EGMONT. Consider what you will be guilty of, if you are wrong: of the most ruinous war that has ever laid waste a country. Your refusal will be the signal which calls all the provinces to arms at once; it will serve to justify every act of cruelty for which Spain has never lacked anything but a pretext. What we have long kept down with the utmost difficulty, you will rouse up with a single call to the most frightful turmoil. Think of the cities, the nobles, the people; of commerce, agriculture, the trades. And think of the destruction, the slaughter! . . . True, in the field the soldier looks calmly upon his dying comrade; but it is the corpses of citizens, children, young women which will float down the rivers to where you stand. So that you will be filled with horror, no longer knowing whose cause you are defending, since those are perishing for whose freedom you took arms. And how will you feel when you have to tell yourself: it was for my safety that I took them?

ORANGE. We are not individual men, Egmont. If it is fitting for us to sacrifice ourselves for the sake of thousands, it is fitting too to spare ourselves for the sake of thousands.

EGMONT. The man who spares himself must become suspicious of himself.

ORANGE. The man who knows himself can advance or retreat with confidence.

EGMONT. The evil which you fear becomes a certainty by your deed.

ORANGE. It is prudent and bold to meet the inevitable disaster.

EGMONT. In a peril so great the slightest hope should be fostered.

ORANGE. There is no room left for the lightest manoeuvre on our part; the abyss lies right in front of us.

EGMONT. Is the King's favour so narrow a ledge?

ORANGE. Not so narrow, but slippery.

EGMONT. By God! You do him an injustice. I will not suffer anyone to think ill of him. He is Charles's son and incapable of baseness.

ORANGE. Kings are never guilty of baseness.

EGMONT. You should get to know him better.

ORANGE. It is that very knowledge which advises us not to await the outcome of this dangerous test.

EGMONT. No test is dangerous if one has the necessary courage.

ORANGE. You are getting excited, Egmont.

EGMONT. I must see with my own eyes.

ORANGE. Oh, if only you would see with mine for once! My

dear friend, because your eyes are open you think that you see. I am going! Wait for Alba's arrival if you must, and God be with you! Perhaps my refusal will save you. Perhaps the dragon will think it has caught nothing if it cannot devour both of us at once. Perhaps it will hesitate, so as to be more sure of success, and perhaps by then you will see the matter in its true light. But be quick then! Quick as lightning! Save yourself. Save yourself, my friend. Farewell. Let nothing escape your watchfulness: the size of his army, how he occupies the city, how much power the Regent retains, how well your friends are prepared. Keep me informed. . . . Egmont—

EGMONT. Well?

ORANGE, *taking his hand*. Let me persuade you. Come with me!

EGMONT. What, Orange, tears in *your* eyes?

ORANGE. To weep for one who is lost is not unmanly.

EGMONT. You regard me as lost?

ORANGE. You are. Think again! You have only the briefest of respites. Farewell.

Exit.

EGMONT, *alone*. Strange that other people's thoughts have such influence on us! It would never have occurred to me, and this man's apprehensions have infected me. . . . Away! It's an alien drop in my blood. Let my sound nature throw it out again! And there's one kind remedy still to bathe away the pensive wrinkles on my brow.

ACT III

The Regent's Palace

MARGARET OF PARMA

REGENT. I should have guessed it. Oh, if one's days are spent in toil and stress, one always thinks one is doing one's utmost; and the person who looks on from afar and gives orders believes he demands only what is possible. . . . Oh, these Kings! . . . I should never have thought that it could grieve me so. It is so pleasant to rule! . . . And to abdicate? . . . I cannot think how my father could do it; and yet I shall do it also.

MACHIAVELLI *appears in the background.*

REGENT. Come closer, Machiavelli! I am just thinking about my brother's letter.

MACHIAVELLI. And may I know what it contains?

REGENT. As much tender attention to me as solicitude for his states. He commends the steadfastness, industry, and loyalty with which I have hitherto upheld the rights of His Majesty in these Provinces. He pities me because the unruly people is causing me so much trouble now. He is so entirely convinced of the profundity of my insight, so extraordinarily pleased with the prudence of my conduct, that I must almost say: the letter is too well written for a King, certainly for a brother.

MACHIAVELLI. This is not the first time he has informed you of his well-deserved satisfaction.

REGENT. But the first time it is a mere figure of rhetoric.

MACHIAVELLI. I don't follow you.

REGENT. You will. For after this induction, he expresses the opinion that without a bodyguard, without a small army, I shall always cut a bad figure here. We were wrong, he says, to withdraw our soldiers from the Provinces because the population complained. An occupation force, he believes, which loads down the citizen's neck prevents him by its weight from indulging in high leaps.

MACHIAVELLI. It would have a most unsettling effect on the people's state of mind.

REGENT. The King, however, is of the opinion—— Are you listening? He is of the opinion that an efficient general, one who does not listen to reason, would very soon put the people and nobility, citizens and peasantry, in their place; and is therefore sending a powerful force commanded—by the Duke of Alba.

MACHIAVELLI. Alba?

REGENT. That surprises you?

MACHIAVELLI. You say he is sending. I suppose he asks you whether he should send.

REGENT. The King does not ask, he sends.

MACHIAVELLI. In that case you will have an experienced military man in your service.

REGENT. In my service? Speak your mind, Machiavelli!

MACHIAVELLI. I am anxious not to anticipate, madam.

REGENT. And I am anxious to disguise the truth! It is very painful to me, very painful. I wish my brother had said what he thinks instead of sending formal epistles which a Secretary of State has drawn up.

MACHIAVELLI. Should we not try to understand . . .

REGENT. But I know them by heart. They want the place cleaned and swept; and since they do not act themselves, they lend their trust to any man who appears broom in hand. Oh, I can see the King and his Council as clearly as if they were embroidered on this tapestry.

MACHIAVELLI. So vividly?

REGENT. Not a single feature is missing. There are good men among them. Honest Rodrick, who is so experienced and moderate, does not aim too high and yet lets nothing fall too low. Honest Alonzo, hard-working Freneda, solid Las Vagas and a few others who will co-operate when the good party comes into power. But on the other side there sits the hollow-eyed Toledan with the brazen brow and the deep, fiery glance, mumbling between his teeth of female softheartedness, misplaced indulgence, and that women may sit a horse already broken, but make poor equerries themselves, and other such pleasantries to which I once had to listen in the company of the political gentlemen.

MACHIAVELLI. You have chosen a good palette for the portrait.

REGENT. Admit it, Machiavelli, of all the colours and shades with which I could choose to paint no tone is as yellow-brown, as gall-black as the colour of Alba's face or as the colour with which he paints. To him, everyone is a blasphemer, a traitor to the King; for on that score he can have them all racked, burnt, hanged, drawn and quartered. . . . The good I have done here probably looks like nothing from a distance, simply because it is good. So he will seize on every caprice long past, recall every disturbance long ago put down; and the King will have such a vision of mutiny, rebellion, and recklessness that he will think the people here devour one another, when we have long forgotten some fleeting, passing misconduct of a nation still rough. Then he will conceive a deep, heartfelt hatred for these poor people; they will seem repulsive to him, indeed like beasts and monsters; he will look around for fire and sword, imagining that that is how to tame men.

MACHIAVELLI. I think you exaggerate a little and take the whole matter too seriously. After all, you will be Regent still.

REGENT. Oh, I know all about that. He will bring a royal directive. I have grown old enough in affairs of state to know how one displaces a person without depriving him of his rank and title. First he will bring a royal directive, which will be twisted and vague; he will make changes all around him, for he has the power, and if I complain he will use the pretext of a secret directive; if I ask to see it, he will prevaricate; if I insist, he will show me a document that contains something quite different; and if I am still not satisfied, he will do no more than he would if I were speaking. Meanwhile he will have done what I fear and irrevocably averted what I wish.

MACHIAVELLI. I wish I could contradict you.

REGENT. What I have calmed with unspeakable patience, he will stir up again by hardheartedness and cruelty. I shall see my work perish before my very eyes and bear the blame for his acts into the bargain.

MACHIAVELLI. Do not anticipate, Your Highness.

REGENT. Well, I still have enough self-control to be quiet. Let him come, I shall make way for him with good grace before he pushes me out.

MACHIAVELLI. And you will take this grave step with such alacrity?

REGENT. It's more difficult for me than you think. If one is accustomed to rule, if it was given to one in youth to hold the fate of thousands daily in one's hand, one descends from the throne as into a grave. But sooner that than remain like a spectre among the living and with hollow gestures lay claim to a place which another has inherited, possesses, and enjoys.

Clare's House

CLARE *and* MOTHER

MOTHER. Never have I seen such love as Brackenburg's; I thought it was only to be found in legends about heroes.

CLARE *walks up and down the room, humming a song with closed lips.* Happy alone
        Is whom love has in thrall.

MOTHER. He suspects how you stand with Egmont. And I think that if you gave him a little encouragement, if you wanted him to, he would still marry you.

CLARE *sings.* Gladdened
        And saddened
        And troubled in vain,
        Longing
        And thronging
        With wavering pain,
        Raised up to heaven,

The deeper to fall,
Happy alone
Is whom love has in thrall.

MOTHER. Oh, leave off the "by-low, lie-low."

CLARE. No, don't say anything against it. It's a powerful song. More than once I've lulled a big child to sleep with it.

MOTHER. You can't think of anything except your love. If only you wouldn't forget everything because of that *one* thing. You should have some respect for Brackenburg, I tell you. He might still make you happy one day.

CLARE. Brackenburg?

MOTHER. Oh yes, there will come a time. . . . You children foresee nothing and will not listen to our experience. Youth and true love, it all comes to an end; and there comes a time when one gives thanks to God for somewhere to lay one's head.

CLARE *shudders, keeps silent, and then bursts out.* Mother, let the time come then, like death. To think of it in advance is horrible! And what if it does come! If we must—then—then we shall face up to it as best we can. To think of losing Egmont!

In tears.

No, it's impossible, quite impossible.

Enter EGMONT *in a riding cloak, his hat pressed down onto his face.*

EGMONT. Clare!

CLARE *utters a scream, totters.* Egmont!

She runs to him.

Egmont!

She embraces him and rests her head on his shoulder.

Oh, my dear, good, darling Egmont! So you've come. You're here!

EGMONT. Good evening, Mother.

MOTHER. Welcome to our house, Your Lordship. My little girl nearly pined away because of your long absence; she spent the whole day, as usual, talking and singing about you.

EGMONT. You'll give me some supper, won't you?

MOTHER. You do us too much honour. If only we had something to offer you.

CLARE. Of course we have. Don't worry about it, Mother; I've made all the arrangements already and prepared something for you. But don't give me away, Mother.

MOTHER. It's paltry enough.

CLARE. Just be patient. And besides, I say to myself: when he's with me, I'm not in the least hungry, so he shouldn't have too big an appetite when I'm with him.

EGMONT. Do you think so?

CLARE *stamps her foot and turns her back on him in a pique.*

EGMONT. What's the matter with you?

CLARE. Oh, you're so chilly to-day. You haven't offered to kiss me yet. Why do you keep your arms wrapped in your cloak like a new-born baby? It isn't right for a soldier or a lover to keep his arms wrapped up.

EGMONT. At times it is, sweetheart, at times. When the soldier is on his guard and trying to get the better of his enemy by stealth, he pulls himself together, puts his arms around himself, and waits till his plan of action has matured. And a lover . . .

MOTHER. Won't you sit down, make yourself comfortable? I must go to the kitchen. Clare forgets everything when you're here. You must excuse me.

EGMONT. Your good will is the best spice.

Exit MOTHER.

CLARE. And what would you call my love?

EGMONT. Anything you like.

CLARE. Compare it to something, if you have the heart.

EGMONT. Well, first of all . . .

He throws off his cloak and stands there splendidly dressed.

CLARE. Goodness!

EGMONT. Now my arms are free.

He hugs her.

CLARE. Stop it! You'll spoil your appearance.

She steps back.

How splendid it is! Now I mustn't touch you.

EGMONT. Are you satisfied? I promised I'd come dressed in Spanish fashion one day.

CLARE. I never asked you again. I thought you didn't want to. . . . Oh, and the Golden Fleece!

EGMONT. Well, there it is for you.

CLARE. And did the Emperor hang it around your neck?

EGMONT. Yes, child. And the chain and the pendant grant the most noble liberties to the man who wears them. There is no one on earth who has the right to judge my actions other than the Grand Master of the Order, together with the assembled company of Knights.

CLARE. Oh, you could let the whole world stand in judgement over you! The velvet is too lovely for words, and the gold thread! And the embroidery! . . . One doesn't know where to begin.

EGMONT. Look your fill.

CLARE. And the Golden Fleece! You told me the story and said it was a symbol of all that is great and precious, only to be earned and won by the most strenuous endeavours. It is very precious—I can compare it to your love. I wear it next to my heart as well—and then . . .

EGMONT. What were you going to say?

CLARE. And then the comparison doesn't apply.

EGMONT. How do you mean?

CLARE. Because I haven't won your love by strenuous endeavours; I haven't earned it.

EGMONT. In love it's different. You have earned it because you don't try to win it, and usually only those people get it who don't chase after it.

CLARE. Did you derive that conclusion from yourself? Did you make this proud observation about yourself? You, whom all the people loves?

EGMONT. If only I'd done something for them! If only I could do something for them. It is their kind will to love me.

CLARE. I suppose you saw the Regent to-day?

EGMONT. I did.

CLARE. Are you on good terms with her?

EGMONT. It looks that way. We are amiable and helpful to each other.

CLARE. And in your heart?

EGMONT. I wish her well. Each of us has his own aims. But that is neither here nor there. She's an excellent woman, knows her men, and would see deep enough even if she weren't suspicious. I cause her a great deal of trouble because she is always looking for secret motives behind my conduct, and I have none.

CLARE. None at all?

EGMONT. Well, yes. A few little reservations. Every wine leaves a deposit of tartar if it's left long enough in the barrel. But Orange provides better entertainment for her all the same, and sets her new puzzles incessantly. He has made people believe that he always harbours some secret project; and so now she is always looking at his forehead wondering what he's thinking, or at his steps, wondering where he may be directing them.

CLARE. Does she conceal her motives?

EGMONT. She's the Regent. What do you expect?

CLARE. Forgive me. What I meant to ask was: is she deceitful?

EGMONT. No more and no less than anyone who wishes to attain his ends.

CLARE. I could never be at home in the great world. But then she has a masculine mind; she's a different kind of woman from us seamstresses and cooks. She is noble, brave, resolute.

EGMONT. Yes, as long as things are not too topsy-turvy. This time she's not so sure of herself.

CLARE. How so?

EGMONT. She has a little moustache too, on her upper lip, and occasional attacks of gout. A real Amazon.

CLARE. A majestic woman! I should be afraid to enter her presence.

EGMONT. You're not usually so shy. But then it wouldn't be fear, only girlish modesty.

CLARE *casts down her eyes, takes his hand, and nestles against him.*

EGMONT. I understand you, my dear. You can raise your eyes.

CLARE. Let me be silent. Let me hold you. Let me look into your eyes: find everything in them, comfort and hope and joy and grief.

She puts her arms around him and looks at him.

Tell me. Tell me. I don't understand. Are you Egmont? Count Egmont, the great Egmont who raises such an ado, whom the newspapers write about, whom the Provinces adore?

EGMONT. No, my little Clare, I am not.

CLARE. What?

EGMONT. You see—— Clare! Let me sit down.

He sits down, she kneels in front of him on a stool, puts her arms on his knees, and looks at him.

That Egmont is an ill-tempered, stiff, cold Egmont, who has to keep up appearances, now make this face, now that; who is tormented, misunderstood, entangled, while other people think he is gay and carefree; loved by a people that does not know its own mind, honoured and carried aloft by a mob for which there is no help; surrounded by friends on whom he must not rely; closely watched by men who desire to harm him in every possible way; toiling and striving, often aimlessly, nearly always unrewarded. . . . Oh, let me say no more about him! How he fares, how he feels! But this one, Clare, this one is calm, candid, happy, beloved and understood by the best of hearts, which he too understands wholly and presses to him with complete love and trust.

He embraces her.

That is *your* Egmont.

CLARE. Then let me die. The world has no joys beyond these!

ACT IV

A Street

JETTER, CARPENTER

JETTER. Hey, there. Hush. Hey, there, neighbour, a word with you!

CARPENTER. Be on your way and keep quiet.

JETTER. Only one word. No news?

CARPENTER. None, except that we've been forbidden to talk of the news.

JETTER. What do you mean?

CARPENTER. Come close to the wall of this house. Keep your eyes and ears open. As soon as he arrived the Duke of Alba issued an order to the effect that if two or three are found talking together in the street they will be declared guilty of high treason without examination or trial.

JETTER. Oh, dreadful!

CARPENTER. The penalty for discussing affairs of state is life imprisonment.

JETTER. All our liberty lost!

CARPENTER. And on pain of death no one is to express disapproval of the government's actions.

JETTER. And our heads likely to be lost as well!

CARPENTER. And great rewards will be promised to induce fathers, mothers, children, relations, friends, servants to reveal what is going on in the home to a special court appointed for that purpose.

JETTER. Let's go home.

CARPENTER. And those who obey are promised that they will suffer no harm in their persons or property.

JETTER. How gracious of them! Didn't I feel aggrieved as soon as the Duke entered our city? Ever since, I've felt as though the sky were covered with black crêpe and hung down so low that one has to bend down to avoid knocking one's head against it.

CARPENTER. And how did you like his soldiers? They're a different kettle of fish to the ones we're used to. Don't you agree?

JETTER. Disgusting! It freezes your marrow to see a body of them march down the street. Straight as posts, their eyes glued on the next man's back, not a single man out of step. And when they're on guard duty and you pass by, you feel as though they could see right into your head, and they look so stiff and grumpy that you seem to see a taskmaster at every corner. They made me feel ill. Our militia, at least, was a gay lot. They took liberties, stood about with legs straddled, wore their hats over one eye, lived, and let live; but those fellows are like machines with a devil inside.

CARPENTER. If one of them calls out "Halt!" and jumps to the alert, do you think one would stop?

JETTER. It would be the death of me at once!

CARPENTER. Let's go home.

JETTER. No good will come of this. Good-bye.

Enter SOEST.

SOEST. Friends! Comrades!

CARPENTER. Quiet. Don't detain us.

SOEST. Have you heard?

JETTER. Only too much!

SOEST. The Regent has left.

JETTER. Now God have mercy on us!

CARPENTER. She was our only hope.

SOEST. Suddenly, and in secret. She didn't get on with the Duke; she sent a message to the nobles to say she will return. No one believes it.

CARPENTER. May God forgive the nobles for allowing this new scourge to descend on our backs. They could have prevented it. All our privileges are lost.

JETTER. Not a word about privileges, for God's sake. I can

smell the powder of a firing squad. The sun refuses to rise, the mists reek of rotten flesh.

SOEST. Orange is gone too.

CARPENTER. That means we've been left to our fate.

SOEST. Count Egmont is still with us.

JETTER. Thank God for that. May all the saints give him strength, so that he'll do his best; he is the only one who can help us.

Enter VANSEN.

VANSEN. Well, fancy that. A few citizens who haven't yet crept away into their dens!

JETTER. Do us a favour: be on your way.

VANSEN. You're not very polite.

CARPENTER. This isn't the time for fine phrases. Are you looking for trouble again? Has your back healed already?

VANSEN. Never ask a soldier about his wounds. If I couldn't take a hiding at times, I shouldn't have got anywhere.

JETTER. Things may become more serious.

VANSEN. It seems that the approaching thunderstorm is making all your limbs feel miserably tired.

CARPENTER. If you don't keep quiet your limbs will soon start moving in a different direction.

VANSEN. Poor little mice, to fall into despair, just because the master of the house has got himself a new cat! Things have changed a bit, that's all; but we shall go about our business just as we did before, never you worry!

CARPENTER. You're a loud-mouthed good-for-nothing.

VANSEN. As for you, brother nitwit, let the Duke do his worst. The old tomcat looks as if he's been eating devils instead of mice, and now he's got indigestion as a result. Just let him get on with it; he has to eat, drink, and sleep like the rest of us. I'm not at all anxious about us, if only we take our time. At the start all goes easily; but later he too will find out that it's more pleasant to live in the larder where the bacon is stored, and to rest at night than to stalk a few mice in the loft, with nothing but fruit all around. Just keep calm. I know what governors are like.

CARPENTER. There's no telling what a fellow like that will blurt out. If I'd ever said anything like it, I shouldn't feel safe for a minute.

VANSEN. Don't you worry, God in heaven doesn't hear anything about worms of your sort, let alone the Regent.

JETTER. Filthy blasphemer!

VANSEN. I know of some people for whom it would be a lot better if they acted the hero less and had a little more discretion instead.

CARPENTER. What do you mean by that?

VANSEN. Hmm! The Count is what I mean.

JETTER. Egmont? What has he got to fear?

VANSEN. I'm a poor devil and could live a whole year on what he loses in one night. And yet he'd do well to give me his income for a whole year if he could have my head for a quarter of an hour.

JETTER. That's what you think. Egmont's got more sense in his hair than you have in your brain.

VANSEN. Say what you like. But he hasn't got more subtlety. It's the great lords who're the first to deceive themselves. He shouldn't be so trusting.

JETTER. Listen to him chatter! A gentleman like Egmont!

VANSEN. That's just it. Because he is indiscreet, like a tailor.

JETTER. Dirty slanderer!

VANSEN. What I wish him is to have your courage just for an hour, so that it could trouble him and make him itch till it drives him out of town.

JETTER. You speak like a fool; he's as safe as a star in the sky.

VANSEN. Have you never seen one shoot off? . . . Gone in a jiffy.

CARPENTER. Who would want to harm him?

VANSEN. Who would want to? Why, do you think you could prevent it? Are you going to start a rebellion when they arrest him?

JETTER. Oh!

VANSEN. Would you risk your skin for his sake?

SOEST. Eh!

VANSEN, *imitating them.* Ee, ah, oo! Run through the whole alphabet to express your surprise! That's how it is and how it will be. God have mercy on him.

JETTER. I'm shocked by your impudence. Such a noble, righteous man—— And you talk of danger?

VANSEN. It's the knave who does well for himself everywhere. On the stool of repentance he makes a fool of the judge; on the judgement seat he delights in making a criminal out of the prosecutor. I once had to copy one of those documents, when the Chief of Police received a load of praise and money from Court because he'd made a self-confessed rascal out of some honest soul they wanted out of the way.

CARPENTER. That's another arrant lie! How can they find any evidence, if the man is innocent?

VANSEN. Oh, my poor sparrow-brain! When there's nothing to be read out of the evidence, they read something into it. Honesty makes you rash—it can make you stubborn too. So they start by asking harmless questions, and the accused is proud of his innocence, as they call it, so he blurts out everything which a sensible man would conceal. Then the prosecutor makes new questions out of the answers and carefully notes any little contradiction that may appear. That's where he attaches his rope, and if the poor fool allows himself to be convinced that he's said too much here, too little there, and perhaps withheld some piece of evidence for no reason at all; or if, in the end, he allows them to frighten him—well, in that case, they're well on the way. And I assure you that the beggar women who pick rags out of the rubbish bins are not more thorough than one of those rogue-makers when he's set his heart on patching together a straw-and-rag scarecrow out of every little crooked, twisted, rumpled, hidden, familiar, denied indication and circumstance, if only to be able to hang his victim in effigy. And the poor fellow has cause to be thankful if he lives to see himself hanged.

JETTER. No one can say he hasn't a fluent tongue in his head.

CARPENTER. That kind of talk may work with flies. But wasps laugh at the yarns you spin.

VANSEN. After the spiders have gone. Look, that tall Duke looks just like one of your garden spiders; not one of the fat-bellied ones—they're less dangerous—but one of the long-legged kind with small bodies that don't get fat with eating and spin very fine threads, though all the tougher for that.

JETTER. Egmont is a Knight of the Golden Fleece: who would dare to lay hands on him? He can only be judged by those of his own kind, by the entire Order. It's your foul mouth and your bad conscience that make you talk such gibberish.

VANSEN. What makes you think I don't wish him well? I've nothing against him. He's an excellent gentleman. He let off a couple of my best friends, who would otherwise have been hanged by now, with a sound whipping. Now, off with you! Get along! That's my advice to you now. I can see a new patrol just starting their rounds over there, and they don't look as if they're going to drink our health. We mustn't be in too much of a hurry, but stand and look on for a while. I've a couple of nieces and an old crony who keeps a tavern; if those men aren't tame by the time they've tasted their wares, they must be as tough as wolves.

Culenburg Palace. The Duke of Alba's Residence

SILVA *and* GOMEZ *meet.*

SILVA. Have you carried out the Duke's instructions?

GOMEZ. Punctiliously. All the daily patrols have been ordered to appear at the appointed time at the different places I have detailed to them; meanwhile, they will patrol the town as usual to maintain the peace. None knows about any of the others; each patrol thinks that the order concerns only its own men, and the cordon can be closed in a moment when necessary so that every approach to the Palace will be cut off. Do you know the reason for this order?

SILVA. I am accustomed to obey orders without questioning them. And who is easier to obey than the Duke, since the outcome will soon prove that his instructions were judicious?

GOMEZ. Oh yes, of course. And I am not surprised to find that you're growing as uncommunicative and monosyllabic as he is, since you have to attend him all the time. It seems strange to me, since I am used to the lighter Italian etiquette. My loyalty and obedience are the same as ever; but I have got into the habit of chattering and arguing. As for you people, you keep silent all the time and never relax. The Duke seems to me like an iron tower without any door to which his staff have the key. The other day I heard him remark at table about some carefree, affable fellow that he was like a bad tavern with a sign advertising brandy to attract idlers, beggars, and thieves.

SILVA. And did he not lead us in silence to this place?

GOMEZ. There's no denying that. Certainly, anyone who witnessed his skill in moving the army here from Italy has seen something worth remembering. How he twined his way, as it were, through friend and foe, through the French, the King's men, and the heretics, through the Swiss and their confederates, maintained the strictest discipline and succeeded in conducting so potentially dangerous a movement with such ease and without giving offence to anyone. We have certainly seen something and learnt something.

SILVA. And here too. Isn't everything peaceful and quiet, as though there had never been any uprising?

GOMEZ. Well, it was quiet in most places when we arrived.

SILVA. The Provinces are a great deal calmer than they were; and if anyone does move now, it's in order to flee. But he will soon put an end to that as well, if I'm not mistaken.

GOMEZ. The King will be pleased with him as never before.

SILVA. And nothing remains more urgent for us than to be sure of *his* pleasure. If the King should come here, the Duke and anyone whom he commends will doubtless be generously rewarded.

GOMEZ. Do you think that the King will come?

SILVA. The many preparations that are being made would suggest that it is very likely.

GOMEZ. They don't convince me.

SILVA. In that case, at least refrain from evincing an opinion on the matter. For if it is not the King's intention to come, what is certain is that we are intended to believe so.

Enter FERDINAND, ALBA's *natural son.*

FERDINAND. Has my father not come out?

SILVA. We are waiting for him.

FERDINAND. The princes will soon be here.

GOMEZ. Are they expected to-day?

FERDINAND. Orange and Egmont.

GOMEZ, *softly to* SILVA. Something has dawned on me.

SILVA. Then keep it to yourself!

Enter the DUKE OF ALBA. *As he enters and comes forward, the others step back.*

ALBA. Gomez!

GOMEZ *comes forward.* My Lord!

ALBA. You have instructed and detailed the guards?

GOMEZ. With the utmost precision. The daily patrols——

ALBA. Very well. You will wait in the gallery. Silva will inform you of the exact moment when you will call them in and occupy the approaches to the Palace. You know the rest.

GOMEZ. Yes.

Exit.

ALBA. Silva!

SILVA. Here I am.

ALBA. Everything I have valued in you—courage, determination, promptness in the execution of orders—all these you must show to-day.

SILVA. I thank you for giving me the opportunity to prove that I am unchanged.

ALBA. As soon as the princes have entered my cabinet, lose no time in arresting Egmont's private secretary. You have made all the necessary arrangements to seize the other persons who have been indicated?

SILVA. Rely on us! Their fate, like a well-calculated eclipse of the sun, will meet them punctually and terribly.

ALBA. You have kept all their movements under observation?

SILVA. Not one has escaped me. Especially not Egmont's. He is the only one whose conduct has not changed since your arrival. Spends the whole day trying out one horse after another, invites guests, is always merry and amusing at table, plays at dice, shoots, and creeps to his sweetheart at night. Whereas the others have made a distinct break in their way of life. They stay at home; the fronts of their houses look like those of men who are ill in bed.

ALBA. Hurry, therefore, before they recover against our will.

SILVA. I shall catch them. At your command we shall overwhelm them with official honours. Panic will seize them. Diplomatically they offer us cautious thanks and feel that it would be wisest to flee; not one of them dares to move one step; they hesitate, cannot get together; and his social sense prevents each one from acting boldly for himself. They would like to avoid all suspicion and yet they become more and more suspect. With the greatest pleasure I foresee the complete success of your stratagem.

ALBA. I take pleasure only in the accomplished act . . . and not easily even in that, for there always remains something to give us cause for thought and anxiety. Fortune, in her obstinate way, may insist on conferring glory on what is base and worthless, and on dishonouring well-considered deeds with a base outcome. Wait here till the princes come, then give Gomez the order to occupy the streets and at once proceed in person to arrest Egmont's secretary and the others that have been indicated to you. When you have done so, come here and report it to my son, so that he may convey the news to me in the cabinet.

SILVA. I hope to have the honour of attending on you tonight.

ALBA *goes to his son, who has been standing on the gallery.*

SILVA. I dare not tell him, but I am losing hope. I fear it will not be as he thinks. I see spirits who, silent and pensive, weigh the destiny of princes and many thousands of men on black scales. Slowly the pointer vacillates, the judges seem deep in thought. At last this scale goes down, that one rises at the breath of obstinate Fortune, and the verdict has been pronounced.

Exit.

ALBA, *stepping forward with* FERDINAND. What was your impression of the city?

FERDINAND. Everything has become very quiet. As though to pass the time of day I rode up and down the streets. Your well-distributed patrols keep their fear so tense that no one dares to breathe a word. The city looks like a field when a thunderstorm flashes in the distance: one doesn't see a bird or an animal that isn't scurrying off to seek shelter.

ALBA. Is that all you saw and encountered?

FERDINAND. Egmont came riding into the market-place with some men. We exchanged greetings; he had an unruly horse, which I was compelled to praise. "Let us lose no time in breaking in horses, we shall need them soon!" he called out to me. He said we should meet again this very day, as he was coming at your request to confer with you.

ALBA. He will meet you again.

FERDINAND. Of all the noblemen I know here I like him best. It seems that we shall be friends.

ALBA. You are still too impetuous and incautious; you always remind me of your mother's fecklessness which drove her unconditionally into my arms. More than once appearances have led you to enter into dangerous relationships precipitately.

FERDINAND. You will find me flexible.

ALBA. Because of your young blood I forgive these impulsive affections, this heedless gaiety. Only never forget what is the work I was called to accomplish, nor what part in it I wish to entrust to you.

FERDINAND. Admonish me and do not spare me, where you think it necessary.

ALBA, *after a pause.* My son!

FERDINAND. My father!

ALBA. The princes will soon be here. Orange and Egmont are coming. It is not out of mistrust that I now reveal to you what will happen. They will not leave this Palace.

FERDINAND. What is your plan?

ALBA. It has been decided to hold them here. . . . You are astonished! Now, hear what you are to do. As for the reasons, you will know them when it is done; there is no time now to go into them. You are the one with whom I would wish to discuss the greatest, most secret issues. A strong bond unites us. You are dear and close to me. I should like to confide everything to you. It is not the habit of obedience alone that I wish to inculcate in you, but also the capacity to plan, to command, to execute—these too I should like to perpetuate in you. To leave you a great inheritance and the King the most useful of servants; to provide you with the best that I have, so that you need not be ashamed to take your place among your brothers.

FERDINAND. How can I ever repay the debt of this love that you bestow on me alone, while a whole Empire trembles with awe of you?

ALBA. Now listen: this is what I want you to do. As soon as the princes have entered, every point of access to the Palace will be occupied. Gomez will see to this. Silva will hasten to arrest Egmont's secretary and other highly suspicious persons. You will supervise the guards at the gate and in the courts. Above all, put your most reliable men into the rooms adjoining this one, then wait in the gallery till Silva returns to bring me some insignificant paper as a sign that his commission has been executed. Then stay in the ante-chamber till Orange leaves. Follow him; I shall detain Egmont here, as if there were something else I wished to discuss with him. At the end of the gallery demand Orange's sword, call the guard, quickly put away the dangerous fellow; and I shall seize Egmont here.

FERDINAND. I shall obey you, Father. For the first time with a heavy heart and with anxiety.

ALBA. I forgive you; it's the first great day you have known.
    Enter SILVA.

SILVA. A messenger from Antwerp. Here is Orange's letter! He is not coming.

ALBA. Is that what the messenger tells you?

SILVA. No, it's my heart that tells me.

ALBA. My evil genius speaks in you.

    After reading the letter he waves his hand at both of them, and they withdraw to the gallery. He remains alone in the front.

He is not coming! And he puts off his explanation till the last moment. He dares *not* to come. So this time, contrary to my expectations, the prudent man was prudent enough not to be prudent. Time presses. Only a little turn more of the minute hand and a great work will have been done or missed, irrevocably missed; for it can neither be repeated nor kept secret. Long ago I had considered every possibility, even this one, and determined what was to be done in this case. And now that it has to be done I can hardly prevent the *pro* and *contra* from vacillating once more in my mind. . . . Is it wise to catch the others if he escapes me? Should I postpone it and let Egmont go with his men, with so many of them, who now, perhaps only to-day, are in my power? Thus Fate compels me, who was invincible. How long I pondered it! How well I prepared it! How fine and great was my plan! How close my hope to its aim! And now, at the moment of decision, I am placed between two evils. As into a lottery urn, I plunge my hand into the dark future: what I draw out is still tightly folded, unknown to me, perhaps a winner, perhaps a blank.

He grows alert, as if he can hear something, and steps to the window.

It's he! Egmont! Did your horse carry you in so easily, without sensing the smell of blood or the spirit with drawn sword who received you at the gate? . . . Dismount! . . . Now you have one foot in the grave; and now both feet! Yes, go on and stroke it, pat its neck for serving you so bravely—for the last time—and to me no choice remains. Never could Egmont hand himself over a second time as dazzled as he is now. . . . Listen!

FERDINAND *and* SILVA *approach hurriedly.*

ALBA. You will do as I commanded; I do not change my mind. I shall detain Egmont as best I can until you, Ferdinand, have brought me news about Silva. Then remain close to me! You, also, Fate deprives of this great merit, to have caught the King's greatest enemy with your own hands.

To SILVA.

Make haste!

To FERDINAND.

Go to meet him!

ALBA, *left alone for a few moments, paces the room in silence.*

Enter EGMONT.

EGMONT. I come to hear the King's will, to discover what service he asks of our loyalty which remains eternally devoted to him.

ALBA. What he desires above all is to know your opinion.

EGMONT. On what matter? Is Orange coming too? I expected to find him here.

ALBA. I much regret his absence at this important hour. The King desires your opinion, your advice, as to how these States can be pacified. Indeed he hopes that you will effectively collaborate in the task of curbing the unrest and establishing complete and lasting order in the Provinces.

EGMONT. You must know better than I that everything is quiet enough already, and indeed was more quiet still before the appearance of the new soldiers filled the people with fear and anxiety.

ALBA. If I am not mistaken, you wish to imply that it would have been most advisable on the King's part never to have placed me in the position of asking your advice.

EGMONT. I beg your pardon. It is not for me to judge whether the King should have sent the army, whether the power of his royal presence alone would not have proved more effective. The army is here; he is not. But we should be very ungrateful, very unmindful, if we did not remember what we owe to the Regent. Let us admit it: by her conduct, as wise as it was brave, she succeeded in quelling the insurgents by force and by esteem, by cunning and persuasion; and, to the astonishment of the whole world, in the space of a few months she recalled a rebellious people to its duty.

ALBA. I don't deny it. The riot has been put down, and everyone seems to have been driven back into the bonds of obedience. But does it not depend on each one's arbitrary whim whether or not he chooses to remain in them? Who will prevent the people from breaking out again? Where is the power that will restrain them? Who guarantees to us that they will continue to prove loyal subjects? Their good will is all the security we have.

EGMONT. And is not the good will of a people the safest and noblest of securities? By God! When can a King feel more secure than when all of them stand by one, and one stands by all? More secure, I mean, from internal and external enemies?

ALBA. Surely we are not going to persuade ourselves that this is the case in these Provinces at present?

EGMONT. Let the King issue a general amnesty, let him set their minds at rest, and we shall soon see loyalty and love return in the train of trust.

ALBA. And let everyone who has profaned the King's majesty, the sanctity of religion, go about scot-free where he pleases? To serve as a walking proof to others that atrocious crimes go unpunished?

EGMONT. But should not a crime of folly, of drunkenness, be excused rather than cruelly punished? Especially where there is well-founded hope, if not certainty, that these evils will not recur? Were kings any less secure, are they not praised by contemporaries and by posterity alike for finding it in them to pardon, pity, or despise an affront to their dignity? Is it not for that very reason that they are likened to God, who is far too great to be affected by every blasphemy?

ALBA. And for that very reason the King must fight for the dignity of God and religion, and we for the King's honour. What the One Above disdains to parry, it is our duty to avenge. Where I am judge, no guilty man shall rejoice in his impunity.

EGMONT. Do you think, then, that you will reach them all? Don't we hear daily that terror is driving them from one place to another, and out of the country? The richest will remove their wealth, themselves, their children, and their friends; the poor will place their hands at their neighbours' service.

ALBA. They will, if we cannot prevent them. That is why the King demands advice and help of all the princes, seriousness of every governor; not only tales about how things are and how they might be if we allowed everything to go on as it is. To look upon a great evil, flatter oneself with hope, put one's trust in time, at the most to deliver one blow, as in a carnival farce, so that one can hear the smack and appear to be doing something when one's desire is to do nothing—might not this arouse the suspicion that one is watching the rebellion with pleasure, unwilling to incite it, yet glad to encourage it?

EGMONT, *about to lose his temper, restrains himself and, after a short pause, says calmly.* Not every intention is manifest, and the intentions of many are early misinterpreted. Thus we are told everywhere that the King's intention is not so much to rule the Provinces in accordance with clear and unambiguous laws, to protect the majesty of religion and grant general peace to his people, as to enslave them absolutely, deprive them of their ancient rights, grasp their possessions, curtail the fine privileges of the aristocracy, for whose sake alone the noble man would dedicate body and soul to his service. Religion, they say, is only a splendid screen behind which every dangerous scheme can be more easily hatched. The people are on their knees and worship the holy embroidered emblems, but behind the screen the bird catcher lurks and listens, waiting to ensnare them.

ALBA. Must I hear this from *you?*

EGMONT. These are not my views. Only what is said and rumoured abroad by great and small, foolish and wise alike. The Netherlanders fear a double yoke; and who has pledged to maintain their freedom?

ALBA. Freedom? A fine word, if only one could understand it! What kind of freedom do they want? What is the freedom of the most free? To do what is right! . . . And in this the King will not hinder them. No, no! They do not feel free if they cannot harm themselves and others. Would it not be better to abdicate than to rule such a people? When foreign enemies press us, of whom no citizen is aware because he is concerned with the most immediate things, and the King asks for help, they will quarrel among themselves and make common cause with their enemies. Far better to hedge them in, to treat them like children, so that one can lead them to their own welfare like children. Believe me, a people does not grow up, or grow wise; a people remains perpetually childish.

EGMONT. How rarely a King attains discretion! And should not the many put their trust in the many rather than in one? And not even in one, but in the few that surround the one, the clan that grows old under its master's gaze? I suppose this clan alone has the right to grow wise.

ALBA. Perhaps it has, just because it is not left to its own devices.

EGMONT. And for that reason is reluctant to leave anyone else to his own devices. Do what you please. I've replied to your question and repeat: it will not work. It cannot work. I know my compatriots. They are men worthy to walk on God's earth; each one a world to himself, a little king, steadfast, active, capable, loyal, attached to old customs. It is hard to win their confidence, easy to keep it. Stubborn and steadfast! Pressure they will bear; oppression never.

ALBA, *who meanwhile has turned his head several times.* Would you repeat all that in the presence of the King?

EGMONT. All the worse, if his presence made me afraid! All the better for him, for his people if he inspired me with courage, gave me confidence to say a great deal more!

ALBA. If what you have to say is useful, I can listen to it as well as he can.

EGMONT. I should say to him: the shepherd can easily drive a whole herd of sheep along, the ox draws its plough without resisting. But if you wish to ride a thoroughbred horse, you must learn to read its thoughts, you must demand nothing foolish nor demand it foolishly. That is why the citizens wish to retain their old constitution, to be ruled by their compatriots, for they know how they will be led and can expect these leaders to be both disinterested and concerned with the people's fate.

ALBA. But shouldn't the Regent be empowered to change

these old traditions? And could not this be the most precious of his privileges? What is permanent in this world? And should one expect a political institution to be permanent? Must not the circumstances change in time, and, for that very reason, must not an old constitution become the cause of a thousand evils, because it takes no account of the present state of the people? I fear that these old rights are so acceptable because they offer dark recesses in which the cunning and the mighty can hide and hold out at the people's cost, at the expense of the whole.

EGMONT. And these arbitrary changes, these unrestricted interferences on the part of the highest authority, do they not forebode that one desires to do what thousands must not do? He desires to liberate himself alone, so that he may gratify every whim, translate every thought into action. And if we were to put all our trust in him, a good wise King, can he speak for his successors? Can he assure us that none will rule without mercy and consideration? Who then would save us from absolute despotism, when he sends us his servants and minions to rule and dispose as they please, without knowledge of our country or of its needs, meet no resistance, and feel free of all responsibility?

ALBA, *who has looked behind him again.* Nothing is more natural than that a King should seek to rule by his own means and prefer to entrust his orders to those who understand him best, endeavour to understand him, and obey his will unconditionally.

EGMONT. And it is just as natural that the citizen should wish to be ruled by those who were born and bred where he was, who were imbued with the same ideas of right and wrong, whom he can look upon as brothers.

ALBA. And yet the aristocracy can hardly be said to have shared equally with these brothers?

EGMONT. This occurred centuries ago and is now accepted without envy. But if new men were sent to us gratuitously to enrich themselves once more at the nation's expense, if the people knew themselves to be at the mercy of a severe, bold, and unlimited avarice, it would cause a ferment that would not easily subside into itself.

ALBA. You tell me what I ought not to hear; I too am a foreigner.

EGMONT. My telling it to you shows that I don't mean you.

ALBA. Even so I would rather not hear it from you. The King sent me in the hope that I should receive the support of the nobility. The King *wills* his will. The King, after long reflection, has seen what the people requires; things cannot go on, cannot remain as they were. It is the King's intention to restrict them for their own good, if need be to thrust their own welfare upon them, to sacrifice the harmful citizens so that the best may live in peace and enjoy the blessing of wise government. This is his resolve. To convey it to the nobility is my charge; and what I demand in his name is advice as to how it is to be done, not what is to be done, for this he has decided.

EGMONT. Unfortunately your words justify the people's apprehension, the general apprehension. For he has decided what no prince has the right to decide. His will is to weaken, oppress, destroy the strength of his people—their self-confidence, their own conception of themselves—so as to be able to rule them without effort. His will is to corrupt the very core of their individuality; doubtless with the intention to make them happier. His will is to annihilate them so that they will become something, a different something. Oh, if his intention is good, it is being misguided. It is not the King whom this people resists; what it opposes is only the King who is taking the first unfortunate steps in a direction utterly wrong.

ALBA. In your state of mind it seems useless for us to try to come to an understanding. You belittle the King and hold his advisers in contempt if you doubt that all this has already been considered, investigated, and weighed up. It is not my business to go into every *pro* and *contra* once more. Obedience is what I ask of the people—and of you, the foremost and greatest, I ask counsel and action as pledges for this absolute duty.

EGMONT. Demand our heads and have done with it! Whether his neck will bend under this yoke or bow to the axe is all one to a noble soul. It was in vain that I spoke at such length. I have shaken the air, and gained nothing more.

Enter FERDINAND.

FERDINAND. Forgive me for interrupting your conversation. The bearer of this letter requires an urgent reply.

ALBA. Excuse me while I see what it contains.

Steps aside.

FERDINAND, *to* EGMONT. That's a fine horse your men have brought to fetch you.

EGMONT. It's not the worst. I've had it for a while; I'm thinking of parting with it. If you like it, perhaps we can come to terms.

FERDINAND. Good. Let's discuss the matter.

ALBA *motions to his son, who withdraws to the back.*

EGMONT. Good-bye. Dismiss me now, for, by God, I can think of nothing more to say.

ALBA. A happy chance has prevented you from betraying your thoughts farther. Recklessly you opened the very folds of your heart and have accused yourself much more severely than any opponent could have done in his malice.

EGMONT. The rebuke does not touch me; I know myself well enough, and am aware how devoted I am to the King—much more than many who serve their own interests in his service. It is with reluctance that I leave this quarrel without seeing it resolved, and only wish that our service of one master, the welfare of the country, will soon unite us. Perhaps a second conference and the presence of the other princes, who are absent to-day, will bring about at some happier moment what to-day seems impossible. With that hope I leave you.

ALBA, *giving a sign to* FERDINAND. Stop, Egmont! Your sword!

The middle door opens; one catches a glimpse of the gallery occupied by guards, who remain immobile.

EGMONT, *after a brief, astonished silence.* So that was your purpose! It was for that you called me?

Clutching his sword, as if to defend himself.

Did you think I'm defenceless?

ALBA. It is the King's order; you are my prisoner.

At the same moment armed men enter from both sides.

EGMONT, *after a silence.* The King? Oh, Orange, Orange!

After a pause, handing over his sword.

Well, take it, then. It has served me more often to defend the King's cause than to protect this body.

Exit through the middle door. The armed men follow him out; also ALBA'S *son.* ALBA *remains standing.*

ACT V

Street at Dusk

CLARE. BRACKENBURG. CITIZENS

BRACKENBURG. Darling. For heaven's sake! What are you doing?

CLARE. Come with me, Brackenburg. You can't know much about people or you wouldn't doubt that we shall free him. For don't they love him dearly? I swear that every one of them is filled with a burning desire to save him, to avert this danger from a precious life and give back freedom to the most free of all. Come on! All that's lacking is a voice to call them together. They haven't forgotten what they owe to him and they know that it's his mighty arm alone that protects them from disaster. On his account and their own they must stake all they have. And what is it we stake? Our lives, at the most, and those are not worth preserving if he dies.

BRACKENBURG. Poor, foolish girl! You don't see the power that fetters us hopelessly!

CLARE. They don't seem unbreakable to me. But let's not waste time on idle words! Here come some of those honest, brave fellows of the old sort. Listen, friends. Listen, neighbours. . . . Tell me, what news of Egmont?

CARPENTER. What does the child want? Tell her to be quiet.

CLARE. Come closer, so that we can talk softly till we're in agreement, and stronger. We haven't a moment to lose. The insolent tyranny that dares to put him in chains is drawing its dagger to murder him. Oh, friends, every minute of the gathering dusk makes me more anxious. I fear this night. Come on! Let's divide into small groups and run through every district, calling the citizens out into the street. Each will take his old weapons. We shall meet again in the market-place, and our stream will sweep everyone along with it. Our enemies will find themselves surrounded and flooded, and will know that they are defeated. How can a handful of slaves resist us? And he, back in our midst, will turn about, know that he's free, and thank us all one day, thank us who were so deeply in his debt. Perhaps he'll see—no, certainly he'll see—another dawn break in an open sky.

CARPENTER. What's the matter with you, girl?

CLARE. Don't you understand me? I'm speaking of the Count! I'm speaking of Egmont.

JETTER. Don't mention that name. It's deadly.

CLARE. Not that name. What? Not mention his name? Who doesn't mention it at every possible opportunity? Who can escape it anywhere? Often I've read it in these stars, every letter of it. And you ask me not to mention it? What can you mean? Oh, friends, dear good neighbours, you're dreaming, come to your senses. Don't stare at me so blankly and timidly. Nor glance about you in that furtive way! I'm only calling out to you what every one of you wants. Isn't my voice the very voice of your own hearts? Who, in this ominous night, before retiring to a restless bed, would not fall on his knees in earnest prayer imploring Heaven for his safety? Ask one another; let each of you ask himself! And who will not say after me: Egmont's freedom or death!

JETTER. God preserve us! This will end in disaster.

CLARE. Don't go. Stay here instead of cringing from his name, which once you welcomed, happily applauded. When rumour announced him, when the news spread: "Egmont is coming! He is coming back from Ghent!" the inhabitants of those streets through which he must pass thought themselves lucky. And when you heard the clatter of his horses each one threw down his work at once, and over all the careworn faces which you thrust out of the windows there passed a gleam of joy and hope like a ray of sunlight cast by his face. Then you lifted up your children on the threshold and pointed out to them: "Look, that's Count Egmont, the tallest, there! That's Egmont! The one from whom you can expect better times than ever your poor fathers knew!" Don't wait to let your children ask one day: "Where is he gone? Where are the times you promised us?" . . . And here we stand chattering! Wasting idle words, betraying him!

SOEST. You should be ashamed of yourself, Brackenburg. Don't let her go on. Stop her before it's too late.

BRACKENBURG. Clare, my dearest, let's go. What will your mother say? Perhaps . . .

CLARE. Do you take me for a child, or a madwoman? Perhaps what? You won't drag me away from this terrible certainty with any hope you can invent. You must listen to me and you shall: for I can see you're deeply troubled and can find no guidance in your own hearts. Just let a single glance pierce through the present danger, back to the past, the recent past. Or turn your thoughts to the future! Can you live at all, *will* you live if he perishes? With his last breath our freedom too expires. What was he to you? For whose sake did he deliver himself up to the most pressing danger? Only for you his wounds bled and healed. The great spirit that supported you all languishes in a cell, and treacherous murder lurks in the dark corners. Perhaps he is thinking of you, placing his hopes in you, though accustomed only to give and to fulfil.

CARPENTER. Come along; let's be off.

CLARE. And I have no strength, no muscles like yours; but I have what all of you lack—courage and contempt for danger! If only my breath could infuse you with some of it! If only I could lend you human warmth and vigour by pressing you to my breast! Come with me! I shall walk in your midst! Just as a floating banner, in itself defenceless, leads a band of noble warriors on, so, flaring over all your heads, my spirit hovers, and love and courage will weld this wavering, scattered people into a terrible army.

JETTER. Get her away from here! I feel sorry for her.

Exeunt CITIZENS.

BRACKENBURG. Clare, my dear. Can't you see where we are?

CLARE. Yes: under the sky that so often seemed to expand more gloriously when noble Egmont walked under it. It's from these windows they looked out, four or five heads, one above the other. In front of these doors they bowed and scraped when he looked down at the lily-livered wretches. Oh, how I loved them then, because they honoured him. Had he been a tyrant, they would have every right to sneak away from him now. But they loved him! Oh, those hands that could raise hats are too feeble to lift a sword. . . . Brackenburg, what about us? Can we reproach them? These arms, that so often held him fast, what are they doing for him? Cunning has always succeeded so well in this world. You know the ins and outs, you know the old Palace. Nothing is impossible. But tell me what to do!

BRACKENBURG. What if we went home?

CLARE. A good idea!

BRACKENBURG. There's one of Alba's patrols on that corner; do listen to the voice of reason. Do you think I'm a coward? Don't you think me capable of dying for you? But we're both out of our senses, I no less than you. Can't you see what's impossible? Try to pull yourself together. You're beside yourself.

CLARE. Beside myself? That's disgusting, Brackenburg. It's you who're beside yourself. When you were loud in your reverence for the hero, called him your friend, your protector, your hope, and cheered him when he appeared— then I stood in my corner of the room, half raised the window, listened, and hid myself, and yet my heart beat faster than the hearts of all you men. And now again it beats faster than all your hearts! You hide yourselves because it's good for you, deny him and don't even feel that you will perish if he dies.

BRACKENBURG. Let's go home.

CLARE. Home?

BRACKENBURG. Only try to think! Look about you. There are the streets where you walked only on Sundays, through which you passed modestly on your way to church, where, with excessive respectability, you were angry with me if I joined you with a friendly word of greeting. Here you stand and talk and act in full view of the public. Only try to think, my dearest. What's the use of it all?

CLARE. Home! Oh yes, I remember. I'm thinking, Brackenburg. Let's go home! Do you know where my home is?
Exeunt.

Prison

Lighted by a lamp, a bunk in the background. EGMONT,
alone.

EGMONT. Old friend, ever-faithful sleep, do you forsake me
too, like my other friends? How willingly once you descended upon my free head and, like a lovely myrtle wreath
of love, cooled my temples. In the midst of battle, on the
wave of love, lightly breathing I rested in your arms like a
burgeoning boy. When gales roared through trees and
foliage, branch and crest creaked as they bent, yet deep
within the heart's core remained unmoving. What is it that
shakes you now? What is it that shivers your steadfast loyal
will? I feel it, it is the sound of the murderous axe that
nibbles at my root. Still I stand fast and upright, but an inward shudder runs through me. Yes, treacherous power
prevails, it is stronger than I. It undermines the high, solid
trunk; before the bark has withered, roaring and shattering,
the crest will fall.

Why, now, you that so often blew away mighty cares
from your head like soap-bubbles, why now can you not
drive off the thousand-limbed forebodings that stir within
your heart? Since when has Death assumed a fearful appearance for you, who once lived calmly with this changing
image as with all the other shapes of the familiar world?
But then, it is not he, the swift enemy, whom the healthy
man longs to meet in close combat; the prison cell it is,
prefiguring the grave, repulsive to the hero and the coward
alike. I found it insufferable enough to sit on my padded
chair when in solemn council the princes endlessly and
repetitively debated what could have been decided in a moment, and when between the gloomy walls of a great hall
the beams of the ceiling seemed to throttle me! Then I
would hurry out as soon as possible and leap upon my

horse's back with a deep breath! Then quickly out where
we belong! Out to the fields, where from the earth all Nature's most immediate remedies, vaporous, rise, and through
the heavens, wafting all the blessings of the planets, en-
wrapping us, descend upon our heads; where, like the earth-
born giant, strengthened by our mother's touch, we rise to
our full height; where we feel wholly human, one with all
that's human, human desire pulsing through every vein;
where the urge to press forward, to be victorious, to seize,
to use one's fists, to possess, to conquer glows in the young
huntsman's soul; where the soldier is quick to arrogate to
himself his inborn claim to all the world and in his terrible
freedom rages like a hailstorm through meadow, field, and
forest, wreaking destruction, and knows no bounds that human hands have set. A mere phantasm, this, this dream of
remembered bliss that so long was mine. What has treacherous Fortune done with it? Does Fortune now refuse to
grant you that quick death you never shunned in the full
glare of the sun, to offer you instead a foretaste of the grave
in nauseous mustiness? How vilely now it breathes upon
me from these stones! Already life congeals; and from my
bed, as from the grave, my foot recoils.

O Care, you that begin your murderous work before the
event, leave off! Since when has Egmont been alone, utterly
alone in this world? It's doubt that makes you helpless now,
not Fortune. Has the King's justice, in which you trusted
all your life, has the Regent's friendship which—why not
admit it now?—was almost love, have these vanished like a
shining, fiery mirage of the night? And do they leave you
lonely now, plunged into darkness, on a dangerous track?
Will not Orange venture out scheming at the head of your
assembled friends? Will not a crowd collect and, with growing force, go out to rescue an old friend?

O walls that now enclose me, do not halt the kindly
progress of so many spirits. And that courage which once
poured out of my eyes into theirs, let it now flow back from
their hearts into mine. Oh yes, they stir in their thousands,
they are coming, to stand by me now. Their pious wishes
wing their way to Heaven and beg for a miracle. And if no
angel comes to my aid from above, I see them take up their

swords and lances. The gates split in two, the bars burst asunder, the wall comes crashing down with their impact, and gladly Egmont steps out towards the freedom of approaching day. How many familiar faces receive me jubilantly. Oh, Clare, if you were a man, I should surely see you here, the very first to welcome me, and I should owe you what it is hard to owe to a King, freedom.

Clare's House

CLARE *comes out of her bedroom with a lamp and a glass of water. She sets down the glass on the table and goes to the window.*

CLARE. Brackenburg? Is that you? What was that noise? No one yet? It was no one. I shall put the lamp on the window sill so that he can see that I'm still awake, that I'm still waiting for him. He promised to bring me news. News? No, horrible certainty. Egmont condemned! What court of law has the right to summon him? And yet they condemn him. Does the King condemn him, or the Duke? And the Regent washes her hands of it. Orange dilly-dallies, and all his friends. . . . Is this the world of whose inconstancy and unreliability I have heard much, but experienced nothing? Is this the world? Who would be so wicked as to be an enemy to him? Could malice be powerful enough to cause the sudden downfall of one so generally loved and esteemed? And yet it *is* so. It is. . . . Oh, Egmont, both from God and men I thought you safe as in my arms! What was I to you? You called me yours, and I was truly yours, wholly devoted and dedicated to you. . . . What am I now? In vain I stretch out my arms towards the noose that grips you. You helpless, and I free! Here is the key to my door. My coming and going depend on my own free will, and yet I am nothing to you. Oh, fetter me to keep me from despair! And cast me down into the deepest dungeon to beat my head against damp walls, to whimper for freedom, dream of how I would help him if I weren't fettered and chained—how I should help him then! But now I'm free, and in that freedom lies the fear of impotence. Fully conscious, yet incapable of moving a finger to help him. Oh, even the smaller part of you, your Clare, is a prisoner as you are and, separated from you, wastes her last strength in a deathly convulsion. . . . I hear someone creeping in—a cough, Brackenburg—yes, he's come. Poor, honest Brackenburg, your fate is always the same. Your sweetheart opens the door to you at night, but oh, for how unhappy, ill-omened a meeting!

Enter BRACKENBURG.

CLARE. You look so pale and harassed, Brackenburg. What is it?

BRACKENBURG. I've passed through dangers and detours to see you. All the main streets are guarded. I stole my way to you through alleys and dark nooks.

CLARE. Tell me what's happening.

BRACKENBURG, *taking a seat.* Oh, Clare, I feel like weeping. I had no love for him. He was the rich man who lured away the poor man's only sheep to a better pasture. I've never cursed him. God made me loyal and softhearted. But all my life dissolved in pain and flowed out of me, and my daily hope was that I should languish away.

CLARE. Forget it, Brackenburg! Forget yourself. Tell me about him. Is it true? He's been condemned?

BRACKENBURG. He has. I know it beyond doubt.

CLARE. And he's still alive?

BRACKENBURG. Yes, he's still alive.

CLARE. How can you be sure about it? Tyranny murders the glorious man overnight. His blood flows where no one can see him. The people lies drugged in anxious sleep and dreams of rescue, dreams the fulfilment of its impotent wish. Meanwhile, dissatisfied with us, his soul forsakes this world. He's gone! Don't deceive me. Don't deceive yourself.

BRACKENBURG. No, he's alive, I assure you. . . . But the Spaniard is preparing a terrible spectacle for the people whom he wants to tread underfoot violently and forever; he will crush every heart that stirs for freedom.

CLARE. Carry on and calmly pronounce my death sentence also. Already I am walking closer and closer to the fields of the blessed and can feel the comfort wafted over from those regions of everlasting peace. Tell me all.

BRACKENBURG. I could tell by the patrol and gather from stray remarks that something gruesome is being prepared in secret in the market-place. Through byways, through familiar passages, I crept to my cousin's house and looked down on the market-place from a back window. Torches flickered in a wide circle of Spanish soldiers. I strained my eyes, unaccustomed to such sights, and out of the night a black scaffold loomed up at me, spacious and high. I felt faint with horror. A great many men were busy around it, draping black cloth around any of the woodwork that was still white and visible. Last of all they covered the steps as well; I saw them do it. They seemed to be dedicating the site for an abominable sacrifice. A white crucifix, which shone in the night like silver, had been erected high up on one side. I looked on and grew more and more certain of the terrible certainty. Still torches swayed about here and there; gradually they vanished or went out. All at once this monstrous progeny of the night had returned to its mother's womb.

CLARE. Quiet, Brackenburg. Be silent now. Let this veil cover my soul. The spectres are gone, and you, lovely night, lend your cloak to the earth that's in ferment inwardly; no longer Earth will bear her loathsome burden but opens her deep jaws and, grating, swallows down the murderous scaffold. And surely an angel will be sent by that God whom they have blasphemously made a witness to their fury; bolts and fetters will break at the messenger's holy touch, and he will surround our friend with a mild radiance; gently and silently he'll lead him through the night to freedom. And my way too leads through that darkness secretly, and I go to meet him.

BRACKENBURG, *detaining her*. Where, child, where? What are you going to do?

CLARE. Quiet, my dear, so that no one will wake up; so that we shan't wake ourselves. Do you know this little bottle, Brackenburg? I took it away from you for a joke, when you used to threaten suicide in your impatience. . . . And now, my friend——

BRACKENBURG. By all the saints!

CLARE. You won't prevent it. Death is my part. And don't begrudge me this quick, gentle death, which for yourself you held in readiness. Give me your hand! At the very moment when I open the dark door which permits no going back, I could tell you by the pressure of this hand how much I loved you and how much I pitied you. My brother died young, it was you I chose to take his place. Your heart protested, tormented itself and me—more and more hotly you demanded what was not meant for you. Forgive me, and farewell. Let me call you brother; it is a name in which a host of other names are contained. And faithfully treasure my last parting gift—accept this kiss. Death unites all things, Brackenburg, and it unites us too.

BRACKENBURG. Then let me die with you. Share it with me, share it! There is enough of it to put out two lives.

CLARE. No, you shall live, you can live. Help my mother, who but for you would die of poverty. Be to her what I can no longer be; live together and weep for me. Weep for your country and for him who alone could have preserved it. The present generation will not recover from this shame, even the fury of revenge will not blot it out. Poor people, drag out your lives through this age that is no age at all. To-day the world comes to a sudden stop; its turning ceases, and my pulse will beat but a few minutes longer. Farewell.

BRACKENBURG. Oh, live with us, as we for you alone! You murder us in you. Oh, live and suffer! Inseparable we shall support you at either side, and always considerate, love shall grant you the comfort of two loving arms. Be ours, because I may not say, be mine.

CLARE. Quiet, Brackenburg, you're not aware how you touch me. What is hope to you is despair to me.

BRACKENBURG. Share that hope with the living. Stay on the brink of the abyss; glance down it once and look back at us.

CLARE. I have conquered; don't call me back into the battle.

BRACKENBURG. You're in a daze; wrapped up in night you seek the depth. But even now not every light is out, still many a day will dawn.

CLARE. Woe to you, woe! Cruelly you tear up the curtain before my eyes. Yes, that day will break! In vain pull all the mists about itself and break against its will. Anxiously the citizen will look out of his window, the night leave behind a black stain; he looks, and, horribly, the murderous scaffold grows in daylight. In renewed anguish the profaned image of Christ will raise an imploring eye to the Father above. The sun will not dare to shine, refusing to mark the hour at which he is to die. Wearily the hands of the clock move on their way, one hour after another strikes. Stop! Now it is time! The premonition of morning drives me to my grave.

She goes to the window as if to look out and secretly drinks.

BRACKENBURG. Clare! Clare!

CLARE *goes to the table and drinks the water.* Here is the rest. I do not ask you to follow. Do what you may, farewell. Put out this lamp quietly and without delay. I am going to lie down. Creep away softly, close the door behind you. Quietly! Don't wake my mother. Go, save yourself! Save yourself! If you don't want to be taken for my murderer. *Exit.*

BRACKENBURG. She leaves me, as usual, for the last time. Oh, if a human soul could know its power to rend a loving heart! She leaves me standing here, left by myself, and death and life are equally loathsome to me now. To die alone! Weep, you lovers, there is no harder fate than mine. She shares the poison with me and dismisses me. Sends me away from her! She drags me after her and pushes me back into life. Oh, Egmont, what a praiseworthy lot is yours! She is the first to set out, you'll take the wreath of victory from her hand; bringing all heaven with her she meets you on your way. . . . And shall I follow? To stand aside again? And carry inextinguishable envy into those celestial realms? On earth there is no staying now for me, and hell and heaven offer equal anguish. How welcome the dreadful hand of annihilation would be to this wretch!

Exit BRACKENBURG. *The stage remains unchanged for a while. Then music, signifying the death of* CLARE, *strikes up; the lamp, which* BRACKENBURG *forgot to extinguish, flares*

*up a few times more, then goes out. Soon the scene changes
to*

Prison

EGMONT *lies sleeping on his berth. There is a rattling of keys,
and the door opens. Servants enter with torches, followed by*
FERDINAND, ALBA'S *son, and* SILVA, *accompanied by armed
men.* EGMONT *wakes up with a start.*

EGMONT. Who are you, who so roughly shake away sleep from
my eyes? What do your defiant, uncertain glances betoken
to me? Why this dreadful procession? What lying nightmare
have you come to present to my half-awakened spirit?

SILVA. The Duke sends us to announce your sentence to you.

EGMONT. Have you brought the hangman too to execute it?

SILVA. Listen to it, then you will know what awaits you.

EGMONT. This befits you well and befits your shameful un-
dertaking. Hatched out at night and carried out at night.
So this insolent deed of injustice may remain hidden. Step
forward boldly, you who keep the sword concealed beneath
your cloak. Here is my head, the freest that ever tyranny
severed from its socket.

SILVA. You are mistaken. What fair judges have resolved they
will not conceal from the face of day.

EGMONT. In that case their insolence exceeds all measure and
conception.

SILVA *takes the verdict from one of the attendants, unfolds it,
and reads.* "In the name of the King, and by authority of a
special power bestowed on us by His Majesty to judge all
his subjects, of whatever station, not excluding Knights of
the Golden Fleece, after due . . ."

EGMONT. Can the King bestow that power?

SILVA. "After due, lawful, and exact examination of the evidence we declare you, Henry, Count Egmont, Prince of
Gavre, guilty of High Treason, and pronounce the sentence:
that at the first break of day you be led from your cell to
the market-place and that there, in the full view of the peo-

ple, as a warning to all traitors, you suffer death by the sword. Signed in Brussels on . . ."

Date and year are read out indistinctly, so that audience do not catch them.

". . . by Ferdinand, Duke of Alba, President of the Court of the Twelve."

Now you know your fate; you have little time left to reconcile yourself to it, put your house in order, and take leave of your nearest and dearest.

Exeunt SILVA *and attendants.* FERDINAND *remains with two torch bearers. The stage is dimly lit.*

EGMONT *has remained standing, deep in thought, and allowed* SILVA *to leave without looking up. He thinks he is alone and as he raises his eyes he sees* ALBA's *son.* You stay behind? Is it your wish to add to my astonishment, my horror, by your presence? Are you perhaps waiting to bring your father the welcome news of my unmanly despair? Go, then! Tell him. Tell him that he deceives neither me nor the world with his lies. At first they will whisper it behind his back, then tell it to him, the ambitious seeker of fame, aloud and more loudly still; and when one day he descends from this peak, thousands of voices will cry it out at him! Not the welfare of the state, not the dignity of the King, not the peace of the Provinces brought him here. For his own sake he counselled war, so that the warrior might prove himself in war! It was he who created this monstrous confusion, so that he would be needed! And I fall as a victim to his vile hatred, his mean jealousy. Yes, I know it and have the right to say it: the dying man, the mortally wounded, may say it. The conceited man envied me; to destroy me was his dear and long-deliberated plan. Even when we were younger and played at dice together, and piles of gold, one after another, speedily moved from his side to mine, he stood there grimly, pretending indifference but inwardly consumed with anger, more at my gain than at his loss. I still recall the glowering gaze, the significant pallor when, at a public festivity, in front of many thousands of people, we competed in a shooting match. He challenged me, and both nations, Spaniards and Netherlanders, stood there betting and wishing. I beat him; his bullet missed, mine hit the mark. A loud cheer broke from my supporters and resounded in the air. Now his shot hits me. Tell him that I know it, that I know him, that the world despises every sign of victory which a petty mind erects for itself by base wiles. As for you, if it is possible for a son to forsake the ways of his father, practise shame in time, by feeling ashamed for him whom you would like to revere with all your heart.

FERDINAND. I listen to you without interrupting. Your reproaches weigh on me like the blows of a club on a helmet. I feel the impact but I am armed. You strike home but you do not wound me. All I feel is the pain that rends my heart. Woe is me that I should have grown up to look on such a sight, that I was destined to act in such a play!

EGMONT. What am I to make of that lamentation? Why should you be moved or troubled? Is it belated remorse at your part in the shameful conspiracy? You are so young, and your appearance promises well. You were so candid, so friendly towards me. As long as I looked at you, I was reconciled to your father. And just as false, more false than he, you lured me into the snare. You are the hideous one! Whoever trusts *him* does so at his peril; but who would suspect any peril in trusting you? Be off with you. Don't rob me of these last moments! Be off, so that I may collect my thoughts, forget the world, and you before all else! . . .

FERDINAND. What can I say to you? I stand and look at you and yet I do not see you nor feel that I am myself. Shall I excuse myself? Shall I assure you that I did not discover my father's intentions till late, till right at the end; that I acted as a passive, inanimate instrument of his will? What can it matter now what you may think of me? You are lost; and I, wretch that I am, only stand here to convince you of it and to bewail you.

EGMONT. What a strange voice, what unexpected comfort to meet on my way to the grave! You, the son of my first, almost my only enemy, you feel sorry for me, you are not on the side of my murderers? Speak up. Tell me! In what light am I to regard you?

FERDINAND. Cruel father! Oh yes, I recognize you in that command. You knew my feelings, my disposition, which so often you rebuked as the inheritance of a tender mother. To mould me in your image you sent me here. To see this man on the edge of his yawning grave, in the grip of a violent death, you compel me; no matter what becomes of me, no matter that I suffer the deepest anguish. If only I become deaf and blind to every kind of plight. If only I become insensitive!

EGMONT. You astonish me! Control yourself! Stand up and speak like a man!

FERDINAND. Oh, that I were a woman! So that one could say to me: what's moving you? What disturbs you so? Tell me of a greater, a more monstrous evil—make me the witness to a more abominable deed. I shall thank you, I shall say: it was nothing.

EGMONT. You forget yourself. Remember where you are!

FERDINAND. Let this passion rage, let me lament unrestrained! I have no wish to appear firm, when all is collapsing inside me. To think that I must see you here! You of all men! Oh, it's horrible. You don't understand me. And should you understand me? . . . Egmont! Egmont!

Falling on EGMONT's *neck.*

EGMONT. Solve me this riddle!

FERDINAND. No riddle.

EGMONT. How can you be so deeply moved by the fate of a stranger?

FERDINAND. No stranger. You're no stranger to me. It was your name that in my first youth shone to me like a star of heaven. How often I listened to tales about you, asked about you! The child's hope is the youth, the youth's hope the man. That is how you strode in front of me, always ahead of me, and always unenvious I saw you in front and followed you, step by step. Then at last I hoped to see you and did see you, and my heart went out to you. You I had chosen for myself, and confirmed my choice when I saw you. Now, only now, I hoped to be with you, to live with you, to grasp you, to—— Well, all that has been cut off now, and I see you here.

EGMONT. My friend, if it is of any help to you, accept my assurance that from the first moment I felt drawn to you. And listen to me. Let's exchange a few calm words. Tell me: is it the strict, serious intention of your father to kill me?

FERDINAND. It is.

EGMONT. This sentence, then, is not an idle show devised to frighten me, to punish me by fear and threats, to humiliate me, only to raise me up again by royal grace?

FERDINAND. No, alas, it is not. At first I consoled myself with this remote hope: and already then I felt pained and troubled to see you in this state. Now it is real, definite. No, I shall not control myself. Who will help me, advise me, how to escape the inevitable?

EGMONT. Then listen to me! If you are possessed by such a mighty urge to save me, if you abhor the superior strength of those who keep me fettered, save me then. Every moment is precious. You are the son of the all-powerful and powerful enough yourself. . . . Let us escape! I know the ways; the means cannot be unknown to you. Only these walls, only a few miles divide me from my friends. Loosen these fetters, take me to them, and be one of us. You can be sure the King will thank you one day for rescuing me. At present he is surprised, and perhaps he hasn't been informed of anything. Your father dares and decides; and His Majesty must approve what has been done, even if he is horrified by it. You are thinking? Oh, think out my way to freedom! Speak, and feed the last hope of my living soul!

FERDINAND. No more, I beg you. Every word you speak adds to my despair. There is no way out, no help, no refuge. . . . This torments me, it lacerates my heart. I myself helped to pull the net tight; I know how strongly and tightly it is knitted; I know how the way has been barred to every bold or ingenious resort. I feel that I share your fetters and those of all the others. Should I be lamenting now if I hadn't tried everything? I have lain at his feet, argued and implored. He sent me here to destroy in one moment all the joy and zest that still remained in me.

EGMONT. And there's no escape?

FERDINAND. None.

EGMONT, *stamping his foot*. No escape! Sweet life, dear lovely habit of living and of being active! I must part from you! And so indifferently too! Not in the tumult of battle, in the uproar of arms. In the scattering of a teeming crowd, do you grant me a brief farewell; you take no brusque leave of me, do not shorten the moment of parting. I am to seize your hand, look into your eyes once more, feel your beauty and worth intensely, poignantly as never before, then resolutely tear myself away and say: Good-bye!

FERDINAND. And I am to stand beside you, looking on, unable to hold or hinder you. Oh, what voice would suffice for this complaint? What heart would not break its bonds at this misery!

EGMONT. Calm yourself!

FERDINAND. You can be calm, you can renounce and take this difficult step like a hero, since Necessity holds you by the hand. What can I do? What should I do? You conquer yourself and us; you have come through. As for me, I survive both you and myself. In the banquet's merriment I shall have lost my light, in the tumult of battle my banner. Dreary, confused, and flat the future seems to me.

EGMONT. Young friend, whom by a strange twist of fortune I win and lose at the same time, who feel my death agony, suffer it on my behalf, look at me now; you do not lose me. If my life to you was a mirror in which you liked to contemplate yourself, let my death be the same. Men are not together only when they meet; even the most distant, the departed lives in us. I live for you and have lived long enough for myself. Every day of my life I was glad to be alive, every day of my life I did my duty with quick efficiency, as my conscience demanded. Now life comes to its end, as it could have done sooner, much sooner, even on the sands of Gravelingen. I cease to live; but at least I *have* lived. Now live as I did, my friend, gladly and with zest, and do not shun death!

FERDINAND. You might have preserved yourself for our sake; you should have done. You killed yourself. Often I've heard people talk about you—wise men, both hostile to you and well-disposed, and heard them debate your worth at great length. But in the end they agreed, no one dared to deny, everyone admitted: yes, he treads a dangerous path. How often I wished I could warn you! Did you have no friends, then?

EGMONT. I was warned.

FERDINAND. And, point by point, I found all these accusations set down once more in the present charge—and your replies! Good enough to excuse you; not pertinent enough to exculpate you——

EGMONT. That is as it may be. Men think that they direct their lives and are in control of themselves; yet their inmost selves are irresistibly pulled towards their destinies. Let's not reflect on it; I can easily rid myself of such thoughts—but not of my concern for this country. Yet even this will be taken care of. If my blood can flow for many and buy peace for my people, it flows willingly. I fear it won't be so. But men should cease to fret where they may no longer act. If you can limit or divert your father's nefarious power, do so! Who will be able to do it? . . . Farewell.

FERDINAND. I can't go.

EGMONT. I heartily commend my servants to you. I have good men and women in my service; see that they are not dispersed or made unhappy! What's become of Richard, my secretary?

FERDINAND. He preceded you. They beheaded him as your abettor in High Treason.

EGMONT. Poor soul! . . . One thing more, and then good-bye. My strength is exhausted. Whatever may preoccupy our minds, in the end Nature exacts her dues and that most insistently; and as a child entwined by a snake enjoys refreshing sleep, so the tired man lies down once more on the very threshold of death and deeply rests, as if a long day's journey lay ahead of him. . . . And one thing more—I know a girl; you will not despise her, since she was mine. Now that I have entrusted her to your care, I die at peace. You are a noble-minded man; a woman who finds such a man is safe from harm. Is my old William alive? Is he at liberty?

FERDINAND. The vigorous old man who always rides out with you?

EGMONT. That's the one.

FERDINAND. He's alive and at liberty.

EGMONT. He knows where she lives; let him take you there and pay him to the end of his days for showing you the way to that treasure. Farewell!

FERDINAND. I am not going.

EGMONT, *pushing him to the door.* Farewell!

FERDINAND. Oh, let me stay!

EGMONT. No leave-taking, friend.

He escorts FERDINAND *to the door and tears himself away from him there.* FERDINAND, *in a daze, hurries away.*

EGMONT, *alone.* Malevolent man! You never thought to render me this favour through your son. Through him I have been relieved of my cares and pain, of fear and every anxious feeling. Gently, yet urgently, Nature demands her last tribute. All is resolved; and all concluded. And that which in the previous night kept me awake on my uncertain bed now lulls my senses with unalterable certainty.

He sits down on his berth. Music.

Sweet sleep! Like purest happiness most willingly you come unbidden, unimplored! You loosen every knot of strenuous thought, consuming all the images of joy and pain; unobstructed flows the circle of inner harmonies, and swathed in agreeable delirium, we sink and cease to be.

He falls asleep; the music accompanies his sleep. Behind his bed the wall seems to open, a radiant apparition enters. Liberty in heavenly raiment, shining, rests upon a cloud. She has CLARE's *features and bows down towards the sleeping hero. She expresses a feeling of compassion, she seems to commiserate with him. Soon she calms herself and, with an enlivening gesture, shows him the quiver of arrows, then her staff and helmet. She invites him to be of good cheer and, by indicating to him that his death will win freedom for the Provinces, acclaims him victor and hands him a laurel wreath. As she approaches his head with the wreath,* EGMONT *moves, like one stirring in his sleep, so that he comes to lie with his face turned up to her. She holds the wreath suspended over his head; from the distance one hears the warlike music of drums and fifes. At the first, soft sound of this the apparition vanishes. The music grows louder.* EGMONT *awakes; the prison is dimly lit by the dawn. His first movement is to put his hand to his head: he rises and looks about, keeping his hand on his head.*

Gone is the wreath! Beautiful image, the light of day has driven you away! But it was they! Truly it was, combined, the two most treasured comforts of my heart. Divine Liberty, borrowing my beloved's features and shape; the sweet girl dressed in the heavenly raiment of her friend. In one solemn moment they appear united, more solemn than charming. With blood-stained soles she came before me, the billowing folds of her garment stained with blood. My blood it was, and that of many noble men. No, it was not shed in vain. Press on, brave people! The goddess of Victory leads you. And as the sea bursts through the dykes you build, so you shall burst and tumble down the mound of tyranny and, flooding all, wash it away from the dear site it has usurped.

Drumbeats come nearer.

Listen! Listen! How often this sound called me to stride freely towards the field of battle and victory! How blithely the companions trod that dangerous, honourable course! I too go from this cell to meet an honourable death; I die for freedom, for which I lived and fought and for which I now passively offer up myself.

The background is filled with a line of Spanish soldiers, carrying halberds.

Yes, go on and summon them! Close your ranks, you won't frighten me. I am accustomed to stand in front of spears, facing spears, and surrounded on all sides by the threat of death, to feel brave life flow through me with redoubled speed.

Drumbeats.

The enemy encircles you! His swords are flashing! Courage, friends, more courage! Behind you parents, wives, and children wait!

Pointing at the guards.

And these, the ruler's hollow words impel, not their true feelings. Protect your property! And to preserve your dearest ones, willingly, gladly fall as my example shows you.

Drumbeats. As he walks towards the guards, towards the back exit, the curtain falls; the music strikes up and concludes in a victorious strain.

DON CARLOS

A DRAMATIC POEM

Friedrich von Schiller

(1787)

English Version by James Kirkup

The Don Carlos of history was born in 1545 and died in 1569. It has been said that his father had him poisoned, and it is certain that Philip was greatly provoked, as Carlos was a cruel, frantic, and probably insane young man. If Schiller departed from history in his portrait of the prince, he liked to think he stayed close to it in his account of the king. "I do not know what kind of monster one expects," he wrote, "when Philip II is mentioned. My drama collapses when such a monster is found in it, and yet I hope to remain true to history, that is, to the chain of events."

E.B.

CHARACTERS

PHILIP II, *King of Spain*
ELIZABETH OF VALOIS, *his queen*
DON CARLOS, *the Crown Prince*
ALEXANDER FARNESE, *Prince of Parma, nephew to the King*
THE INFANTA CLARA EUGENIA, *a child of three*
THE DUCHESS OF OLIVAREZ, *chief lady-in-waiting*
THE MARCHIONESS OF MONDECAR
THE PRINCESS EBOLI ⎬ *ladies attending the queen*
THE COUNTESS OF FUENTES
THE MARQUIS OF POSA, *Chevalier of the Order of the Knights of Malta*
THE DUKE OF ALBA
THE COUNT LERMA, *Colonel of the King's Guard*
THE DUKE OF FERIA, *Knight of the Order of the Golden Fleece*
THE DUKE OF MEDINA SIDONIA, *Admiral of the Fleet*
DOMINGO, *the King's confessor*
THE GRAND INQUISITOR
THE PRIOR *of a Carthusian monastery*
THE QUEEN'S PAGE

Other ladies of the court, grandees, officers, pages.
The members of the King's bodyguard.

ACT I

SCENE 1

THE ROYAL GARDEN AT ARANJUEZ

DON CARLOS. DOMINGO

DOMINGO. The pleasant days in Aranjuez
Are nearly over now. Your Royal Highness
Has not improved in spirits. Our stay here
Has been in vain. But break
This curious silence, Prince: open your heart
To your father. No monarch can afford
To grudge his son—his only son—
Peace of heart and mind.

CARLOS *looks down and is silent.*

Prince, this elaborate display of silence
Which we have suffered now for eight long months,
Has cost His Majesty many sleepless nights
And given your mother bitter grief.

CARLOS, *suddenly turning on him.*
Mother? Mother did you say?
O God! I only wish I could forget
The man who made me call her that!

DOMINGO. Prince!

CARLOS, *recollecting himself.* Reverend sir,
I haven't had much luck with mothers.
When I first saw the light of day,
My birth was the murder of my mother.

DOMINGO. But surely, Prince, you cannot still
Reproach yourself with that?

CARLOS. And my new mother—has she not already
Cost me my father's love?

He hardly ever really loved me but required merely
That I should be his only son.
Then she gave him a daughter. Who knows
What history is plotting in the dark of time?

DOMINGO. Now you are hardly serious, Prince. All Spain
Adores his queen, and only you
Look upon her with the eye of hate. Why, Prince?
Carlos cannot hate a queen so loved by all.
Be careful. Do not let it come to her ears
How much she displeases you. It would hurt her grievously.

CARLOS. Do you really think so?

DOMINGO. If Your Highness will recollect
The last tourney at Saragossa,
When the King was wounded by a splintering lance,
The Queen was sitting with her ladies
In the seat of honour, watching the contest.
The cry went up: "The King is bleeding!"
There was suddenly a disturbance,
And the rumour reached the Queen.
"Is the Prince hurt?" she cried,
Jumping to her feet in sudden fear.
"No, it is the King himself," they told her.
Whereupon she sat down calmly once again and said,
"Get the doctors!"

After a pause.

Well, Prince? What do you say to that?

CARLOS. I am surprised that the King's excellent confessor
Should be so well-grounded in the gossip of the court.
I've always understood that those
Who spy on people's every word and gesture
Have done more evil in this world
Than the dagger and the poison of the murderer.
You might have saved yourself the trouble, sir.
If you require thanks, the King will give them gladly.

DOMINGO. You do well, Prince, to guard yourself against
A certain kind of person: but use discrimination.
Take care that you do not repulse
Both friend and enemy. I say it for your own good.

CARLOS. Then don't let my father know about it,
Or you'll lose your cardinal's hat.

DOMINGO. What?

CARLOS. You know what I mean.
Didn't he promise you should have
That honour conferred upon you? The first in Spain?

DOMINGO. Prince, you are pleased to joke . . .

CARLOS. Heaven forbid that I should joke
With the man whose word
Can save or damn my father!

DOMINGO. I shall not presume, Prince,
To inquire the nature of your secret pain.
I would only beg Your Highness to remember
That the church holds comfort for
Distress of conscience in confession,
To which no monarch keeps the key,
In which all evil deeds are locked
Beneath the seal of sacrament. You know, Prince,
What I mean.

CARLOS. Never would I seek to place my thoughts
Beneath your sacramental seal.

DOMINGO. Prince, this distrust will do you harm.
I am your most faithful servant.

CARLOS *takes his hand.* Then it would be better
To renounce your services to me.
The world knows you are a holy man, yet—
Let me be frank—I feel you have too many interests
Unworthy of a man of God.
You take the longest road to heaven, sir.
Too much knowledge would be a burden to you.
Tell that to my father when you see him.
I know he sent you here.

DOMINGO. Sent me . . . ?

CARLOS. That is what I said. Oh, I know
Only too well what traitors stand around me here:
I know that a thousand eyes
Are paid and prompted to observe my every move;
That the King has sold his son

To the meanest spies, who catch his every word;
And these ignoble whisperings
Are paid more highly than
One good deed. I know . . . but, oh,
If I once begin to tell you . . . Already
I have said too much.

DOMINGO. The King has decided to return
This evening to Madrid. You are to make
Your preparations, Prince,
And follow with the court.

CARLOS. Very well.

DOMINGO *goes. A pause.*

Poor, pitiable Philip, pitiable as your son.
You bleed already from the poisoned serpent's bite,
Whose dreadful revelations will make you mad!

SCENE 2

DON CARLOS. MARQUIS OF POSA

CARLOS. Who . . . Why, it's Roderich!

MARQUIS OF POSA. Carlos!

CARLOS. It's not possible . . . It just can't be you . . .
They embrace.
Oh, but it *is.* . . . How wonderful!
Now everything will be well again,
Even my own unhappy sickness . . .

MARQUIS OF POSA. Unhappy? Sickness? *What* is well again?
What is it had to be made well again?

CARLOS. And how is it you've come from Brussels,
So unexpectedly?

MARQUIS OF POSA. I hardly know, Prince, what to say.
I did not expect to find Don Philip's son
In such a state. This is not the lion-hearted youth
A subjugated race of heroes sent me to!
For I do not stand before you as

The companion of your youth but
As a representative of all mankind:
The provinces of Flanders
Send me to implore your aid.
Your beloved country will be ruined
If Alba's murderous fanaticism
Imposes Spanish laws on Brussels:
The country's final hope now rests
Upon the Emperor Karl's illustrious grandson.
All hope for her is ended, if his noble heart
Has forgotten how to share
The beating pulse of her oppressed humanity.

CARLOS. Then all hope for her
Is ended.

MARQUIS OF POSA. What do you mean?

CARLOS. All that is over now.
The friend you see before you now
Is not the one you used to know:
He is long since dead and buried.
Once, when we were fellow students
And I took my leave of you in Alcalá,
I had the sweet and heady dream
Of being the creator of a new and glorious Spain.
It was a childish fancy.
All that is finished now. My dreams are dead.

MARQUIS OF POSA. Dreams? Were they just dreams?

CARLOS. My father is a king, and yet
I do not know what it must be
To have a father.
You are the only friend I have,
The only one who knows my heart.
When we were boys together,
You were always faithful and,
Of all my companions, you
Were the truest and most loving friend.
And yet at first—do you remember?—
You would coldly kneel before me,
Offering respect, the formal homage
Which you said was due to sons of kings.

CARLOS. Yes, and whatever else you may require of me
  I shall gladly promise.

MARQUIS OF POSA. The king is returning to the capital.
  The time is short. If you wish to speak
  In secret with the queen, it must be
  Here in Aranjuez.

CARLOS. That was what I longed to do,
  But it's hopeless.

MARQUIS OF POSA. Not altogether. I am going now
  To present myself before her.
  If she is still the same, I know
  I shall find her of an open heart and mind,
  As she was in France, at Henri's court.
  If I can read a word of hope in what she says,
  If I can discover her inclined to meet you,
  If I can find a way of drawing off her ladies . . .

CARLOS. Most of them would give me their support. Especially
  The Marchioness of Mondecar, whose son
  Is now my page.

MARQUIS OF POSA. All the better. Be close at hand, Prince,
      and ready
  To approach us when I give the sign.

CARLOS. I shall be there. Now hurry!

MARQUIS OF POSA. Not a minute shall be wasted.

  Both depart in different directions.

SCENE 3

THE QUEEN'S COURT IN ARANJUEZ

*A simple country setting, with an avenue of trees, near
the Queen's summer palace*

QUEEN. DUCHESS OF OLIVAREZ. PRINCESS EBOLI *and* MAR-
CHIONESS OF MONDECAR, *coming up the avenue.*

QUEEN, *to the* MARCHIONESS.

    You must stay beside me, Mondecar.

    The Princess's bright eyes have plagued me

    All this morning. Look,

    She hardly knows how to conceal her happiness

    Because we are to leave the countryside.

PRINCESS EBOLI. I shan't deny, Your Majesty,

    That I shall be glad to see Madrid again.

MARCHIONESS OF MONDECAR. Doesn't Your Majesty feel the same?

    Are you so unwilling to leave Aranjuez?

QUEEN. This—lovely countryside—yes.

    Here I feel that I am in

    My own part of the world again.

    This is my favourite spot.

    The air of France seems to be blowing here.

    And one's own land—that is something

    One can never forget.

PRINCESS EBOLI. But how lonely it is here!

    How sad and lifeless! It's almost

    Like being shut away in La Trappe.

QUEEN. I find that quite the opposite is true.

    Madrid is dead. Now what does our duchess say to that?

DUCHESS OF OLIVAREZ. It is my opinion, Your Majesty,

    That we should preserve the old tradition,

    Passing one month here, another in Pardo,

    And the winter in the Residencia

    As long as there are kings in Spain.

QUEEN. Yes, Duchess, you know all the rules.

    We two shall never quite agree

    On these formalities.

MARCHIONESS OF MONDECAR. And how exciting it will be this season in Madrid!

    The Plaza Mayor is being made ready now

    For bullfights, and we are promised too

    An auto-da-fé. . . .

QUEEN. Promised it? How can my sweet and gentle Mondecar

    Talk with such zest for blood?

MARCHIONESS OF MONDECAR. But why not? The ones who
  will be burned

  Are heretics.

DUCHESS OF OLIVAREZ. Princess Eboli, you have not told us yet
  Whether Gomez will find his suit requited.

  When may we congratulate the bride?

QUEEN. I'm glad you reminded me, dear Duchess.

  To the PRINCESS.

  I have been asked to intercede with you.

  But how can I do that? The man whom I reward
  With Princess Eboli must be one worthy of her.

DUCHESS OF OLIVAREZ. And so he is, Your Majesty, a worthy
  man,

  One whom we know our king
  Has been pleased to honour with his favours.

QUEEN. That must have gratified Don Gomez very much, I'm
  sure.

  But what we want to know is,
  Can he inspire love? Can he return it too?

  Now, Eboli, you must tell us what you think.

PRINCESS EBOLI *pauses, then, confused, throws herself at*
QUEEN'S *feet.*

  Oh, Your Majesty, have pity on me.

  Do not let me—in heaven's name—do not let me
  Be offered up in marriage to . . .

QUEEN. Offered up? A sacrifice? That's all I need to hear.

  Come, do not kneel to me. I believe in your distress.

  Is it long since you and Count Gomez fell out?

PRINCESS EBOLI. Oh, months ago. Prince Carlos

  Was still in Alcalá, at the university.

QUEEN *starts and looks keenly at her.*

  Have you asked yourself upon what grounds
  You must refuse him?

PRINCESS EBOLI. I could never, never marry him, Your
  Majesty,

  And for a thousand reasons.

QUEEN. Only one should do. You do not love him.
That is enough for me. We'll speak of him no more.
To the other ladies.
I still have not seen the Infanta to-day.
Marchioness, go bring her to me.

DUCHESS OF OLIVAREZ, *looking at her watch.*
It is not yet time for that,
Your Majesty.

QUEEN. I thought there was always time
To be a mother.

A PAGE *enters and whispers to the* LADY-IN-WAITING, *who
turns to address the* QUEEN.

DUCHESS OF OLIVAREZ. The Marquis of Posa, Your Majesty?

QUEEN. Of Posa?

DUCHESS OF OLIVAREZ. He has come through France from the
Netherlands,
And begs the favour of presenting you
With letters from your mother, the Queen Regent.

QUEEN. And is that permitted?

DUCHESS OF OLIVAREZ. The particular case has not, so far,
Come within my jurisdiction: I do not know
What etiquette would require when
A Castilian grandee comes from a foreign court
With letters for the Queen of Spain as she sits
Among her ladies in her summer garden.

QUEEN. Then I shall take the risk upon my own head,
And invite him to present himself.

DUCHESS OF OLIVAREZ. Then I must ask permission to withdraw myself.

QUEEN. As you please, Duchess.

DUCHESS goes, and the QUEEN *makes a sign to the* PAGE,
who departs at once.

SCENE 4

QUEEN. PRINCESS EBOLI. MARCHIONESS OF MONDECAR
and MARQUIS OF POSA

QUEEN. Welcome, Chevalier, to Spanish soil.
Your journey, so I hear,
Has taken you through France.
What news do you bring me from
My mother and my dear brothers?

MARQUIS OF POSA. I found your mother ill, cut off
From every pleasure in this world, but that
Of knowing that her daughter now is Queen of Spain
And fortunate and happy.

QUEEN. How can I not be, at the thought
Of such sweet remembrances from those I love?
. . . Well, you have seen so many foreign courts, sir,
I fear that you will find Madrid far from your taste.
It is very—quiet in Madrid.

MARQUIS OF POSA. That is something the rest of Europe does
      not know
But would be glad to enjoy once more: a quiet peace.

QUEEN. Princess Eboli, I think I see a hyacinth
Blooming over there. Will you bring it to me?

PRINCESS *goes.* QUEEN, *softly to* MARQUIS.

Chevalier, unless I am very much mistaken,
Your arrival here has made at least
One more happy person in this court.

MARQUIS OF POSA. I found a most unhappy one,
Who, to be happy, needs . . .

PRINCESS EBOLI, *returning with flower.* The Chevalier has seen
So many lands. He must have lots to tell us.

MARQUIS OF POSA. To be sure. And it is of course well known
That seeking for adventure is the true knight's duty:
And the pleasantest duty of all
Is to protect fair ladies such as I find here.

MARCHIONESS OF MONDECAR. But there are no more ogres,
  No more giants left.

MARQUIS OF POSA. Power, lady, is at all times
  A giant to the weak and helpless.

QUEEN. The Chevalier is right. There are still giants in the
     world,
  But, alas, there are no more gallant knights.

  Turning to EBOLI.

  Now I really think it's time for me
  To see my daughter. Princess, have her brought to me.

  The latter goes. The MARQUIS *makes a sign to a* PAGE, *who
  disappears. The* QUEEN *opens the letters and appears to be
  overcome by astonishment. Meanwhile the* MARQUIS *is talking very surreptitiously with* MONDECAR. *The* QUEEN, *having read the letters, turns a searching gaze upon the*
  MARQUIS.

  You seem uneasy, Marquis. Whom are you looking for?

MARQUIS OF POSA. I am just thinking how very happy it would
     make
  A certain person, whom I dare not name,
  To be where I am now.

QUEEN. And whose fault is it, sir,
  That he isn't here?

MARQUIS OF POSA. Why—— Am I allowed, Your Majesty,
  To interpret that as—consent?
  He would find favour with you, if he were to come here
     now . . .

QUEEN, *shocked.* Come here? Now? What do you mean, sir?

MARQUIS OF POSA. May he hope for . . . hope for . . . your
     approval?

QUEEN. You frighten me, Marquis. Surely
  He could never . . .

MARQUIS OF POSA. Here he is.

SCENE 5

QUEEN. DON CARLOS. MARQUIS OF POSA *and* MARCHIONESS OF
MONDECAR *move away.*

CARLOS, *kneeling before the* QUEEN.
And so the moment has arrived
At last, and I may touch this hand!

QUEEN. This is too rash a step. Stand up, Prince,
Or we shall be discovered. . . .

CARLOS. No, I will not stand.
Here I shall kneel forever,
Bound by a spell to this enchanted ground.

QUEEN. You are out of your mind, sir!
Remember, it is your mother
You say these foolish things to.
Do you not realize that I
Shall have to tell the King of this?

CARLOS. Even if it means death, I shall not go from here:
One moment lived in Paradise
Is not too dearly bought with death.

QUEEN. And your Queen . . . What will become of her?

CARLOS, *standing.* Then I must go, since you command it.
Oh, Mother, Mother, how cruelly you wrong me.
Give me one look, one sign, before I go.

QUEEN. Go! Go! I beg of you,
Before my ladies—before my jailer—
Find you here alone with me
And take their stories to your father.

CARLOS. I await my destiny, whether it be life or death.
I have built my hopes so long
On this one moment, I cannot let it go.

QUEEN. What do you want of me?

CARLOS. Oh, I have struggled hard, so hard!
Harder than any mortal ever did,
As God is my witness, Mother,

My struggle has been bitter—and in vain.
I cast away my hero's name. And I submit.

QUEEN. No more of that. Leave me some little peace
Of mind and heart.

CARLOS. You were mine. Before all the world
You were promised to me from the steps
Of two great thrones. Nature herself
Intended us to be betrothed. And then
Philip, Philip—he took you from me——

QUEEN. He is your father.

CARLOS. And your husband.

QUEEN. Who brings you the greatest empire in the world.

CARLOS. And you—— Not as my bride but as
My mother!

QUEEN. Mad—this is madness——

CARLOS. But does he even realize how rich he is,
What priceless treasure he possesses in yourself?
I should not complain,
No, I should forget forever
How happy I would be with you,
If only *he* were happy.
But he's not! That is what makes my hell.
He *is* not and never will be happy with you!
You robbed me of my hope of heaven,
Only to destroy its promises in Philip's arms!

QUEEN. No. . . . Do not say such things. . . .

CARLOS. Oh, I know, I know the way he wooed you.
I know the sort of love that he demands.
And what do you stand for here in Spain?
Are you really his queen? No, never!
How could you be Queen within a land where Alba
Massacres all human freedom?
If you were Queen,
How could Flanders now be bleeding for its faith?
No, it could never be.

QUEEN. Who told you that my place at Philip's side
Was so despicable, so totally unworthy?

CARLOS. It was my heart, the passionate longing of my heart,

That told me what great worth that place would have
If only it were at my own devoted side.

QUEEN. Oh, the vanity of youth and manhood!
And what if my own heart said the opposite?
What if Philip's thoughtful tenderness
And the unprotesting demonstrations of his love
Moved me far more than all his son's
Impassioned, fiery speeches?
What if the devotion of an ageing man . . .

CARLOS. That would be different. Then—and only in that
case—
I would ask forgiveness. . . .
I did not know you loved the King.

QUEEN. My one desire is to reverence and respect him.

CARLOS. Then you have never been in love?

QUEEN. What a strange question!

CARLOS. Have you never been in love?

QUEEN. I am in love no more.

CARLOS. Because your heart forbids it, or your marriage vows?

QUEEN. Prince, you must go. Leave me now,
And never say such things to me again.

CARLOS. Is it your heart forbids it, or your marriage vows?

QUEEN. Because my duty . . . Oh, why, why must we obey?
Why must we be condemned by fate?

CARLOS. *Must* obey? *Must* be condemned?

QUEEN. Why are you so serious? What do you want with me?

CARLOS. So much. I cannot think of "must"
When all I know is "will."
I do not intend to be
Always unhappy, even if it means
The reversal of all my country's laws.

QUEEN. If I understand you correctly, then,
You still have hopes? You still dare to hope,
Even now, when everything is lost?

CARLOS. Nothing is ever completely lost,
Except in death.

QUEEN. And you still set your hopes on me, your mother?

And . . . Why not? Oh, the new King
Could hope for more than that. He could destroy
The dead one's terrible decrees with fire and sword,
Could overthrow his images, deface his portraits.
And even . . . why not? . . . take the embalmed body
Out of its long repose in the Escorial,
Out into the light and candour of the sun and strew
To all four winds its desecrated dust . . .

CARLOS. No more, I beg of you, no more!

QUEEN. And then, to make a fitting consummation, he
Could take the widowed mother to a bridal bed!

CARLOS. Damned, doomed, accursèd son!
Yes, now you have said the worst.
What I dared never say, now you have spoken it.
Now I see clearly
What must remain forever dark to me.
You are forever far beyond my reach . . .
Far, far beyond. . . . The die now is cast,
And I have lost, for you are lost to me.
Oh, hell, hell is in that terrible reality;
And yet another hell, more terrible than this,
Would come from my possessing you. . . .
Oh, I am lost, lost! My senses reel, I cannot,
Cannot bring my mind to understand
How lost I am. . . .

QUEEN. Poor Carlos . . . poor, dear Carlos,
How I feel for you! I too feel as if it were my own,
The pain that harrows you in heart and soul.
A pain that like your love will never end.
Yet you must be strong and conquer it,
For the reward would be so great.

CARLOS. It is too late, too late!

QUEEN. Too late to be a hero and a man?
Oh, Carlos, how great is virtue,
If we call on it to conquer
The desires of our heart.
Go, seek the rewards of heaven,
Learn to live without the weaknesses of mortal flesh,

And make a sacrifice
As great as any that was ever made.

CARLOS. That I could do, I know. Yes, I could be a hero.
In order to win you, I could command
A giant's strength. But if I must give you up,
I have no courage left.

QUEEN. Be candid with yourself, Carlos. You must realize
That it is spite and bitterness and envy,
Pride too, wounded pride, that draws you to your mother.
The love you so extravagantly offer me
Belongs rather to those kingdoms and those peoples
That one day you must rule. That is your love's first duty.
Until now you have deflected it, and wrongly,
Upon your mother. Oh, Carlos, keep it for
The kingdoms and the peoples of the future
And learn, instead of the dagger of an evil conscience,
The use of mercy, as if you were a god!
Elizabeth was your first love. Your second
Must be Spain: and how gladly, Carlos,
I renounce that love, if you may learn to know
A better one!

CARLOS *casts himself at her feet.* Oh, you heavenly being,
How noble and how truly great you are! Yes,
Everything you ask of me I shall perform.

He rises.

I swear by heaven that from now
My lips shall never speak the love I feel for you.
But in my heart there shall be forever
Talk of you, for I shall never,
Never be able to forget that love. Never!

QUEEN. How could I ask of you
What I myself could never do?

MARQUIS OF POSA, *appearing suddenly from the avenue.* The
King!

QUEEN. Oh! Carlos!

MARQUIS OF POSA. Come, Prince, away!

QUEEN. If he should find you here . . . If he suspects . . .
His rage is terrible . . .

CARLOS. I'm staying here.

QUEEN. And who, then, will bear the fury of his rage?

CARLOS. Come, let us go!

Seizing the MARQUIS *by the arm, he begins to leave, then returns.*

Tell me one last thing. What
Message may I take from you, to comfort me?

QUEEN. You have the friendship of your mother.

CARLOS. Friendship . . . Mother . . .

QUEEN. And these sad, broken-hearted cries
Out of the weeping Netherlands.

She gives him the letters. CARLOS *and* MARQUIS *go. The* QUEEN *looks round uneasily for her ladies, who are nowhere to be seen. As she is about to withdraw, the* KING *enters.*

SCENE 6

KING. QUEEN. DUKE OF ALBA. COUNT LERMA.
DOMINGO. *Several* COURT LADIES *and* GRANDEES *in background*

KING, *looking about him with displeasure. It is some time before he speaks.*
What's this? Why are you here? Why are you alone,
      madam?
Where are your ladies? Not one of them here!
Why are you alone?

QUEEN. My gracious husband——

KING. Why are you alone?

To his entourage.

I shall require the fullest explanation of
This unpardonable oversight.

QUEEN. Oh, sir, do not be angry with them.
It is I who am at fault: Princess Eboli,
At my own request, withdrew a little way from here.

KING. At your own request?

QUEEN. It was to call the nurse, because
I was longing to see the Infanta.

KING. That would account for one lady only.
Where were the others?

MARCHIONESS OF MONDECAR, *who meanwhile has returned and joined the others, comes up to the* KING.
Your Majesty, I feel I am at fault——

KING. Then you can spend the next ten years
In banishment, far from Madrid. Perhaps
That will give you time to think it over.

The MARCHIONESS *draws back, her eyes full of tears. There is a general silence. All look, perplexed, at the* QUEEN.

QUEEN. Dear lady, whom are you weeping for?

To the KING.

Sir, if I have failed in my duty, then at least
The crown of Spain should spare me
This public humiliation.
I never asked to be your queen.
Forgive me, sir, but I am not accustomed
To let those who serve me faithfully
Be brought to tears. . . . Mondecar!

She takes off a belt of gold and gives it to MONDECAR.

You have caused the King displeasure, but not me.
Take this remembrance of my favour,
And of this unhappy day. Leave the country:
It is only Spain you have offended.
In my country you will find the French
Will gladly dry these tears for you.
Why must I always be reminded of my native land?

She lays her face on OLIVAREZ' *shoulder.*

Oh, how different it was in France!

KING, *somewhat disturbed.*
How could a reproach caused by my love
Upset you so?

QUEEN. Sir, if I have offended you . . .

KING. The sun never sets upon my state.
I am rich. And yet all that I possess

Belonged once to another and it will in turn
Belong to someone else. Only one thing is really mine
And it is my greatest fortune: Elizabeth
Belongs to Philip; she alone
Makes me a vulnerable mortal.
To lose her would be death to me.

QUEEN. Are you afraid, sir?

KING. Does not my greying hair betray me?
But if I once felt fear, now
I am afraid no more.

To the GRANDEES.

I am counting the great ones in my court.
The very first among them is not here.
Where is my son, Don Carlos?

No one answers.

The boy is beginning
To be afraid of me, it seems.
He avoids my presence ever since
He returned from the university at Alcalá.
His blood is young and fiery:
Why is his look so cold?
Be careful with him. I am warning you. Watch him.

DUKE OF ALBA. I do. As long as a heart beats in my panther's
        breast,
Don Philip may sleep in peace.

COUNT LERMA. May I venture to contradict most humbly
The wisest of all kings? I revere too profoundly
The majesty of Spain to judge his son
So rashly and severely.
I fear his fiery blood but not his heart.

KING. Well spoken, Lerma, but your kindness
Might unwittingly betray me. The Duke of Alba
Shall be my best support in this affair.

Turning to the court.

Now we must hasten to Madrid.
The duties of a king demand my presence there.
My people are infected with the plague of heresy,
And in the Netherlands revolts are breaking out.

The hour has come. A terrible example must be made
Of those mistaken souls.
You are all invited to
This edifying spectacle.

He leads the QUEEN *away, and the rest follow.*

SCENE 7

DON CARLOS *with letters in his hand and* MARQUIS OF POSA
enter from opposite sides.

CARLOS. My mind's made up. Flanders must be saved.
She implores my aid. That is enough.

MARQUIS OF POSA. Then we have no time to lose. They say
The Duke of Alba has been elected by the cabinet
To be their governor.

CARLOS. I shall seek an audience with my father in Madrid.
I wish to be given that position. It will be
The first request that I have ever made to him.
I hope, moreover, in this interview,
To put our strained relations on a friendlier footing.

MARQUIS OF POSA. Now that is my old friend Carlos speaking.
Now at last you are yourself again!

SCENE 8

DON CARLOS. MARQUIS OF POSA. COUNT LERMA

COUNT LERMA. His Majesty has just left Aranjuez.
My orders are——

CARLOS. Very good, Count Lerma. I'm coming.

MARQUIS OF POSA, *pretending to be going away. Ceremoni-
ously.* Has Your Highness
Any further commands for me?

CARLOS. Nothing more, Chevalier. I wish you a good journey
To Madrid. There you must tell me

More of the news from Flanders.
To COUNT LERMA, *still waiting.*
I shall be with you in a moment.
Exit LERMA.

SCENE 9

DON CARLOS. MARQUIS OF POSA

CARLOS. We understand each other.
Here is my hand.

MARQUIS OF POSA. And mine, forever.

CARLOS. And will it be the same when I am King?

MARQUIS OF POSA. I swear it will be so.

CARLOS. Now to the King. With you beside me,
I fear nothing. Come!
I call out the future into the lists of life!
Exeunt.

ACT II

SCENE 1

IN THE ROYAL PALACE IN MADRID

KING PHILIP, *sitting under a canopy on the throne.* DUKE OF
ALBA, *some distance away from the* KING, *his head covered.* DON CARLOS.

CARLOS *enters.* Our country has precedence. I gladly
Stand aside, in deference to your minister's authority.
He speaks for Spain. I am its royal house's only son.
He steps back with a bow.

KING. The Duke will remain here, and you may speak.

CARLOS. Then I would beg of your kindness, Duke,
To let me have my father to myself.
It is only for a little while.

KING. Your father's friend stays here.

CARLOS. Am I too worthy of that friendship?

KING. *Can* you be worthy of it? I do not like sons
Who think they can make better choices than their father.

CARLOS. Can Alba's noble pride
Suffer without a blush
This little scene?

KING, *leaving the throne and casting an angry glance at*
CARLOS. Leave us for the moment, Alba!
The latter is about to leave by the main doorway, but the
KING *signals him to a smaller one.*
No, wait in my cabinet room until I call you.

SCENE 2

KING. DON CARLOS

CARLOS, *going to the* KING *as soon as* ALBA *has left, and falling on his knees before him.*
Now at last I have my father once again! My thanks
For this great favour! Oh, Father,
Give me your hand! Why have you kept me
As a stranger to your heart? What is my fault?

KING. No speeches, I beg of you!
They do not come from the heart.

CARLOS, *rising.* I heard your courtiers speaking there.
Oh, Father, not everything they tell you,
Not everything your priest confides in you
Is good. I am not evil, Father:
My faults are rashness, and my crime is youth.
But my heart is true——

KING. Your heart, I know, is good.

CARLOS. Oh, Father, have pity on me!
Let us be reconciled!
Kneels before PHILIP.

KING. No more of this play acting! Stand up!

CARLOS. Forgive me! Is the devotion of your only son
No more to you than that? Forgive me!

KING. I do not care to see you weep.
Tears are unmanly. Go away, out of my sight.
If you had come to me
Bearing the honours of glorious battles,
My arms would have opened to receive you.
Honour alone repays a coward's guilt.

CARLOS. Who has set you against me? Who?
How did the priest turn father against son?
What has Alba done that has betrayed me?

KING. No more! These men you dare to slander

Are my proved and chosen ministers.
You will give them your respect.

CARLOS. Never! I know that what the Duke of Alba has to do
Can also be performed by me. What right has a hireling
To sue for favours in a court that never will belong to him?
What does he care, if Philip's hair is grey
And turns to the hoary white of age?
But Carlos would have loved you more than ever then.
I shudder at the thought
Of sitting on a throne, alone and friendless.

KING. I am alone and friendless.

CARLOS. You *were* alone! If you will only cease to hate me,
I shall give you all the fiery love
That burns my breast. Only
Do not hate me any more.

KING. Oh, my son! My son! But love is something
You have never felt for me.

CARLOS. That is not true! You yourself
Shut me from your heart, and until now
The Crown Prince of Spain has been a stranger
In the land that one day
Shall be his own.
Father, may I ask one favour of you?

KING. Another request? What is it now?

CARLOS. Let me lead an army into Flanders!
They love me in the Netherlands,
And I would give my life's hot blood for them.
How glorious it would be
To do this for the honour of my country,
And for my father's approbation, and his wide renown!

KING. I wish to send a man and not a boy——

CARLOS. Better to send a human being, Father:
That is something Alba has never been.

KING. Humanity and pity would be out of place.
Your heart, Prince, is too soft and generous.
But the Duke is feared. I cannot grant you your request.

CARLOS. Oh, Father, send me at your army's head
To Flanders. My name alone would give us victory.

Alba is no more than your public executioner.
Oh, Father, grant the first request I ever made!
Send me to Flanders!

KING. And lose the flower of my troops?

CARLOS. O God, after all these years of waiting,
Will it only come to this
Cold denial? Show me you trust and honour me,
And send me with your army into Flanders!

KING. I do not wish to hear you speak that name again.

CARLOS. For the last time I brave
My king's royal anger and his just displeasure:
Let me have Flanders! I must and shall leave Spain.
Madrid's air hangs over me
Like a threat of murder. Only a change of sky
Can bring me to myself again, and it must be soon!
Father, if you wish to save your son,
Send me to Flanders!

KING. Those who are sick, my son, as you appear to be,
Require the care of doctors. You will remain in Spain.
The Duke of Alba shall go to Flanders.

CARLOS. Oh, now, my good spirits, come to my aid!

KING, *retreating a step*. Why, what is this?

CARLOS. Father, is your decision
Irrevocable?

KING. It was given by your king.

CARLOS. Then my decision too is made.

He leaves, in great excitement.

SCENE 3

PHILIP *remains sunk in thought for a while, then walks
slowly up and down.* ALBA *approaches.*

KING. Hold yourself in readiness
To leave for Brussels at any moment.

DUKE OF ALBA. Everything is ready, Your Majesty.

KING. Take your leave of the Queen and of my son.

DUKE OF ALBA. I saw him leave this instant, like a madman.
What was the subject of your conversation, may I ask?

KING. The Duke of Alba. I do not mind that he
Should hate the laws I make. I do not like to know
That he despises them.

ALBA *is startled and blanches.*

I give you my permission to excuse his rashness.

DUKE OF ALBA. Sire!

KING. Who was it warned me first against my son?
I gave my ear to you and not to him.
I have decided to take the risk, Duke.
Soon my son shall stand a little closer to
His father's throne. Now go!

The KING *enters his cabinet room.* ALBA *leaves by another door.*

SCENE 4

AN ANTEROOM TO THE
QUEEN'S APARTMENTS

DON CARLOS *comes in, talking to a* PAGE. *The* COURTIERS
present drift away on their arrival.

CARLOS. A letter? For me? And what is this key for?
Why do you deliver them so secretly? Come closer.
Where did you get them. Eh?

PAGE. The lady would rather let her identity remain unknown.

CARLOS. Lady? Whom do you mean? Who are you?

PAGE. A page of noble family in the service of the Queen.

CARLOS, *horrified, going up to him and putting his hand over
the* PAGE'S *mouth.* No more! That's all I need to know!
*He hurriedly breaks the seal and goes to one side to read
the letter. Meanwhile, the* DUKE OF ALBA, *unnoticed by the*
PRINCE, *enters and goes into the* QUEEN'S *apartments. The*
PRINCE, *having read the letter, stands speechless for a moment, staring at the letter. Finally he turns to the* PAGE.

Did you receive this letter from the lady herself?

PAGE. Yes, Your Highness.

CARLOS. She gave it you herself? By heaven,
    If you are trying to play a trick on me——

PAGE. On you, sire?

CARLOS. It wasn't the King gave you this letter?

PAGE. Sire, have I done anything
    To merit these suspicions?

CARLOS, *reading letter aloud*. This key unlocks the room
    At the rear of the Queen's pavilion. Here
    You may confess your love freely, without fear.
    Then it is true! She loves me!

PAGE. Come, Prince, I shall take you there.

CARLOS. I shall find my own way. But before you go,
    Remember that not one word of this
    Must pass your lips.

PAGE. And I, Prince, shall be proud
    To keep this secret for you.

CARLOS. Someone's coming. Go!

    ALBA *comes out of the* QUEEN's *apartments.*

PAGE. Be sure you find the right room!

CARLOS. The Duke! Keep calm, Prince! Calm!

SCENE 5

DON CARLOS. DUKE OF ALBA

DUKE OF ALBA. I should like a word with you, sir.

CARLOS. Very well, but it must be some other time.
    Going.

DUKE OF ALBA. This place does not indeed
    Lend itself to what I have to say.
    Perhaps in your own apartments——

CARLOS. Come, get it over.

DUKE OF ALBA. What really brought me here

And dug the furrows where the seeds of faith were sown.
As God rules in heaven, so did I on earth——

CARLOS. Whether you were God or devil hardly matters.
You were his right arm. I know that. And now
No more of this, I beg of you.
I would rather not remember certain things.
I respect my father's choice. He needs an Alba.
You are a great man. That may well be.
Only I fear you came three centuries too soon.
I should have thought an Alba was the sort of man
Who would appear towards the very end of time.
Then, when heaven's patience finally is overcome
By the dread fertility of evil
And needs a reaper for its ghastly harvest,
Then would be the time for men like you.
O God! Flanders! But I must think no more of that.
They say you are taking with you
A plentiful stock of death sentences.
I must commend your foresight. Oh, my father,
How completely I mistook your meaning!
I accused you—you!—of cruelty,
Because you would not let me perform the bloody task
That Alba will carry out with such
Conspicuous success. I see now, Father,
It was the beginning of your true esteem for me.

DUKE OF ALBA. Prince! I cannot let such words
Go undefended——

CARLOS, *startled*. What?

DUKE OF ALBA. The King's son hides himself behind his father's
name.

CARLOS, *drawing his sword*. I'll have your blood for that!
Draw your sword!

DUKE OF ALBA, *coldly*. Against whom, pray?

CARLOS. Unsheathe your sword! I'll run you through!

DUKE OF ALBA. Well, if it has to be——
They fight.

SCENE 6

QUEEN. DON CARLOS. DUKE OF ALBA

QUEEN, *running, terrified, out of her apartments.* Put up your
swords!

To the PRINCE, *indignantly, pleadingly.*

Carlos!

CARLOS, *beside himself at sight of the* QUEEN. Forgive me,
Duke!

DUKE OF ALBA. By heaven, this is strange!

PRINCE *kisses him, falls at the* QUEEN'S *feet, then hurries
away.*

QUEEN, *after a pause moves slowly towards her apartments,
turning at the door to speak to* ALBA. Come with me, Duke.

ALBA *follows her into her apartment.*

SCENE 7

THE PRINCESS EBOLI'S APARTMENTS

PRINCESS EBOLI, *beautifully but simply dressed, is playing
the lute and singing. Enter the queen's* PAGE.

PRINCESS EBOLI, *hurriedly rising.* Is he coming?

PAGE. Are you alone? I am surprised
That he is not already here. He should be with you now
At any moment. . . . Princess,
He loves you, loves you as you can never be loved again
By anyone.

PRINCESS EBOLI. Quick, tell me what he said!
What did he do?

PAGE. I gave him the key and the letter
In the queen's antechamber. He gave a start
And stared at me, when I told him that
A woman had sent me.

PRINCESS EBOLI. He started? Good! What next?

PAGE. I wanted to speak further, but he turned
Quite white and snatched the letter from my hand.
Then he looked threateningly upon me and said
That he knew everything. He read the letter through:
Overcome by emotion, he began to tremble.

PRINCESS EBOLI. He said that? Said he knew . . . everything?

PAGE. Yes. And asked me three, four times at least
If it was really you who had sent it.

PRINCESS EBOLI. If it was really me? Did he?
Did he mention my name?

PAGE. No. He said there were spies
Who might report the matter to the King
If they should chance to hear him speak of you.

PRINCESS EBOLI, *astonished*. Did he really say that?

PAGE. He said the King would give
A very great deal to know the contents of your letter.

PRINCESS EBOLI. The King? Are you sure you heard aright?
The King?
Was that the word he used?

PAGE. Yes. He said it was a dangerous secret,
And warned me to be on my guard,
To watch my every move and every word,
In order that the King might not suspect . . .

PRINCESS EBOLI. It can't be possible! The Prince
Must know the whole story! Who
Could have betrayed the secret?
Only the eagle eye of love
Could have detected it. . . . But go on!
He read the letter . . .

PAGE. And assured me the joy it held for him
Was almost too much to bear: never, he said,
Could he have dreamt of such a happiness.
But then, unfortunately, the Duke of Alba
Entered the antechamber and compelled us . . .

PRINCESS EBOLI, *angrily*. But what in the world
Is the Duke doing there?
What concern is it of his?

What right has that honourable man
To stand between me and my happiness?
The prince could just have left him there,
Or simply sent him away . . . Oh, truly,
The Prince, it seems, knows just as little about love
As he does about the hearts of women.
He does not realize
How precious moments are, when we await our love. . . .
But listen! I can hear someone coming. Go, now!
It's the Prince!

PAGE *hurries off.*

SCENE 8

PRINCESS EBOLI, *and, in a moment,* DON CARLOS

PRINCESS *has cast herself down upon an ottoman and plays her lute.*

CARLOS *rushes in. He recognizes the* PRINCESS *and starts. He stands dumbfounded.* Why . . . What place is this?

PRINCESS EBOLI, *laying her lute aside.* Ah, Prince Carlos!
She goes to him.

CARLOS. Where am I? I have come to the wrong room!

PRINCESS EBOLI. How clever of you, Prince, to hit upon the
     very room
Where a lady may not be compromised.

CARLOS. Princess . . . Forgive me . . . I . . . I found
The door to the antechamber open. . . .

PRINCESS EBOLI. But how could that be? I'm almost certain
I closed it myself.

CARLOS. No, it was not closed. I heard
Someone playing on a lute. . . . It was
A lute, wasn't it? Ah, yes,
There it is. . . . And heaven knows,
I love more than anything the music of a lute.
I heard it and became all ears,
Was led by it, and stumbled into this

Apartment of the sweet musician who
Had so wonderfully laid her spell upon me.

PRINCESS EBOLI. That shows a commendable curiosity, and
   one
Which now, it would appear, has been quite easily satisfied.
After a little pause, meaningfully.

Oh, I prize the man who, to spare a woman's blushes,
Can bring himself to tell such stories!

CARLOS. Princess, I feel I am only making worse
What I wanted to put right. Release me, I beg of you,
From a part which I am hardly fitted to perform.
You came here to find a refuge from the world
In the quiet and solitude of your own thoughts:
And now I have disturbed your dream. . . . Forgive me.
I shall take my leave.

He is about to go.

PRINCESS EBOLI, *surprised and disappointed.* Prince! Oh,
That was hardly worthy of you!

CARLOS. I understand how painful
My sudden entry into your apartment must have been
And I respect the virtuous distress you show.
I abhor the man who makes a woman blush!
And it makes me unhappy to see a woman tremble so.

PRINCESS EBOLI. Can it be possible? A young man, and a king's
   son,
With such a conscience? Now you must stay.
What woman would ever tremble in the presence of
Such honourable conduct? Your entrance surprised me
In the middle of my favourite aria.
She leads him to the sofa and takes up her lute.

I must play it again, Prince, and your punishment
Shall be to listen to me.

CARLOS *sits rather unwillingly beside the* PRINCESS.
A punishment
That fits the crime. And indeed
What I heard had such a lovely sound,
I could hear it many times again.

PRINCESS EBOLI. So you have already heard it all?

That was most ungallant of you, Prince.
There was talk, I believe, of love in it?

CARLOS. And if I am not mistaken, of happy love—
Of love returned. A lovely theme upon
Such lovely lips, and yet its beauty
Was greater than its truth.

PRINCESS EBOLI. Do you doubt its truth, sir?

CARLOS. I very much doubt whether Carlos and
The Princess Eboli would understand each other
If there were talk of love.

The PRINCESS *starts. He notices it and goes on in a tone of gallant banter.*

For who would ever think these roses in her face
Conceal a secret passion, a raging fire?
There is no danger that her sighs
Would go unheard or unrewarded. Only he
Who loves without hope of a return can know
What love must be.

PRINCESS EBOLI, *with her former gaiety.* Oh no, no, Prince!
Those are dreadful sentiments. . . . Although it seems
That such a fate pursues you, yes, you,
Particularly now . . .

Seizing his hand and speaking with flattering concern.

Dear Prince, you are not happy. . . . You are suffering,
I know it. Yet why should you, of all men,
Suffer for love? You, a great king's son,
And gifted in your cradle with much else,
With looks and talents that eclipse your royal fame.
Why should you, of all men, be unhappy?
Oh, heaven, you who gave him everything,
Why do you not give him eyes to see
The victory that he is blind to?

CARLOS, *who during her speech has been sunk in thought, comes to his senses when she stops speaking and rises quickly.* Wonderful! Sing that passage to me once again.
Only you could sing it as you did.

PRINCESS EBOLI, *astonished.* Prince, where were your thoughts?

CARLOS. Yes, by heaven, I'm glad you have reminded me.
I have to go.

PRINCESS EBOLI, *holding him back*. But where?

CARLOS. To seek my freedom. Let me go, Princess.
I feel as if the world were going up in flames
Behind my back——

PRINCESS EBOLI, *dragging him back*.
What is the matter with you?
Why this unnatural, unkind behaviour?

CARLOS *remains silent a moment, and she seizes this opportunity to lead him back to the sofa.*

You must rest, Carlos, you are distressed about something.
Sit here beside me and forget your black and fevered dreams.
Do you not understand the thing that so oppresses you?
And even if you did, do you not think that there would be
One person—one sympathetic woman in this court—
To listen to your sad complaint and cure you of it?
Is there no woman worthy of that honour?

CARLOS, *lightly, thoughtlessly*. Perhaps—Princess Eboli——

PRINCESS EBOLI, *gladly, promptly*. Really?

CARLOS. Give me—write me a letter to my father,
Recommending me as worthy of his favour.
They say your word counts with him.

PRINCESS EBOLI. *Who* say it? (Ah, so it was suspicion
That made you hold your tongue!)

CARLOS. Apparently that is the story going round.
I have a strong desire to go to Flanders,
There to win my spurs. My father will not let me.

PRINCESS EBOLI. Carlos, you are trying to deceive me. Now
tell the truth.
You simply choose this means to get away from me.
Look me in the eyes!
Will he who only dreams of knightly deeds
Descend so low as to steal ribbons when
They fall from a lady's neck, and—
Forgive me——

She has been loosing his ruff, and takes out a bow of ribbon that had been concealed beneath it.

And then to guard them with such jealous love——

CARLOS, *astonished, stepping back.* Princess! No, you go too
     far! Were they—your ribbons?
I am betrayed! You, however, cannot be deceived.
You are in league with evil spirits.

PRINCESS EBOLI. And does that surprise you? I wager
I can bring back things to your remembrance—
Moments, incidents which gave me hope:
If only a passing mood, the sound of a word
Stammered half-heard upon the air and then
Disguised in a more serious vein;
If only an appearance, or a gesture
When you were off your guard—these things
Did not escape me. Did I not understand aright?

CARLOS. You credit me with feelings
Of which I myself was ignorant;
These are things I never was aware of.

PRINCESS EBOLI. Never, Prince? Look deeper in your heart,
And look around you too. This room
Is not the Queen's apartment. . . . You start?
And why this sudden blush? . . . Oh, indeed,
Who could be so clever and so cunning,
And, alas, so persevering, as to spy
On Carlos, Carlos, who refuses to believe
That he is spied upon?
Did no one notice how, at the last court ball,
He left the Queen, his partner, standing,
And separated the next couple in the dance
And gave his hand to Princess Eboli instead?
That was a bad mistake, which even the King,
Who at that moment had just arrived,
Did not fail to notice.

CARLOS. Indeed?

Giving an ironic smile.

So even he
Noticed it? It mattered least of all to him.

PRINCESS EBOLI. As little, perhaps, as on that occasion in
The royal chapel, which Prince Carlos

Will surely not remember now. You knelt
In prayer at the feet of the Virgin,
When suddenly you heard the rustling
Of certain ladies' dresses behind you.
Then Don Philip's valorous son
Began to tremble like a sacred candle flame:
The prayers died upon his lips, disordered by
The tumult of his passions. . . . Oh, it was
An amusing sight, to see him seize the cold
And marble hand of the Madonna and rain
His fiery kisses on it——

CARLOS. You do me wrong, Princess. I was praying.

PRINCESS EBOLI. And then there was the time
When Carlos was at cards with the Queen and myself,
And with extraordinary skill
Stole this glove from me——

CARLOS *jumps up.*

Instead of leading with his ace!

CARLOS. Oh, heavens! What have I done?

PRINCESS EBOLI. Nothing, I hope, that you need be sorry for.
What a happy shock it was for me,
When I found in one of the fingers of the glove
A little note, which you had hidden there!
It was the most romantic piece of——

CARLOS. Verses, nothing more! My brain
Often throws off such airy nothings,
That die as soon as they are written.
It was nothing more. Let us forget it.

PRINCESS EBOLI, *astonished, moves away from him and looks
at him thoughtfully from a distance.* I am exhausted.
All my well-laid schemes
Appear to run like water from the back
Of this most strange and unimpressionable creature!
She is silent for a few moments.

Enlighten me, Prince! I feel that I am standing
In front of a magic chest to which
I cannot find the key.

CARLOS. I feel the same, Princess, in front of you.
(By heaven, how beautiful she is!)

PRINCESS EBOLI. The man I choose
Shall have my heart completely. I shall give
My all for him and give it forever.

CARLOS. (How can it be that I have only now
Discovered such a woman? In all Madrid
There is no one to equal her.)

PRINCESS EBOLI. I would long ago have left this court and left
The world, to immure myself in a religious order,
But one thing held me back, something
That binds me irresistibly to life——
A phantom, perhaps, a dream—— But so dear to me!
I am in love, Prince, but
I am not loved in return.

CARLOS, *passionately, moving towards her.* You are!
As true as God is in the heavens, I swear you are!
You *are* loved—more than words can say!

PRINCESS EBOLI. You swear it? You?
Oh, that was an angel voice that spoke those words!
If *you* say so, Carlos, then
I believe it: my love is returned.

CARLOS, *taking her tenderly in his arms.*
Sweet, angelic creature!
I stand before you, and can only look, and listen,
And it is all enchantment, all a miracle.
Who could have seen you and not known
He loved you? Yet why should you be here,
At Philip's court? This is no place for angels.
But I shall put my arms around you
And bear you safely through its dreadful hells!
Yes! Let me be your angel, your guardian angel!

PRINCESS EBOLI, *with a look full of love.* Oh, Carlos,
How little I knew you! But how rich is the reward
Of learning to know the secrets of your heart!
She seizes his hand and tries to kiss it.

CARLOS, *pulling his hand away.*
Princess, what do you mean by this?

PRINCESS EBOLI, *taking his hand again and gazing at it.*
How fine a hand!
How rich it is! . . . Prince, this hand can give
Two precious gifts: a crown, and Carlos' heart,
And both, perhaps, to *one* blessed mortal.
It is almost too much for one
Human heart to bear. . . . But may I know the name
Of this fortunate woman?

CARLOS. You may. I shall reveal my heart to you,
To your innocence, your purity. You alone
In all this court—you alone are the worthiest,
The only one, the first to understand my heart.
Yes, I must confess it to you now:
I am in love.

PRINCESS EBOLI. Was it so difficult to make, Carlos? A
    confession
That should have been so easy?
If you have found me worthy of your love,
Could you not find me worthy of your pity too?

CARLOS *starts.* What? What do you mean?

PRINCESS EBOLI. Carlos, it was hardly kind of you
To keep me in suspense so long!
Even to pretend you did not have the key!

CARLOS. The key? The key!
He is deep in thought.
Ah, yes. So that was it. Now I see. Oh, God!
*He staggers, and supports himself against the back of a
chair. Both are silent.*

PRINCESS EBOLI *gives a loud cry and falls to the ground.*
What have I done?

CARLOS, *drawing himself up again.*
To be dashed to earth again,
In sight of heaven! Oh, how terrible!

PRINCESS EBOLI, *burying her face in a cushion.*
What have I discovered?
Oh, heavens!

CARLOS, *casting himself down before her.* I am not to blame.

Passion—an unhappy misunderstanding—by God in heaven,
I swear I am not to blame!

PRINCESS EBOLI, *thrusting him away.* Out of my sight!

CARLOS. Never! How could I leave you in such desolation?

PRINCESS EBOLI. For pity's sake, leave me alone!
Do you want to kill me? I hate the sight of you!

As CARLOS *is about to go.*

Give me back my letter and the key.
And where is the other letter?

CARLOS. The other letter? What other letter?

PRINCESS EBOLI. The one from the King.

CARLOS, *starting.* From the King!

PRINCESS EBOLI. The one I gave you before——

CARLOS. From the King? To whom? To you?

PRINCESS EBOLI. Oh, heavens! How terrible is this confusion!
The letter! Give it to me! I must have it back!

CARLOS. Letters from the King—to *you?*

PRINCESS EBOLI. I beg of you, in the name of all that's holy,
Give me back the letter!

CARLOS. So it came from the King! Well, Princess,
That puts a different face on things.

Triumphantly waving the letter in the air.

This is a letter without price:
All Philip's empires could not buy it back.
This letter I shall keep.

He strides off.

PRINCESS EBOLI. Oh, God! I am lost forever!

SCENE 9

PRINCESS EBOLI, *alone*

PRINCESS EBOLI. One moment, Prince! Just one word—— Oh,
he's gone!
Now he despises me! I am abandoned, rejected, alone,

Terribly alone! I have been beaten by a rival.
He is in love, there's no doubt of that.
And it would appear he loves where he should not.
He hides his guilty passion from the King. But why?
The King would be glad to see him happy,
And the Queen——

*She suddenly stops, astonished at her discovery. She looks
at the bow of ribbon* CARLOS *has given her, and recognizes
it.*

Oh, what a fool I have been!
Now I understand! Those passionate glances were
For her, not me! And to think that he should love her
Without hope—he who might have had whatever wife he
        chose!
But I shall be revenged on her! The King shall know of this!
A pause.
Yes, that is the way to gain his ear.
She goes.

SCENE 10

A ROOM IN THE ROYAL PALACE

PRINCESS EBOLI. DOMINGO

DOMINGO. What happy chance has brought me
   This longed-for meeting with Your Highness?
   A pause, as he waits for her answer.
   Do not be afraid to speak. We are alone.
   Have you at last discovered
   A way to grant the wishes of His Majesty?
   You know he loves you. Are there grounds for hope?——

PRINCESS EBOLI. Did you give my answer to the King?

DOMINGO. I decided not to give him such a bitter wound.
   There is still time, lady.

PRINCESS EBOLI. Go now, and tell the King that I shall wait
   upon him.

DOMINGO. Am I to take that for consent? Is it the truth?

PRINCESS EBOLI. Would I joke about such a thing?
You frighten me. What have I done, what have I said,
That you—even you—turn pale?

DOMINGO. Princess, the surprise—it is all
So unexpected—— I can hardly believe——

PRINCESS EBOLI. It would indeed be better if you didn't.
I would to God you couldn't——
Things have completely changed since when
I rejected his advances so indignantly, for then
I believed him to be happy in the love
Of a most lovely queen, whom I felt worthy
Of the sacrifice I made when I denied
His pressing claims, repulsed his promises.
But now—— Oh, I know better now!

DOMINGO. Dear Princess, tell me more.
I think we understand one another——

PRINCESS EBOLI. She has given herself away.
I cannot spare her any longer.
The sly thief is found out. She has betrayed
The King, and me, and Spain. She has deceived us all.
She is in love. I know she is in love
With someone. . . . I can bring you proofs
That will make you tremble.
The King is deceived, but by heaven,
It shall not go unavenged by me!
The price I have to pay is terrible, yet——
That itself shall be my triumph and my joy.
For you, it will bring an even greater one.

DOMINGO. The moment now is ripe.
With your permission, I shall call the Duke.
He goes.

PRINCESS EBOLI. Call the Duke——!

SCENE 11

PRINCESS EBOLI. DUKE OF ALBA. DOMINGO

DOMINGO, *leading in the* DUKE. Our other plans
Now pale to insignificance. The Princess
Has discovered, so she claims, a secret——
The one that we had planned to tell her.

DUKE OF ALBA. Then my presence here will not disturb her
Quite so much. I cannot believe my eyes.
Such discoveries can only come from women's hearts.

PRINCESS EBOLI. Discoveries?

DOMINGO. We should like to know the place and hour——

PRINCESS EBOLI. To-morrow morning I shall expect you.
This secret can no longer
Be hidden from the King.

DUKE OF ALBA. That is my own opinion. The King
Must be informed. And by you.
Who else but you could better undeceive him—
You, the intimate companion of his Queen?

DOMINGO. Who else but you, dear Princess, who with a word,
A single look, can have him in your power?

DUKE OF ALBA. I am the Prince's enemy. He knows it too.

DOMINGO. It will be assumed that I am also.
But you, Princess Eboli, are unsuspected.
Where we must hold our peace, you
Are in a position where it is your duty
To tell him everything. The King cannot deny us then.
Then we can bring our labours
To a satisfactory conclusion.

DUKE OF ALBA. But it must be soon. Every moment
Is valuable. At any time
I may be called away to Brussels.

DOMINGO. Would there by any chance be letters—
Letters from the Prince? They would help our case.

Now, let me see. Yes. You share, I believe,
The Queen's bedchamber. Is that not so?

PRINCESS EBOLI. Why?

DOMINGO. Have you observed
Where the key to her writing-case
Is usually kept?

PRINCESS EBOLI. Yes, that might give us something.
I think I know where the key is to be found.

DOMINGO. Letters require messengers. The Queen's suite
Is numerous. If only we could find out something there!
Perhaps a promise of a monetary nature——
Money works wonders!

DUKE OF ALBA. Has no one noticed if the Prince
Has a particular friend, someone he confides in——

DOMINGO. Not one. Not in all Madrid.

DUKE OF ALBA. That is curious.

DOMINGO. It's true. He despises the entire court.
I have ways of knowing.

DUKE OF ALBA. And yet I seem to recollect,
When I was leaving the Queen's apartments
After bidding her farewell, I saw the Prince
Conversing with a page. They were whispering together——

PRINCESS EBOLI. No. That was something else.

DOMINGO. And may we inquire what it was, dear Princess,
That something else? The circumstances
Seem highly suspicious.

To DUKE.

And did you recognize
The page?

PRINCESS EBOLI. All that is quite without importance.
I know what it was all about. It was nothing.
Well, we shall meet again soon,
Before I make my revelation to the King.
Meanwhile, much may be discovered.

DOMINGO, *leading her to one side.* And the King has hopes of——
May I announce the happy news to him? Yes?
And when the hour will come, when he may hear

From you the words that grant him
All those things that he so ardently desires?

PRINCESS EBOLI. In a day or two, I shall fall sick.
In such cases it is customary
For me to leave the Queen's apartments.
I shall be in my rooms, alone.

DOMINGO. How very convenient! How fortunate!
The great wager is almost won, and that despite
All the machinations of the Queen.

PRINCESS EBOLI. I must go now. They are calling for me.
I must attend Her Royal Majesty. Farewell.

She hastens away.

SCENE 12

DUKE OF ALBA. DOMINGO

DOMINGO. Well, Alba, what with these sweet revelations,
And your great victories in Flanders——

DUKE OF ALBA. And with the aid of your great God——
I'd like to see what power could upset our plans!

They go.

SCENE 13

IN A CARTHUSIAN MONASTERY

DON CARLOS. PRIOR

CARLOS, *to* PRIOR, *as they enter.* Has he been here already?

PRIOR. Three times already this morning.
He left about an hour ago——

CARLOS. He'll be coming back?

PRIOR. Before noon, he said.

CARLOS, *at a window, looking out.* Your cloister
  Lies far from the city's busy streets.
  In the distance I can see the towers of Madrid.
  And here the Manzanares flows. The landscape
  Is just as I would have it. Everything fits
  The keeping of a secret, for everything
  Is quiet as a secret truly kept.

PRIOR. Like the entry to the other world.

CARLOS. Into the keeping of your honest soul
  I have given my most precious and most holy thoughts.
  No mortal man must know
  With whom I have spoken here so secretly.
  Are we quite safe from prying eyes?
  Do you remember your promise to me?

PRIOR. You can put your trust in me. The suspicions
  Of kings cannot investigate a grave.
  The world stops outside these walls.

CARLOS. You must be thinking that
  A guilty conscience lies uneasily behind
  This fearful dissimulation?

PRIOR. I do not think anything.

CARLOS. You are wrong, then, holy Father.
  I am afraid of my secret in the eyes of men,
  But not in the eyes of God.

PRIOR. My son, that concerns us
  Very little. This freedom of thought
  Is as liable to sin as holy innocence.
  Whether what you intend to do is good
  Or evil is a matter for your own
  Conscience, heart, and soul.

CARLOS. Your God cannot find dishonour
  In what we must conceal. For it is His own
  Most beautiful and holy work. Even to you
  I could reveal the secrets of my heart.

PRIOR. But to what end? I would rather, Prince,
  That you did not. The world and all its laws
  Will long be locked away on that long journey
  That we all must make. Why, in the little time

That's left to me, should I renew again
My knowledge of a world I have abjured?
Happiness depends on very little. The less we have,
The happier we are. . . . Now the bell sounds the hour.
I shall go and pray.

PRIOR *goes*.

SCENE 14

DON CARLOS. *Enter* MARQUIS OF POSA.

CARLOS. Oh, at last! At last!

MARQUIS OF POSA. What a test for the patience of a friend!
Quick, tell me, did the King forgive you?
Are you reconciled?

CARLOS. Reconciled? With whom?

MARQUIS OF POSA. With Philip. And did he make a decision in
your favour
About Flanders?

CARLOS. The Duke of Alba leaves to-morrow
For Flanders. That is the decision.

MARQUIS OF POSA. But that cannot be. Can all Madrid
Be mistaken? They say you had
A secret audience with the King, and he——

CARLOS. Remained unmoved. We are forever
Set against one another, even more so
Than we were before.

MARQUIS OF POSA. Then you're not going to Flanders?

CARLOS. No!

MARQUIS OF POSA. Oh, all my great hopes in you——

CARLOS. That's nothing. Oh, Roderich,
Since I saw you last, what have I not been through!

MARQUIS OF POSA. Is it your mother? No! Then what can it be?

CARLOS. I may allow myself some hope.
But more of that another time. Just now
I want to know how I can speak to her.

MARQUIS OF POSA. What is this? On what do you base
This heated dream?

CARLOS. It *is* no dream! It's true! True!

Drawing out EBOLI'S *letter from the* KING.

I have obtained this letter written by the King
To Princess Eboli. He is in love with her.
This letter will set my mother free.
Read it.

MARQUIS OF POSA. What? From the King himself? To Eboli?

CARLOS. To the Princess Eboli. The day before yesterday
A page brought me from an unknown lady
A letter and a key. A room in the left wing of the palace
Where the Queen lives was pointed out to me: there
A certain lady was to wait for me, one
Whom I had loved a long, long time.
I followed the directions——

MARQUIS OF POSA. Oh, Carlos, why?

CARLOS. I did not recognize the writing in the letter.
And I know only one lady whom I have loved so long.
Who else would ask for Carlos to be sent to her?
Filled with a heady rapture, I flew to the room,
Opened the door, and—— Whom do you think I found?
Can you imagine my horror?

MARQUIS OF POSA. It was the Princess Eboli, and not——

CARLOS. Oh, Roderich, I was lost, hopelessly lost,
Or rather, would have been, had I not fallen into
An angel's hands. Oh, but how unfortunate it is!
Misled by the ardour of my silent glances,
She imagined it was she herself I loved!
Moved by my soul's unspoken love,
She then decided, out of the greatness of her heart,
To let me know it was reciprocated, but——
By *her,* not by the Queen!
Respect for her made me keep silence. But
She was bold enough to break it and
Confess her love to me.

MARQUIS OF POSA. You tell it all so calmly. Oh, Carlos,
How could you have been so blind?
The Princess Eboli has seen through your disguise.
You do not need to tell me, for I know

She drew that inmost secret from your heart.
Hell has no fury like a woman spurned.
You have offended her, it's clear. She's dangerous.
The King would commit the greatest follies for her favours.

CARLOS, *confidently*. She is pure and good and virtuous.

MARQUIS OF POSA. Only with the selfishness of love. I fear that
        virtue.
I know that sort of virtue and I fear it
More than any other thing. It is a bastard growth.
Think! Will she ever be able to forgive the Queen
That a man rejected her so jealously-defended,
Much sought-after virtue, simply to consume his heart
In unrequited ardour for Don Philip's wife?

CARLOS. Do you know her as well as that?

MARQUIS OF POSA. The Princess was faithful to you
    Only because she thought you loved her.
    Now you have rejected her, and she will fall.

CARLOS, *vigorously*. No! It cannot be!
    Oh, Roderich, how meanly it becomes you
    To destroy your friend's belief in humankind!

MARQUIS OF POSA. Did I deserve that? No, that was not my
        meaning.
    Oh, this Eboli—she might have been an angel,
    And I am as reluctant as yourself to pull her down.
    But once you had given her your secret——

CARLOS. How idle are your fears! What other proofs has she,
    Than those which will involve herself in shame?
    Would she buy the sad pleasure of revenge
    With her honour?

MARQUIS OF POSA. Many have brought shame upon themselves
    In order to retrieve a moment when their pride was humbled.

CARLOS. No! That is too awful to conceive . . .
    She is proud and noble: I know her
    And fear nothing from her. It is in vain
    You try to rob me of my hopes. No more of that.
    . . . Now I must speak to my mother.

MARQUIS OF POSA. But how?

CARLOS. I can spare myself no longer.

I must know my fate. You must find a way
Of bringing me into her presence.

MARQUIS OF POSA. And do you really wish to show her
This letter from the King to Eboli?

CARLOS. That's not the question at the moment.
The first thing is to find a way to speak to her.

MARQUIS OF POSA. Did you not tell me once you loved your
mother?
And still you intend to show this letter to her?

CARLOS *looks down and is silent.*

Carlos, I have never seen you quite like this before.
Why do you turn your eyes away from me?
Have I read your meaning rightly?
Let me see the letter.

CARLOS *gives him the letter. The* MARQUIS *tears it up.*

CARLOS. Roderich! Are you mad?
Truly, I must confess I had great hopes
Of this incriminating letter.

MARQUIS OF POSA. So I thought. That is why I tore it up.
Tell me, what has the desecration of the royal bed to do
With real love—the true love you have for her?
Oh, how mistaken I have been: I thought
You loved her truly.

CARLOS. Why, what do you mean?

MARQUIS OF POSA. I see now I must alter my ideas.
Once, yes, once it was different.
You were so rich in love, the globe itself
Could have contained itself within your noble heart.
Now all that has gone, devoured
By your selfish lust and by a woman's envy.
Your heart has withered, Carlos. It holds
Not one tear for the devastated provinces,
Not one! Oh, Carlos, how poor you are,
How poor you have become, since you began
To love no other but yourself!

CARLOS. I know I have lost your friendship and regard.

MARQUIS OF POSA. Not so, Carlos! I know these emotional
flights of yours.

They are the aberrations of a noble heart.
The Queen belonged to you, was stolen from you by
The King your father: yet until now
You have hesitated to defend your rights.
Philip perhaps was worthy of her: you did not venture
To bring the matter to a crux. The letter
Decided for you. You were the only one
Worthy of her love. Then with joy and pride
You saw the possibility of taking fate in hand
And overthrowing tyranny and persecution.
You were delighted to be the wounded and insulted one,
For great souls delight in suffering injustices.
But at this point your imagination led your heart astray.

CARLOS. No, Roderich, you are mistaken.
I did not have such noble thoughts by far
As those that you would give me credit for.

MARQUIS OF POSA. Carlos, when you are at fault,
I always seek to find some virtue in your actions.
We understand each other better now.
You shall speak to the Queen—*must* speak to her.

CARLOS. Oh, how ashamed you make me feel!

MARQUIS OF POSA. You can depend on me. You have my word.
A bold, wild plan is forming in my mind.
You shall hear of it, dear Carlos,
From the Queen herself. I am going to her now.
Perhaps to-morrow will finally resolve our problems.
Meanwhile, remember Flanders!

CARLOS. I shall remember everything.

MARQUIS OF POSA. I hear your courtiers coming.
Now for a while again we shall become
Crown Prince and servant.

CARLOS. Are you returning to Madrid at once?

MARQUIS OF POSA. At once.

CARLOS. Be careful! Letters to Brabant are opened by the
King.

MARQUIS OF POSA. I'll send them through Germany. Farewell!
They leave in different directions.

ACT III

SCENE 1

THE KING'S BEDROOM. TOWARDS DAWN

Two night lamps burning on a side table. PAGES *asleep on their knees at rear. The* KING, *half-undressed, is standing before a table in a thoughtful posture. Papers and a medallion lie on the table.*

KING. So she has had a lover. It cannot be denied.
I could never give her love, and yet
Did she ever appear to feel its need?
It is proved. She has been false to me.

                          Where was I?
Is the King the only one here left awake?
The lights are burning out. It will soon be day.
Another day. There is no sleep for me. A King
Has little time to spare
To make up for troubled nights.

He puts out the lights and opens the curtains over the windows. He paces up and down and notices the sleeping PAGES, *before whom he stands for a moment in silence. Then he pulls a bell-rope.*

SCENE 2

KING. COUNT LERMA

COUNT LERMA. Is Your Majesty unwell?

KING. There were pistol shots in the left wing. Did you not hear them?

COUNT LERMA. No, Your Majesty.

KING. How can that be? Do you think I was dreaming?
  Doesn't the Queen sleep in that wing?

COUNT LERMA. Yes, Your Majesty.

KING. The dream frightened me. Give orders for the guards
  To be doubled outside the Queen's pavilion.

COUNT LERMA. Your Majesty should try to sleep a little.

KING. Sleep? I shall have my fill of sleep
  In the Escorial.

  To PAGES, *who by now have woken up.*

  Call the Duke of Alba!

  PAGES *go.*

  Come here, Count. Tell me, is it true?
  Do you swear to me that it is true?
  Am I deceived? Am I?

COUNT LERMA. True? Deceived by whom, sir?

KING. Nothing. It doesn't matter. Leave me.

  The COUNT *is about to leave but is called back.*

  Are you married, Lerma? Are you a father?

COUNT LERMA. Yes, Your Majesty.

KING. Married, you say, and you dare to spend
  One night keeping watch over your master?
  Go back home and you will find your wife
  Abandoned to your son's incestuous embraces.
  You must believe your King. Queens
  Should never spot their virtue.
  If you doubt it——

COUNT LERMA. Who can doubt it, sir?
  In all my master's provinces
  Who is bold and dastardly enough
  To sully her angelic virtue
  With the poison of suspicion?
  The best of queens——

KING. The best? And *your* best friend, no doubt.
  She has some very ardent friends among my court.
  You may go. Let the Duke appear.

COUNT LERMA. I hear him coming through the antechamber——

KING, *more mildly.*

Count, before you go, I beg your forgiveness.
My head is burning with the fire of sleepless nights.
Forget what I just said to you. It was an evil dream.
Do you hear? Forget it. You have the favour of your King.

He holds out his hand for LERMA *to kiss.* LERMA *goes, opening the door for the* DUKE OF ALBA.

SCENE 3

KING. DUKE OF ALBA

DUKE OF ALBA, *approaching the* KING *in some uncertainty.*
This unexpected call—at this unusual hour——
Dear sir, you are not well!

KING. I am sick to the death, wounded
With a deadly wound. And no one warned me!
Do you recognize this writing?

DUKE OF ALBA. It is Don Carlos' hand.

KING. Well, do you not suspect anything?
You warned me against his proud ambition.
Was ambition all you should have guarded me against?

DUKE OF ALBA. Ambition is a great, a far-reaching word,
Covering all kinds of possibilities.

KING. And had you nothing more to tell me?
Was ambition the only thing?

DUKE OF ALBA. Not everything I know
Is fit for royal ears.

KING, *handing him the letter.* Read this letter.

DUKE OF ALBA *reads and turns a horror-stricken face towards
the* KING.
Who was the madman who put
This unhappy letter in Your Majesty's hands?

KING. What? You know what it's about, then?
The writer, I believe, takes care to omit the signatures.

DUKE OF ALBA. I know the person it was addressed to.

KING. So I must be the last to find it out!

DUKE OF ALBA. Your Majesty, I confess my great mistake.
I am ashamed now of my cowardly cleverness
That counselled me to silence in a matter
That concerned my master's honour.
Your Majesty perhaps remembers an occasion
In the Queen's garden at Aranjuez.
You discovered the Queen alone, with a distracted mien,
In a secluded arbour. We know now
That the Prince, Don Carlos, had been there with her.

KING. And she wept, when I spoke angrily to her!
She made me feel ashamed before the entire court!
Oh, it is all as clear as day! Now I understand!
The Queen did wrong to hide from me
The contents of these letters and to conceal
Don Carlos' presence in the garden.
Her generous nature led her to protect him.
I shall find means to have her punished.

To PAGE, *who goes.*

Have Domingo sent to me.
I forgive you, Alba, for your cowardice.

ALBA *departs.*

SCENE 4

KING. DOMINGO

DOMINGO. How glad I am to find you, sir,
So tranquil and composed.
Heaven be praised, my fears were groundless!

KING. Your fears? What had you to fear?

DOMINGO. Your Majesty, I cannot conceal from you
That I am already acquainted with
A certain secret——

KING. And have I expressed a desire to share it with you?
    I do not care for your presumption.

DOMINGO. Your Majesty, it was imparted to me
    Under seal of the confessional.
    It was confessed to me by one
    Whose tender conscience is tormented by her deed,
    And who seeks the grace of heaven.
    The Princess weeps too late for
    An action which she did not realize would bring
    Such terrible consequences for her Queen.

KING. Really? Ah, she has a true and noble heart!
    You have guessed correctly
    My reason for summoning you here.
    You must help me find my way
    Out of this dark labyrinth to which my rash
    Enthusiasms have led me.
    From you I expect, and demand, the truth.
    Be frank with me. What must I believe? What must I do?

DOMINGO. Sire, if it were not my holy duty
    To impose sweet penance on you,
    I should recommend Your Majesty
    To pass your discovery over in
    Dignified silence.
    What has been found out can be forgiven.
    One word from the King . . . and the Queen has never
        sinned.
    A monarch's will confers both happiness and virtue.
    And only a dignified and noble calm
    Can defeat the rumours—

KING. Rumours?—— About me?

DOMINGO. Lies! Nothing but lies! I swear they are.

KING. By heaven!

DOMINGO. A good name is the most priceless and the only
        treasure
    A woman, whether she be queen or serving girl,
    Must carefully preserve.

KING. Her good name, I hope, is not in question?

    DOMINGO *does not reply.*

You have something bad to tell me.
Do not put it off. Out with it!
What are my people saying against the Queen?

DOMINGO. They cannot forget the time when
For two long months you were on the point of death,
Confined by sickness to your chamber. Yet
In only thirty weeks from then, your people hear
The Queen has been delivered of a child——

KING *jumps up and goes to bell-pull.* ALBA *enters*—DOMINGO
is taken aback.

KING, *going up to* ALBA. Toledo!
You are a man. Protect me from this priest.

DOMINGO, *exchanging embarrassed glances.*
If we had only known
How the bringing of this news would be revenged——

KING. A bastard, did you say? I had hardly left
A bed of almost mortal sickness
Before she found herself with child?
If I am not mistaken, that was when
You gave your thanks in all our churches
For the almighty wonder of my great recovery!
If it was then a miracle, why is it not one now?
You lied to me then, or else
You lie to me now. What do you expect me to believe?
Oh, I have seen through everything! I see now
That if your plot had come to full fruition then,
This holy man had forfeited ambitious dreams
Of power in the cabinet and in the Church.
The time was not yet ripe for my betrayal!

DUKE OF ALBA. Betrayal! Plot!

KING. Do you mean to tell me you are not
Both hand in glove? Is that it?
Do you think I have not noticed
How greedily you swooped upon your prey?
How keenly exercised you were
To rouse a dreadful anger in me?
How could I fail to see the eagerness
With which the Duke came begging favours
That should more suitably be given to my son?

How impudently you, the man of piety,
Concealed your petty schemes behind
The threat of royal anger? You think
That I am just the bow that must be bent
At will, to shoot the poisoned arrows of your foul desires?
No!
My will is still my own, and I intend to use it.
I shall begin on you.

DUKE OF ALBA. We did not think our loyalty
Would be rewarded thus.

KING. Loyalty!
Loyalty would have warned me of a threatened crime.
You bring me to the brink of an abyss
And leave me on the point of falling.

DOMINGO. What better proofs could there be found
Than the evidences of our eyes?

KING, *to* DOMINGO.
I shall assemble the great ones of my realm
To a most solemn trial of you both and I
Myself shall sit in judgement!
There you may bring, if you have effrontery enough,
Your charges against the Queen.
Denounce her, if you dare, before a court of law,
As an adulteress! As a paramour, a prostitute!
The Prince must die. But, if she can defend and prove
Her innocence, then *you* shall be the one to die.
Would you be prepared to make
Such an offering to the truth? No? Why don't you answer?
Make your decision, man. You show the courage of a liar.

DUKE OF ALBA, *who has remained quietly in the background,*
steps forward. I will do it.

KING, *staring at him*. That's very bold of you, though I recall
That you have risked your life in fierce battles
On a much slighter thing: the absurdity of fame.
I reject your offer. Go, and await me
In the audience chamber.
Both go.

SCENE 5

THE AUDIENCE CHAMBER

DON CARLOS *in conversation with the* PRINCE OF PARMA. DUKES OF ALBA, FERIA *and* MEDINA SIDONIA. COUNT LERMA *and other* GRANDEES *with papers in their hands. All await the* KING.

DUKE OF MEDINA SIDONIA, *obviously avoided by all the others, turns to the* DUKE OF ALBA, *who is walking up and down, alone, and in deep thought.*

DUKE OF MEDINA SIDONIA. You have been speaking with His
    Majesty.
How did you find him? What kind of mood is he in?

DUKE OF ALBA. A very bad one, thanks to you and your news.

DUKE OF MEDINA SIDONIA. The fire of the English galleons
    Was easier for me to bear than this.

CARLOS, *who has been watching him with silent sympathy, now approaches him and shakes his hand.*

Thank you for that kind gesture.
You see how everyone avoids me. I am ruined.

CARLOS. Hope for the best from my father,
From your innocence and his graciousness.

DUKE OF MEDINA SIDONIA. I lost his fleet for him, a fleet
Whose like had never sailed the seas before.
What is one fallen head against
Seventy sunken galleons? What breaks my heart
Is the loss of my five sons, all
With futures bright as yours before them.

SCENE 6

The KING, *and the already assembled characters. All remove their hats and make way for him, forming a semicircle round him. Silence.*

KING. The Prince of Parma!

PARMA *approaches with* CARLOS.

Your mother, nephew,
Would like to know how pleased we are with you
Here in Madrid.

PRINCE OF PARMA. We must first await the outcome of my
first engagement.

KING. You can be confident of that.

To DUKE OF FERIA.

What have you brought me, sir?

DUKE OF FERIA, *kneeling before the* KING. The Grand Master
Of the Order of Calatrava died this morning.
I have brought you his cross of knighthood.

KING *takes the Order and looks round the circle.* Who deserves
best to wear it after him?

He beckons to ALBA, *who kneels to him as he places the Order round his neck.*

You are my first commander-in-chief.
I assure you that you shall always have my favour.

He notices the DUKE OF MEDINA SIDONIA.

Admiral!

DUKE OF MEDINA SIDONIA *approaches, kneels, and bends his head.* Your Majesty,
This head is all I have to offer in exchange for
The blasting of the flower of Spain,
Our fallen youth, and your Armada.

KING. God is greater than I.
I sent you out against men and not
Against storms and cliffs.

He holds out his hand to be kissed.

What else is there? I thank you, Princes.

CARLOS and PARMA leave. The remaining noblemen approach and present their papers to the KING on bended knee. He leafs through them hastily and gives them to ALBA.

Put them in the cabinet room. Is that all?

Silence.

How is it that I do not see
The Marquis of Posa among my courtiers?

COUNT LERMA. The Chevalier has only recently arrived
Here in Madrid and awaits your command
Before presenting himself before Your Majesty.

KING. I know how good a servant he has been;
How brave in the service of my fame. I am astounded
That such a man has not appeared before
To sue for favours. I must speak to him.
Alba, when we have heard Mass,
You will bring him to me.

ALBA goes.

The KING signs to FERIA.

You, sir, will preside
Over the council in my absence.

He goes.

DUKE OF FERIA. The King is very kind to-day.

DUKE OF MEDINA SIDONIA. Say rather that he is a god.
He has acted like one to me.

COUNT LERMA, *as they all leave.* How rich he has made you,
And with no more than a word or two!

SCENE 7

THE KING'S CABINET

MARQUIS OF POSA *and* DUKE OF ALBA

MARQUIS OF POSA, *entering.*
Wants to see *me?* The King? It can't be!

What could he want of me?

DUKE OF ALBA. He wishes to get to know you. Make good use
of the occasion.

I leave you under a good star.

Goes.

SCENE 8

MARQUIS OF POSA, *alone*

MARQUIS OF POSA. There was some truth in what he said.
One must seize the moment as it flies
And make the most of every opportunity.
That practised old courtier gave good advice,
If not in his own sense, then in mine.

*He walks up and down several times and finally stops be-
fore a portrait, at which he is gazing when the* KING *enters.
The* KING *watches the* MARQUIS *for a while without being
seen.*

SCENE 9

KING. MARQUIS OF POSA

The latter goes to the KING *and kneels before him, then rises
and stands before him without any trace of uneasiness.*

KING, *gazing at him in astonishment.*
Have you ever spoken to me before?

MARQUIS OF POSA. No.

KING. You have served the throne well.
Why have you never let me thank you?
I am not accustomed to being in my servants' debt.
You may ask a favour of me.

MARQUIS OF POSA. Sire, I wish for nothing.

KING. You are leaving my service, so I hear?

MARQUIS OF POSA. To make way for a better man.

KING. I am sorry to hear it.

MARQUIS OF POSA. I am most grateful for your kindness
And for the gracious interest of Your Majesty.
But—— I cannot serve kings and princes.
I cannot be a courtier.

KING. What do you mean?

MARQUIS OF POSA. I have an independent spirit. I love freedom.
The services my arm and mind performed for you
Were also for myself. My own integrity
Is more to me than the approval of the throne.
I love humanity. If I served a monarch
I could only love myself.

KING. That shows a worthy spirit.
Find yourself some post within my kingdom
That will give these high ideals fuller scope.

MARQUIS OF POSA. There is no such post.

KING. Then I shall create one.

MARQUIS OF POSA. No, sire. Is what Your Majesty commands
    of me
The furtherance of human happiness, the happiness
That my disinterested love would give? No!
That sort of happiness would make a monarch tremble.
The crown has its own conceptions
Of what a human's happiness should be.
You have your profile stamped on every coin;
It is a likeness of the truth you fashion for yourself,
The only truth that you can bear. All others that
Would give that truth the lie are cast away,
The mould destroyed. But that is something I cannot accept.

KING. You must be a Protestant.

MARQUIS OF POSA. My religion, sire, is your own.
But you may find me dangerous, because
I think for myself. You would be mistaken.
The times have not yet come
In which my new philosophies could find fulfilment.
They can be no more than dreams, and dreams
That one word from you could utterly destroy.

KING. A great truth lies in what you say.
　I need integrity like yours.

MARQUIS OF POSA. I beg of you, sire,
　Dismiss me from your service. My nature
　Does not fit me for a courtier's life.

COUNT LERMA *enters and whispers a few words to the* KING.
The latter signs to him to leave.

KING. I feel there is something else you want to say.
　What is it?

MARQUIS OF POSA. Sire, lately I returned from Flanders and
　　　Brabant—
　A lovely country, and a fine, strong race of people.
　How wonderful, I thought, to be the father of
　Such a splendid nation! But then
　I came upon heaps of charred and human bones——

Here he falls silent, his eyes resting on the KING, *who tries
in vain to return his look.*

　Yes. You are right. You have to do it. But
　That you *could* do it—that
　Fills me with amazement and with horror.
　Yet one day milder times will come and bring
　A better wisdom: then ordinary men
　Will walk with kings and princes,
　The state will let its children dance,
　And human need once more will find a human heart
　To succour it.

KING. And when do you think these happy times would have
　　　arrived
　If I had been afraid of the present century's curses on
　My policy? Look round you now in Spain and you will see
　That human happiness can flourish under cloudless skies
　In peace. That peace I wish to bring to Flanders.

MARQUIS OF POSA. The peace of a graveyard! And do you
　　　really hope
　To bring to a conclusion what you have begun?
　Hope to retard the present springtime
　That brings a revolution in the Christian faith?
　Would you set yourself against the climates of opinion in

The whole of contemporary Europe? Already
The citizens whom you have lost to the faith
Have fled to England, and there have been received
By Elizabeth with open arms. Now Britain flourishes
With all the arts that have been banished from
Their native lands. Granada now lies desolate,
Abandoned by the Christians of a newer faith;
And Europe rejoices at the sight of Philip
Weltering in the blood of self-inflicted wounds.

The KING *is moved.* MARQUIS *comes nearer.*

How can you cultivate the future,
If it is death you sow? It hurts me
To hear your noble name in company with those
Of Nero and Busiris: for you were a good man.
But, even now, it is not too late!
Never did a mortal man possess such power as yourself.
You are no god, but you could use that power
Like a god. Go and take council with the kings of Europe.
They respect your name: your signature could change
The face of all this continent. Freedom of thought
Is what our peoples need!

KING.   I have been much moved and touched by what you say.
Now let me address you as a man, not as a king.
You have spoken honestly and frankly,
And for that reason I shall overlook
The nature of the things you uttered and
The circumstance that brought them to my ear. But——
Flee my Inquisition.
                     Now go and tell the world
That I judge men as I find them. But I know
You would think otherwise of men if you
Knew what I know about them.
                              I must see more of you.
What can I do to win you back?

MARQUIS OF POSA.   Allow me, sire, to remain as I am now. A
    free man.

KING.   I cannot tolerate such self-sufficiency.
From this moment you are in my service. No!
A pause.

There shall be no refusal.
Was it not truth I asked for?
I have received from you, Chevalier,
More than I bargained for. You have found out
The secrets of the throne: have you discovered also
The secrets of my house?

The MARQUIS *does not reply.*

I see you have. Why can I, the unhappiest of fathers, not
Find happiness in marriage?

MARQUIS OF POSA. The prince has a good and noble mind.

KING. But I know differently. What he has taken from me
Can never be retrieved by any crown. And she
Was such a virtuous queen!

MARQUIS OF POSA. Who could dare to hint that——

KING. The world! Evil tongues! You, yourself!
Here I hold proofs that tell unquestionably
All her guilt. I shall soon receive others,
Whose nature fills me with a terrible foreboding.
How could she have done it? How could she
Have let her honourable name be trampled in the dust?
How happy I would be to know that Princess Eboli
Has slandered her! Does Domingo not despise
Both Eboli and Carlos? And how do I know
What Alba may be plotting? My wife
Is worth more than all of them.

MARQUIS OF POSA. Sire, there still is something left
That can preserve a woman from all evil words: her virtue.

KING. Yes, that is what I think too. Posa,
You know what men and women are.
I have long wanted such a man as you,
And that is why I have chosen you——

MARQUIS OF POSA. I, sire?

KING. You stood before your King and asked
For nothing for yourself. Never before have I encountered
Such a person. You will be just, I know, and passion
Will not warp your judgement. Get to know my son's
Most inner thoughts and try to seek the confidence

Of the Queen. I grant you full authority
To speak to them alone. Now leave me!

Rings bell.

MARQUIS OF POSA. This day is the most wonderful I've ever
lived.

KING, *holding out his hand to be kissed.* I too
Feel that I have not lived through it in vain.

The MARQUIS *rises and goes. Enter* LERMA.

KING. In future the Chevalier may enter unannounced.

ACT IV

SCENE 1

A ROOM IN THE QUEEN'S APARTMENTS

QUEEN. DUCHESS OLIVAREZ. PRINCESS EBOLI.
COUNTESS OF FUENTES, *and other ladies of the court*

QUEEN, *addressing* OLIVAREZ, *who rises.*
Was the key never found again?
Then the lock of my writing-cabinet must be forced,
Because I cannot——
Seeing EBOLI *approaching her to kiss her hand.*
                          Welcome back among us, Princess!
I am delighted to see you here once more, although
You still seem a little pale——

COUNTESS OF FUENTES, *rather spitefully.*
Caused by that wretched fever, I'm sure.
It plays havoc with the nerves, does it not, Princess?

QUEEN. I wanted so much to visit you, dear friend.
But as you know, that is not allowed.

DUCHESS OF OLIVAREZ. The Princess did not lack for company,
at any rate.

QUEEN. I can well believe it. Why, what is wrong, my dear?
You are trembling!

PRINCESS EBOLI. Nothing—it's nothing, Your Majesty.
I would ask your gracious permission to withdraw.

QUEEN. You are trying to hide something from us. I'm sure
You are more ill than you would want to say.
I can see that standing is too much for you.
Countess, fetch a stool for the Princess and
Place it beside me, where I can watch over her.

PRINCESS EBOLI. I shall feel better after—after a breath of air——

Goes.

QUEEN. Countess, go with her. What an alarming change!

A PAGE *enters and speaks to the* DUCHESS, *who turns to the* QUEEN.

DUCHESS OF OLIVAREZ. The Marquis of Posa, Your Majesty. He comes
On the authority of the King for private audience.

QUEEN. Let him come in.

PAGE *opens door to* MARQUIS.

SCENE 2

MARQUIS OF POSA. *The assembled characters*

The MARQUIS *kneels before the* QUEEN, *who motions to him to rise, and to the others to leave. They go.*

QUEEN. I can hardly believe my eyes, Marquis.
You, sent to me by the King?

MARQUIS OF POSA. Does Your Majesty consider that
So very extraordinary? I do not.

QUEEN. It's as if the sun and stars had left their courses.
His Majesty—and *you*—I must confess——

MARQUIS OF POSA. It does sound somewhat improbable. But the present time
Is full of many strange and remarkable possibilities.

QUEEN. Then this must be the strangest and the most remarkable.
But what message did he send with you?

MARQUIS OF POSA. The King would ask your gracious Majesty
Not to receive the French ambassador to-day.
That was my official commission.

QUEEN. And is that all you have to tell me?

MARQUIS OF POSA. No, Your Majesty. That was not what brought me here.

Don Carlos——

QUEEN. What news have you of him?

MARQUIS OF POSA. Ready to die for his love. Here are
A few words written by his hand.

Gives QUEEN *a letter.*

QUEEN, *after a hasty glance.* He says he must speak to me.

MARQUIS OF POSA. I think so too.

QUEEN. How could it make him happy
To see my own unhappiness?

MARQUIS OF POSA. It would help him to act and make a
decision.

QUEEN. About what?

MARQUIS OF POSA. The Duke of Alba is being sent to Flanders.

QUEEN. So I heard.

MARQUIS OF POSA. We know the King's unalterable obstinacy;
He will never change his mind. But the Prince
Must not stay here. And Flanders must not be made
Another bloody sacrifice to Spain.

QUEEN. How can it be stopped?

MARQUIS OF POSA. Perhaps, though the means is almost
As dangerous as the thing we wish to avoid—
Only to you, my Queen, dare I reveal it.
Only from your lips would Carlos
Consent to hear my plan, which might be called
By a rather sinister name——

QUEEN. Revolt.

MARQUIS OF POSA. He must disobey the orders of the King
And go to Brussels secretly, where the people
Are waiting to welcome him with open arms.
At one word from Carlos, all the Netherlands
Would rise in arms. He could make the throne of Spain
Tremble before his power. What his father has refused him
here
He may grant him in Brussels.

QUEEN. You can say that, after speaking to the King?

MARQUIS OF POSA. Because I spoke to him.

QUEEN. Your plan both terrifies me and gives me hope.

I believe you are right. Does the Prince know of it?

MARQUIS OF POSA. He shall hear it first from you, Your
Majesty.

QUEEN. I can vouch for the support of France and also
Of Savoy. I am entirely in agreement with you.
The Prince must act, and quickly.
But such a plan needs money.

MARQUIS OF POSA. That too is all arranged.
Then may I inform him of your pleasure?
Will you consent to see him?

QUEEN. I must think it over.

MARQUIS OF POSA. Your Majesty, Carlos demands an answer
now.
I must not return to him with empty hands.

Handing his notebook to the QUEEN.

A few words are all that's needed.

QUEEN, *writing.* Shall I be seeing you again?

MARQUIS OF POSA. As often as Your Majesty wishes.

QUEEN. As often as I wish? I still cannot believe it.
If only this new freedom
Might spread to all of Europe!

MARQUIS OF POSA. I knew—I knew you would understand me.

OLIVAREZ *appears in the doorway.*

QUEEN, *suddenly cold to the* MARQUIS. Whatever orders come
From the King, I shall observe them to the letter,
As if they were laws. Go and reassure him of
My submissive respect and loyalty.

She gives him a sign. MARQUIS *goes.*

SCENE 3

A GALLERY

DON CARLOS. COUNT LERMA

CARLOS. Here we can talk undisturbed.
What have you to tell me?

COUNT LERMA. The Marquis of Posa has had a private audi-
ence with the King.
He was there at least two hours.
The matters they discussed were of no small moment.

CARLOS. I can well believe it.

COUNT LERMA. I often heard your own name mentioned.

CARLOS. I hope that it will bring no more bad news for me.

COUNT LERMA. There was mention of the Queen also.

CARLOS. No!

COUNT LERMA. When the Marquis left, I was commanded
That in future he was to enter
His Majesty's apartments unannounced.

CARLOS. How extraordinary!

COUNT LERMA. Quite unprecedented.

CARLOS. And in what way was the Queen mentioned?

COUNT LERMA. No, it would be failing in my duty to the King
To tell you that.

CARLOS. Why should you tell me one thing and conceal the
other?

COUNT LERMA. It was my duty to tell you the first but not
the second.

CARLOS. You are right.

COUNT LERMA. I had always thought the Marquis to be
A man of honour.

CARLOS. Then you have judged him correctly.

COUNT LERMA. If he is still a man of honour,

Then my suspicions do him no injury
And you, Prince, have double cause
For treasuring his friendship.

CARLOS. No, treble cause, for I see you are my friend.
You have made me win one and not lose the other.

Takes his hand. LERMA *goes.*

SCENE 4

THE KING'S CABINET ROOM

KING *sitting. Beside him the* INFANTA CLARA EUGENIA

KING. She *is* my daughter. There's no doubt of that.
Nature tells the truth and cannot lie.
Those blue eyes are mine! And in each feature
I find myself again.
Dear child, let me press you to my heart.
You are my own—my flesh and blood.

He gives a start.

My blood! Oh, when will my fears find an end?
Are these features not *his* also?

*He takes the medallion and looks from its portrait to a mir-
ror and back again. Finally he throws the medallion to the
floor, stands up quickly, and thrusts the* INFANTA *away from
him.*

Away! Away!

SCENE 5

COUNT LERMA. KING

COUNT LERMA. Her Majesty the Queen is in the antechamber.
She asks for the favour of an audience.

KING. What, now? At this unusual hour? No!
I cannot see her now—I cannot——

COUNT LERMA. Here comes Her Majesty.

He goes.

SCENE 6

The KING. *The* QUEEN *enters. The* INFANTA *runs towards her
and throws herself into her arms. The* QUEEN *kneels to the*
KING, *who stands speechless and bewildered.*

QUEEN. My lord, my husband—— I must—— I am compelled——
To ask for justice. I have been treated
Most ignominiously in your court.
My writing-case has been broken into,
And things of great value stolen from it——

KING. Stand up, I beg of you.

QUEEN. Not before you promise, sire,
To use your kingly authority to catch the thief——

KING. Please, rise, I cannot bear to see you kneel to me——

QUEEN, *standing.*
That he must be a person of wealth and influence
Is plain, for there were precious jewels also in the box.
But he was satisfied with my letters and with a medallion
Of the Prince. The letters were from him too.

KING. From the Prince? To you? Do you dare to tell me that?

QUEEN. Why not, sire? You must remember the letters
Which, with the consent of both our kingdoms,
Don Carlos wrote to me in Saint Germain.
Whether he had permission also
To send the medallion or not is not for me to say.
If it was hasty rashness on his part, then
It is easily forgivable—I can vouch for that.
For in those days he did not know
He was sending his portrait to—his mother.

She notices the INFANTA'S *movement.*

What is it? What have you got there?

INFANTA, *who, meanwhile, has found the medallion on the floor and has been playing with it, brings it to the* QUEEN. Look here, Mother! Look at the pretty picture!

QUEEN. Where, my dear?——

She recognizes the portrait and stands in speechless astonishment. KING *and* QUEEN *look hard at one another.*

Truly, sire, I find this way of testing your queen's heart
Very kinglike, very noble. I should like to ask you
One more question.

KING. It is for me to ask the questions.

QUEEN. My own suspicions
Shall not bring suffering upon the innocent.
If this theft was committed on your orders——

KING. It was.

QUEEN. Then I have no one left to turn to,
No one more to pity but yourself,
Whose wife did not deserve such treatment.

KING. Madam, you shall not deceive me
A second time, as you deceived me in Aranjuez.
I know you better now. Is it true
That you spoke with no one there?
With no one? Is it really true?

QUEEN. I spoke with the Prince——

KING. Now it is out. What impudence! What boldness!
Why did you deny the truth?

QUEEN. Because, sire, I am not accustomed
To being treated like a common evil-doer
In the presence of my court.
When the truth is asked for honourably
And with kindness, I do not deny it.
That was hardly how Your Majesty asked for it in Aranjuez.
I granted the Prince an interview
Which he had pleaded for most pressingly.
I did so, sire, because it was my wish.

KING. These are bold words, Madam.

QUEEN. Why should I conceal my thoughts?
I love the Prince as one

Who is most near and dear to me.
I will not be commanded to despise and hate
Because your policy requires it.

KING. Elizabeth! Until now
You have only known my gentler side:
You think to take advantage of that mildness.
I warn you now
That fury can unleash a raving monster in me
That will not spare the Prince or you.

QUEEN. What fault have I committed?

KING. However small your fault,
If fault it can be proved to be,
If I have been deceived by you—and even
In the most trifling way—I shall have
No mercy for you. I shall overcome
All tenderness, all pity, and bring down all
My terrible revenges on you both.
Woe then to you and me and all of us, Elizabeth!

QUEEN. Tell me what fault I have committed?

KING. Blood must flow!

QUEEN. Oh, has it come to this?

KING. I am no more the husband you have known.
You honour no respect, no law of nature,
No marriage treaty, and disown
The treaties made between our countries for our common
good.

QUEEN. How much I pity you!

KING. I want no pity from a whore and an adulteress,
An incestuous paramour——

INFANTA. The King is angry, and my pretty mother weeps.

The KING *thrusts the child away from the* QUEEN.

QUEEN. This child shall not be made
A party to your cruelty and wrath.
Come with me, my love. If the King
Will have no more of me,
Then I shall have protection from across the Pyrenees.
France shall revenge these terrible injustices.

She prepares to go.

I can bear no more. It is too much.

She reaches the door and falls, with the child in her arms, on the threshold.

KING, *hurrying to her.* Why, what's the matter?

INFANTA. My mother's bleeding! My mother——

She runs out.

KING. Blood! Did I deserve this punishment?
Stand up! There are people coming!
Must this be a spectacle for all the court?
I beg of you, stand up!

She rises, supported by the KING.

SCENE 7

Enter DUKE OF ALBA *and* DOMINGO. *Ladies follow.*

KING. Conduct the Queen to her apartments,
She is not well.

The QUEEN *goes with her ladies.*

DUKE OF ALBA. The Queen in tears, her head bleeding——

KING. And that surprises you, you devils, does it?
You are the cause of this——

DOMINGO. We——?

KING. You said enough to bring me
Out of my mind with rage:
But it does not convince me yet.

DUKE OF ALBA. We simply told you what we knew——

KING. I hope you are damned to hell for it.
You made me do a thing
That all my life I shall remember with
The bitterest remorse. She could not have spoken thus
If she had had a guilty conscience.

MARQUIS OF POSA, *off.* Is it possible to see the King?

SCENE 8

MARQUIS OF POSA. *The assembled characters*

KING. Ah, here he is! You are most welcome, Marquis.
   I do not need you any more, Alba. Leave us alone.
   ALBA *and* DOMINGO *go, bewildered.*

SCENE 9

KING. MARQUIS OF POSA

KING. What news do you bring?

MARQUIS OF POSA. I found occasion to take some papers from
   The Prince's portfolio, which I hope
   Will cast some light upon——

KING, *looking through papers.* A letter from
   The Emperor, my father—plans for a party—
   A few thoughts scribbled out of Tacitus——
   And what is this? I should know this hand.
   It is a lady's—— What does she say?
   "This key will open—the Queen's
   Inner apartments"—— Ha! What's this?
   "There you may freely speak your love—
   A hearing will be granted—a good reward"——
   What devilish deception! Now I know whose hand it is——

MARQUIS OF POSA. The Queen's? Impossible!

KING. Princess Eboli—— Marquis,
   I find myself in a most terrible dilemma!
   This—this woman opened, broke open,
   The Queen's writing-cabinet—I received
   The first warning from the Princess——
   Who knows how much the monk may know of this?
   I have been utterly misled—— Oh, Marquis,

I begin to feel I have misjudged my wife
Most grievously——

MARQUIS OF POSA. If there was any understanding
Between Don Carlos and Her Majesty,
Then it was something quite, quite different
From what they are accused of.
I have quite definite confirmation
That the Prince's desire to go to Flanders
Was put into his head by the Queen herself.

KING. I always suspected it.

MARQUIS OF POSA. Would you like me to find out
If she is in love with him? Or he with her?
I think it is a matter we might profitably investigate.

KING. Do so.

MARQUIS OF POSA. I must have full authority——

KING. It is granted.
You are my good angel. How thankful I am to you
For this great help!
To LERMA, *who has entered on these words.*
How is the Queen?

COUNT LERMA. Still very weak, sire, after her collapse.
He looks meaningfully at POSA *and goes.*

MARQUIS OF POSA. One more precaution I think is necessary.
The Prince may be warned—he has friends in plenty,
Perhaps connections with the rebels in Ghent.
Fear might lead him into rash decisions. And so
I advise you to take measures
To prevent any untoward event.

KING. You are quite right. But how——

MARQUIS OF POSA. A secret warrant of arrest, which Your
Majesty
Will draft for me, in case of danger.
It would remain a state secret.

KING, *going to writing-desk.* The kingdom is at stake.
The circumstances require extraordinary measures.
Writes.

Here, Marquis. I do not need to recommend
Particular consideration——

MARQUIS OF POSA, *taking the warrant.*
It shall be used, Your Majesty,
Only in the most pressing extremity.

KING. Now go, Marquis, and set my mind at rest.
Through you I may find sleep again at night.
Both depart in different directions.

SCENE 10

A GALLERY

CARLOS *enters, very agitated.* COUNT LERMA.

CARLOS. Is it true?
Did he stab her with a dagger?

COUNT LERMA. She fell in a faint and hurt her head.
That was all.

CARLOS. No other danger?

COUNT LERMA. Not for the Queen. But certainly for you.
Prince, I gave you a warning yesterday
Which you refused to listen to.
Do not be so heedless of my second warning.

CARLOS. What is it?

COUNT LERMA. If I am not mistaken, Prince,
You have a portfolio of letters
Bound in blue silk, with a silhouette
Embroidered with gold and pearls upon the cover——

CARLOS. That is so.

COUNT LERMA. When I entered the King's apartments,
I saw it in his hands, and beside him stood
The Marquis of Posa——

CARLOS. That cannot be true.

COUNT LERMA. Then I am a liar.
But I remember what the King was saying.

"How thankful I am to you," he said,
"For this great help!"

CARLOS. No! No!

COUNT LERMA. They say that the Duke of Alba
Is fallen from favour, that the great Seal of State
Has been taken from Prince Ruy Gomez
And handed over to the Marquis.

CARLOS. And he kept all this from me!

COUNT LERMA. The whole court now looks upon him as
An all-powerful minister, the first in the King's favour.

CARLOS. He loved me once. I know he did.
But now his love embraces millions,
And he has none for me.
His heart was too great for one good friend,
And Carlos' love too small a thing.
I've lost him. I have lost my friend.

COUNT LERMA. My dear Prince, what can I do for you?

CARLOS. Go to the King and betray me too.

COUNT LERMA. Do you not wish to save yourself?

CARLOS. Save myself! I am past caring.

COUNT LERMA. Past caring even for the safety of another?

CARLOS. My mother! The letter I gave him—
I did not want to, but he persuaded me
To give him a letter from my mother—from *her!*
I must go to her. Oh, Lerma, I have no one left
To send to her. But I have *you*—
I still have one friend left!
Come!

He hurries off.

COUNT LERMA, *following.* Prince! Where are you going?

SCENE 11

A ROOM IN PRINCESS EBOLI'S APARTMENTS

PRINCESS EBOLI. CARLOS *enters*.

PRINCESS EBOLI. So it is true, this extraordinary rumour
That all the court is whispering about?

CARLOS. Do not be afraid, Princess!
I shall be as gentle as a child with you.

PRINCESS EBOLI. Prince—this terrible surprise!

CARLOS. Do you still feel injured? Insulted?

PRINCESS EBOLI. Prince——!

CARLOS. *Do* you? I want to know!

PRINCESS EBOLI. What do you mean? You seem to forget——
What do you want with me?

CARLOS, *seizing her hand*. Will you never forget your hatred?
Can injured love never forgive?

PRINCESS EBOLI, *trying to free herself*. Why do you remind
me——

CARLOS. I want you to remember
Your own kindness and my ungratefulness.
Oh, I know, only too well,
How terribly I hurt you, tore your heart,
Brought bitter tears into those angel's eyes!

PRINCESS EBOLI. Let me go——

CARLOS. I have come to you because
You are a good, sweet, and gentle creature;
Because I build my hopes upon the goodness of your soul.
I have no other friend left now. You are
The only one left to me in the world.
Once you were so kind, so lovingly disposed towards me.
You must not always hate me, not always
Close your heart to me!

PRINCESS EBOLI, *turning her face away.* I beg of you, no more!

CARLOS. Let me remind you once again
Of those golden days when you did love **me**
And of that love which I rejected so unworthily.

PRINCESS EBOLI. Oh, Carlos, do not torture me——

CARLOS. Rise above your woman's heart! Forget
The hurts and injuries it suffered.
I am asking you to do a thing
No woman has ever done before.
I beg of you—upon my knees I beg of you—
Allow me to speak a few words with my mother——

SCENE 12

PRINCESS EBOLI. DON CARLOS

MARQUIS OF POSA *rushes in with two officers of the* KING'S
bodyguard.

MARQUIS OF POSA, *beside himself, thrusts* EBOLI *and* CARLOS
apart.
What has he told you? Do not believe him!

CARLOS, *still on his knees.* By heaven——

MARQUIS OF POSA, *interrupting.* He is raving mad, I tell you.
Pay no heed to what he says.

CARLOS, *pressingly, to* EBOLI. It is a matter of life and death.
Take me to her! Let me speak to her!

MARQUIS OF POSA, *pulling* EBOLI *roughly to him.* I shall kill you
If you listen to him.

To an officer.

In the name of the King, and by virtue of
This warrant for Don Carlos' arrest,
I command you to take him prisoner!

CARLOS *stares at him thunderstruck. The* PRINCESS *gives a
shriek and tries to escape, but finds the way barred by the
officers. The* MARQUIS *is trembling with emotion.*

Prince, I must ask you for your sword.
Princess Eboli, you will remain here.

To officers.

Gentlemen, you will see to it that His Highness
Speaks to no one—no one—not even to yourselves.
I shall give His Majesty an account of this.
Prince, we shall meet again, within the hour.

CARLOS *lets himself be led away. As he goes, he gives the*
MARQUIS *a last stunned glance.* MARQUIS *holds* EBOLI.

SCENE 13

PRINCESS EBOLI. MARQUIS OF POSA

PRINCESS EBOLI. For pity's sake, leave me alone——

MARQUIS OF POSA, *dragging her downstage.*
You miserable woman,
What did he say to you?

PRINCESS EBOLI. Nothing! Nothing——! Leave me alone!

MARQUIS OF POSA, *even more severely.* What did he tell you?
You won't get away this time.
You'll never tell a soul what he has said,
I swear you won't——

PRINCESS EBOLI. Oh, God! Do you mean to murder me?

MARQUIS OF POSA, *drawing his dagger.*
I do, if you won't tell me!
Now! Be quick!

PRINCESS EBOLI. What have *I* done? Oh, heaven help me!

MARQUIS OF POSA, *pointing the dagger at her breast.*
There is still time. The poison has not yet
Passed your lips. I can destroy you,
And everything will be as it was before—— To think
The fate of Spain hangs on this wretched woman's life!
He keeps the dagger at her breast.

PRINCESS EBOLI *sinks to her knees.*
Well, what are you waiting for?

I do not ask for mercy. I deserve to die. I am ready.

MARQUIS OF POSA, *lowering the dagger.*

Then I should be a coward

As well as a murderer! No! Thank God! There's another
way!

He drops the dagger and hurries out. PRINCESS EBOLI *runs
through another door.*

SCENE 14

A ROOM IN THE QUEEN'S APARTMENTS

QUEEN. COUNTESS FUENTES

QUEEN, *to* COUNTESS FUENTES.

What is all the uproar in the palace?

It frightens me. Go and find out what it is.

The COUNTESS *goes.* PRINCESS EBOLI *rushes in.*

PRINCESS EBOLI. Your Majesty, help! He is taken prisoner.

QUEEN. Who?

PRINCESS EBOLI. The Marquis of Posa arrested him

On the orders of the King.

QUEEN. But who? Who?

PRINCESS EBOLI. The Prince!

QUEEN. Well, at least he is in good hands, thank heaven!

PRINCESS EBOLI. How can you be so calm, so cold?

It is no small offence he has committed.

He will be put to death——

QUEEN. No!

PRINCESS EBOLI. And I am—his executioner!

QUEEN. Put to death? Do you know what you are saying?

PRINCESS EBOLI. Oh, if I had known that it would come to this!

QUEEN *takes her gently by the hand.* Princess,

You are beside yourself. Try to tell me calmly

What has happened.

PRINCESS EBOLI. You are so kind, so noble, you do not suspect
  What a she-devil you have in your court.
  I, who have always been your friend—
  I am the one who broke into your writing-desk,
  And handed those letters to the King——

QUEEN. You?

PRINCESS EBOLI. And it was I who had the cowardly temerity
  To denounce you to the King——

QUEEN. You! How could *you*——

PRINCESS EBOLI. Revenge, passion, madness——
  I hated you and loved the Prince.

QUEEN. Because you loved him——

PRINCESS EBOLI. Because I confessed my love to him,
  And he did not return it.

QUEEN. Ah, now I begin to understand.
  You loved him—for that I can forgive you.
  All that is now forgotten. Come, rise, and sit beside me——

PRINCESS EBOLI. No! No! There is something else I must
      confess—
  A terrible thing—— The King—seduced me. Oh,
  You turn away from me! The crime of which
  I dared to accuse you—— It was not you,
  But I who committed it——

She casts herself down from her knees to the ground. The
QUEEN *goes away. After a moment* OLIVAREZ *enters and finds*
the PRINCESS *still in this attitude. The latter, hearing her*
coming, raises her head, and jumps despairingly to her feet
when she sees the QUEEN *has gone.*

SCENE 15

PRINCESS EBOLI. DUCHESS OF OLIVAREZ

PRINCESS EBOLI. Oh, God! She has left me! There is no hope
  now.

DUCHESS OF OLIVAREZ. Princess Eboli——

PRINCESS EBOLI. I know why you have come, Duchess.
  The Queen has sent you—— Tell me, quickly,
  What is my fate?

DUCHESS OF OLIVAREZ. I have orders from Her Majesty
  To divest you of your Order,
  And to take back the key you stole——

PRINCESS EBOLI, *taking a gold star from her breast and giving
  it to* OLIVAREZ. May I not kiss her hand once more?

DUCHESS OF OLIVAREZ. You will enter a convent and there
  Await her gracious decision——

PRINCESS EBOLI. Shall I not see the Queen again?

DUCHESS OF OLIVAREZ, *embracing her.* Farewell!

  She quickly walks away. The PRINCESS *follows her to the
  door of the* QUEEN's *apartments, which is closed in her face.
  The* PRINCESS *hurries away, with her face in her hands.*

SCENE 16

QUEEN. MARQUIS OF POSA

QUEEN. Marquis! At last! Thank heaven you are here!

MARQUIS OF POSA. You probably know already——

QUEEN. Carlos is taken prisoner and by your hand?
  So it is true? I could not believe it.

MARQUIS OF POSA. It is true.

QUEEN. I respect your actions, even when I do not understand
  them.
  But this time—— I fear you are playing a dangerous game.

MARQUIS OF POSA. I have lost it. But he is safe.
  It is I who am lost. But he is safe!
  Whatever the price I have to pay,
  He is safe! But only for to-day.
  He must make the most
  Of the short time left to him.
  He must leave Madrid to-night.
  Arrangements have been made.

Letters await him in the Carthusian monastery
Which was once our meeting-place.
But here, in the heart of his Queen,
I leave my last will and testament:
He will find it here, when I
Am here no more to give it him.

QUEEN. Those are the words of a dying man——
Do you mean what you are saying?

MARQUIS OF POSA. Tell the Prince that he must not forget
The vow we made. I have kept my part
And am true to him, to the death——

QUEEN. To the death?

MARQUIS OF POSA. Tell him to make our dreams reality,
Our dreams of a new and better state.
It might have been my own lot
To bring a new morning to this land.
The King gave me his confidence and friendship.
He called me his son. If I had had my way,
Your Albas and Domingos would be no more.
You are weeping! Oh, I know those tears.
They are tears of joy. But all that is over now.
It was either Carlos or myself. It was
A frightful choice to make. One of us was lost,
And I wanted that one to be myself.

QUEEN. At last I begin to understand what you have done.

MARQUIS OF POSA. I renounce the friendship of the King.
Of what further use can I be to the King?
No more roses flower for me
In this ungrateful soil. The fate of Europe
Hangs upon the actions of the Prince.
I leave Spain to him, however much hot blood
His father spills. . . . I hope I have not chosen wrongly.
But no. I am sure. I know Carlos. He will not fail me.
And you, Your Majesty, are my guarantee of that!

A pause.

I saw it grow, your love for one another.
And I did nothing to prevent its growth.
Rather I fostered it. The world can judge me otherwise,

But I do not regret my long devotion to
Its furtherance. Will you promise me
To love him always?

QUEEN. My heart, I promise you, shall always be
The only judge of what I love.

MARQUIS OF POSA. Then I shall die content. My work is done.

He bows and is about to go.

QUEEN. Shall we—see one another again?

MARQUIS OF POSA. Certainly.

QUEEN. Why have you thrown your life away?

MARQUIS OF POSA. It was either he or I.

QUEEN. Is there no hope?

MARQUIS OF POSA. None.

QUEEN. Cannot I do anything?

MARQUIS OF POSA. Not even you.

QUEEN. You do not know me—I can fight.

MARQUIS OF POSA. I know it.

QUEEN. And still there is no hope?

MARQUIS OF POSA. None.

QUEEN, *covering her face.* Go! I can respect no man again.

MARQUIS OF POSA. Your Majesty! Life is so wonderful——

He goes swiftly away. The QUEEN retires.

SCENE 17

THE KING'S ANTECHAMBER

DUKE OF ALBA *and* DOMINGO. PRINCE OF PARMA.
DUKES OF FERIA *and* MEDINA SIDONIA
with other GRANDEES

PRINCE OF PARMA. Can I speak to the King?

DUKE OF ALBA. No.

PRINCE OF PARMA. Who is with him?

DUKE OF FERIA. The Marquis of Posa, without a doubt.

DUKE OF ALBA. He is expected at any moment.
Letters have been discovered, sent by him
To Brussels, to William, Prince of Nassau and Orange.

PRINCE OF PARMA. We have just this moment arrived from
Saragossa.
All Madrid is in a turmoil at the news.

DUKE OF FERIA. Is it really true? The Prince has been arrested?
And by Posa, on the King's orders?

DOMINGO. Yes, it is true.

PRINCE OF PARMA. But why? No one seems to know.

DUKE OF ALBA. His Majesty and Posa know, but no one else
does.

PRINCE OF PARMA. But without trial or anything?

COUNT LERMA, *rushing out of the cabinet room.*
The Duke of Alba!

DOMINGO. At last! Praise be to God!

ALBA *hurries into the cabinet room.*

COUNT LERMA. When the Marquis arrives
He must be shown in to the King immediately.

DOMINGO. What has happened? You are as pale as a ghost.

COUNT LERMA. It was terrible. The King wept.

DOMINGO. Wept?

SCENE 18

PRINCESS EBOLI *and the foregoing*

PRINCESS EBOLI. Where is the King? I must speak to him.
To FERIA.
You, sir, take me to him.

DUKE OF FERIA. The King is engaged. It is a matter of the
highest gravity.
No one can be allowed to see him.

PRINCESS EBOLI. Is he already signing the death warrant?

He has been deceived. I must tell him how he was deceived.

DOMINGO. Princess Eboli!

PRINCESS EBOLI. So you are here too! Good. I need you.
You shall support me in the declaration
I must make to the King.

DOMINGO. You are not in your right mind, Princess.

DUKE OF FERIA. Stay here. The King cannot see you now.

PRINCESS EBOLI. He must see me, listen to me.
He must hear the truth.

DOMINGO. Keep away!

PRINCESS EBOLI. Nothing will keep me away from him——

She is about to enter the cabinet room when ALBA *rushes
out.*

DUKE OF ALBA, *triumphant.*
Have a Te Deum sung in all the churches.
We have won.

DOMINGO. Won?

DUKE OF ALBA, to GRANDEES.
Now you may go in to see His Majesty.
You will hear more from me later.

ACT V

SCENE 1

A ROOM IN THE ROYAL PALACE, DIVIDED FROM A COURTYARD BY A LARGE BARRED GATE. GUARDS IN COURTYARD

CARLOS *sitting at a table with his head buried in his arms as if asleep. At the rear of the room a few officers. The* MARQUIS OF POSA *enters unseen by the* PRINCE *and whispers to the officers, who withdraw. He goes towards* CARLOS *and gazes at him silently and sadly. Then makes a movement that rouses the latter.* CARLOS, *rising, becomes aware of the* MARQUIS *and shrinks with fear. Then he looks at him for a moment with wide and staring eyes and passes a hand over his forehead, as if trying to recollect his thoughts.*

MARQUIS OF POSA. Here I am, Carlos.

CARLOS, *holding out his hand.*

You can still bring yourself to see me?
That is kind of you.

MARQUIS OF POSA. I thought you perhaps would need a friend.

CARLOS. I am glad of that. I knew that you would never leave
me.
But I know what your action must have cost you.
How your heart must have bled when you prepared
The sacrifice for the altar!

MARQUIS OF POSA. Carlos! What do you mean?

CARLOS. Now it must be you who brings our dreams to real
life.
I cannot do that now.
You will bring the golden days to Spain.
I can do nothing more. I am lost to all your hopes

And dreams. Providence or chance
Led you to the King—it cost me my secret
But made you his—you are his good angel now.
There is no more hope for me.

MARQUIS OF POSA. Here are a few of the letters
You gave into my keeping. Take them.

CARLOS. Why?

MARQUIS OF POSA. I am returning them to you, because
They will be safer in your hands than mine.

CARLOS. But did the King not read them?

MARQUIS OF POSA. These letters?

CARLOS. Did you not show him all of them?

MARQUIS OF POSA. He still has the other letters.

CARLOS. Why am I here?

MARQUIS OF POSA. As a precautionary measure only.
I wanted to prevent you
From taking people like the Princess Eboli
Into your confidence again.

CARLOS. Ah, now I begin to see the light!

MARQUIS OF POSA. Who is this coming?

SCENE 2

DUKE OF ALBA. *The foregoing characters*

DUKE OF ALBA, *going to* PRINCE *and keeping his back turned
to* MARQUIS.
Prince, you are free. The King sends me
To acquaint you with his decision.
I count myself fortunate, Prince, to be the first
To bring you this good news——

CARLOS. But why? First I am imprisoned and then set free.
But no one tells me why!

DUKE OF ALBA. It was an error. The King was led astray
By some unscrupulous person.

CARLOS. But it was all the same on the King's orders
    That I was imprisoned here?

DUKE OF ALBA. Yes, through a mistake on His Majesty's part.

CARLOS. I am really sorry to hear it. If the King
    Made a mistake, then let him come in person
    To retrieve it. I cannot take back
    My dagger from hands such as yours.
    I shall stay here until the King consents
    To come in person and lead me from this prison.
    That is my answer. Take it to him.

    ALBA *goes. He is seen for a moment in the courtyard giving*
    orders.

SCENE 3

DON CARLOS. MARQUIS OF POSA

CARLOS. What is all this? Are you not Chief Minister any
    longer?

MARQUIS OF POSA. I *was* and am no more. Oh, Carlos,
    The plan has worked! It has worked!

CARLOS. What do you mean?

MARQUIS OF POSA. You are safe, Carlos. And free!

CARLOS. And you?

MARQUIS OF POSA. How sweet this moment is! I have bought it
    With everything I hold most dear.
    Now we must say good-bye to one another.
    Take it like a man, Carlos. Do not pity me.
    You are losing your friend: you will not see him
    For a long, long time—fools call it
    Eternity. You do not answer? Come,
    I shall explain it to you.
    The day after I met you in the Carthusian monastery,
    The King requested that I should be brought to him.
    You and all Madrid, know what success for me
    Followed upon that meeting. But what you do not know
    Is that your secret was betrayed to him.

He told me himself
That letters from you to the Queen
Had been stolen for him from Her Majesty;
And with those words
He took me into his confidence, and I was his.
Yes, Carlos, I myself conceived the plot
That brought your downfall. The truth was out.
It was too late to warn you. All that was left to me
Was to make certain that his wrath would fall on me
And not on you. And so I became your enemy,
But only in order to serve you better.
Are you listening?

CARLOS. Yes, yes! Go on.

MARQUIS OF POSA. Then what I had feared came to pass.
You were told of the Queen's long interview
With him, that ended with her bleeding head:
You heard the horror of the court.
There was Lerma's unhappy zeal. At last
Your heart was overwhelmed with doubt and fear.
You believed that I was lost to you forever.
And yet, such was your friendship for me,
You tried to explain my betrayal in a charitable way.
Abandoned by your only friend, you ran
To Princess Eboli and told her all—Eboli,
The one who had betrayed you to the King!
I found you with the Princess. It was too late.
You had already confessed everything to her.
There was no further hope for you——

CARLOS. No, no! She was touched and moved most deeply
And sincerely by what I told her. You are mistaken.

MARQUIS OF POSA. Then a terrible darkness came upon my
mind.
Desperation made me mad. I drew my dagger
And laid its point against her heart.
I would have murdered her. But then
A ray of light fell on my darkness.
What if I were to mislead the King?
If I could succeed in appearing the guilty one?
Then I could buy you time to fly to Brabant.

CARLOS. And would you really have done that for me?

MARQUIS OF POSA. I wrote a letter to the Prince of Orange
Saying that I loved the Queen, and that
I had succeeded in turning his suspicions on to you.
That I had found a way, through the King's
Affection for me, to carry off the Queen.
I added that I was afraid to be discovered;
That you, warned of my passion, had gone
To Princess Eboli, asking her to tell the Queen
Of my intentions. I said that I had taken you
A prisoner and that, as everything was lost,
I should be travelling at once to Brussels.
I put this letter in the post.

CARLOS. But I warned you that His Majesty
Reads all the letters sent to Brussels!

MARQUIS OF POSA. The letter was delivered to the King.

CARLOS. God! Then there is no hope left for me!

MARQUIS OF POSA. For *you!* Why?

CARLOS. Because you have no hope left yourself.
I must go and see the King. It must not be.

MARQUIS OF POSA. You must not, must not go!

CARLOS. Do not try to stop me. Perhaps even now
He is writing your sentence of death.

MARQUIS OF POSA. That makes my time all the more precious.
We have many things to say to one another.
And remember, Carlos, I was not so prompt
To right a wrong when we were boys, and you
Took punishment for me. Go to Flanders!
Your mission is to save the Crown, and mine—to die!

CARLOS. No! No! I will take you to him,
And say: "Father, this is what a friend has done for me."
That will appease his wrath. It will move and touch him.
He is not altogether lacking in humanity.
Yes, we will go together——

A shot is heard through the barred gate. CARLOS *jumps up.*
Who was that for?

MARQUIS OF POSA. I think it was—for me.

He falls to the ground.

CARLOS, *giving a cry of horror.* Oh, God!

MARQUIS OF POSA, *in a dying voice.*

The King—— He acts quickly——
I hoped for—a longer time—— Save yourself——
Do you hear?—— Your mother—knows everything now—
Carlos—I cannot—cannot——

CARLOS *kneels beside the dead body. After a while the* KING *comes in with* GRANDEES *and starts back at the spectacle. The grandees gather round him and* CARLOS, *who is now lying across the body and giving no sign of life. The* KING *looks at them both with silent calm.*

SCENE 4

KING. DON CARLOS. DUKES OF ALBA, FERIA, *and* MEDINA
SIDONIA. PRINCE OF PARMA. COUNT LERMA.
DOMINGO *and many* GRANDEES

KING. My son, I have granted your request.
Here I have come, with all the nobles of my kingdom,
To bring you freedom.

CARLOS *looks up and does not answer.*

Take back your sword. Your arrest was a mistake.

He goes to CARLOS *and helps him to rise.*

Come to your rightful place, my son,
Here in your father's arms.

CARLOS. I cannot embrace you, Father. You smell of murder.

KING, *about to go.* Follow me, my noblemen.

CARLOS. You will not leave this place——

He seizes him by both hands and manages to unsheath the sword his father has brought with him.

KING. Would you draw a sword against your father?

All GRANDEES *draw their weapons.*

CARLOS. Put your swords up. Do you think I'm mad?

No, I'm not mad. But it does me good to feel
How his life trembles at the point of my sword.
I beg of you, withdraw a little. This
Has nothing to do with you. See,
How his finger bleeds! Do you see?

KING. Draw back, sirs. There is nothing to fear.
Are we two not father and son?
What evil trick could nature play upon us?

CARLOS. Nature? I know nothing of that.
Murder is now the only way.
The bonds of common humanity are broken.
You yourself, sire, have broken them.
Look! Look here! Never was there such a murderous day
As this. Do you know what you have done?
No. He does not know that he has snatched
Out of the world a life far greater and far nobler
Than he will ever find again.
It is my friend you have murdered!
And do you know why he died? He died for me!

The KING *stares motionless at the body.*

He was so far above you—and yet
All you could do was kill him!

DUKE OF ALBA, *fearfully approaching the* KING. Sire,
Break this deathly stillness. Look around you!
Look at us! Speak to us!

CARLOS *sinks down again across the body.*

KING. You must all of you bow your heads, as I do,
And look upon the ground. Cover your faces.

*Silence again. In the distance a sound of growing tumult.
A murmur of fear passes through the nobles.*

COUNT LERMA. The storm is breaking.

DUKE OF ALBA. I fear it is.

SCENE 5

An OFFICER *of the King's Guard. The others*

OFFICER. It is rebellion! Open rebellion! Where's the King?
  All Madrid is up in arms! Thousands are storming
  Round the royal palace, and there are ugly rumours
  That the Prince's life is in danger.
  He must show himself to the people,
  Or all Madrid will go up in flames.
  General commotion.

DUKE OF ALBA. Your Majesty, fly at once! There is danger here.
  We do not know yet how the people got their arms,
  Or who incited them.

KING, *rousing himself.* Is my throne still standing?
  Am I still king in my own land? No.
  I will have no more of it. These cowards are in tears,
  All because of a boy. They are waiting only
  To see what the outcome will be, before abandoning
  Their King. I am betrayed by rebels.

DUKE OF ALBA. Oh, sire, how can you say such things?

KING. Away from me! Kneel down here, before
  The new young King! I am King no more, but only
  A grey-haired, impotent old man!

DUKE OF ALBA. So it has come to this! Spaniards!
  Show your devotion and respect.
  All crowd round the KING *and kneel before him with bared swords.* CARLOS *alone with the corpse.*

KING, *tearing off his cloak and throwing it away.*
  Put the royal robes upon him!
  He collapses in the arms of ALBA *and* LERMA.

DUKE OF ALBA. Take him to his bedchamber. Meanwhile
  I shall calm the multitude.
  He goes. The KING *is carried away, and grandees follow him.*

SCENE 6

THE KING'S ANTEROOM

DUKES OF ALBA *and* FERIA *enter, talking.*

DUKE OF ALBA. The city is calm again. How was the King
    when you left him?

DUKE OF FERIA. In a terrible mood. He has made his decision.
His anger against Don Carlos knows no bounds.
No one knows what may happen now. The Marquis'
Treachery seems to have changed him in an hour
To a different man. We can recognize our King in him
No longer.

DUKE OF ALBA. I must speak to him. A Carthusian monk
Was discovered entering secretly the Prince's apartments
And was arrested and interrogated. The fear of death
Drew from him the confession that
He bore papers of great importance
Which he had been commanded to deliver to the Prince.
These papers inform us that Don Carlos
Is supposed to be leaving Madrid before dawn.

DUKE OF FERIA. What plot is this?

DUKE OF ALBA. Other papers tell us that a ship lies ready
In the harbour at Cadiz, to take him to Flushing,
And that the Netherlands are only waiting for
His prompt arrival to throw off the Spanish yoke forever.

DUKE OF FERIA. What a dastardly plan!

DUKE OF ALBA. Other letters announce that a fleet has left
    Rhodes
To do battle with the King's navy in the Mediterranean.
And that is against the treaties we have signed.

DUKE OF FERIA. Can it be possible?

DUKE OF ALBA. These very letters inform us also
Of the reason for the late Marquis' voyages in Europe.
They had no other purpose but to rouse the Northern powers
Into arms to help the Netherlands.

DUKE OF FERIA. A spy! He was a spy!

DUKE OF ALBA. The letters also contain a detailed plan
  Of the entire campaign. Everything is there.
  The plan is devilish, but I must confess
  Most masterly in conception.

DUKE OF FERIA. What a traitor he was!

DUKE OF ALBA. There is also mention in the letters
  Of a secret interview the Prince should have
  At midnight with the Queen.
  I have given my orders. But there is not
  One minute to lose. I must see the King——
  He is about to go, when the KING *appears.*

SCENE 7

KING. DUKE OF ALBA. DUKE OF FERIA. DOMINGO. GRANDEES

They are astonished at the KING's *appearance. He moves
like a sleep-walker. His clothes are disarranged and his face
is working frightfully. He walks slowly past the* GRANDEES
as if he did not see them. Finally he pauses and speaks.

KING. Give the body back to me.
  I must have his body.

DOMINGO, *to* ALBA. Speak to him.

KING. He did not care for me and died.
  I must have him back again.
  I long for him to think better of me now.

DUKE OF ALBA. Sire——

KING. Who's that? Who dares to speak to me?
  Have you forgotten who I am?
  Why do you not kneel before me, creature?
  I am still the King. I demand obedience.
  Must I lose all respect, because one man despised me?

DUKE OF ALBA. Sire, speak no more of him.
  There is a worse enemy in our midst——

DUKE OF FERIA. Prince Carlos——

KING. The Prince had a friend
  Who gave his life for him! That friend,
  If he had been mine, would have shared my kingdom!
  If only he were still alive!
  I would give the Indies for him. But
  He would have none of me and died.

DUKE OF ALBA. Sire, you must listen to me.
  These papers were left by the Marquis
  To be handed on his death to Carlos.

KING, *looking distractedly through the papers and putting
  them aside.* Call me the Grand Inquisitor. Ask him to grant
  me an interview.

  A GRANDEE *hurries away.*

KING. So it must be to-night!

DUKE OF FERIA. At two o'clock the post will halt
  Outside the Carthusian monastery.

DUKE OF ALBA. And I have information that several pieces of
  luggage,
  All clearly bearing the Prince's monogram,
  Were taken secretly into the monastery for him.

DUKE OF FERIA. Moorish agents are said to have provided
  enormous sums
  Of money in the name of the Queen.

KING. Where did you leave the Prince?

DUKE OF ALBA. Beside the dead Marquis.

KING. Is there still light in the Queen's apartments?

DUKE OF ALBA. She dismissed her ladies earlier than usual.
  The Duchess of Arcos, the last to leave,
  Said she was sound asleep.

  Enter an OFFICER *of the guard, who speaks to* ALBA *and*
  FERIA. *They speak to* DOMINGO *and others. Murmurs.*

KING. What is it?

DUKE OF FERIA. The strangest news, sire.

DOMINGO. Two Switzers say that in the left wing of the palace
  They saw the ghost of the late Emperor
  Walking past them with slow and solemn stride.
  The apparition entered, so they say,
  The apartments of the Queen.

KING. And in what form did he appear?

OFFICER. In the same habit he wore for the last time
At Justi, when he was a monk.
They knew he was the Emperor
By the sceptre he carried in his hand.

DOMINGO. They say they have often seen him wandering so.

KING. Did no one speak to him?

OFFICER. No one ventured to. The watch said their prayers
And let him pass reverently through.

KING. And the spectre entered the Queen's apartments?

OFFICER. Into her antechamber.

General silence.

KING. What have you to say?

DUKE OF ALBA. Sire, we are dumbfounded.

KING, *to* OFFICER. Put my garden under armed guard,
And close every entrance in the left wing.
I should like to have a word with this—ghost.

OFFICER *off. Enter* PAGE.

PAGE. Sire! The Grand Inquisitor.

KING, *to* COURTIERS. Leave us together.

The GRAND INQUISITOR *enters, a grey-haired man of ninety,
blind, leaning on a stick and led by two Dominicans. As
he walks through the crowd, all fall to their knees and touch
the hem of his robes. He gives the sign of the cross over
them. All depart.*

SCENE 8

KING. GRAND INQUISITOR

A long pause.

GRAND INQUISITOR. Am I in the presence of His Majesty the
King?

KING. Yes.

GRAND INQUISITOR. My pupil Carlos, your great father,
Never needed to ask me for advice.

KING. He was more fortunate than I. Cardinal,
  I have done a murder, and my peace of mind——

GRAND INQUISITOR. What was the reason for the murder?

KING. It was a betrayal the like of which
  Has never been known before.

GRAND INQUISITOR. I knew of it.

KING. Knew what? Who told you? When?

GRAND INQUISITOR. I have known for many years
  What has been known to you since sunset.
  His life history is recorded in
  The holy registers at the Santa Casa.

KING. And he was allowed total freedom?

GRAND INQUISITOR. The tight rope he was walking
  Was long, and unbreakable.

KING. His movements took him outside my kingdom.

GRAND INQUISITOR. Wherever he went, there I was too.

KING. Why was I not told?

GRAND INQUISITOR. Why did you not ask? When you threw
      yourself into his arms,
  One calm glance would have shown you he was a heretic.
  Why did you rob the Holy Office of its victim?
  When a King becomes a hole-and-corner thief,
  And has an understanding—behind our backs—
  With our most base, ignoble enemies,
  What are we to do? If one is spared, with what right
  Are tens of thousands offered up?

KING. He has been offered up.

GRAND INQUISITOR. No! He has been murdered. Criminally.
      Infamously.
  The blood that should have gloriously flowed in our honour
  Has been spattered and wasted by an assassin's hand.
  The man was ours. What right had you
  To lay your hands upon our Order's sacred property?
  He was there to be killed by us. That was my plan.
  Now the work of many years is in the dust.
  We have been robbed, and you are left
  With nothing more than bloody hands.

KING. It was passion drove me to it. Forgive me.

GRAND INQUISITOR. Passion? Is that Philip speaking? Passion!

KING. I am still untutored in these things.
Have patience with me.

GRAND INQUISITOR. No! I am not satisfied with you.
What is resolution, what is constancy,
What is human trust, if in a single sentimental moment
A rule of sixty years melts to nothing
Like a woman's whim?
What need had you of such a creature?
What new thing could he have shown you
That you did not already know? Did the windy words
Of world reformers ring so strangely in your ear?
How could you write the sentence of death?

KING. I wanted one man. Domingo——

GRAND INQUISITOR. Why do you want men about you? Men
should be mere ciphers to you.

KING. I am a poor, weak man. You demand
What only the Creator could provide.

GRAND INQUISITOR. No, sire. I am not deceived.
I see through you. You want to run away from us.
The chains of our Order lie too heavily upon you.
You want to be alone and free.

KING. Do not take that tone with me!
I command you, restrain your tongue!
I will not have it. I will not be spoken to so.

GRAND INQUISITOR. Will you tell me why I have been brought
here?
What is there for me to do? I have no desire
To repeat this visit.

KING. There is one more task for you. The last one.
Then you may leave this world in peace.
Let the past be forgotten,
And let peace reign between us.
Are we reconciled?

GRAND INQUISITOR. If Philip will bow to me in all humility.

KING. My son is inciting a rebellion.

GRAND INQUISITOR. What is your decision?

KING. All—or nothing.

GRAND INQUISITOR. And what do you mean by nothing?

KING. I shall let him escape if
I cannot bring myself to have him killed.

GRAND INQUISITOR. Well, sire?

KING. Can you instruct me in another faith
Which would sanction the bloody murder of my son?

GRAND INQUISITOR. The Son of God died on the cross
To atone for the eternal sin.

KING. Do you wish to instil that thought throughout
The whole of Europe?

GRAND INQUISITOR. Throughout all lands in which the cross is
worshipped.

KING. I shall blaspheme against Nature. Can you silence
Her great voices?

GRAND INQUISITOR. In the eyes of faith,
The mysteries of Nature signify nothing.

KING. I lay my power of decision in your hands.

GRAND INQUISITOR. Give him to me.

KING. He is my only son.

GRAND INQUISITOR. Authority, not laxity.

KING. We are agreed. Come.

GRAND INQUISITOR. Where are we going?

KING. Where you may receive the sacrifice at my own hands.
Leads him away.

SCENE 9

THE QUEEN'S APARTMENTS

DON CARLOS. QUEEN. *Finally the* KING *and followers*

CARLOS *in his monk's habit, a mask over his face, which he
now removes, and a naked sword in his hand. It is quite
dark. He approaches a door, which is opened. The* QUEEN

comes out in her night attire, carrying a light. CARLOS *sinks to his knee before her.*

CARLOS. Elizabeth!

QUEEN. So we see each other once again?

CARLOS. We see each other once again!

A pause.

QUEEN. Stand up, Carlos. We must not make each other weak.
He who is dead so gloriously
Cannot be honoured by idle tears. Let us keep tears
For lesser tragedies! He gave his life for you!
Bought your safety with his own dear life.
And has his blood been shed to feed a ghost's imaginings?
Carlos! I gave myself as security for you.
Will you make of me a liar?

CARLOS. I shall build him a memorial
Greater than any king has ever had,
And a paradise shall blossom from his ashes.

QUEEN. That is what I wished to hear.
That was the real meaning of his death.
He chose me to execute his final wish. I warn you:
I shall not rest until my oath has been fulfilled.
He left me something else to tell you.
My heart must speak. I am afraid of no one any more.
Did he say our love was virtuous?
I believe his words, not what my heart would speak.

CARLOS. Say no more. I have been asleep, and dreamed
A long and heavy dream. I loved someone——
Now I am awake. Let the past be forgotten!
Here are your letters back. My own you will destroy.
Everything is over now. A pure fire
Has burned my passion clean. No mortal desire
Shall ever move my heart again.

QUEEN. Carlos!

CARLOS. Mother, I came to say good-bye.
Now I shall be leaving Spain and never,
Never shall I see the King again.
My love for him is dead forever.
I haste to rescue my people, sore oppressed

By his hard tyrant's hand. Madrid
Shall see me return
A king, or I shall not return at all.
And now, for the last time, good-bye! Farewell!

He kisses her.

QUEEN. Oh, Carlos!

CARLOS. Am I not strong, Elizabeth?
I hold you in my arms and do not falter—
All that is over now.

QUEEN. It is over now.

CARLOS. Listen! What was that sound?

QUEEN. Only the awful bell that takes you far from me.

CARLOS. Good night, then, Mother. You shall receive
My first letter from Ghent, to tell you of our victories.
And now I must go and see my father.
There must be no more secrets between us any more.
This is my last deception——

He is about to take off his mask. The KING *steps in.*

KING. It is your last indeed!

The QUEEN *falls senseless.*

CARLOS, *holding her in his arms.* Is she dead? Dead! Dead!

KING, *coldly, to the* GRAND INQUISITOR. Cardinal, I have done
My duty. Now do yours.

He goes.

MARY STUART

A TRAGEDY

Friedrich von Schiller

(1800)

*Translated by Joseph Mellish
and adapted by Eric Bentley*

"But her marriage with Darnley, his murder by Bothwell at the Kirk of Field, and her too hasty marriage with the murderer, led her subjects to suppose her precognizant of the deed . . . She was obliged to fly from Scotland. She elected . . . to take refuge with Elizabeth whose throne she challenged and endangered. What did she expect? If she looked for romantic generosity she had come to the wrong door. Or did she trust her own sharp wits to fool her rival? From the moment that Mary made herself Elizabeth's captive, the politics of England, and indeed of all Europe, turned on the hinges of her prison door . . . Urged by the Pope, Spain, and the Jesuits, the more extreme English Catholics laid plot after plot to place her on Elizabeth's throne, through assassination, rebellion, and foreign conquest . . . England's final act of defiance to all comers, the execution of Mary, was the volition of the people rather than of their sovereign . . . When the discovery by Walsingham of Babington's plot to murder Elizabeth revealed Mary as acquainted with the design, Mary's prolonged existence raged like a fever in men's blood, for if she survived Elizabeth, either she would become Queen and the work of the Reformation be undone, or else there would be the worst of civil wars . . . The prospect was too near and too dreadful to leave men time to pity a most unhappy woman. Parliament, people and Ministers at length prevailed on Elizabeth to authorize the execution. Her attempt to avoid responsibility for the death warrant by ruining her Secretary Davison was in her worst manner . . ."

Trevelyan's *History of England.*

CHARACTERS

In this English version there are twenty speaking parts— fourteen male, six female. Some degree of "doubling" is possible. The presence of the many non-speaking lords, soldiers, etc., is advantageous but not necessary.

ELIZABETH, *Queen of England*
MARY STUART, *Queen of Scots, a prisoner in England*
ROBERT DUDLEY, *Earl of Leicester*
GEORGE TALBOT, *Earl of Shrewsbury*
WILLIAM CECIL, *Lord Burleigh, Lord High Treasurer*
EARL OF KENT
SIR WILLIAM DAVISON, *Secretary of State*
SIR AMIAS PAULET, *Keeper of Mary*
SIR EDWARD MORTIMER, *his nephew*
COUNT AUBESPINE, *the French Ambassador*
COUNT BELLIÈVRE, *Envoy Extraordinary from France*
O'KELLY, *Mortimer's friend*
SIR ANDREW MELVIL, *Mary's House-Steward*
BURGOYNE, *her physician*
HANNAH KENNEDY, *her nurse*
MARGARET CURL, *her attendant*
Two Women of the Chamber
Officer of the Guard
Page
Non-speaking parts: Sheriff of the County, assistant to Paulet, soldiers, French and English lords, Elizabeth's Servants of State, Mary's servants and attendants

THE TIME: *As the date of Mary Stuart's death is known to be February 8, 1587, it can be deduced from passages in the text that Act V belongs to that day, Acts II, III, and IV to February 7, and Act I to February 6. But Schiller deliberately took many liberties with history. For example, though February 1587 would make Elizabeth fifty-four and Mary forty-four years old, Schiller stated in a letter: "In the play Mary is about 25, Elizabeth at most 30."*

THE PLACE: *London and Fotheringay Castle, which Schiller takes to be in the neighborhood of London, though it was actually some seventy-five miles away. How much poetic license Schiller could take with place is shown in Act III, Scene 1, where Mary sees from Fotheringay to the Scots border!*

ACT I

SCENE 1

A COMMON APARTMENT IN THE CASTLE OF FOTHERINGAY

HANNAH KENNEDY *contending violently with* PAULET, *who is about to break open a closet. His assistant has an iron crow.*

KENNEDY. How now, sir? What fresh outrage have we here?
Back from that cabinet!

PAULET.   Whence came the jewel?
I know that it was thrown into the garden
From a window. You would suborn the gardener!
In spite of all my caution and my searching,
Still treasures here, still costly gems concealed!
Advancing towards the cabinet.

KENNEDY. Intruder, back! Here lie my lady's secrets.

PAULET. Exactly what I seek.

Drawing forth papers.

KENNEDY.   Mere trifling papers,
The amusements only of an idle pen
To cheat the dreary tedium of a dungeon!
Those writings are in French.

PAULET.   So much the worse:
That tongue betokens England's enemy.

KENNEDY. Sketches of letters to the Queen of England.

PAULET. I'll be their bearer. Ha! What glitters here?

He touches a secret spring and draws out jewels from a private drawer.

A royal diadem enriched with stones
And studded with the fleur-de-lis of France!

He hands it to his assistant.

Here, take it, sirrah, lay it with the rest.
Exit the assistant.

KENNEDY, *supplicating.* Oh, sir, be merciful, deprive us not
  Of the last jewel that adorns our life!

PAULET. 'Twill be restored to you with scrupulous care.

KENNEDY. Who that beholds these naked walls could say
  That majesty dwelt here? Where is the throne?
  Where the imperial canopy of state?
  With common pewter which the lowliest dame
  Would scorn they furnish forth her homely table.

PAULET. Thus did she treat her spouse at Stirling once
  And pledged the while her paramour in gold!

KENNEDY. Even the mirror's trifling aid withheld.

PAULET. The contemplation of her own vain image
  Incites to hope and prompts to daring deeds.

KENNEDY. Books are denied her to divert her mind.

PAULET. The Bible still is left to mend her heart.

KENNEDY. Even of her very lute she is deprived.

PAULET. Because she tuned it to her wanton airs.

KENNEDY. Is this a fate for her, the gentle born,
  Who in her very cradle was a Queen;
  Who, reared in Catherine's luxurious court,
  Enjoyed the fullness of each earthly pleasure?
  Was it not enough to rob her of her power,
  Must you then envy her its paltry tinsel?

PAULET. These are the things that turn the human heart
  To vanity, which should collect itself
  In penitence. For a lewd, vicious life,
  Want and abasement are the only penance.

KENNEDY. If youthful blood has led her into error,
  With her own heart and God she must account.

PAULET. She shall have judgement where she has trans-
  gressed.

KENNEDY. Her narrow bonds restrain her from transgression.

PAULET. And yet she found the means to stretch her arm
  And, with the torch of civil war, inflame
  This realm against our Queen (whom God preserve)

And arm assassin bands. Did she not rouse
From out these walls the malefactor Parry
And Babington to the detested crime
Of regicide? And did this iron grate
Prevent her from decoying to her toils
Norfolk himself? Whose head we then saw fall
A sacrifice for her upon the block.
The bloody scaffold bends beneath the weight
Of her new daily victims; and we shall
Not see an end till she herself, of all
The guiltiest, be offered up upon it.
Oh, curses on the day when England took
This Helen to its hospitable arms!

KENNEDY. Did England then receive her hospitably?
Oh, hapless Queen, who, since that day when she
First set foot in England as a suppliant
And from her sister begging sanctuary
Has been condemned, despite the law of nations,
To weep away her youth in prison walls!
And now, when she hath suffered long in prison,
Foully accused and summoned to the bar,
She's forced to plead for honour and for life!

PAULET. She came among us as a murderess,
Chased by her very subjects from a throne
Which she had oft by vilest deeds disgraced.
Sworn against England's welfare came she hither
To call the times of Bloody Mary back,
Betray our church to Romish tyranny
And sell our dear-bought liberties to France.
For, why disdained she to resign her claim
To England's crown and with one single word
Throw wide her prison gates? Because she trusts
To hourly plotting schemes of mischief, hopes
To conquer from her prison all this isle!

KENNEDY. You mock us, sir, and edge your cruelty
With words of bitter scorn. That *she* should form
Such projects! She, who's here immured alive!
Who hath so long no human face beheld,
Save her stern gaoler's unrelenting brows,

Till now of late in your uncourteous nephew
She sees a second keeper and beholds
Fresh bolts and bars around her multiplied!

PAULET. How do I know these bars are not filed through?
Fear scares me from my rest, and in the night
I try the strength of every bolt and test
Each guard's fidelity. I see with fear
The dawning of each morn which may confirm
My apprehensions. Yet, thank God, there's hope
That all my fears will soon be at an end.

KENNEDY. Here comes the Queen.

PAULET.   Christ's image in her hand,
Pride and all worldly lusts within her heart.

SCENE 2

THE SAME

Enter MARY, *veiled, a crucifix in her hand.*
KENNEDY, *hastening towards her.*
O gracious Queen, they tread us underfoot.
Each coming day heaps fresh indignities,
New sufferings on your royal head.

MARY.   Be calm.
Tell what has happened.

KENNEDY.   See, your cabinet
Is forced—your papers and your only treasure——

MARY. Basely indeed they may behave to us
But they cannot debase us. I have learnt
To use myself to many a change in England;
I can support this too. Sir, you have taken
By force what I this very day designed
To have delivered to you. There's a letter
Among these papers for my royal sister
Of England. Pledge me, sir, your word of honour
To give it to Her Majesty's own hands
And not to the deceitful care of Burleigh.

PAULET. I shall consider what is best to do.

MARY. Sir, you shall know its import. In this letter
I beg a favour, a great favour of her,
That she herself will give me audience—she
Whom I have never seen. I have been summoned
Before a court of men whom I can never
Acknowledge as my peers. The Queen
Is of my family, my rank, my sex.
To her alone—a sister, queen, and woman—
Can I unlock my heart.

PAULET.   Too oft, my lady,
Have you entrusted both your fate and honour
To men less worthy your esteem than these.

MARY. I, in the letter, beg another favour.
I have in prison missed the Church's comfort,
The blessing of the sacraments; yet she
Who robs me of my freedom and my crown,
Who seeks my very life, can never wish
To shut the gates of heaven upon my soul.

PAULET. Whenever you wish, the dean shall wait upon you.

MARY, *interrupting him sharply.*
Talk to me not of deans. I ask the aid
Of one of my own church—a Catholic priest.

PAULET. That is against the published laws of England.

MARY. I am not England's subject. I have never
Consented to its laws and will not bow
Before their cruel and despotic sway.
I also wish a public notary
And secretaries to prepare my will.
My sorrows and my prison's wretchedness
Prey on my life. My days, I fear, are numbered.
I would indite my will and make disposal
Of what belongs to me.

PAULET.   This liberty
May be allowed to you, for England's queen
Will not enrich herself by plundering you.

MARY. I have been parted from my faithful women
And from my servants. Tell me, where are they?

PAULET. All of your servants have been cared for, madam.
Going.

MARY. And will you leave my presence thus again?
Thanks to the vigilance of your hateful spies
I am divided from the world; no voice
Can reach me through these prison walls; my fate
Lies in the hands of those who wish my ruin.
A month of dread suspense is passed already
Since when the forty High Commissioners
Surprised me in this castle and erected,
With most unseemly haste, their dread tribunal.
They forced me, stunned, amazed, and unprepared,
Without an advocate, from memory,
Before their unexampled court, to answer
Their weighty charges artfully arranged.
They came like ghosts; like ghosts they disappeared,
And since that day all mouths are closed to me.
In vain I seek to construe from your looks
Which has prevailed—my cause's innocence
And my friends' zeal or my foes' cursèd counsel.

PAULET. Close your accounts with heaven.

MARY.   From heaven I hope
For mercy, sir; and from my earthly judges
I hope and still expect the strictest justice.

PAULET. Justice, depend upon it, will be done you.

MARY. Is the suit ended, sir?

PAULET.   I cannot tell.

MARY. Am I condemned?

PAULET.   I cannot answer, lady.

MARY. Dispatch is here the fashion. Is it meant
The murderer shall surprise me, like the judges?

PAULET. Still entertain that thought, and he will find you
Better prepared to meet your fate than they did.

MARY, *after a pause.*
Sir, nothing can surprise me which a court,
Inspired by Burleigh's hate and Hatton's zeal,
However unjust, may venture to pronounce.

But I have yet to learn how far the Queen
Will dare in execution of the sentence.

PAULET. What justice hath decreed her fearless hand
Will execute before the assembled world.

SCENE 3

THE SAME

MORTIMER *enters and, without paying attention to the*
QUEEN, *addresses* PAULET.

MORTIMER. Uncle, you're sought for.

He retires. The QUEEN *remarks it and turns towards* PAULET,
who is about to follow him.

MARY.   Sir, one favour more.
If *you* have aught to say to me—from *you*
I can bear much; I reverence your grey hairs
But cannot bear that young man's insolence.
Spare me in future his unmannered rudeness.

PAULET. He is not, truly, one of those poor fools
Who melt before a woman's treacherous tears.
He has seen much—has been to Rheims and Paris
Yet brings us back a loyal English heart.
Exit.

SCENE 4

MARY, KENNEDY

KENNEDY. How dares the ruffian use such language to you?

MARY, *lost in reflection.*
In the fair moments of our former splendour
We lent to flatterers a too willing ear.
It is but just, good Hannah, we should now
Be forced to hear the bitter voice of censure.

KENNEDY. So downcast, so depressed, my dearest lady!

MARY. I see the bleeding Darnley's royal shade
  Rising in anger from his darksome grave;
  And never will he make his peace with me
  Until the measure of my woes be full.

KENNEDY. What thoughts are these?

MARY.   You may forget it, Hannah,
  But I've a faithful memory. 'Tis this day
  Another wretched anniversary
  Of that regretted, that unhappy deed—
  Which I must celebrate with fast and penance.

KENNEDY. The penitence of many a heavy year,
  Of many a suffering, has atoned the deed.

MARY. This long atonèd crime arises fresh
  And bleeding from its lightly covered grave.
  My husband's restless spirit seeks revenge.
  No sacred bell can exorcise, no host
  In priestly hands dismiss it to his tomb.

KENNEDY. You did not murder him—'twas done by others.

MARY. But it was known to me; I suffered it
  And lured him with my smiles to death's embrace.

KENNEDY. Your youth extenuates your guilt. You were
  Of tender years.

MARY.   So tender, yet I drew
  This heavy guilt upon my youthful head.

KENNEDY. You were provoked by direst injuries
  And by the rude presumption of the man.
  Before your eyes he had your favorite singer,
  Poor Rizzio, murdered. You did but avenge
  With blood the bloody deed——

MARY.   And bloodily,
  I fear, too soon 'twill be avenged on me!

KENNEDY. The madness of a frantic love possessed you
  And bound you to a terrible seducer,
  The wretched Bothwell. That despotic man
  With all his philtres and his hellish arts
  Inflamed your passions.

MARY.   All the arts he used
Were man's superior strength and woman's weakness.

KENNEDY. No, no, my Queen. The most pernicious spirits
Of hell he must have summoned to his aid.
Your ear no more was open to the voice
Of decency. Soft female bashfulness
Deserted you. Those cheeks, which were before
The seat of virtuous blushing modesty,
Glowed with the flames of unrestrained desire
And the flagitious daring of the man
Overcame your natural coyness. You exposed
Your shame unblushingly to public gaze.
You let the murderer, whom the people followed
With curses through the streets of Edinburgh,
Before you bear the royal sword of Scotland
In triumph. You begirt your parliament
With armèd bands and, by this shameless farce,
You forced the judges of the land to clear
The murderer of his guilt, and then, O God——

MARY. I gave my hand in marriage to the murderer.

KENNEDY, *after a pause*.
I nursed your youth myself. Your heart is framed
For tender softness; 'tis alive to shame,
And all your fault is thoughtless levity.
Since this misdeed, which blackens thus your life,
You have done nothing ill; your conduct has
Been pure; myself can witness your amendment;
Nor are you guilty here. Not England's queen,
Nor England's Parliament can be your judge.
Here *might* oppresses you: you may present
Yourself before this self-created court
With all the fortitude of innocence.

MARY. A step!

KENNEDY.   'Tis Paulet's nephew. Pray withdraw!

SCENE 5

THE SAME

Enter MORTIMER, *approaching cautiously.*

MORTIMER, *to* KENNEDY.
Step to the door and keep a careful watch.

MARY, *with dignity.*
I charge you, Hannah, go not hence. Remain!

MORTIMER. Fear not, my gracious lady: learn to know me.
*He gives her a card. She examines it and starts back
astonished.*

MARY. Heavens! What is this?

MORTIMER, *to* KENNEDY.   Retire, good Kennedy.
See that my uncle come not unawares.

MARY, *to* KENNEDY, *who hesitates and looks at the* QUEEN
inquiringly. Go in. Do as he bids you, my good Hannah.
KENNEDY *retires, with signs of wonder.*

SCENE 6

MARY, MORTIMER

MARY. From France? The Cardinal of Guise, my uncle?
She reads.
"Confide in Mortimer, who brings you this.
You have no truer, firmer friend in England."
Looking at him with astonishment.
The nephew of my jailer, whom I thought
My most inveterate enemy?

MORTIMER, *kneeling.*   Oh, pardon,
My gracious liege, for the detested mask,

Yet through such means alone have I the power
To see you and to bring you help and rescue.

MARY. Arise, sir; you astonish me. I cannot
So suddenly emerge from the abyss——

MORTIMER. Our time is brief: each moment I expect
My uncle, whom a hated man attends.
Hear, then, before his terrible commission
Surprises you, how heaven prepares your rescue.

He hesitates.

Allow me of myself to speak.

MARY.   Say on.

MORTIMER. I scarce, my liege, had numbered twenty years,
Brought up in deadliest hate to Papacy,
When, led by irresistible desire
For foreign travel, I resolved to leave
My country and its puritanic faith
Far, far behind me; bent my course through France
On to the plains of far-famed Italy.
'Twas then the time of the great Jubilee
And crowds of palmers filled the public roads.
Each image was adorned with garlands; 'twas
As if all humankind were wandering forth
In pilgrimage towards the heavenly kingdom.
The tide of holy pilgrims bore me on
Into the streets of Rome. What was my wonder,
As the magnificence of stately columns
Rushed on my sight! The vast triumphal arches,
The Colosseum's grandeur, left me speechless!
I had never felt the power of art till now.
The church that reared me hates the charms of sense:
It tolerates no image, it adores
But the unseen, the incorporeal word.
What were my feelings, then, as I approached
The threshold of these churches and within
Heard heavenly music floating in the air
While from the walls and high-wrought roofs there streamed
Crowds of celestial forms in endless train—
When the Most High, Most Glorious, pervaded
My captivated sense in real presence,

And when I saw those great and godlike visions,
The Salutation, the Nativity,
The Holy Mother, and the Trinity's
Descent, the luminous Transfiguration
And last the Pontiff, clad in all the glory
Of his office, bless the people!

MARY. Spread no more
Life's verdant carpet out before my eyes!
Remember I am wretched and a prisoner.

MORTIMER. Full many noble Scots who saw my zeal
Encouraged me, and with the gallant French
They led me to the Cardinal of Guise,
Your princely uncle. What a royal priest!

MARY. You've seen him then, the much loved, honoured man,
Who was the guardian of my tender years!

MORTIMER. That holy man descended from his height,
Taught me true faith, and banished all my doubts.
He showed me that the glimmering light of reason
Serves but to lead us to eternal error;
That what the heart is called on to believe
The eye must see; so I returned, my lady,
Back to the bosom of the holy Church.

MARY. Then of those happy thousands, you are one
Whom he, with his celestial eloquence,
Converted!

MORTIMER. I was sent by him to Rheims,
Where, by the Jesuits' anxious labour, priests
Are trained to preach our holy faith in England.
There, 'mongst the Scots, I found the noble Morgan
And your true Lesley, Ross's learnèd bishop,
Who pass in France their joyless days of exile.
They fortified my faith. As I one day
Roamed through the bishop's dwelling, I was struck
With a fair female portrait; it was full
Of touching, wondrous charms; it moved my soul.
"Well," cried the bishop, "may you linger thus,
For the most beautiful of womankind
Is also matchless in calamity."

MARY *is in great agitation. He pauses.*

MARY. Excellent man! All is not lost, indeed!

MORTIMER. Then he began, with moving eloquence,
To paint the sufferings of your martyrdom.
He proved to me that you alone have right
To reign in England, not this upstart queen,
The base-born fruit of an adulterous bed,
Whom Henry's self rejected as a bastard!

MARY. Oh, this unhappy right! 'Tis this alone
Which is the source of all my sufferings.

MORTIMER. Just at this time the tidings reached my ears
Of your committal to my uncle's care.
It seemed to be a loud decree of fate
That it had chosen me to rescue you.
My friends concur with me; the Cardinal
Instructs me in the subtle task of feigning.
His plan digested, I set out for England.
Ten days ago, I landed. Oh, my Queen,
I saw then, not your picture, but yourself.

He pauses, gazes upon her.

Oh, what a prudent policy in her
To hide you here! For if the youth of England
Beheld their captive queen, through all the isle
They'd rise in mutiny——

MARY.   'Twere well with her
If every Briton saw her with your eyes!

MORTIMER. Never on this threshold can I set my foot
That my poor heart with anguish is not torn,
Not ravished with delight at gazing on you!
Yet fearfully the fatal time draws near.
I can no longer hide my news——

He stops.

MARY.   My sentence?

MORTIMER. It is pronounced. The two-and-forty judges
Have given the verdict: "Guilty." Parliament
Demands the execution of the sentence.
The Queen alone still craftily delays
That she may be constrained to yield but not
From feelings of humanity or mercy.

MARY, *collected.*

 I know their aim: they mean to keep me here
 In everlasting bondage and to bury
 My vengeance with me and my rightful claims.

MORTIMER. They stop not there. As long as you shall live,
 Distrust and fear will haunt the English queen:
 Your death alone can make her throne secure.

MARY. Will she then dare, regardless of the shame,
 Lay my crowned head upon the fatal block?

MORTIMER. Most surely will she dare it, doubt it not.

MARY. And fears she not the dread revenge of France?

MORTIMER. With France she makes an everlasting peace
 And gives to Anjou's Duke her throne and hand.

MARY. Were this a spectacle for British eyes?

MORTIMER. This land, my Queen, has, in these latter days,
 Seen many a royal woman from the throne
 Descend and mount the scaffold. Her own mother
 And Catherine Howard trod this fatal path.
 And was not Lady Grey a crownèd head?

MARY, *after a pause.*

 It is not, sir, the scaffold that I fear:
 I never lift the goblet to my lips
 Without an inward shuddering, lest the draught
 May have been mingled by my sister's love.

MORTIMER. No! Neither open nor disguisèd murder
 Shall ever prevail against you! Fear no more.
 All is prepared. Twelve nobles of the land
 Are my confederates and have pledged to-day,
 Upon the Sacrament, their faith to free you.
 Count Aubespine, the French Ambassador,
 Knows of our plot and offers his assistance.
 'Tis in his palace that we hold our meetings.

MARY. Know you, then, what you risk? Are you not scared
 By Babington and Tichburn's bloody heads
 Set up as warnings upon London Bridge?
 Fly, if there yet be time for you, before
 That crafty spy, Lord Burleigh, track your schemes!

Fly hence! As yet success has never smiled
On Mary Stuart's champions.

MORTIMER.   I'm not scared
By Babington and Tichburn's bloody heads
Set up as warnings upon London Bridge.
Both of them found therein immortal honour!

MARY. It is in vain. Nor force nor guile can save me.
My enemies are watchful, and the power
Is in their hands. It is not Paulet only
And his dependent host; all England guards
My prison gates; Elizabeth's free will
Alone can open them.

MORTIMER.   Expect not that.

MARY. There is a man, too, who could open them.

MORTIMER. Then let me know his name.

MARY.   Lord Leicester.

MORTIMER *starts back in wonder.*   He!
The Earl of Leicester! Your most bloody foe,
The favourite of Elizabeth! Through him——

MARY. If I am to be saved at all, 'twill be
Through him and him alone. Go to him, sir.
Freely confide in him and, as a proof
You come from me, present this paper to him.

She takes a paper from her bosom. MORTIMER *draws back
and hesitates to take it.*

For it contains my portrait. Take it, sir;
I've borne it long about me, but your uncle's
Close watchfulness has cut me off from all
Communication with him. You were sent
By my good angel.

He takes it.

MORTIMER.   Oh, my Queen, explain
This mystery.

MARY.   Lord Leicester will resolve it.
Who comes?

KENNEDY, *entering hastily.*
'Tis Paulet; and he brings with him
A nobleman from court.

MORTIMER.   It is Lord Burleigh.
Collect yourself, my Queen, and strive to hear
The news he brings with equanimity.
He retires through a side door, and KENNEDY *follows him.*

SCENE 7

Enter LORD BURLEIGH *and* PAULET.

PAULET, *to* MARY.
You wished to-day assurance of your fate.
My Lord of Burleigh brings it to you now.

BURLEIGH. I come deputed from the court of justice.

MARY. Lord Burleigh lends that court his willing tongue,
Which was already guided by his spirit.

PAULET. You speak as if no stranger to the sentence.

MARY. Lord Burleigh brings it; therefore do I know it.
But to the matter, sir.

BURLEIGH.   You have acknowledged
The jurisdiction of the two-and-forty.

MARY. It is enacted by the English laws,
That every one who stands arraigned of crime
Shall plead before a jury of his equals.
Who is my equal in this High Commission?
Kings only are my peers.

BURLEIGH.   But yet you heard
The points of accusation, answered them
Before the court——

MARY.   'Tis true. I was deceived
By Hatton's crafty counsel. He advised me
To listen to the points of accusation
And prove their falsehood. This, my lord, I did
From personal respect for the lords' names,
Not their usurpèd charge, which I disclaim.

BURLEIGH. Acknowledge you the court or not, that is
Only a point of mere formality
Which cannot here arrest the course of justice.

You breathe the air of England; you enjoy
The law's protection and its benefits;
You, therefore, are its subject.

MARY.   Sir, I breathe
The air within an English prison's walls;
I am no member of this realm; I am
An independent and a foreign queen.

BURLEIGH. And do you think that the mere name of queen
Can serve you as a charter to foment
This bloody discord? Where would be the state's
Security, if the stern sword of justice
Could not as freely smite the guilty brow
Of the imperial stranger as the beggar's?

MARY. I do not wish to be exempt from judgement,
It is the judges only I disclaim.

BURLEIGH. The judges? How now, madam! Are they then
Base wretches, snatched at hazard from the crowd?
Are they not men who rule a generous people
In liberty and justice, men whose names
I need but mention to dispel each doubt,
Each mean suspicion which is raised against them?
Say, then, could England's sovereign do more
Than, out of all the monarchy, elect
The very noblest and appoint them judges
In this great suit? And were it probable
That party hatred could corrupt *one* heart,
Can forty chosen men unite to speak
A sentence just as passion gives command?

MARY, *after a short pause.*
Oh, how shall I, a weak, untutored woman,
Cope with so subtle, learned an orator?
Yes, truly, were these lords as you describe them,
I must be mute; my cause were lost indeed,
Beyond all hope, if they pronounced me guilty.
But, sir, these men whom you are pleased to praise,
I see performing in the history
Of these dominions very different parts.
I see this high nobility of England
Make statutes and annul them, ratify

A marriage and dissolve it, as the voice
Of power commands. To-day it disinherits
And brands the royal daughters of the realm
With the vile name of bastards and to-morrow
Crowns them as queens and leads them to the throne.
I see them in four reigns, with pliant conscience,
Four times abjure their faith; renounce the Pope
With Henry, yet retain the old belief;
Reform themselves with Edward; hear the Mass
Again with Mary; with Elizabeth,
Who governs now, reform themselves again——

BURLEIGH. You say you are not versed in England's laws.
    You seem well read, methinks, in her disasters.

MARY. And these men are my judges?

As LORD BURLEIGH *seems to wish to speak.*

                              My Lord Treasurer,
I well believe that, not your private ends,
Your sovereign and your country's weal alone
Inspire your counsels and direct your deeds.
Therefore, my noble lord, you should the more
Distrust your heart, should see that you mistake not
The welfare of the government for justice.
I do not doubt, besides yourself, there are
Among my judges many upright men,
But they are Protestants, are eager all
For England's quiet, and they sit in judgement
On me, the Queen of Scotland and the Papist.
It is an ancient saying that the Scots
And English to each other are unjust;
And hence the rightful custom that a Scot
Against an Englishman, or Englishman
Against a Scot, cannot be heard in judgement.
Deep policy oft lies in ancient customs;
My lord, we must respect them. Nature cast
Into the ocean these two fiery nations
Upon this plank, then she divided it
Unequally and bade them fight for it.
No foe oppresses England but the Scot
Becomes his firm ally; no civil war

Inflames the towns of Scotland but the English
Add fuel to the fire. This raging hate
Will never be extinguished till, at last,
One Parliament in concord shall unite them,
One common sceptre rule throughout the isle.

BURLEIGH. And from a Stuart, then, should England hope
This happiness?

MARY.   Yes! Why should I deny it?
Yes, I confess, I cherished the fond hope!
I thought myself the happy instrument
To join in freedom, 'neath the olive's shade,
Two generous realms in lasting happiness!

BURLEIGH. An evil way you took to this good end:
To set the realm on fire and, through the flames
Of civil war, to strive to mount the throne!

MARY. When did I strive at that? Where are your proofs?

BURLEIGH. The great majority of forty voices
Hath found that you have contravened the law
Last year enacted and have now incurred
Its penalty.

Producing the verdict.

MARY.   Upon this statute, then,
My lord, is built the verdict of my judges?

BURLEIGH, *reading.* Last year it was enacted: "If a plot
Henceforth should rise in England, in the name
Or for the benefit of any claimant
To England's crown, that justice should be done
On such pretender, and the guilty party
Be prosecuted unto death." Now, since——

MARY. Can you deny it, sir, that this same statute
Was *made* for my destruction and nought else?

BURLEIGH. It should have acted as a warning to you:
You saw the precipice which yawned before you,
Yet, truly warned, you plunged into the deep.
With Babington, the traitor, and his bands
Of murderous companions, were you leagued.
You knew of all and from your prison led
Their treasonous plottings with a deep-laid plan!

MARY. When did I that, my lord? Let them produce
  The documents!

BURLEIGH.   You have already seen them:
  They were, before the court, presented to you.

MARY. Mere copies written by another hand.
  Show me the proof that I dictated them——

BURLEIGH. Before his execution, Babington
  Confessed they were the same which he received.

MARY. Why was he in his lifetime not produced
  Before my face? Why was he then despatched
  So quickly that he could not be confronted
  With her whom he accused?

BURLEIGH.   Besides, my lady,
  Your secretaries, Curl and Nau, declare
  On oath they are the very selfsame letters
  Which, from your lips, they faithfully transcribed.

MARY. And on my menials' testimony, then,
  I am condemned! Upon the word of those
  Who have betrayed me, *me*, their rightful queen!

BURLEIGH. You said yourself you held the wretched Curl
  To be an upright, conscientious man.

MARY. He ever was an honest man but weak
  In understanding; his sly comrade Nau
  And instruments of torture may have forced him
  To write and to declare more than he knew.
  He hoped to save himself by this false witness,
  And thought it could not injure me—a queen.

BURLEIGH. The oath he swore was free and unconstrained.

MARY. Let them appear against me, face to face,
  And there repeat what they have testified!
  I heard from Talbot's mouth, my former keeper,
  That in this reign a statute had been passed
  Which orders that the plaintiff be confronted
  With the defendant. Is there such a law?

PAULET. Madam, there is.

MARY.   There is! Well then, my lord,
  Why was not Babington confronted with me?
  Why not my servants, who are both alive?

BURLEIGH. Be not so hasty, lady. 'Tis not only
    Your plot with Babington——

MARY.   'Tis that alone
    Which arms the law against me; that alone
    From which I'm called upon to clear myself.

BURLEIGH. It has been proved that you have corresponded
    With the Ambassador of Spain, Mendoza——

MARY. Stick to the point, my lord.

BURLEIGH.   —that you have formed
    Conspiracies to overturn the fixed
    Religion of the realm, that you have called
    Into this kingdom foreign powers and roused
    All kings in Europe to a war with England——

MARY. Even suppose it were so: I am kept
    Imprisoned here against all laws of nations.
    I came not into England, sword in hand;
    I came a suppliant. And at the hands
    Of my imperial kinswoman I claimed
    The sacred rights of hospitality
    When power seized upon me and prepared
    To rivet fetters where I hoped protection.
    Say, is my conscience bound, then, to this realm?
    I should but exercise a sacred right,
    Derived from sad necessity, if I
    Roused and incited every state in Europe
    For my protection to unite in arms.
    Murder alone would stain, dishonour me:
    Dishonour me, my lord, but not condemn me,
    Nor subject me to England's courts of law.
    For 'tis not justice but mere violence
    Which is the question between me and England.

BURLEIGH, *significantly*.
    Madam, the dreadful right of power is seldom
    On the prisoner's side.

MARY.   Let her then confess
    That she hath exercised her power alone!
    Let her not borrow from the law the sword
    To rid her of her hated enemy!
    Let her not clothe in a religious garb

The bloody daring of licentious might!
Let her dare to seem the thing she is!
Exit.

SCENE 8

BURLEIGH, PAULET

BURLEIGH. She scorns us, she defies us, will defy us
Even at the scaffold's foot.

PAULET. And yet, my lord,
Irregularities have been allowed
In these proceedings: Babington and Ballard
Should have been brought, with Curl and Nau, her servants,
Before her, face to face.

BURLEIGH. No, Paulet, no,
That was not to be risked. Her influence
Upon the human heart is too supreme.
Her secretary Curl would straight shrink back
And fearfully revoke his own confession.

PAULET. Then England's enemies will fill the world
With rumours. These proceedings to the minds
Of all will signalize an act of outrage.

BURLEIGH. Had but this lovely mischief died before
She set her faithless foot on English ground!

PAULET. Amen, say I!

BURLEIGH. Had sickness but consumed her—

PAULET. England had been secured from such misfortune!

BURLEIGH. And yet, if she had died in nature's course,
The world would still have called us murderers.

PAULET. 'Tis true, the world will think, despite of us,
Whatever it likes.

BURLEIGH. Yet could it not be proved,
And it would make less noise.

PAULET.   Why, let it make
What noise it may! It is not clamorous blame,
But only righteous censure that can wound.

BURLEIGH. We know that holy justice cannot escape
The voice of censure, and the public cry
Is ever on the side of the unhappy.
The sword of justice, which adorns the man,
Is hateful in a woman's hand; the world
Will give no credit to a woman's justice,
If woman be the victim. Vain that we,
The judges, spoke what conscience dictated:
She has the royal privilege of mercy.

PAULET. And therefore——?

BURLEIGH.   Should she live? No! She should not!
'Tis this disturbs the Queen, whose eyes demand:
"Who'll save me from this sad alternative:
Either to tremble in eternal fear
Upon my throne or else to sacifice
A queen of my own kindred on the block?"

PAULET. 'Tis even so, nor can it be avoided——

BURLEIGH. Well might it be avoided, thinks the Queen,
If she had only more attentive servants.

PAULET. How more attentive?

BURLEIGH.   Such as could interpret
A silent mandate.

PAULET.   What? A silent mandate?

BURLEIGH. Who, when a poisonous adder is delivered
Into their hands, would keep the treacherous charge
As if it were a sacred, precious jewel?

PAULET. A precious jewel is the Queen's good name;
One cannot guard it with sufficient care.

BURLEIGH. When, out of Shrewsbury's hand, the Queen of
Scots
Was trusted to Sir Amias Paulet's care——

PAULET. Let me not think I am indebted for it
To anything but my unblemished name!

BURLEIGH. Spread the report she wastes; grows sicker still
And sicker; and expires at last in peace.

Thus will she perish in the world's remembrance;
And your good name is pure.

PAULET.   But not my conscience.

A pause.

BURLEIGH. Though you refuse us, sir, your own assistance,
You will not, sure, prevent another's hand?

PAULET. Her life's a sacred trust. To me the head
Of Queen Elizabeth is not more sacred.
You are the judges; judge, and break the staff;
And when 'tis time, then let the carpenter
With axe and saw appear to build the scaffold;
My castle's portals shall be open to him,
The sheriff, and the executioners.
Till then, she is entrusted to my care.

Exeunt.

ACT II

SCENE 1

LONDON. A HALL IN THE PALACE OF WESTMINSTER

The EARL OF KENT *and* SIR WILLIAM DAVISON, *meeting.*

DAVISON. Is that my lord of Kent? So soon returned?
  Is then the tourney, the carousal over?

KENT. How now? Were you not present at the tilt?

DAVISON. My office kept me here.

KENT.   You have missed
  The fairest show which ever taste devised:
  For *Beauty's* virgin fortress was presented,
  As by *Desire* assaulted. The Earl Marshal,
  The Lord High Admiral, and ten other knights
  Belonging to the Queen, defended it,
  And France's cavaliers led the attack.
  A herald marched before the gallant troop
  And summoned, in a madrigal, the fortress;
  And from the walls the chancellor replied;
  And then the artillery played, and nosegays,
  Breathing delicious fragrance, were discharged
  From pretty cannons; but in vain, the storm
  Was valiantly resisted, and *Desire*
  Was forced, unwillingly, to raise the siege.

DAVISON. A sign of evil boding, good my lord,
  For the French suitors.

KENT.   Why, you know that this
  Was but in sport; when the attack's in earnest,
  The fortress will, no doubt, capitulate.

DAVISON. Ha! Think you so? I never can believe it.

KENT. The hardest article of all is now

Adjusted and acceded to by France:
The Duke of Anjou is content to hold
Catholic worship in a private chapel,
And publicly he promises to honour
And to protect the realm's established faith.
Had you but heard the people's joyful shouts
Wherever the tidings spread! For it has been
The country's constant fear the Queen might die
Without immediate issue of her body,
And England bear again the Romish chains
If Mary Stuart should ascend the throne.

DAVISON. This fear appears superfluous: she goes
Into the bridal chamber; Mary Stuart
Enters the gates of death.

KENT.   The Queen approaches.

SCENE 2

Enter ELIZABETH, *led in by* LEICESTER, COUNTS AUBESPINE,
BELLIÈVRE, LORDS SHREWSBURY *and* BURLEIGH, *with other
French and English Gentlemen.*

ELIZABETH, *to* AUBESPINE.
Count Aubespine, I know how you must miss
The sparkling splendour of St. Germain's court.
Such pompous festivals of godlike state
I cannot furnish as the royal court
Of France. A sober and contented people
Which crowd around me with a thousand blessings
Whenever I present myself in public:
This is the spectacle which I can show,
And not without some pride, to foreign eyes.
The splendour of the noble dames who bloom
In Catherine's beauteous garden would, I know,
Eclipse myself and my more modest merits.

AUBESPINE. The court of England has one lady only
To show the wondering foreigner, but all
That charms our hearts in the accomplished sex
Is seen united in her single person.

BELLIÈVRE. Great Majesty of England, suffer us
    To take our leave, and to our royal master,
    The Duke of Anjou, bring the happy news.

ELIZABETH. Press me no further now, Count Bellièvre,
    It is not now a time, I must repeat,
    To kindle here the joyful marriage torch.
    A fatal blow is aimed against my heart.

BELLIÈVRE. We only ask Your Majesty to promise
    Your royal hand when brighter days shall come.

ELIZABETH. My wish was ever to remain unmarried
    That men hereafter on my tomb might read:
    "Here rests the Virgin Queen." But my subjects think
    And clamorously assert, 'tis not enough
    That blessings now are showered upon this land,
    They ask a sacrifice for future welfare:
    That I should cede my virgin liberty,
    To satisfy my people. 'Tis by this
    I see that I am nothing but a woman
    In their regard; and yet methought that I
    Had governed like a man, yes, like a king.
    Well know I that it is not serving God
    To quit the laws of nature; and that those
    Who here have ruled before me merit praise
    For opening the cloister gates and giving
    Thousands of victims of ill-taught devotion
    Back to the duties of humanity . . .
    But yet a Queen, who has not spent her days
    In fruitless, idle contemplation; who,
    Without a murmur, indefatigably,
    Performs the hardest of all duties; *she*
    Should be exempted from that natural law
    Which does ordain one half of humankind
    Shall ever be subservient to the other.

AUBESPINE. Great Queen, you have upon your throne done
       honour
    To every virtue; nothing now remains
    But to the sex whose greatest boast you are
    To be the leading star and great example.
    'Tis true, the man exists not who deserves you,

Yet if there were a prince alive to-day
Deserving of this honour——

ELIZABETH.   Without doubt,
My Lord Ambassador, a marriage union
With France's royal son would do me honour.
If I must yield unto my people's prayers,
I do not know in Europe any prince
To whom with less reluctance I would yield.
Let this confession satisfy your master.

BELLIÈVRE. It gives the fairest hope, and yet it gives
Nothing but hope; my master wishes more.

ELIZABETH *takes a ring from her finger and examines it.*
This common token marks one common duty,
One common servitude; the ring denotes
Marriage; and 'tis of rings a chain is formed.
Convey this present to His Highness. 'Tis
As yet no chain; it binds me not as yet;
But out of it may grow a link to bind me.

BELLIÈVRE, *kneeling.* This present I receive and press the kiss
Of homage on the hand of her who is
Henceforth my princess.

ELIZABETH, *to the* EARL OF LEICESTER, *whom she, during the
last speeches, had continually regarded.*

                    By your leave, my lord.

She takes the Order of the Garter from his neck and invests
BELLIÈVRE *with it.*

Invest His Highness with this ornament.
"Honi soit qui mal y pense." So be it.
And let the bond of confidence unite
Henceforth the crowns of Britain and of France.

BELLIÈVRE. See! mercy beams upon your radiant brow:
Let the reflection of its cheering light
Fall on a wretched princess who concerns
Britain and France alike!

ELIZABETH.   No further, Count.
Let us not mix two inconsistent things:
If France be truly anxious for my hand,

It must partake my interests and renounce
Alliance with my foes.

AUBESPINE.   In your own eyes
Would she not seem to act unworthily
If in this joyous treaty she forgot
That hapless Queen, the widow of her King?

ELIZABETH. France has discharged her duties as a friend.
I will fulfil my own as England's Queen.

She bows to the French AMBASSADORS, *who, with the other
Gentlemen, retire respectfully.*

SCENE 3

Enter BURLEIGH, LEICESTER, *and* SHREWSBURY. *The* QUEEN
takes her seat.

BURLEIGH. Illustrious sovereign, you crown to-day
The fervent wishes of a loyal people.
Now but one only care disturbs this land:
It is a sacrifice which every voice
Demands. Oh, grant but this, and England's peace
Will be established now and evermore.

ELIZABETH. What wish is this, my lord? Speak.

BURLEIGH.   They demand
The Stuart's head. If to your people you
Would now secure the precious boon of freedom
And the fair light of truth so dearly won
Then she must die. If we are not to live
In endless terror for your precious life
The enemy must fall. For well you know
Romish idolatry still has its friends
In secret in this island, and they're leagued
With the fell Cardinal of Guise, her uncle.
Rheims is his see and Rheims his arsenal.
Rheims is the Guise's school of regicide.
Thence come their missionary spies. From thence
Have we not seen the third assassin come?
While in her castle sits, at Fotheringay,

The Ate of this everlasting war
And with a torch of love sets fire to all.
To set her free, young men resolve to die.
To set her free? That's a pretence. The aim
Is to establish her upon your throne!

ELIZABETH. Lord Burleigh, there is wisdom in your speech
And yet I hate this wisdom when it calls
For blood. I hate it in my inmost soul.
Think of a milder counsel. Good my Lord
Of Shrewsbury, we crave your judgement here.

SHREWSBURY. Long may you live, my Queen, to be our joy!
Never hath this isle beheld such happy days
Since it was governed by its native kings.
Ere it shall buy its happiness with its
Good name, may Talbot's eyes be closed in death!

ELIZABETH. Forbid it, Heaven, that our good name be stained!

SHREWSBURY. Then must you find some other way than this
To save your kingdom, for the sentence passed
Of death against the Stuart is unjust.
You cannot upon her pronounce a sentence
Who is not subject to you.

ELIZABETH.   Then, it seems,
My council and my parliament have erred:
Each bench of justice in the land is wrong,
Which did with one accord admit this right.

SHREWSBURY, *after a pause.*
The proof of justice lies not in the voice
Of numbers. England's not the world nor is
Your parliament a focus to collect
The vast opinion of the human race.
This present England is no more the future,
Than 'tis the past; as inclination changes,
Thus ever ebbs and flows the unstable tide
Of public judgement. Do not say that you
Must act as stern necessity compels,
That you must yield to the importunate
Petitions of your people. Every hour
You can experience that your will is free.
Make trial and declare that you hate blood

And that you will protect your sister's life,
And you shall see how stern necessity
Can vanish, and what once was titled justice
Into injustice be converted.

A pause.

Yourself must pass the sentence, you alone.
God has not planted rigour in the frame
Of woman; and the founders of this realm,
Who to the female hand have not denied
The reins of government, intend by this
To show that mercy, not severity,
Is the best virtue to adorn a crown.

ELIZABETH. Lord Shrewsbury is a fervent advocate
For mine and England's enemy. I must
Prefer those counsellors who wish *my* welfare.

SHREWSBURY. I do not take the part of her misdeeds.
They say 'twas she who planned her husband's murder;
'Tis true that she espoused his murderer.
A grievous crime this was but then it happened
In the stern agony of civil war.
God knows what arts were used to overcome her!
For woman is a weak and fragile thing.

ELIZABETH. Woman's not weak! There are heroic souls
Among the sex, and in my presence, sir,
I do forbid to speak of woman's weakness.

SHREWSBURY. Misfortune was for you a rigid school,
You were not stationed on the sunny side
Of life, you saw no throne from far before you:
The grave was gaping for you at your feet.
The father of this land taught you your duty
At Woodstock and in London's gloomy Tower.
No flatterer sought you there: far from the world
Your soul learnt there to commune with itself
And estimate the real goods of life.
How different was the lot of that poor woman:
Transplanted in her youth to giddy France
She was deluded by the glare of vice
And carried forward on the stream of ruin.
Hers was the vain possession of a face;

For she outshone all others of her sex
As much in beauty as nobility.

ELIZABETH. Those charms must surely be without compare
Which can engender, in an elder's blood,
Such fire!

A pause.

My lord of Leicester, you are silent.

LEICESTER. Astonishment possesses me, I own,
To think this queen who, in her days of freedom,
Was but your puppet should, as your prisoner,
Be so formidable. What makes her so?
That she lays claim to England? That the Guises
Will not acknowledge you as England's queen?
And is not she, by Henry's will, passed over
In silence? Is it probable that England
Should throw itself into this papist's arms?
From you, the sovereign it adores, desert
To Darnley's murderess? What will they then,
These restless men who even in your lifetime
Torment you with a successor, who cannot
Dispose of you in marriage soon enough
To rescue church and state from fancied peril?
Stand you not blooming there in youthful prime
While each step leads her towards the expecting tomb?
By heaven, I hope you will full many a year
Walk over the Stuart's grave and never be
Yourself the instrument of her sad end.

BURLEIGH. Lord Leicester hath not always held this tone.

LEICESTER. 'Tis true I in the court of justice gave
My verdict for her death; here in the council
I may consistently speak otherwise.
Here, right is not the question but advantage.
Is this a time to fear her power when France,
Her succour, has abandoned her, and you
Prepare to give your hand to France's son?
Then hasten not her death: she's dead already.
Contempt and scorn are death to her; take heed
Lest ill-timed pity call her into life.
'Tis therefore my advice to leave the sentence

By which her life is forfeit in full force.
Let her live on, but let her live beneath
The headsman's axe, and, at the very hour
Aught is attempted for her, let it fall.

ELIZABETH *rises*.

My lords, I now have heard your several thoughts.
With God's help, I will weigh your arguments
And choose what best my judgement shall approve.

SCENE 4

Enter SIR AMIAS PAULET *and* MORTIMER.

ELIZABETH. Sir Amias Paulet! Well, noble sir,
What tidings bring you?

PAULET.   Gracious Sovereign,
My nephew, who but lately is returned
From foreign travel, kneels before your feet
And offers you his first and earliest homage.

MORTIMER, *kneeling on one knee*.
Long live my royal mistress! Happiness
And glory form a crown to grace her brows!

ELIZABETH. Arise, Sir Knight; and welcome here in England.
You've made the tour I hear, have been in France
And Rome, and tarried too some time at Rheims.
Tell me what plots our enemies are hatching.

MORTIMER. May God confound them all, my gracious liege.

ELIZABETH. Did you see Morgan and the wily Bishop
Of Ross?

MORTIMER. I saw, my Queen, all Scottish exiles
Who forge at Rheims their plots against this realm.

PAULET. Private despatches they entrusted to him,
In ciphers, for the Queen of Scots, which he
With loyal hand hath given up to us.

ELIZABETH. Say, what are then their latest plans of treason?

MORTIMER. It struck them all as 'twere a thunderbolt
That France should leave them and with England close

This firm alliance. Now they turn their hopes
Towards Spain——

ELIZABETH.   This Walsingham has written us.

LEICESTER. England no more is frightened by such arms.

BURLEIGH. They're always dangerous in bigots' hands.

ELIZABETH, *looking steadfastly at* MORTIMER.
Your enemies have said that you frequented
The schools at Rheims and have abjured your faith.

MORTIMER. So I pretended, that I must confess:
Such was my anxious wish to serve my Queen.

ELIZABETH, *to* PAULET, *who presents papers to her.*
What have you there?

PAULET.   'Tis from the Queen of Scots.
'Tis a petition, and addressed to you.

BURLEIGH, *hastily catching at it.* Give it to me.

PAULET, *giving it to the* QUEEN.   My lord, she ordered me
To bring it to Her Majesty's own hands.

The QUEEN *takes the letter: as she reads it,* MORTIMER *and*
LEICESTER *speak some words in private.*

BURLEIGH, *to* PAULET.
Idle complaints, from which one ought to screen
The Queen's too tender heart.

PAULET.   She asks a boon.
She begs to be admitted to the grace
Of speaking with the Queen.

BURLEIGH.   It cannot be.

SHREWSBURY. Why not? Her supplication's not unjust.

BURLEIGH. For her, the base encourager of murder,
Her who has thirsted for our sovereign's blood——

SHREWSBURY. And if the Queen is gracious, sir, are you
The man to hinder pity's soft emotion?

BURLEIGH. She is condemned to death; 'twould ill become
The Queen to see a death-devoted head.
The sentence cannot have its execution
If the Queen's majesty approaches her
For pardon still attends the royal presence.

ELIZABETH, *having read the letter, dries her tears.*

Oh, what is man? What is the bliss of earth?
To what extremities is she reduced
Who with such proud and splendid hopes began?
Who, called to sit on the most ancient throne
Of Christendom, misled by vain ambition,
Hoped with a triple crown to deck her brows?
How is her language altered since the time
When she assumed the arms of England's crown
And by the flatterers of her Court was styled
Sole monarch of the two Britannic isles!
Forgive me, lords, my heart is cleft in twain
To think that earthly goods are so unstable
And that the dreadful fate which rules mankind
Should threaten mine own house and scowl so near me!

SHREWSBURY. Stretch forth your hand, to raise this abject
    Queen,
And, like the luminous figure of an angel,
Descend into her gaol's sepulchral night!

BURLEIGH. Be steadfast, mighty Queen. Let no emotion
Of seeming laudable humanity
Mislead you. Take not from yourself the power
Of acting as necessity commands.

LEICESTER. The law of England, not the monarch's will,
Condemns the Queen of Scotland, and 'twere worthy
Of the great soul of Queen Elizabeth
To follow the soft dictates of her heart.
But the Queen's wise and does not need our counsel.

ELIZABETH. Retire, my lords. We shall, perhaps, find means
To reconcile the tender claims of pity
With what necessity imposes on us.
But now retire——

The LORDS *retire. She calls* SIR EDWARD MORTIMER *back.*
                Sir Edward Mortimer!

SCENE 5

ELIZABETH, MORTIMER

ELIZABETH, *having measured him for some time, with her eyes, in silence.*

He who has timely learnt to play so well
The difficult dissembler's needful task
Becomes a perfect man before his time.
Fate calls you to a lofty scene of action:
I prophesy it and can, happily
For you, fulfil myself my own prediction.

MORTIMER. Illustrious mistress, what I am and all
I can accomplish is devoted to you.

ELIZABETH. You've made acquaintance with the foes of
England.
Their hate against me is implacable;
Their fell designs are inexhaustible.
As yet, indeed, almighty Providence
Has shielded me, but on my brows the crown
Forever trembles while *she* lives who fans
Their bigot zeal and animates their hopes.

MORTIMER. She lives no more as soon as you command it.

ELIZABETH. The sentence is pronounced—what gain I by it?
It must be executed, Mortimer,
And I must authorize the execution.
The blame will ever light on me. I must
Avow it nor can save appearances.
That is the worst——

MORTIMER.   But can appearances
Disturb your conscience where the cause is just?

ELIZABETH. You are unpractised in the world, Sir Knight.
What we appear is subject to the judgement
Of all mankind, but what we are, of no man.
No one will be convinced that I am right:

I must take care that my connivance in
Her death be wrapped in everlasting doubt.

MORTIMER, *seeking to learn her meaning.*
Then it perhaps were best——

ELIZABETH, *quickly.*   Ay, surely 'twere
The best; my better angel speaks through you.
You are in earnest; you examine deep;
Have quite a different spirit from your uncle.

MORTIMER, *surprised.*
Have you imparted then your wishes to him?

ELIZABETH. I am sorry that I have.

MORTIMER.   Excuse his age.
The old man is grown scrupulous, I fear.
My hand I'll lend you; save then as you can
Your reputation——

ELIZABETH.   Well, sir, if you could
But waken me some morning with the news:
"This Mary Stuart, your bloodthirsty foe,
Breathed yesternight her last"——

MORTIMER.   Depend on me.

ELIZABETH. When shall my head lie calmly down to sleep?

MORTIMER. The next new moon will terminate your fears.

ELIZABETH. And be the selfsame happy day the dawn
Of your preferment. So God speed you, sir.
Be not aggrieved, sir, that my gratitude
Must wear the mask of darkness. Silence is
The happy suitor's god. The closest bonds,
The dearest, are the work of secrecy.
Exit.

SCENE 6

MORTIMER, *alone*

MORTIMER. Go, false deceitful Queen! As you delude
The world, even so I cozen you; 'tis right,
Thus to betray you; 'tis a worthy deed.

Trust only to my arm and keep your own
Concealed; assume the pious outward show
Of mercy 'fore the world, while reckoning
In secret on my murderous aid; and thus
By gaining time we shall ensure *her* rescue.
You will exalt me, show me from afar
The costly recompense, but even were
Yourself the prize and all your woman's favour,
What are you, poor one, and what can you proffer?
I scorn ambition's avaricious strife.
With her, with her, is all the charm of life!
I can effect her rescue, I alone.
Be danger, honour, and the prize my own!
——I must attend Lord Leicester and deliver
Her letter to him—'tis a hateful charge—
I have no confidence in this court puppet——
As he is going, PAULET *meets him.*

SCENE 7

MORTIMER, PAULET

PAULET. What said the Queen to you?

MORTIMER.   'Twas nothing, sir,
Nothing of consequence——

PAULET, *looking at him earnestly.*

                          Hear, Mortimer!
It is slippery ground on which you tread.
I know the deed the Queen proposed to you.
Have you then pledged your promise, have you?——

MORTIMER.   Uncle!

PAULET. If you have done so, I abandon you,
And lay my curse upon you——

LEICESTER, *entering.*   Worthy sir!
I with your nephew wish a word. The Queen
Is graciously inclined to him. She wills
That to his custody the Scottish queen

Be with full powers entrusted. She relies
On his fidelity.

PAULET.   The Queen relies
On him; and I, my noble lord, rely
Upon myself and my two open eyes.
Exit.

SCENE 8

LEICESTER, MORTIMER

LEICESTER, *surprised*. What ailed the knight?

MORTIMER.   The confidence, perhaps,
The Queen so suddenly confers on me.

LEICESTER. Are you deserving, then, of confidence?

MORTIMER. That would I ask of you, my lord of Leicester.

LEICESTER. You said you wished to speak with me in private.

MORTIMER. Assure me first that I may safely venture.

LEICESTER. I see you, sir, exhibit at this court
Two different aspects. One of them must be
A borrowed one, but which of them is real?

MORTIMER. The selfsame doubts I have concerning you.

LEICESTER. Who then shall pave the way to confidence?

MORTIMER. He who, by doing it, is least in danger.

LEICESTER. Well, that are you——

MORTIMER.   No, you! The evidence
Of such a weighty, powerful peer as you
Can overwhelm my voice. My accusations
Were weak against your rank and influence.

LEICESTER. Sir, you mistake. In everything but this
I'm powerful here, but in this tender point
Which I am called upon to trust you with
The poorest testimony can undo me.

MORTIMER. If the all-powerful Earl of Leicester deign
To stoop so low to meet me, and to make

Such a confession to me, I may venture
To think a little better of myself.

Producing suddenly the letter.

Here is a letter from the Queen of Scotland.

LEICESTER, *alarmed, catches hastily at the letter.*
Speak softly, sir! What see I?—— Oh, it is
Her picture!——

Kisses and examines it with speechless joy. A pause.

MORTIMER, *who has watched him closely the whole time.*
               Now, my lord, I can believe you.

LEICESTER, *having run hastily through the letter.*
You know the purport of this letter, sir?

MORTIMER. Not I.

LEICESTER.   She surely has informed you——

MORTIMER.   She said
You would explain this riddle to me—— 'Tis
To me a riddle that the Earl of Leicester,
The far-famed favourite of Elizabeth,
The open, bitter enemy of Mary,
Should be the man from whom the Queen expects
Deliverance from her woes; and yet it must be.
Your eyes express too plainly what your heart
Feels for the hapless lady.

LEICESTER.   Tell me, sir,
First, how it comes that you should take so warm
An interest in her fate; and what it was
Gained you her confidence?

MORTIMER.   My lord, I can:
A letter from the Cardinal Archbishop
Was my credential with the Queen of Scots.

LEICESTER. Each remnant of distrust be henceforth banished!
Your hand, sir; pardon me these idle doubts.
Knowing how Walsingham and Burleigh hate me
And, watching me, in secret spread their snares,
I feared you were their instrument, their creature,
To lure me to their toils.

MORTIMER.   How poor a part

So great a nobleman is forced to play
At court! My lord, I pity you.

LEICESTER.   With joy
I rest upon the faithful breast of friendship.
You seem surprised, sir, that my heart is turned
So suddenly towards the captive Queen.
In truth, I never hated her; the times
Have forced me to appear her enemy.
She was, as you well know, my destined bride
Long since, ere she bestowed her hand on Darnley,
While yet the beams of glory round her smiled.
Coldly I then refused the proffered boon.
Now, at the hazard of my life, I claim her,
Though she's confined and at the brink of death.

MORTIMER. True magnanimity, my lord of Leicester.

LEICESTER. Ambition made me all insensible
To youth and beauty. Mary's hand I held
Too insignificant for me. I hoped
To be the husband of the Queen of England.

MORTIMER. It is well known she gave you preference
Before all others.

LEICESTER.   So, indeed, it seems.
Men call me happy!—— Did they only know
What the chains are for which they envy me!
For I have sacrificed ten bitter years
To the proud idol of her vanity,
Submitted with a slave's humility
To every change of her despotic fancies,
The plaything of each little wayward whim.
At times by seeming tenderness caressed,
As oft repulsed with proud and cold disdain,
Alike tormented by her grace and rigour,
Watched like a prisoner by the Argus eyes
Of jealousy, examined like a schoolboy,
And railed at like a servant—— Oh, no tongue
Can paint this hell!

MORTIMER.   My lord, I feel for you.

LEICESTER. To lose, and at the very goal, the prize!
'Tis not her hand alone this envious stranger

Threatens, he'd rob me of her favour too:
She is a woman, and he, formed to please.

MORTIMER. He is the son of Catherine. He has learnt,
In a good school, the arts of flattery.

LEICESTER. As fall these hopes, I turn towards the hope
Of former days. Within me Mary's image
Renews itself, and youth reclaims its rights.
No more 'tis cold ambition; from my heart
I yearn to have my jewel back again.
I have already sent the Queen the news
Of my conversion to her interests,
And in this letter which you brought me she
Assures me that she pardons me and offers,
If I rescue her, herself as guerdon.

MORTIMER. But you attempted nothing for her rescue.
You let her be condemned without a word.
You voted for her death——

LEICESTER.   I was obliged,
Before the world, to persecute her still,
But do not think that I would patiently
Have seen her led to death. No, sir, I hoped,
And still I hope, to ward off all extremes,
Till I can find some certain means to save her.

MORTIMER. These are already found: my lord of Leicester,
Your generous confidence in me deserves
A like return. *I* will deliver her.

LEICESTER. What say you? You alarm me—— How?—— You
would——?

MORTIMER. I'll open forcibly her prison gates.
I have confederates, and all is ready.

LEICESTER. Alas, in what rash enterprise would you
Engage me? And these friends, know they *my* secret?

MORTIMER. Fear not. Our plan was laid without your help.
Without your help it would have been accomplished
Had she not signified her resolution
To owe her liberty to you alone.

LEICESTER. And can you then with certainty assure me
That in your plot my name has not been mentioned?

MORTIMER. You wish to rescue Mary and possess her;
    You find confederates; sudden, unexpected,
    The readiest means fall, as it were, from heaven;
    Yet you show more perplexity than joy.

LEICESTER. We must avoid all violence. It is
    Too dangerous an enterprise.

MORTIMER.   Delay
    Is also dangerous.

LEICESTER.   I tell you, sir,
    It is not to be attempted——

MORTIMER.   It is
    Too hazardous for you who would possess her,
    But we, who only wish to rescue her,
    We are more bold.

LEICESTER.   You will not weigh the matter.
    With blind and hasty rashness you destroy
    The plans which I so happily had framed.

MORTIMER. And what were, then, the plans which you had
        framed?
    And how, if I were miscreant enough
    To murder her as was proposed to me
    This moment by Elizabeth, and which
    She looks upon as certain, only name
    The measures you have taken to protect her?

LEICESTER. Did the Queen give you then this bloody order?

MORTIMER. She was deceived in me, as Mary is
    In you.

LEICESTER. And have you promised it? Say, have you?

MORTIMER. That she might not engage another's hand,
    I offered mine.

LEICESTER.   Well done, sir, that was right.
    This gives us leisure, for she rests secure
    Upon your bloody service; and the sentence
    Is unfulfilled the while and we gain time.

MORTIMER, *angrily.* No, we are losing time!

LEICESTER.   The Queen depends
    On you and will the readier make a show
    Of mercy—so may I prevail on her

To give an audience to her adversary.
And by this stratagem we tie her hands.

MORTIMER. And what is gained by that? When she discovers
That I am cheating her, that Mary lives,
Are we not where we were? She never will
Be free. The mildest doom which can await her
At best is but perpetual confinement.
A daring deed must one day end the matter:
Why will you not with such a deed begin?
Fight a good fight for her! You know you are
Lord of the person of the Queen of England.
Invite her to your castle. She's been there
Before. Then show that you're a man. Keep her
Confined till she release our Queen!

LEICESTER.   Know you
The deeps and shallows of this court? Know you
The potent spell this female sceptre casts
Upon men's minds? In vain you seek the old
Heroic energy of this our land:
A woman holds it under lock and key——
Someone approaches. Go!

MORTIMER.   Yet Mary hopes!
Shall I return to her with empty comfort?

LEICESTER. Bear her my vows of everlasting love!

MORTIMER. Bear them yourself! I offered my assistance
As her deliverer not your messenger.
Exit.

SCENE 9

ELIZABETH, LEICESTER

ELIZABETH. Was someone here? I heard the sound of voices.

LEICESTER, *turning quickly and perplexedly round, on hearing
the* QUEEN. It was young Mortimer——

ELIZABETH.   How now, my lord!
Why so confused?

LEICESTER, *collecting himself.*
                    Your presence is the cause.
My sight is dazzled by your heavenly charms.
Oh!——

ELIZABETH. Whence this sigh?

LEICESTER.   Have I no reason, then,
To sigh? When I behold you in your glory,
I feel anew, with pain unspeakable,
The loss which threatens me.

ELIZABETH.   What loss, my lord?

LEICESTER. Anjou has never seen you, can but love
Your splendour and the splendour of your reign;
But I love you, and were you born of all
The peasant maids the poorest, I, the first
Of kings, would lay my sceptre at your feet.

ELIZABETH. Pity me, Dudley; 'tis not my fortune
To place upon the brows of him, the dearest
Of men to me, the royal crown of England.
The Queen of Scotland was allowed to make
Her hand the token of her inclination;
She has had every freedom, and has drunk,
Even to the very dregs, the cup of joy.

LEICESTER. And now she drinks the bitter cup of sorrow.

ELIZABETH. She never did respect the world's opinion.
Life was to her a sport; she never courted
The yoke to which I bowed my willing neck.
And yet, methinks, I had as just a claim
As she to please myself and taste the joys
Of life. But I preferred the rigid duties
Which royalty imposed on me. Yet she,
She was the favourite of all the men,
And youth and age became alike her suitors.
Thus are the men—voluptuaries all!
For did not even Talbot, though grey-headed,
Grow young again when speaking of her charms?

LEICESTER. Forgive him. Talbot was her keeper once,
And she has fooled him with her cunning wiles.

ELIZABETH. And is it really true that she's so fair?

Pictures are flattering, and description lies:
I will trust nothing but my own conviction.
Why gaze you at me thus?

LEICESTER.   I placed in thought
You and this Mary Stuart side by side.
Yes! I confess, I oft have felt a wish,
If it could be but secretly contrived,
To see you placed beside the Scottish Queen.
Then would you feel, and not till then, the full
Enjoyment of your triumph. She deserves
To be thus humbled. She deserves to see
Herself surpassed, to feel herself overmatched.

ELIZABETH. In years she has the advantage——

LEICESTER.   Has she so?
I never should have thought it. Can her griefs
Have brought down age upon her ere her time?
And it would mortify her more to see you
As bride. She has already turned her back
On each fair hope of life and she would see you
Advancing towards the open arms of joy!

ELIZABETH, *with a careless air*.
I'm teased to grant this interview.

LEICESTER.   She asks it
As a favour; grant it as a punishment.
For though you should conduct her to the block,
Yet would it less torment her than to see
Herself extinguished by your beauty's splendour.
Thus can you murder her, as she has wished
To murder you. Could she but see your beauty,
Exalted by the splendour of the crown
And blooming so with tender bridal graces,
Now were the hour of her destruction come!

ELIZABETH. Now? No—not now. No, Leicester, this must be
Maturely weighed. I must with Burleigh——

LEICESTER.   Burleigh!
To him you are but sovereign, and as such
Alone he seeks your welfare. But your rights,
Derived from womanhood, this tender point
Must be decided by your own tribunal!

ELIZABETH. But would it then become me to behold
    My kinswoman in infamy and want?

LEICESTER. You need not cross her threshold. Hear my counsel.
    The hunt you mean to honour with your presence
    Is in the neighbourhood of Fotheringay.
    Permission may be given to Lady Stuart
    To take the air. You meet her in the park,
    As if by accident.

ELIZABETH, *after a pause.*
                    I should not care
    To cross your merest whim, for I have grieved you.
    And may not our affection grant more than
    We do approve? But let it be—your whim.

She speaks the last sentence with tenderness. LEICESTER
prostrates himself before her.

ACT III

SCENE 1

OUTSIDE THE CASTLE OF FOTHERINGAY

In the foreground, trees; in the background, a distant prospect

> MARY *advances, running from behind the trees.* HANNAH
> KENNEDY *follows slowly.*

KENNEDY. You fly before, my lady, as on wings.

MARY. *Let me enjoy my new-found liberty!*
Let us be children! Be a child with me!
We'll find the wingèd step of youth again
Upon the verdant carpet of the plain!
> *I have escaped the prison's sadness*
> > *And left behind the house of care!*
> > *O, let me in my hungry gladness*
> > > *Drink in the free, celestial air!*

KENNEDY. Your gaol has been extended but a little.
The walls are barely hidden by those trees.

MARY. *I thank you, friendly trees, that hide from me*
> *My darksome prison's dread seclusion!*
I fain would dream myself happy and free!
> *Why wake me from my dream's illusion?*
Free and unfettered are my eyes!
The vault of heaven about me lies.
Space is a wide immeasurable sea.
> *There, where the misty mountains soar,*
I can my Scotland's boundary descry,
While the swift clouds that southward fly
> *Seek the French kingdom's distant shore!*

KENNEDY. Fond, fruitless wishes! See you not from far
How we are followed by observing spies?

MARY, *oblivious*. I recognise in this the mighty arm
  Of Leicester. They will by degrees expand
  My prison; will accustom me, through small,
  To greater liberty; until at last
  I'll see the face of him whose hand will dash
  My fetters off!

KENNEDY.   Their chains are also loosed
  Whom everlasting liberty awaits.

  Hunting horns are heard.

MARY. *O painful memory yet dear!*
  It ever was my joy to hear
  The hound and horn
  Salute the morn
  In the glens of the highlands, loud and clear!

SCENE 2

Enter PAULET.

PAULET. Well? Have I acted right at last, my lady?
  Do I for once, at least, deserve your thanks?

MARY. How? Do I owe this favour, sir, to you?

PAULET. Why not to me? I gave the Queen your letter.

MARY. And is this freedom which I now enjoy
  The happy consequence?

PAULET, *significantly*.
                    Nor that alone.
  You heard the hunting horns?

MARY, *starting back with apprehension*.
                    You frighten me!

PAULET. The Queen is hunting in the neighbourhood——

  MARY, *gives a short cry*.

  In a few moments she'll appear before you.

KENNEDY, *hastening towards* MARY, *who is trembling and
  about to fall*. How fare you, dearest lady? You grow pale.

PAULET. Is it not well? Was it not then your prayer?

MARY. Now I am not prepared for it. Not now!
  What, as the greatest favour, I besought
  Seems to me now most fearful. Hannah, come,
  Lead me into the house till I collect
  My spirits.

PAULET.   Stay, you must await her here.

SCENE 3

Enter the EARL OF SHREWSBURY.

MARY. Worthy Shrewsbury! Save me from this sight!

SHREWSBURY. Command yourself, your Majesty. Have
      courage!
  'Tis the decisive moment of your fate.

MARY. For this I've studied, weighed, and written down
  Each word within the tablet of my memory
  That was to touch and move her to compassion.
  Yet nothing lives within me at this moment
  But the fierce, burning feeling of my wrongs!

SHREWSBURY. However much the inward struggle cost
  You must submit to stern necessity.
  The power is in *her* hand; therefore be humble.

MARY. To her? I never can.

SHREWSBURY.   Speak with respect
  And strive to move her magnanimity.
  Insist not now upon your rights, not now——

MARY. Rather in love could fire and water meet,
  The timid lamb embrace the roaring tiger!
  I have been hurt too grievously; she has
  Too grievously oppressed me. No atonement
  Can make us friends.

SHREWSBURY.   First see her, face to face.
  Did I not see how she was moved at reading
  Your letter? How her eyes were drowned in tears?

MARY, *seizing his hand.*
  They have indeed misused me, Shrewsbury.

SHREWSBURY. Let all be now forgot, and only think
　　How to receive her with submissiveness.

MARY. Is Burleigh with her too, my evil genius?

SHREWSBURY. No one attends her but the Earl of Leicester.

MARY. Lord Leicester?

SHREWSBURY.　　　　　Fear not him. It was his work
　　That here the Queen has granted you this meeting.

MARY. Ah, well I knew it!

SHREWSBURY.　　　　　What?

PAULET.　　　　　　The Queen approaches.

　　They all draw aside; MARY *alone remains, leaning on*
　　KENNEDY.

SCENE 4

THE SAME

ELIZABETH, EARL OF LEICESTER, *and Retinue*

ELIZABETH, *to* LEICESTER. What seat is that, my lord?

LEICESTER.　　　　　　　　'Tis Fotheringay.

ELIZABETH, *to* SHREWSBURY.
　　My lord, send back our retinue to London.
　　The people crowd too eager in the roads.
　　We'll seek a refuge in this quiet park.

　　TALBOT *sends the train away. She looks steadfastly at* MARY
　　as she speaks further with LEICESTER.

　　My honest people love me overmuch.
　　Thus should a god be honoured, not a mortal.

MARY, *who the whole time has leaned, almost fainting, on*
　　KENNEDY, *rises now, and her eyes meet the steady, piercing
　　look of* ELIZABETH; *she shudders and throws herself again
　　upon* KENNEDY's *bosom.*
　　Alas, from out those features speaks no heart.

ELIZABETH. What lady's that?

A general, embarrassed silence.

LEICESTER. You are at Fotheringay,
My liege!

ELIZABETH, *as if surprised, casting an angry look at* LEICESTER.
Who has done this, my lord of Leicester?

LEICESTER. 'Tis past, my Queen; and now that Heaven has led
Your footsteps hither, be magnanimous!

SHREWSBURY. But cast your eyes on this unhappy one
Who stands dissolved in anguish!

MARY *collects herself and begins to advance towards* ELIZA-
BETH, *stops, shuddering, halfway; her action expresses the
most violent internal struggle.*

ELIZABETH. How, my lords?
Which of you had announced to me a prisoner
Bowed down by woe? I see a haughty one
In no way humbled by calamity.

MARY. Farewell high thought and pride of noble mind!
I will forget my dignity and all
My sufferings. I will fall before her feet
Who has reduced me to this wretchedness.

She turns towards the QUEEN.

The voice of Heaven decides for you, my sister.
Your happy brows are now with triumph crowned.
I bless the Power Divine which thus has raised you.

She kneels.

But in your turn be merciful, my sister.
Stretch forth your hand, your royal hand, to raise
Your sister from the depths of her distress.

ELIZABETH, *stepping back.*
You are where it becomes you, Lady Stuart,
And thankfully I prize my God's protection
Who has not suffered me to kneel a suppliant
Thus at your feet as you now kneel at mine.

MARY, *with increasing energy of feeling.*
Think on all earthly things, vicissitudes,
For there are gods who punish haughty pride!
Before these strangers' eyes, dishonour not
Yourself in me! Profane not nor disgrace

The royal blood of Tudor! In my veins
It flows as pure a stream as in your own.
Oh, for God's pity, stand not so estranged
And inaccessible, like some tall cliff
Which shipwrecked sailors try to reach in vain.
My all, my life, my fortune now depend
Upon the influence of my words and tears.
That I may touch your heart, O set mine free!
If you regard me with those freezing looks
My shuddering heart contracts and turns to ice.

ELIZABETH, *cold and severe.*
What would you say to me, my lady Stuart?
You wished to speak with me; and I, forgetting
The Queen and all the wrongs I have sustained,
Fulfil the pious duty of the sister
And grant the boon you wished for of my presence.
Yet I, in yielding to the generous feelings
Of magnanimity, expose myself
To rightful censure that I stoop so low.
For well you know you would have had me murdered.

MARY. Oh, how shall I begin? Oh, how shall I
So artfully arrange my cautious words
That they may touch yet not offend your heart?
I cannot speak without impeaching you,
And that most heavily. I wish not so.
You have not, as you ought, behaved to me.
I am a Queen, like you, yet you have held me
Confined in prison. As a suppliant
I came to you, yet you in me insulted
The pious use of hospitality;
Slighting in me the holy law of nations,
Immured me in a dungeon; tore from me
My friends and servants. To unseemly want
I was exposed and hurried to the bar
Of a disgraceful, insolent tribunal.
No more of this! In everlasting silence
Be buried all the cruelties I suffered!
See—— I will throw the blame of all on fate.
An evil spirit rose from the abyss
To kindle in our hearts the flames of hatred.

It grew with us, and bad, designing men—
Frantic enthusiasts with sword and dagger—
Armed the uncalled-for hand. This is the curse
Of kings, that they, divided, tear the world
In pieces and let loose hell's raging furies!

Approaching her confidently, and with a flattering tone.

Now stand we face to face; now, sister, speak;
Name but my crime, I'll fully satisfy you.
Alas, had you vouchsafed to hear me then,
When I, so earnest, sought to meet your eye,
It never would have come to this, my sister—
This so distressful, this so mournful meeting!

ELIZABETH. Accuse not fate. Your own deceitful heart
It was, the wild ambition of your house.
As yet no enmities had passed between us
When your imperious uncle, the proud priest,
Whose shameless hand grasps at all crowns, attacked me
With unprovoked hostility and taught
You, but too docile, to assume my arms
And meet me in the lists in mortal strife.
What means employed he not to storm my throne?
The curses of the priests, the people's sword,
The dreadful weapons of religious frenzy—
Even here in my own kingdom's peaceful haunts
He fanned the flames of civil insurrection.
But God is with me, and the haughty priest
Has not maintained the field. The blow was aimed
Full at my head. But yours it is that falls!

MARY. I'm in the hand of Heaven. You never will
Exert so cruelly the power it gives you.

ELIZABETH. Who shall prevent me? Ha? Did not your uncle
Set all the kings of Europe the example—
How to conclude a peace with those they hate?
Be mine the school of Saint Bartholomew:
The church can break the bonds of every duty,
It consecrates the regicide, the traitor.
I only practise what your priests have taught.
Say, then, what surety can be offered me,
Should I magnanimously loose your chains?

MARY. Had you declared me heir to your dominions,
    As is my right, then gratitude and love
    In me had fixed, for you, a faithful friend
    And kinswoman.

ELIZABETH.   Your friendship is abroad,
    Your house is popery, the monk your brother.
    Name *you* my successor! Oh, treacherous snare!
    That in my life you might seduce my people,
    And when I——

MARY.   Sister, rule your realm in peace:
    I give up every claim to these domains.
    Alas, the pinions of my soul are lamed;
    Greatness entices me no more; your point
    Is gained. I am but Mary's shadow now.
    You have destroyed me in my bloom. Now speak
    The word which to pronounce has brought you hither.
    Pronounce this word. Say: "Mary, you are free.
    You have already felt my power, learn now
    To honour too my generosity."

ELIZABETH. So: you confess at last that you are conquered?
    Are all your schemes run out? No more assassins
    Now on the road? Will no adventurer
    Attempt again, for you, the sad achievement?
    Yes, madam, it is over. You'll seduce
    No mortal more. The world has other cares.
    None is ambitious of the dangerous honour
    Of being your fourth husband!

MARY, *starting angrily.*   Sister, sister!
    Grant me forbearance, all ye powers of heaven!

ELIZABETH *regards her long, with a look of proud contempt.*
    Those then, my Lord of Leicester, are the charms
    Which no man with impunity can view,
    Near which no woman dare attempt to stand?
    In sooth, this honour has been cheaply gained.
    She who to all is common may with ease
    Become the common object of applause!

MARY. This is too much!

ELIZABETH, *laughing insultingly.* You show us now, indeed,
    Your real face! Till now, 'twas but the mask!

MARY, *burning with rage, yet dignified and noble.*
  My sins were human and the faults of youth.
  Superior force misled me. I have never
  Denied or sought to hide it. I despised
  All false appearance as became a queen.
  The worst of me is known, and I can say
  That I am better than the fame I bear.
  Woe to you when in time to come the world
  Shall strip the robe of honour from your deeds!
  Virtue was not your portion from your mother:
  Well know we what it was that brought the head
  Of Anne Boleyn down on the fatal block!

SHREWSBURY, *stepping between both* QUEENS.
  Is this the moderation, the submission,
  My lady?——

MARY.   Moderation! I've supported
  What human nature can support. Farewell,
  Lamb-hearted resignation, passive patience,
  Fly to your native heaven! Burst at length
  In all your fury, long-suppressèd rancour!

SHREWSBURY. She is distracted. My liege, forgive her.

ELIZABETH, *speechless with anger, casts enraged looks at*
MARY.

LEICESTER, *in the most violent agitation. He seeks to lead*
ELIZABETH *away.* Away from this disastrous place!

MARY, *raising her voice.*   A bastard
  Profanes the English throne! The generous Britons
  Are cheated by a juggler! Her whole person
  Is false and painted—heart as well as face!

  Into ELIZABETH'S *face.*

  If right prevailed, you'd be lying in the dust
  Before me! For I am your rightful queen!

ELIZABETH *hastily quits the stage; the* LORDS *follow her in
consternation.*

SCENE 5

MARY, KENNEDY

KENNEDY. Now all hope is over.

MARY, *still quite beside herself.* Gone hence in wrath!
  Falling on KENNEDY's *bosom.*
  Now I am happy, Hannah! Now, at last,
  After whole years of sorrow and abasement,
  One moment of victorious revenge!
  A weight falls off my heart, a weight of mountains!

KENNEDY. Unhappy lady! Frenzy overcomes you!

MARY. I have abased her before Leicester's eyes.
  How I did hurl her from her haughty height!
  He saw it; he was witness of my triumph.

SCENE 6

Enter MORTIMER.

KENNEDY. Oh, sir! What a disaster!

MORTIMER.   I heard all——
  *Gives the nurse a sign to repair to her post, and draws
  nearer; his whole appearance expresses the utmost violence
  of passion.*
  Yours is the palm. You trod her in the dust.
  Now I adore you as a deity!

MARY, *with vivacity and expectation.*
  You spoke with Leicester? Gave my letter to him?

MORTIMER, *beholding her with glowing looks.*
  You are the fairest woman upon earth!

MARY. What says his lordship? Say, sir, may I hope?

MORTIMER. Who? He?—— He is a wretch, a very coward!

MARY. What say you?

MORTIMER.   He deliver and possess you?
  Why, let him dare it! He! He must with me
  In mortal contest first deserve the prize!

MARY. Will he do nothing for me?

MORTIMER.   Speak not of him.
  I will release you, I alone.

MARY.   Alas,
  What power have you?

MORTIMER.   Deceive yourself no more.
  The moment that the Queen thus quitted you,
  And that your interview had taken this turn,
  All hope was lost, each way of mercy shut.
  You must be free before the morning break!

MARY. What say you, sir? To-night?—— Impossible!

MORTIMER. Hear what has been resolved. I led my friends
  Into a private chapel, where a priest
  Heard our confession and, for every sin
  We had committed, gave us absolution.
  He gave us absolution too, beforehand,
  For every crime we might commit in future.

MARY. Oh, God!

MORTIMER.   We scale the castle walls to-night.
  The keys are in our power. The guards we kill,
  Then from your chamber bear you forcibly.
  None must remain that might disclose the deed:
  We'll murder every living soul——

MARY.   But Paulet?
  He'd sooner spill his dearest drop of blood——

MORTIMER. He falls the very first beneath my steel!

MARY. What, sir! Your uncle? What? Your second father?

MORTIMER. Must perish by my hand. I murder him.

MARY. Sin upon sin!

MORTIMER.   No! We have been absolved
  Beforehand. I may perpetrate the worst.
  I can, I will do so!

MARY.   But it is dreadful!

MORTIMER. And should I be obliged to kill the Queen,

I've sworn upon the Host it shall be done!

MARY. No, Mortimer, ere so much blood for me——

MORTIMER. What is the life of all compared to you
And to my love? The bond that holds the world
Together may be loosed, a second deluge
Come rolling on and swallow all creation;
Henceforth I value nothing. Ere I quit
My hold on you, may earth and time be ended!

MARY, *retiring.* You frighten me!

MORTIMER, *with unsteady looks, expressive of quiet madness.*
                              Life's but a moment. Death's
But a moment. Let them drag me to Tyburn,
Tear me limb from limb with red-hot pincers——
Violently approaching her with his arms extended.
—If only I can hold you in my arms!

MARY. Madman, stand back!

MORTIMER.   To rest upon this bosom,
To press upon this passion-breathing mouth——

MARY. Leave me, for God's sake, sir! Let me go in——

MORTIMER. I will deliver you: What though it cost
A thousand lives, I'll do it. But I swear,
As God's in heaven, I will possess you too!

MARY. Do hate and love conspire alike to fright me?

MORTIMER. Yes, glowing as their hatred is my love!
They would behead you, they would wound this neck,
So dazzling white, with the disgraceful axe!
Then offer to the living god of joy
What you would sacrifice to bloody hate!

MARY. My woe, my sufferings should be sacred to you!

MORTIMER. The crown is fallen from your brows, O Queen.
Your moving form alone remains, the high,
The godlike influence of your heavenly beauty.
This bids me venture all, this arms my hand
With might and drives me towards the headsman's axe!

MARY. Will no one save me from his raging madness?

MORTIMER. Why shed their blood the daring? Is not life
Life's highest good? And he a madman who

Casts life away? First will I rest my head
Upon the breast that glows with love's own fire!

He presses her violently to his bosom.

MARY. Must I then call for help against the man
Who would deliver me?

MORTIMER.　　　　　　　　You're not unfeeling!
You made the minstrel Rizzio blest and gave
Yourself a willing prey to Bothwell's arms.

MARY. Presumptuous man!

MORTIMER.　　　　　　　*He* was indeed your tyrant.
Well, then—if only terror can obtain you—
By the infernal gods!——

MARY.　　　　　　　　Away—— You're mad!

MORTIMER. I'll teach you now to tremble before me!

KENNEDY, *entering suddenly.*
They're coming—they approach—the park is filled
With men in arms.

MARY flies towards the house, KENNEDY *following.*

MORTIMER, *starting, and catching at his sword.*
　　　　　　　I will defend you—I——

SCENE 7

MORTIMER. PAULET *and* DRURY *rush in, in the greatest consternation.* ATTENDANTS *hasten over the stage.*

PAULET. Shut all the portals—draw the bridges up——

MORTIMER. What is the matter, Uncle?

PAULET.　　　　　　　　Where is the murderess?

MORTIMER. What is the matter? What has passed?

PAULET.　　　　　　　　　The Queen!

MORTIMER. The Queen! What Queen?

PAULET.　　　　What Queen? The Queen of England!
She has been murdered on the road to London.

Hastens into the house.

SCENE 8

MORTIMER. *Soon after*, O'KELLY

MORTIMER, *after a pause.*
  Am I then mad? Came not one running by
  But now and cried aloud: "The Queen is murdered!"
  O'Kelly! Comrade——

O'KELLY, *rushing in.*   Flee, our cause is lost!

MORTIMER. What's this? What—lost?

O'KELLY.   Stand not on question. Think
  On speedy flight.

MORTIMER.   What has occurred?

O'KELLY.   That madman
  Sauvage struck at the Queen!

MORTIMER.   Then it is true?

O'KELLY. True, true! Go save yourself!

MORTIMER, *exultingly.*   The Queen is murdered
  And Mary shall ascend the English throne!

O'KELLY. Is murdered? Who said so?

MORTIMER.   Yourself.

O'KELLY.   She lives!
  And I and you and all of us are lost!

MORTIMER. She lives!

O'KELLY.   The blow was badly aimed. Her cloak
  Received it. Shrewsbury disarmed the murderer.

MORTIMER. She lives!

O'KELLY.   She lives to whelm us all in ruin.
  Come! They surround the park——

MORTIMER.   And it was one of
  Our number did this deed!

O'KELLY.   Sauvage, the monk
  From Toulon, whom you saw immersed in thought
  As in the chapel the Pope's bull was read

Which poured anathemas on England's Queen.
He wished to take the nearest, shortest way
To free with one bold stroke the church of God.
He struck the blow upon the road to London.

MORTIMER, *after a long silence.*

Unhappy Mary! Now your death is fixed.
Your very angel has prepared your fall.

O'KELLY. Whither will you take your flight, sir? I go
To hide me in the forests of the north.

MORTIMER. I will remain and still attempt to save
My Queen. If not, my bed shall be her grave.

Exeunt at different sides.

ACT IV

SCENE 1

LONDON. AN ANTECHAMBER IN THE PALACE OF WESTMINSTER

COUNT AUBESPINE, *the* EARLS OF KENT *and* LEICESTER

AUBESPINE. How did it happen? Was it possible
That in the midst of this most loyal people——

LEICESTER. The deed was not attempted by the people.
The assassin was a subject of your King,
A Frenchman.

AUBESPINE.   Sure a lunatic.

LEICESTER.   A Papist,
Count Aubespine.

SCENE 2

Enter BURLEIGH *in conversation with* DAVISON.

BURLEIGH.   Sir, let the death warrant
Be instantly made out, and pass the seal.
The Queen must sign it.

DAVISON.   Sir, it shall be done.

Exit.

AUBESPINE. Praised be almighty Heaven that has averted
Assassination from our much-loved Queen!

BURLEIGH. Praised be His name, who thus has turned to scorn
The malice of our foes!

AUBESPINE.   May Heaven confound
The perpetrator of this cursèd deed!

BURLEIGH. Its perpetrator and its base contriver!

AUBESPINE. Please you, my lord, to bring me to the Queen,
That I may lay the warm congratulations
Of my imperial master at her feet.

BURLEIGH. There is no need of this.

AUBESPINE, *officiously.* My lord of Burleigh,
I know my duty.

BURLEIGH. Sir, your duty is
To quit this kingdom and without delay.

AUBESPINE, *stepping back with surprise.* What? How is this?

BURLEIGH. The sacred character
Of an Ambassador to-day protects you,
But not to-morrow.

AUBESPINE. What's my crime?

BURLEIGH. Should I
Once name it, there were then no pardon for it.

AUBESPINE. I hope, my lord, my charge's privilege——

BURLEIGH. Screens not a traitor.

LEICESTER *and* KENT. Traitor! What?

AUBESPINE. My lord,
Consider well—

BURLEIGH. Your passport was discovered
In the assassin's pocket.

KENT. Righteous Heaven!

AUBESPINE. Sir, many passports have been signed by me.
I cannot know the secret thoughts of men.

BURLEIGH. He in your house confessed and was absolved.

AUBESPINE. My house is open——

BURLEIGH. —to our enemies.

AUBESPINE. My monarch is insulted in my person:
He will annul the marriage contract.

BURLEIGH. That
My royal mistress has annulled already.
England will not unite herself with France.
My lord of Kent, I give to you the charge
To see Count Aubespine embarked in safety.

The furious populace has stormed his palace
Where a whole arsenal of arms was found.
Should *he* be found, they'll tear him limb from limb.
Conceal him till their fury is abated.

AUBESPINE. I leave a kingdom where they sport with treaties
And trample underfoot the laws of nations.

Exeunt KENT *and* AUBESPINE.

SCENE 3

LEICESTER, BURLEIGH

LEICESTER. And thus you loose, yourself, the knot of union
Which you officiously, uncalled-for, tied!

BURLEIGH. My aim was good, though fate declared against it.
Happy is he who has so fair a conscience!

LEICESTER. Now you are in your element, my lord.
A monstrous outrage has been just committed,
And darkness veils, as yet, its perpetrators.
Now will a court of inquisition rise;
Each word, each look be weighed; men's very thoughts
Be summoned to the bar. You are, my lord,
The mighty man, the Atlas of the state!

BURLEIGH. In you, my lord, I recognise my master,
For such a victory as your eloquence
Has gained I cannot boast.

LEICESTER.   What means your lordship?

BURLEIGH. You were the man who knew, behind my back,
To lure the Queen to Fotheringay Castle.

LEICESTER. Behind your back! When did I fear to act
Before your face?

BURLEIGH.   *You* led Her Majesty?
Oh no, *you* led her not—it was the Queen
Who was so gracious as to lead *you* thither——

LEICESTER. What do you mean, my lord, by that?

BURLEIGH.   The noble part

You forced the Queen to play! The glorious triumph
Which you prepared for her! Too gracious princess,
So shamelessly, so wantonly to mock
Your unsuspecting goodness, to betray you
So pitiless to your exulting foe!
This is the magnanimity, the grace
Which suddenly possessed you in the council!
The Stuart is for *this* so despicable,
So weak an enemy, that it would scarce
Be worth the pains to stain us with her blood!

LEICESTER. Unworthy wretch! This instant follow me
And answer at the throne your insolence!

BURLEIGH. You'll find me there, my lord, and look you well,
That now your eloquence desert you not!
Exit.

SCENE 4

LEICESTER, *alone; then* MORTIMER

LEICESTER. I am detected. All my plot's disclosed.
Alas, if he has proofs, if she should learn
That I have held a secret correspondence
With her worst enemy, how criminal
Shall I appear to her! How false will then
My counsel seem, and all the fatal pains
I took to lure the Queen to Fotheringay!
I've shamefully betrayed, I have exposed her
To her detested enemy's revilings!
All will appear as if premeditated.
The bitter turn of this sad interview,
The triumph and the tauntings of her rival,
Yes, even the murderous hand, which had prepared
A bloody, monstrous, unexpected fate,
All, all will be ascribed to my suggestions!

MORTIMER *enters, in the most violent uneasiness, and looks with apprehension round him.*

MORTIMER. My lord! Are we alone?

LEICESTER.   What seek you here?

MORTIMER. Be vigilant.

LEICESTER.   Get you away!

MORTIMER.   They know
That private conferences have been held
At Aubespine's——

LEICESTER.   What's that to me?

MORTIMER.   They know too
That the assassin——

LEICESTER.   That is your affair——
Audacious wretch! To dare to mix my name
In your detested outrage. Go! Defend
Your bloody deeds yourself!

MORTIMER.   But only hear me.

LEICESTER, *violently enraged.*
I know you not—I make no common cause
With murderers!

MORTIMER.   You will not hear me then.
I came to warn you: you too are detected.

LEICESTER. What?

MORTIMER.   Lord Burleigh went to Fotheringay
Just as the luckless deed had been attempted,
Searched with strict scrutiny the Queen's apartments,
And found there——

LEICESTER.   What?

MORTIMER.   A letter which the Queen
Had just addressed to you——

LEICESTER.   Unhappy woman!

MORTIMER. In which she calls on you to keep your word,
Renews the promise of her hand, and mentions
The picture which she sent you.

LEICESTER.   Death and hell!

MORTIMER. Lord Burleigh has the letter.

LEICESTER.   I am lost!

During the following speech of MORTIMER, LEICESTER *goes up and down, as in despair.*

MORTIMER. Improve the moment. Be beforehand with him,
And save yourself—save her! An oath can clear
Your fame: contrive excuses to avert
The worst. *I* am disarmed, can do no more.
My comrades are dispersed—to pieces fallen
Our whole confederacy. For Scotland I,
To rally such new friends as there I may.
'Tis now your turn, my lord.

LEICESTER *stops suddenly, as if resolved.* Sir, you are right.
Goes to the door, opens it, and calls.

Who waits without? Guards! Seize this wretched traitor——
To the OFFICER, *who comes in with* SOLDIERS.

—And guard him closely! A most dreadful plot
Is brought to light. I'll to Her Majesty.

MORTIMER *stands for a time petrified with wonder; collects himself soon; and follows* LEICESTER *with his looks expressive of the most sovereign contempt.*

Over my head he strides. Upon my fall
He builds the bridge of safety. Be it so.
I would not join you, no, even in death.
Life is all a scoundrel has—then keep it!

To the OFFICER OF THE GUARD, *who steps forward to seize him.*

What will you, slave of tyranny, with me?
I laugh to scorn your threatenings: I am free.
Drawing a dagger.

OFFICER. He's armed! Rush in!
They rush upon him; he defends himself.

MORTIMER, *raising his voice.* Curse and destruction
Light on you all! You have betrayed your faith,
Your God, and your true sovereign, and, false
Both to the earthly Mary and the heavenly,
Sell yourselves to a bastard!

OFFICER.   Forward! Seize him!

MORTIMER. Belovèd Queen, I could not set you free.
Yet take a lesson from me how to die.

Mary, Thou holy one, O pray for me
And take me to Thy heavenly home on high!

Stabs himself and falls into the arms of the GUARD.

SCENE 5

THE APARTMENT OF
QUEEN ELIZABETH IN THE
PALACE OF WESTMINSTER

ELIZABETH, *with a letter in her hand;* BURLEIGH

ELIZABETH. The traitor! Thus to lead me, as in triumph,
Into the presence of his paramour!

BURLEIGH. I cannot yet conceive what potent means,
What magic he exerted, to surprise
The prudence of my Queen.

ELIZABETH.   I die for shame!
I thought to humble her and was myself
The object of her bitter scorn!

BURLEIGH.   By this
You see how faithfully I counselled you.

ELIZABETH. Yes, I am sorely punished, that I turned
My ear from your wise counsels; yet I thought
I might confide in him. Who could suspect,
Beneath the vows of faithfullest devotion,
A deadly snare? Leicester, whom I have made
The greatest of the great and in this Court
Allowed to play the master and the king!

BURLEIGH. Yet in that very moment he betrayed you.

ELIZABETH. Now shall she pay me for it with her life!
Is the death warrant there?

BURLEIGH.   It is prepared
As you commanded.

ELIZABETH.   She shall surely die.
He shall behold her fall and fall himself.

Conduct him to the Tower and let him feel
In its full weight the rigour of the law.

BURLEIGH. But he will seek your presence; he will clear——

ELIZABETH. How can he clear himself? Does not the letter
Convict him? All his crimes are manifest!

BURLEIGH. But you are mild and gracious! His appearance——

ELIZABETH. I will never see him. Are orders given,
Not to admit him, should he come?

BURLEIGH. They are.

PAGE, *entering*. The Earl of Leicester!

ELIZABETH. The presumptuous man!
I will not see him. Tell him that I will not.

PAGE. I am afraid to bring my lord this message,
Nor would he credit it.

ELIZABETH. And I have raised him
So high that my own servants tremble more
At him than me!

BURLEIGH, *to the* PAGE. The Queen forbids his presence.

The PAGE *retires slowly.*

ELIZABETH, *after a pause.*
And yet, and yet, might it not be a snare
Laid by the cunning Scot to sever me
From my best friend? The ever-treacherous harlot,
She might have writ the letter just to ruin
The man she hates.

BURLEIGH. No, gracious Queen, consider——

SCENE 6

LEICESTER *bursts open the door and enters with an imperious
air.*

LEICESTER. Forbid me the apartments of my Queen!

ELIZABETH, *avoiding his sight.* Audacious slave!

LEICESTER. To turn me from the door!

If for a Burleigh she be visible
She must be so for me!

BURLEIGH.   My lord, you are
Too bold, without permission to intrude——

LEICESTER. My lord, you are too arrogant, to take
The lead in these apartments. What? Permission?

Humbly approaching ELIZABETH.

'Tis from my Sovereign's lips alone that I——

ELIZABETH, *without looking at him.*
Out of my sight, deceitful, worthless traitor!

LEICESTER. You have lent him your ear. I ask the like.

ELIZABETH. Speak, shameless wretch! Increase your crime—
deny it——

LEICESTER. Dismiss this troublesome intruder first.
Retire——!

ELIZABETH, *to* BURLEIGH. Remain, my lord; 'tis my command.

LEICESTER. What has a third to do 'twixt you and me?
I have to clear myself before my Queen,
And I insist upon it that my lord
Retire.

ELIZABETH. This haughty tone befits you well.

LEICESTER. Am not I the man to whom your favour
Has given the highest station? Then what
Your favour gave, by heavens I will maintain!

ELIZABETH. Think not with cunning words to hide the truth.

To BURLEIGH.

My lord, produce the letter.

BURLEIGH.   Here it is.

LEICESTER, *running over the letter without losing his presence
of mind.* It is the Stuart's hand——

ELIZABETH.   Read it, Lord Leicester.

LEICESTER, *having read it quietly.*
I will not by appearances be judged.

ELIZABETH. Can you deny your secret correspondence
With Mary? That *she* sent and *you* received
Her picture? That you gave her hopes?

LEICESTER.   I confess
That she has said the truth.

ELIZABETH.   Well then! You wretch!

BURLEIGH. His own words sentence him——

ELIZABETH.   Out of my sight!
Away! Conduct the traitor to the Tower!

LEICESTER. I am no traitor; it was wrong, I own,
To make a secret of this step to you.
Yet pure was my intention. It was done
To search into her plots and to confound them.

ELIZABETH. Vain subterfuge!

BURLEIGH.   And do you think, my lord——

LEICESTER. I've played a dangerous game. I know it well.
And none but Leicester dare be bold enough
To risk it at this court. The world must know
How I detest this Stuart while my rank
Must sure suffice to——

BURLEIGH.   If the course was good,
Wherefore conceal it?

LEICESTER.   You are used, my lord,
To prate before you act. That is your manner.
But mine is first to act and then to speak.

BURLEIGH. Ay, now you speak—because you must.

LEICESTER, *measuring him proudly and disdainfully with his
    eyes.*   And *you*
Boast of a wonderful, a mighty action,
That *you* have saved the Queen, have snatched away
The mask from treachery. All is known to *you*.
And yet despite your cunning, Mary Stuart
Was free today, had *I* not hindered it!

BURLEIGH. *You*, sir?

LEICESTER.   Yes, I, my lord. The Queen confided
In Mortimer: she opened to the youth
Her inmost soul. Yes, she went farther still:
She gave him too a secret bloody charge.
Say, is it so, or not?

The QUEEN *and* BURLEIGH *look at one another with astonishment.*

BURLEIGH. Whence know you this?

LEICESTER. And where, my lord, where were your thousand eyes,
Not to discover Mortimer was false?
That he, the Guise's tool, a raging Papist,
Was come to free the Stuart and to murder
The Queen of England!

ELIZABETH, *with the utmost astonishment.*
Edward Mortimer?

LEICESTER. This very day she was to have been torn
From her confinement. He this very moment
Disclosed his plan to me. I took him prisoner
And gave him to the guard, when in despair
He slew himself.

ELIZABETH. Mortimer! I have been
Deceived beyond example! Mortimer!

BURLEIGH. This happened then but now? Since last we parted?

LEICESTER. For my own sake I must lament the deed—
That he was thus cut off. His testimony,
Were he alive, had fully cleared my name.
I was surrendering him to open justice
To verify and fix my innocence
Before the world.

BURLEIGH. He killed himself, you say.
Is it so? Or did *you* kill him?

LEICESTER *goes to the door and calls.* Officer!

Enter the OFFICER OF THE GUARD.

Sir, tell the Queen how Mortimer expired.

OFFICER. I was on duty in the palace porch
When suddenly my lord threw wide the door
And ordered me to take the knight in charge,
Denouncing him a traitor. Mortimer
Straight drew a dagger out and plunged the steel
Into his heart.

The OFFICER *withdraws.*

ELIZABETH.   Abyss beneath abyss
Of monstrous deeds!

LEICESTER.   Who was it then, my Queen,
Who saved you? Was it Burleigh?

BURLEIGH.   Mortimer
Died most conveniently for *you,* my lord.

ELIZABETH. What I should say I know not. I believe you
And I believe you not. A curse on her
Who caused me all this anguish!

LEICESTER.   She must die.
I formerly advised you to suspend
The sentence till some arm was raised anew
On her behalf; and now the case has happened.

BURLEIGH. You give this counsel? You?

LEICESTER.   However it wound
My feelings to be forced to this extreme,
Yet now I see most clearly, now I *feel*
That the Queen's welfare asks this bloody victim.

BURLEIGH, *to the* QUEEN.
Since then his lordship shows such earnest zeal,
Such loyalty, 'twere well, were he appointed,
To see to the execution of the sentence.

LEICESTER. Who? I?

BURLEIGH.   Yes, you. You surely could not find
A better means to shake off the suspicion
Which rests upon you still than to command
Her, whom 'tis said you love, to be beheaded.

ELIZABETH, *looking steadfastly at* LEICESTER.
My lord advises well. So be it, then!

LEICESTER. A man who stands so near the royal person
Should have no knowledge of such fatal scenes;
But yet, to prove my zeal to satisfy
My Queen, I waive my charge's privilege.

ELIZABETH. Lord Burleigh shall partake this duty with you.
To BURLEIGH.
So: be the warrant instantly prepared.

BURLEIGH *withdraws. A tumult heard without.*

SCENE 7

Enter the EARL OF KENT

ELIZABETH. How now, my lord of Kent? What uproar's this
    I hear without?

KENT.   My Queen, it is your people,
    Who, round the palace ranged, impatiently
    Demand to see their sovereign.

ELIZABETH.   What's their wish?

KENT. A panic terror has already spread
    Through London that your life has been attempted;
    That murderers commissioned from the Pope
    Beset you; that the Catholics have sworn
    To rescue from her prison Mary Stuart,
    And to proclaim her Queen. Your loyal people
    Believe it and are mad. They want her head.

ELIZABETH. What? Will they force me then?

KENT.   They are resolved——

SCENE 8

Enter BURLEIGH *and* DAVISON, *with a paper.*

ELIZABETH. Well, Davison?

DAVISON *approaches earnestly.* Your orders are obeyed,
    My Queen——

ELIZABETH.   What orders, sir?

    *As she is about to take the paper, she shudders and starts
    back.*

                 Alas!

BURLEIGH.   Obey
    Your people's voice: it is the voice of God.

ELIZABETH. But who will give me the assurance, sir,

That what I now hear *is* the people's voice?
If I should listen to this multitude
Do I not have to fear a different voice
Will soon be heard, a different multitude?
And that the men who force me to this step
Will heavily condemn me when 'tis taken?

SCENE 9

Enter the EARL OF SHREWSBURY, *with great emotion.*

SHREWSBURY. Hold fast, my Queen, they wish to hurry you.

Seeing DAVISON *with the paper.*

Or is it then decided?

ELIZABETH.   I'm constrained——

SHREWSBURY. Who can constrain *you?* You are Queen of
    England.
Here must your majesty assert its rights:
Command those savage voices to be silent
Who take upon themselves to put constraint
Upon your royal will and rule your judgement.

BURLEIGH. Judgement has long been passed. It is not now
The time to pass, but execute the sentence.

KENT, *who, on* SHREWSBURY's *entry, had retired, comes back.*
The tumult gains apace. There are no means
To moderate the people.

ELIZABETH, *to* SHREWSBURY. See, my lord,
How they press on.

SHREWSBURY.   I only ask a respite.
A single word traced by your hand decides
The peace, the happiness of all your life.
Wait for a moment of tranquillity.

BURLEIGH, *violently.*
Wait for it—pause—delay—till flames of fire
Consume the realm—until the fifth attempt
At murder be successful! God, indeed,
Had thrice delivered you. Your late escape

Was marvellous, but to expect again
A miracle would be to tempt the Lord!

SHREWSBURY. Yet think of this. You tremble now before
The living Mary: you would tremble more
Before a murdered, a beheaded Mary.
When you have done the bloody deed, *then* go
Through London, seek your people which till now
Delighted swarmed about you: you shall see
Another London and another people.
No more the dignity of godlike justice
Will beam about you. Fear, the dread ally
Of tyranny, will march before you shuddering
And make a wilderness of every street!

ELIZABETH, *after a pause.*

I'm weary of my life and of my crown.
If heaven decree that one of us two Queens
Must perish to secure the other's life—
And sure it must be so—why should not I
Be she who yields? My people must decide:
I give them back the sovereignty they gave.
God is my witness that I have not lived
For my own sake but for my people's welfare.
If they expect from this false, fawning Stuart,
The younger sovereign, more happy days,
I will descend with pleasure from the throne
And back repair to Woodstock's quiet bowers
Where once I spent my unambitious youth
And far removed from all the vanities
Of earthly power found within myself
True majesty. I am not made to rule——

BURLEIGH. You say you love your people above yourself:
Then prove it. Choose not peace for your own heart
And leave your kingdom to the storms of discord.
Think on the church. Shall, with this Papist queen,
The ancient superstition be renewed,
The monk resume his sway, the Roman legate
In pomp march hither, lock our churches up,
Dethrone our monarchs? I demand of you

The souls of all your subjects! As you now
Shall act, they all are saved or all are lost!
A pause.

ELIZABETH. I would be left alone. I'll lay my doubts
Before the Judge of all. I am resolved
To act as He shall teach. Withdraw, my lords.
To DAVISON, *who lays the paper on the table.*
You, sir, remain in waiting, close at hand.
The LORDS *withdraw.* SHREWSBURY *alone stands for a few
moments before the* QUEEN, *regards her significantly, then
withdraws slowly and with an expression of the deepest
anguish.*

SCENE 10

ELIZABETH, *alone*

ELIZABETH. O servitude of popularity!
Disgraceful slavery! How weary am I
Of flattering this idol which my soul
Despises in its inmost depth! O when
Shall I once more be free upon this throne?
I must respect the people's voice and strive
To win the favour of the multitude
And please the fancies of a mob, whom nought
But jugglers' tricks delight. Do not call him
A king, who needs must please the world about him.
But have I practised justice all my life
Only to bind my hands against this first
Unavoidable act of violence?
Had I but been a tyrant, like my sister,
My predecessor, I could fearless then
Have shed this royal blood, but am I now
Just by my own free choice? No, I am forced
By stern necessity to use this virtue,
Necessity which binds even monarchs' wills.
Surrounded by my foes, my people's love

Alone supports me on my envied throne.
All Europe's powers confederate to attack me;
The Pope declares me excommunicate;
While France betrays me with a kiss; and Spain
Prepares a great Armada to destroy me.
Thus stand I in contention with the world,
A poor defenceless woman. I must now
Remove the stain in my imperial birth
By which my father cast disgrace upon me.
In vain with princely virtues would I hide it:
My enemies uncover it again.

Walking up and down, with quick and agitated steps.

The hated name of every ill I feel
Is Mary Stuart. Were she but no more
On earth, I should be free as mountain air.

Standing still.

With what disdain did she look down on me!

Advancing to the table hastily and taking the pen.

I am a bastard, am I? Hapless wretch,
Your death will make my birth legitimate.

*She signs with resolution; then lets her pen fall: and steps
back with an expression of terror. After a pause, she rings.*

SCENE 11

ELIZABETH, DAVISON

ELIZABETH. Where are their lordships?

DAVISON.   They are gone to quell
The tumult of the people. The alarm
Was instantly appeased when they beheld
The Earl of Shrewsbury. "That's he!" exclaimed
A hundred voices. "That's the man—he saved
The Queen. Hear *him*—the bravest man in England!"
And now began the gallant Talbot, blamed
In gentle words the people's violence
And used such strong, persuasive eloquence

That all were pacified and silently
They slunk away.

ELIZABETH.   The fickle multitude!
Which turns with every wind. Unhappy he
Who leans upon this reed!

As he is going towards the door.

                        And, sir, this paper,
Receive it back; I place it in your hands.

DAVISON *casts a look upon the paper and starts back.*
My gracious Queen—your name! 'Tis then decided.

ELIZABETH. I had but to subscribe it—I have done so—
A paper sure cannot decide—a name
Kills not——

DAVISON.   Your name, my Queen, beneath this paper
Is most decisive—kills. This fatal scroll
Commands the Sheriff and Commissioners
To take departure straight for Fotheringay
And to the Queen of Scots announce her death
Which must at dawn be put in execution.
As soon as I have parted with this writ
Her race is run——

ELIZABETH.   Yes, sir, the Lord has placed
This weighty business in your feeble hands;
Seek Him in prayer, to light you with His wisdom.
I go, and leave you, sir, to do your duty.
Going.

DAVISON. But leave me not till I have heard your will.
Say, have you placed this warrant in my hands
To see that it be speedily enforced?

ELIZABETH. That you must do, as your own prudence dictates.

DAVISON, *interrupting her quickly, and alarmed.*
Permit me, in this weighty act, to be
Your passive instrument, without a will.
Tell me in plain undoubted terms your pleasure.

ELIZABETH. Its name declares its meaning.

DAVISON.   Do you, then,
My liege, command its instant execution?

ELIZABETH. I said not that; I tremble but to think it.

DAVISON. Shall I retain it, then, till further orders?

ELIZABETH. At your own risk; you answer the event.

DAVISON. I! Gracious Heavens!—— O speak, my Queen, your
  pleasure!

ELIZABETH. My pleasure is that this unhappy business
  Be no more mentioned to me! That at last
  I may be freed from it, and that forever!

DAVISON. What shall I do with this mysterious scroll?

ELIZABETH. I have declared it. Plague me, sir, no longer.

DAVISON. You have declared it, say you? But, my Queen,
  You have said nothing——

ELIZABETH *stamps on the ground.* Insupportable!
  Exit.

SCENE 12

DAVISON, *then* BURLEIGH

DAVISON. She goes. She leaves me. How to act I know not.
  Should I retain it? Should I forward it?
  To BURLEIGH, *who enters.*
  Oh, I am glad that you are come, my lord.

BURLEIGH. The Queen was with you.

DAVISON.   She has quitted me
  In bitter anger. Pray advise me, help me,
  Save me from this fell agony of doubt.
  My lord, here is the warrant: it is signed.

BURLEIGH. Indeed? Indeed? Then give it me!

DAVISON.   I may not.

BURLEIGH. What?

DAVISON.   She has not yet explained her final will.

BURLEIGH. Explained! She has subscribed it. Give it me.

DAVISON. I am to execute it and I am not.

Great Heavens, I know not what I am to do!

BURLEIGH, *urging more violently*

It must be now, this moment, executed—
The warrant, sir. You're lost if you delay.

DAVISON. So am I also if I act too rashly.

BURLEIGH. What strange infatuation! Give it me!

Snatches the paper from him, and exit with it.

DAVISON. What would you? Stop! You will be my destruction!

ACT V

SCENE 1

THE SCENE IS THE SAME AS IN ACT I

HANNAH KENNEDY, *in deep mourning, her eyes still red from weeping, in great but quiet anguish is employed in sealing letters and parcels. Her sorrow often interrupts her occupation, and she is seen at such intervals to pray in silence.* PAULET, *also in mourning, enters, followed by many* SERVANTS, *who bear golden and silver vessels, mirrors, paintings, and other valuables, and fill the back part of the stage with them.* PAULET *delivers to the* NURSE *a box of jewels and a paper and seems to inform her by signs that it contains the inventory of the effects the Queen had brought with her. At the sight of these riches, the anguish of the* NURSE *is renewed. She sinks into a deep melancholy, during which* PAULET *and the* SERVANTS *silently retire.*

MELVIL *enters.*

KENNEDY *screams as soon as she observes him.*
  Melvil! Can it be you I see again?

MELVIL. Yes, faithful Kennedy, we meet once more.

KENNEDY. You come——?

MELVIL.   To take an everlasting leave.

KENNEDY. And now at length, now on the fatal morn
  Which brings her death, they grant our royal lady
  The presence of her friends.

MELVIL.   Restrain your grief,
  And when the rest give way to tears we two
  Will lead her with heroic resolution
  And be her staff upon the road to death!

KENNEDY. Melvil, you are deceived if you suppose
  The Queen has need of our support to meet

Her death with firmness. She it is, my friend,
Who will exhibit the undaunted heart.

MELVIL. Received she firmly, then, the sad decree
Of death? 'Tis said that she was not prepared.

KENNEDY. Freedom was promised us. This very night
Had Mortimer engaged to bear us hence.
And thus the Queen, perplexed 'twixt hope and fear,
Sat waiting for the morning. On a sudden
Our ears are startled by repeated blows
Of many hammers, and we think we hear
The approach of our deliverers. Then suddenly
The portals are thrown open. It is Paulet
Who comes to tell us that the carpenters
Erect beneath our feet the murderous scaffold.
She turns aside, overpowered by anguish.

MELVIL. How bore the Queen this terrible affliction?

KENNEDY, *after a pause in which she has somewhat collected
herself.* Not by degrees can we relinquish life.
Quick, sudden, in the twinkling of an eye
The separation must be made, and God
Imparted to our mistress at that moment
His grace, to cast away each earthly hope
And, firm and full of faith, to mount the skies.

MELVIL. Where is she now? Can you not lead me to her?

KENNEDY. She spent the last remainder of the night
In prayer, and from her dearest friends she took
Her last farewell in writing. Then she wrote
Her will with her own hand.

MELVIL.   Who attends her?

KENNEDY. None but her women and physician Burgoyne.

SCENE 2

Enter MARGARET CURL.

KENNEDY. How, madam, fares the Queen? Is she awake?

MARGARET CURL, *drying her tears.*
She is already dressed—she asks for you.

KENNEDY, *to* MELVIL, *who seems to wish to accompany her.*
Follow me not, good Melvil, till the Queen
Has been prepared to see you.

Exit.

MARGARET CURL.   Melvil? You're
The ancient steward?

MELVIL.   Yes.

MARGARET CURL.   My name is Curl.

A pause.

You come from London, sir. Can you give me
No tidings of my husband?

MELVIL.   It is said
He will be set at liberty as soon——

MARGARET CURL. As soon as our dear Queen shall be no more!
He is our lady's murderer. They say
It was his testimony which condemned her.

MELVIL. That is so.

MARGARET CURL. Curse him! He has borne false witness!

MELVIL. Think, madam, what you say.

MARGARET CURL.   I will maintain it
With every sacred oath before the court!
I will repeat it in his face! I say
That she dies innocent!

MELVIL.   God grant it true!

SCENE 3

Enter BURGOYNE, *followed by* HANNAH KENNEDY.

BURGOYNE. Melvil!

MELVIL.   Burgoyne!

They silently embrace.

BURGOYNE, *to* MARGARET CURL. Go fetch a cup of wine.
'Tis for our lady.

Exit MARGARET CURL.

MELVIL. Is Queen Mary sick?

BURGOYNE. Deceived by the sublimity of courage
She thinks she has no need of nourishment.
I would not give her enemies that triumph
To say that it was fear that blanched her cheek.

MELVIL. May I approach her now?

KENNEDY. She'll come herself.

SCENE 4

Enter two WOMEN OF THE CHAMBER *weeping, and in deep mourning.*

FIRST WOMAN. She has sent us from her——

SECOND WOMAN. Bade us leave her
Alone. She is communing with her God.

SCENE 5

Enter MARGARET CURL, *bearing a golden cup of wine. She places it hastily upon the table and leans, pale and trembling, against a chair.*

MELVIL. How, madam? What has frightened you?

BURGOYNE. Speak, madam!

MARGARET CURL. As I went down the staircase which conducts
To the great hall below, a door stood open——
O Heaven!

MELVIL. What saw you?

MARGARET CURL. All the walls were hung
With black. A spacious scaffold overspread
With sable cloth was raised above the floor,
And in the middle of the scaffold stood
A dreadful sable block. Upon it lay
A naked, polished axe. The hall was full
Of cruel people crowding round the scaffold,

Who, with a horrid thirst for human blood,
Seemed waiting for the victim.

MELVIL.   She approaches.

SCENE 6

Enter MARY *in white and sumptuously arrayed, as for a festival. She wears, hanging from her neck on a row of small beads, an Agnus Dei; a rosary hangs from her girdle; she bears a crucifix in her hand and a diadem of precious stones binds her hair; her large black veil is thrown back. On her entrance, all present fall back on both sides with the most violent expressions of anguish.* MELVIL *falls involuntarily upon his knees.*

MARY, *with quiet majesty, looking round the whole circle.*
Why these complaints? Why do you weep? You should
Rejoice with me that now at length the end
Of my long woe approaches; that my shackles
Fall off, my prison opens, and my soul,
Delighted, mounts on seraph's wings and seeks
The land of everlasting liberty.
Then do not weep. Death is a helpful friend.
The foulest criminal's ennobled by his
Sufferings. Now I feel the crown upon
My brows, and dignity possess my soul.

Advancing a few steps.

What? Melvil here? My worthy sir, not so;
Arise. You rather come in time to see
The triumph of your mistress than her death.
How have you fared, sir, in this hostile land?

MELVIL. No other evil galled me but my grief
For you and that I wanted power to serve you.

MARY. Sir, to your loyal bosom I commit
My latest wishes. Bear then, sir, my blessing
To the most Christian king, my royal brother.
I bless the Cardinal, my honoured uncle.
I bless the Holy Father, the Vicegerent

Of Christ on earth, who will, I trust, bless me.
They are remembered in my will, good Melvil.

Turning to her servants.

I have bequeathed you to my royal brother
Of France who will give you another home.
Swear by this image of our suffering Lord
To leave this fatal land when I'm no more.

MELVIL, *touching the crucifix.*

I swear obedience in the name of all.

MARY. What I still possess be shared among you,
And what I wear upon the way to death!

To the LADIES OF HER CHAMBER.

To Alice, Gertrude, Rosamund, I leave
My clothes, my pearls, my trinkets. Margaret,
That I have not avenged your husband's fault
On you I hope my legacy will prove.
My memory will be to you, my Hannah,
The dearest jewel. Take this handkerchief.
I worked it for you, Hannah. You will bind
My eyes with it when it is time. Now come!

She stretches forth her hands; the women violently weeping, fall successively at her feet, and kiss her outstretched hand.

Margaret, farewell. My Alice, fare thee well.
Thanks, Burgoyne, for your honest faithful service.
Gertrude, your lips are hot. I too was loved.
May a deserving husband bless my Gertrude!
Bertha, you have made the better choice of heaven.
So haste you to fulfil your vows. The goods
Of earth are all deceitful. You may learn
This lesson from your Queen. No more. Farewell,
Farewell, farewell, my friends, farewell forever.

She turns suddenly from them; all but MELVIL *retire at different sides.*

SCENE 7

MARY, MELVIL

MARY, *after the others are all gone.*
Melvil, one thought alone there is which binds
My troubled soul nor suffers it to fly
Delighted and at liberty to heaven.

MELVIL. Disclose it to me. Ease your bosom, madam.

MARY. A priest of my religion is denied me.
And I disdain to take the sacrament
From priests of a false faith. I die believing
In my own church, for she alone can save.

MELVIL. Compose your heart. The fervent, pious wish
Is prized in heaven as high as the performance.
The word is dead. 'Tis faith which brings to life.

MARY. Our faith must have some earthly pledge to ground
Its claims to the high bliss of heaven. For this
Our God became incarnate and inclosed
Mysteriously his unseen heavenly grace
Within the outward figure of a body.
Ah, happy they, who for the glad communion
Of pious prayer, meet in the house of God!
The altar is adorned, the tapers blaze,
The bell invites, the incense soars on high,
The bishop stands enrobed, he takes the cup
And, blessing it, declares the mystery,
The transformation of the elements,
While the believing people fall delighted
To worship and adore the present Godhead.
Alas, that I should be debarred from this.

MELVIL. The withered staff can send forth verdant branches,
And he who from the rock called living water
Can change——
Seizing the cup, which stands upon the table.
                    ——the earthly contents of this cup

Into a substance of celestial grace!

MARY. Melvil! Oh yes, I understand you, Melvil!
Here is no priest, no church, no sacrament.
But the Redeemer says: "When two or three
Are in my name assembled, I am with them."

MELVIL. You err. Here *is* a priest—here *is* a God.
A God descends to you in real presence.

*At these words he uncovers his tonsured head and shows a
Host in a golden vessel.*

I am a priest, O Queen, I have received
Upon my head the seven consecrations.
I bring you from His Holiness this Host
Which he himself has deigned to bless for you.

MARY. As an immortal one on golden clouds
Descends, as once the angel from on high
Delivered the Apostle from his fetters—
He scorns all bars, he scorns the soldier's sword,
He steps undaunted through the bolted portals,
And fills the dungeon with his native glory—
So here the messenger of heaven appears
When every earthly champion had deceived me.

She sinks before him on her knees.

MELVIL, *making over her the sign of the cross.*
Hear, Mary Queen of Scotland. In the name
Of God the Father, Son, and Holy Ghost,
Do you swear in your confession here before me
To speak the truth before the God of truth?

MARY. Before my God and you my heart lies open.

MELVIL. Declare the sin which weighs so heavily
Upon your conscience since your last confession.

MARY. I hope forgiveness of my sins from God,
Yet could I not forgive my enemy.

MELVIL. Do you repent the sin? Are you, in sooth,
Resolved to leave this world at peace with all?

MARY. As surely as I wish the joys of heaven.

MELVIL. What other sin has armed your heart against you?

MARY. My heart was vainly turned towards the man
Who left me in misfortune, who deceived me.

MELVIL. Do you repent the sin? And have you turned
Your heart from this idolatry to God?

MARY. It was the hardest trial I have passed:
This last of earthly bonds is torn asunder.

MELVIL. What other sin disturbs your guilty conscience?

MARY. By my connivance fell the King, my husband.
I gave my hand and heart to a seducer.
By rigid penance I have made atonement,
Yet in my soul the worm is gnawing still.

MELVIL. And has your heart no other accusation
Which has not been confessed and washed away?

MARY. You have heard all with which my heart is charged.

MELVIL. Think on the punishments with which the church
Threatens imperfect and reserved confession:
This is the sin to everlasting death.

MARY. I have hid nothing.

MELVIL.   Will you then conceal
From God the crime for which you are condemned?
You tell me nothing of the share you had
In Parry's treason and in Babington's!

MARY. Within the narrow limits of an hour
I shall appear before my Judge's throne:
But, I repeat it, my confession's ended.

MELVIL. Consider well. The heart is a deceiver.
You have perhaps, with sly equivocation,
The *word* avoided which would make you guilty
Although your *will* was party to the crime.

MARY. I swear that, neither by intent nor deed,
Have I attempted my oppressor's life.

MELVIL. Your secretaries must have witnessed falsely!

MARY. It is as I have said. What they have witnessed
The Lord will judge.

MELVIL.   Then, satisfied of your
Own innocence, you mount the fatal scaffold?

MARY. God in his mercy lets me now atone
　My youth's misdeeds by undeservèd death.

MELVIL, *making over her the sign of the cross.*
　Sink a devoted victim on the altar:
　Thus shall your blood atone the blood you spilt.
　And so, by the authority which God
　Hath unto me committed, I absolve you
　From all your sins. Be as your faith your welfare!

　He gives her the Host.

　Receive the body which for you was offered.

　*He takes the cup which stands upon the table, consecrates
　it with silent prayer, then presents it to her.*

　Receive the blood which for your sins was shed.

　She takes the cup.

　So may you henceforth, in His realm of joy,
　A fair transfigured spirit, join yourself
　Forever with the Godhead and forever!

　*He sets down the cup; hearing a noise, he covers his head
　and goes to the door;* MARY *remains in silent devotion on
　her knees.* MELVIL, *returning.*

　Have you the strength to smother every impulse
　Of malice and of hate?

MARY.   I have to God
　Devoted both my hatred and my love.

MELVIL. Prepare then to receive my lords of Burleigh
　And of Leicester.

SCENE 8

Enter BURLEIGH, LEICESTER, *and* PAULET. LEICESTER *remains in the background, without raising his eyes;* BURLEIGH,
*who remarks his confusion, steps between him and the
Queen.*

BURLEIGH.   I come, my Lady Stuart,
　To receive your last commands.

ARY.   Thanks, my lord.

My will declares my last desires on earth:
I've placed it in Sir Amias Paulet's hands
And humbly beg that it may be fulfilled.

PAULET. You may rely on that.

MARY.   I beg that all
My servants unmolested may return
To France or Scotland as their wishes lead.

BURLEIGH. It shall be as you wish.

MARY.   And since my body
Is not to rest in consecrated ground,
I pray you suffer this my faithful servant
To bear my heart to France.

BURLEIGH.   It shall be done.
What wishes else?

MARY.   Unto Her Majesty
Of England bear a sister's salutation.
Tell her I pardon her my death, repent
The passion of my speech to her. God save
The Queen!

BURLEIGH.   You still refuse the dean's assistance?

MARY. My lord, my peace with God is made.

To PAULET.

Good sir,
I have unwittingly caused you much sorrow:
Your nephew was your age's only stay—

PAULET, *giving her his hand.*
Go your way in peace! The Lord be with you!

SCENE 9

HANNAH KENNEDY *and* QUEEN MARY'S *other women crowd
into the room with marks of horror. The* SHERIFF *follows
them, a white staff in his hand. Behind are seen, through
the open doors, men under arms.*

MARY. What ails you, Hannah? Yes, my hour is come.

The Sheriff's here to lead me to my fate,
And part we must. Farewell!

KENNEDY *and* MARGARET CURL. We will not leave you!
We will not part from you!

MARY, *to* MELVIL. You, worthy sir,
And my dear faithful Hannah, shall attend me.

BURLEIGH. For this I have no warrant.

MARY. How, my lord?

BURLEIGH. 'Tis ordered that no woman shall ascend
The scaffold steps with you. Their tears and moans——

MARY. She bore me on her arms into this life,
Let her then gently lead me to my death.
She shall not weep, my lord, she shall not moan.

PAULET, *to* BURLEIGH. Yield to her wishes.

BURLEIGH. Be it so.

MARY. I now
Have nothing in this world to wish for more.

She takes the crucifix and kisses it.

As once Thy arms were stretched upon the cross,
Let them be now extended to receive me!

*She turns round to go. At the same moment her eyes fall
upon* LEICESTER, *who, on her going, starts involuntarily and
turns his eyes towards her. At this sight* MARY *trembles, her
knees fail her, she is about to fall, when* LEICESTER *catches
at her and receives her in his arms. She regards him for
some time earnestly and in silence. He cannot support her
looks. At length she speaks.*

You keep your word, my lord of Leicester. For
You promised me your arm to lead me forth
From prison and you lend it to me now
As now I leave these dismal halls forever.
All is fulfilled, and you have saved your honour.

*He stands as if annihilated; she continues, with a gentle
voice.*

Led by your hand and happy in your love,
I hoped once more to taste the joys of life.
Yes, Leicester, I may venture to confess

Without a blush the frailty I have conquered.
Farewell, my lord, and, if you can, be happy!
To woo two queens has been your daring aim.
You have disdained a tender, loving heart,
Betrayed it, in the hope to win a proud one.
Kneel at the feet of Queen Elizabeth.
May your reward not prove your punishment!
Farewell: I now have nothing more on earth.

She goes, preceded by the SHERIFF, *at her side* MELVIL *and her* NURSE. BURLEIGH *and* PAULET *follow. The others, wailing, follow her with their eyes till she disappears; they then retire through the other two doors.*

SCENE 10

LEICESTER, *remaining alone.*
She's gone, a spirit purged from earthly stain,
And the despair of hell remains for me!
Where is the purpose now with which I came
To see her head descend upon the block
With unaverted and indifferent eyes?
How does her presence wake my slumbering shame?
Must she in death surround me with love's toils?
Lost, wretched man! No more it suits you now
To melt away in womanly compassion!
Pity be dumb! Mine eyes be petrified!
I'll see! I *will* be witness of her fall!

He advances with resolute steps towards the door through which MARY *passed; but stops suddenly halfway.*

I cannot see her die. Hark! What was that?
They are already there. Beneath my feet
The bloody business is preparing. Hark!
I hear their voices. Hence! Away, away!

He attempts to escape by another door, finds it locked, and returns.

How? Does some demon chain me to this spot
To hear what I would shudder to behold?

That voice—it is the dean's, exhorting her—
She interrupts him—— Hark! She prays aloud.
Her voice is firm. Now all is still, quite still,
And sobs and women's moans are all I hear.
Now they undress her—they remove the stool—
She kneels upon the cushion—lays her head——

*Having spoken these last words and paused awhile, he is
seen with a convulsive motion suddenly to shrink and faint
away. A confused hum of voices is heard at the same moment from below and continues for some time.*

SCENE 11

THE APARTMENT OF QUEEN ELIZABETH
(AS IN THE SECOND PART OF ACT IV)

ELIZABETH, *entering from a side door, her gait and action ex-
pressive of the most violent uneasiness.*
No message yet? And no one here? O God,
Will evening never come? Stands the sun still?
Is it accomplished?—— Is it not?—— I shudder
At both events and do not dare to ask.
My lord of Leicester comes not—— Nor Lord Burleigh———
Who's there?

SCENE 12

Enter a PAGE.

ELIZABETH.   Returned alone? Where are the lords?
PAGE. My Lord High Treasurer and the Earl of Leicester——
ELIZABETH. Where are they?
PAGE.   They are not in London.
ELIZABETH.   No?
Where are they then?
PAGE.   That no one could inform me.

Before the dawn, mysteriously, in haste,
They quitted London.

ELIZABETH, *exultingly*. I am Queen of England!

Walking up and down in the greatest agitation.

Go—— Call me—— No, remain, boy! She is dead.
Now have I room upon the earth at last.
Why do I shake? And whence the dread? The grave
Covers my fears. Who dares say I did it?
I have enough tears left to weep her fall.

To the PAGE.

Command my secretary Davison
To come to me this instant. Let the Earl
Of Shrewsbury be called. But here he comes.

Exit PAGE.

SCENE 13

Enter SHREWSBURY.

ELIZABETH. Welcome, my noble lord. What tidings? Speak!

SHREWSBURY. My liege, the doubts that hung upon my heart
Directed me this morning to the Tower,
Where Mary's secretaries, Curl and Nau,
Are now confined as prisoners, for I wished
Once more to put their evidence to proof.
On my arrival the lieutenant seemed
Embarrassed and perplexed; refused to show me
His prisoners. But my threats obtained admittance.
With hair dishevelled, on his pallet lay
This Curl, like one tormented by a fury.
The miserable man no sooner saw me
Than at my feet he fell and there with screams
Implored, conjured me to acquaint him with
His sovereign's destiny, for vague reports
Had somehow reached the dungeons of the Tower
That she had been condemned to suffer death.
When I confirmed these tidings, adding too

That on his evidence she had been doomed,
He started wildly up, caught by the throat
His comrade Nau, with the giant strength
Of madness tore him to the ground and tried
To strangle him. No sooner had we saved
The wretch from his fierce grapple than at once
He turned his rage against himself and beat
His breast with savage fists, and cursed himself.
Curl's evidence was false; the fatal letters
To Babington which he had sworn were true
He now denounced as forgeries. For he
Had set down words the Queen had never spoken;
The traitor Nau had led him to this treason.
Then ran he to the casement, threw it wide
With frantic force, and cried into the street
So loud that all the people gathered round:
"I am the man, Queen Mary's secretary,
The traitor who accused his mistress falsely!
I bore false witness and am cursed forever!"

ELIZABETH. You said yourself that he had lost his wits.
A madman's words prove nothing.

SHREWSBURY.   Yet this madness
Serves in itself to swell the proof. My liege,
Give order for a new inquiry!

ELIZABETH.   Sir,
To set your mind at rest, the inquiry shall
Be straight renewed. Well that 'tis not too late!

SCENE 14

Enter DAVISON.

ELIZABETH. The sentence, sir, which I but late entrusted
Unto your keeping—— Where is it?

DAVISON, *in the utmost astonishment.* The sentence!

ELIZABETH, *more urgent.*
Which yesterday I gave into your charge.

DAVISON. Into my charge, my liege!

ELIZABETH.   The people urged
And baited me to sign it. I perforce
Was driven to yield obedience to their will.
To gain time was my purpose. You remember
What then I told you. Now, the paper, sir!

SHREWSBURY. Restore it, sir, affairs have changed since then.
The inquiry must be set on foot anew.

DAVISON. Anew! Eternal mercy!

ELIZABETH.   Why this pause,
This hesitation? Where, sir, is the paper?

DAVISON. I have it not!

ELIZABETH.   What? What, sir?

SHREWSBURY.   God in heaven!

DAVISON. It is in Burleigh's hands—since yesterday.

ELIZABETH. Did I not lay my strict injunction on you
To keep it carefully?

DAVISON.   No such injunction
Was laid on me, my liege——

ELIZABETH.   Give me the lie?
Opprobrious wretch! When did I order you
To give the paper into Burleigh's hands?

DAVISON. Never, expressly—in so many words——

ELIZABETH. If evil come of this officious deed
Your life shall answer the event to me.
Earl Shrewsbury, you see how my good name
Has been abused.

SHREWSBURY.   I see. Would I did not!

SCENE 15

Enter BURLEIGH.

BURLEIGH, *bowing his knee before the* QUEEN.
Long life and glory to my royal mistress,
And may all enemies of her dominions
End like this Stuart!

SHREWSBURY *hides his face.* DAVISON *wrings his hands in despair.*

ELIZABETH.   Speak, my lord. Did you
From me receive the warrant?

BURLEIGH.   No, my Queen;
From Davison.

ELIZABETH.   And did he in my name
Deliver it?

BURLEIGH.   No, that I cannot say.

ELIZABETH. Just was the sentence; we are free from blame
Before the world. Yet it behoved you not
To intercept our natural clemency.
For this, my lord, I banish you my presence.

Exit BURLEIGH.

To DAVISON.

For, you, sir, who have traitorously betrayed
A sacred pledge entrusted to your care
A more severe tribunal is prepared:
Let him be straight conducted to the Tower,
And capital arraignments filed against him.

DAVISON *is led away.*

My honest Talbot, you alone have proved,
Of all my counsellors, an upright man:
You shall henceforward be my guide, my friend.

SHREWSBURY. Oh, banish not the truest of your friends
Nor cast those into prison who for you
Have acted, who for you are silent now!
And suffer me, great Queen, to give the seal
Which these twelve years I've borne unworthily
Back to your royal hands and take my leave.

ELIZABETH, *surprised.*
No, Shrewsbury. You surely would not now
Desert me? No, not now!

SHREWSBURY.   Pardon. I am
Too old, and this right hand is grown too stiff
To set the seal upon your later deeds.

ELIZABETH. Will he forsake me who has saved my life?

SHREWSBURY. 'Tis little I have done; I could not save
Your nobler part. Live, Queen! Henceforth you have
Nothing more to fear, need stop at nothing.

Exit.

ELIZABETH, *to the* EARL OF KENT, *who enters.*
Send for the Earl of Leicester.

KENT.   He desires
To be excused. He is embarked for France.

PENTHESILEA

A TRAGEDY

Heinrich von Kleist

(1808)

English Version by Humphry Trevelyan

CHARACTERS

PENTHESILEA, *Queen of the Amazons*

PROTHOE
MEROE   } *Amazon Princesses*
ASTERIA

THE HIGH PRIESTESS OF DIANA

ACHILLES
ODYSSEUS
DIOMEDE   } *Grecian Kings*
ANTILOCHUS

GREEKS *and* AMAZONS

SCENE: *a Battlefield near Troy*

Enter ODYSSEUS *and* DIOMEDE *from one side,* ANTILOCHUS
from the other, with attendant SOLDIERS.

ANTILOCHUS. Greetings, great chiefs! Tell me now how things
    go
  Since last we met before the walls of Troy?

ODYSSEUS. Badly, Antilochus. You see upon this field
  The armies of the Greeks and Amazons
  Locked in dread conflict like two rav'ning wolves.
  And, by the gods, neither can tell the cause!
  If Mars in anger, or our lord Apollo,
  Do not restrain them, or the Thunderer
  With levin-bolts do not divide the hosts,
  They die, in hate inseparable,
  The fangs of either deep in other's throat.

To a SOLDIER.

  Bring me a helmet full of water, friend!

ANTILOCHUS. These Amazons—what do they want of us?

ODYSSEUS. At Agamemnon's word we started out
  With the whole company of the Myrmidons,
  I and Achilles; for 'twas said that she,
  Penthesilea, from her Scythian forests
  Had broken out as leader of a host
  Of Amazons, in scaly snakeskins clad,
  All hot with battle-lust, and fast approaching
  Through mountain tracks to raise the siege of Troy.
  Scamander's bank scarce reached, we hear yet more:
  Deiphobus, old Priam's son, with an arm'd power
  Has left the Trojan stronghold with intent
  To seek the Queen in friendship and to greet
  Her who brings help. We, hearing this, devour
  The dusty miles in hope to plant ourselves
  Between the dread alliance of such foes;
  All night we march, hasting o'er winding tracks.

Yet as the dawn comes creeping up the sky
Amazement seizes us, Antilochus;
For there in the wide valley at our feet
Fiercely engaged with all the Trojan force
We see the Amazons! Penthesilea,
As storm winds sweep and rend the scudding wrack,
Tumbles the fleeing Trojans down the vale
As though her only thought across the Hellespont,
Ay, off earth's orb itself, to scatter them.

ANTILOCHUS. Strange, by my soul!

ODYSSEUS.   We quickly close our ranks
To meet the Trojan rout which falls upon us
Thund'ring, a torrent, and to hurl it back;
Our spear points make a wall against the foe.
At sight of this Deiphobus stops short,
And we in panting council soon decide
To greet the Amazon queen as our ally;
The while she too halts her triumphant course.
Could there be better or more obvious counsel?
Pallas herself, if I had asked her mind,
Could she have spoke more sensibly and well?
By Mars, she must, this virgin Queen, she must—
Falling from heav'n thus sudden, fully armed,
Plump in the middle of our quarrel—she
Must seek her friends on this side or on that;
And we may well believe her friend to us
Since to the Trojans she is patent foe.

ANTILOCHUS. What else? She has no other choice.

ODYSSEUS.   Very well!
Great Peleus' son and I—we find her there
The Scythian queen, in war's rich panoply,
Short-kilted, at the head of all her host
Immobile; from her crest the plume waves free;
And still her palfrey, tossing with eager head
His gold and crimson tassels, stamps the ground.
A moment long with blank, unseeing eye,
Expressionless, she looks into our ranks
As though mere blocks of stone we stood before her.
My bare palm here, this flat unseeing hand

Has more expression than her face then had.
Till suddenly her eye falls on Achilles,
And in a trice her brow, her cheeks, her throat
Are flushed with gules, as though the whole world round
At sight of him had sunk in leaping flame.
Then with a sudden spasm swings herself
—The while she darkly glances on Achilles—
Down from her horse, leaving with careless hand
Her reins to an attendant, and inquires
Why with such pomp and state we do approach her.
To which I then: that we were wondrous glad
To meet in arms so doughty a foe of Troy;
What hatred long burned in the Grecian's breast
Against the sons of Priam; how opportune
To her and us a sure alliance could be;
And what more in such strain the moment taught.
Yet with amazement, in mid flood of my speech,
I see she does not heed me, turns away,
Her face lit up with eager wonderment
(Like any silly girl, scarce yet sixteen,
Whose head is turned by some Olympic victor),
And to a friend who stands beside her, calls:
"Oh, such a man as this, dear Prothoe,
My mother, Otrere, never can have seen!"
Her friend, shamefaced, astonished, holds her peace,
While we exchange in wonder laughing glances.
And she herself, unconscious, infatuate,
Stands drinking in the Peleid's gleaming form;
Until her friend reminds her timidly
That she still owes an answer to my words.
She then, her mantling cheek, with rage or shame,
Ruddying her harness even to the waist,
Confus'dly, proudly, almost wildly, turns
To me and cries: "I am Penthesilea,
Queen of the Amazons, too soon ye shall
Have wingèd answer from our Scythian bows."

ANTILOCHUS. So word for word your messenger reported,
   Yet no one of us in the Grecian camp
   Could see what this——

ODYSSEUS.   We now still ignorant

What from this strange retort we might expect,
In shame and fury turn to regain our ranks,
The while the Trojans, who with mocking glee
Have marked all our discomfiture from far,
Triumphant stand; and soon, mistakenly
Deeming themselves the favour'd ones, and that
Some error merely, soon to be put right,
Had loosed on them the fury of this maid,
Resolve through herald's voice to offer her
Once more their heart and hand, which she had scorned.
Yet e'er the herald, chosen to this task,
Had shak'n the dust from armour and from arms,
Crashes upon us both, Trojan and Greek,
This centaur queen with all her reckless band,
Like mountain torrent's headlong, swirling flood
Sweeping both us and them to utter wrack.

ANTILOCHUS. Incredible, my friends!

ODYSSEUS.   There then begins
A struggle such as never yet was seen
Since hate began, upon the fields of Earth.
Each force in Nature, creates its opposite
And fights with this; no room for any third.
What quenches fire will not make water boil
And turn to steam; likewise the opposite.
Yet here appears a deadly foe of both,
That makes fire doubt: should it not flow like water?
And water: should it haply burn like fire?
The hard-press'd Trojan, fleeing the Amazon
Shelters behind a Grecian shield; the Greek
Defends him from the maiden's blade, and both
Trojan and Greek are almost forced, despite
The rape of Helen, to hold each other friends
And join to fight a common enemy.

A Greek brings him water.

Thanks, friend! A grateful draught.

DIOMEDE.   From that day on
The battle rolls unceasing on these plains,
Its slack'ning rage ever again renew'd,
Like to a grumbling thunderstorm hemm'd in

By mountain peaks. But yesterday as I
Brought rested pow'rs to stay the fainting Greeks,
She was in act to cleave our wav'ring ranks
As with intent to smite the whole Greek race
And lay it, root and branch, forever low.
The noblest boughs, Astyanax, Ariston,
Lie scattered by the storm—Menander too—
The grace and loveliness of their young limbs
But dung about the roots of that high laurel
That grows for her, the dreaded daughter of Mars.
And prisoners she has victorious taken
More than she leaves us eyes to mark their loss
Or valiant arms to fight for their release.

ANTILOCHUS. But what she wants of us—is that still dark?

DIOMEDE. Quite dark—that is the strangest—cast where'er
We will the lead line of our searching thought.
Sometimes, to judge by that unnatural rage
With which she seeks in every broil the son
Of Thetis, we have deemed her heart was full
Of some especial hatred for his person.
Not more untiringly the rav'ning she-wolf
Pursues through snow-lapped forests still her prey
That she has marked her with gaunt, hungry eye,
Than throughout all our battle she Achilles.
Yet lately once, when for a moment's time
She held his life within her blood-stained hand,
Smiling she gave it him again; in truth
He stood on Lethe bank, had she not held him.

ANTILOCHUS. What? Had not who? The Queen, you say?

DIOMEDE.   The Queen!
For as at sundown yesterday those two,
Penthesilea and Achilles met
At point to fight, appears Deiphobus,
Ranges him at the warrior-maiden's side
And strikes great Thetis' son, the Peleid,
An underhand blow, that all his harness rings,
And from the topmost elms the sound re-echoes.
The Queen, death-colour, two whole minutes long
Hangs limp her arms: then shaking free her locks

Unschooled about her flaming cheeks, she stands
High in her gleaming stirrups towering up,
Then down as from the firmament itself
She drives her blade into the Trojan's neck,
That he—poor meddling fool—to earth down crashing
Rolls in his gore at our great Peleid's feet.
He then, Achilles, in his gratitude
Will serve her in like manner; but the Queen,
Pressed flat into her dappled charger's mane,
Who, straining at the bit, curvets and rears,
Avoids his murd'rous blow and shakes the reins
And, turning in the saddle, smiles and is gone.

ANTILOCHUS. Most strange indeed!

ODYSSEUS.   What brings you here from Troy?

ANTILOCHUS. Our lord, great Agamemnon, sends me here
To ask if 'twere not wiser, things so changed,
That you should sound retreat; since our true purpose
To raze the towers of Ilium, not interpose
Ourselves between a wand'ring princess' host
And her far aim, to us indifferent.
If then you have acquired good certainty
'Tis not to succour Troy she comes in arms,
He is desirous you should straight return,
Not weigh the cost, and shelter once again
Behind the Argive ramparts by the shore.
If she pursue you, he, great Atreus' son,
Will sally forth in person with the host,
To see with his own eyes upon which side
This riddling sphinx will throw her battled power.

ODYSSEUS. By Jupiter, these orders like me well!
Can you suppose Laertes' son is glad
To fight where neither sense nor reason bid?
But first get him away: him—him—Achilles!
For, as the hound unleashed with dreadful bay
Flings herself on the stag's wide-branching antlers,
The huntsman fears for her and calls her off,
But she, her teeth firm closed in the shaggy throat
Is dragged through streams, o'er mountains, clinging still,
Into the deepest forest's gloom; so he,

Infatuate since he's flushed such noble game
So strange, so lovely, from the coverts of war.
Though with an arrow you should pierce his thighs
To hobble him, yet never will he leave
The scent, he swears it, of this Amazon
Till he has dragged her by her silken hair
Off her pied tiger-steed into the dust.
Try it, Antilochus, try it yourself and see
What subtlest words can do against his madness.

DIOMEDE. Let us as one oppose an icy wedge
Of reason to his mad resolve and split it.
You, friend, of many wiles will doubtless find
The chink of weakness where we can break in.
If he is stubborn still, I'll pick him up
And, with two more Aetolians, on our backs
We'll carry him, a clod quite reft of sense,
And pitch him in the Argive camp.

ODYSSEUS.   Lead on!

ANTILOCHUS. What now? Who is it hurries thus to us?

DIOMEDE. It is Adrastes, pale and all distraught.

SCENE 2

Enter a CAPTAIN.

ODYSSEUS. What bring'st thou?

DIOMEDE.   News?

CAPTAIN.   For you the dismallest
That ever yet you heard.

DIOMEDE.   What news?

ODYSSEUS.   Speak out!

CAPTAIN. Achilles—captive of the Amazons;
So Ilium's walls will never now be razed.

DIOMEDE. Ye gods in heav'n, be kind!

ODYSSEUS.   O hateful news!

ANTILOCHUS. When did this fearful thing, and where, take
place?

CAPTAIN. A new onslaught of these daemoniac maids,
    This brood of Mars, like searing thunderbolt,
    Melted too fast the Aetolians' stalwart ranks
    And poured them down upon us Myrmidons,
    Till then unconquered, like a swirling flood.
    Vainly we strive, close-knit and firm, to stem
    Their fleeing hordes; in headlong inundation
    Swept from the field in welter and wrack we fly;
    And nowhere can we halt our swift career
    Till far from Peleus' son we stand aghast.
    At length he struggles, threaten'd on every side,
    Out of the battle's thickest gloom, and seeks
    His fearful course down a smooth-sloping hill.
    Towards us now he wings his way. Already
    Rejoicing, jubilant we call to him,
    But soon the grateful shout dies on our lips;
    For suddenly before his horses' hoofs
    A chasm gapes, and down from giddy height
    He gazes, frozen, into yawning depths.
    Vain now the skill in which he so excels,
    Deftly to guide the chariot to the goal:
    His team turn terrified their rearing heads
    Backwards against their driver's furious blows.
    And now in chaos of tangled harness lie
    Chariot and steeds, a sprawling, huddled mass,
    And with them in the wreck Achilles' self,
    Powerless as lion in the hunter's snare.

ANTILOCHUS. Insensate! Whither would he——?

CAPTAIN.   Automedon
    His stalwart charioteer at once springs down
    And leaps to loose the tangle of steeds and harness;
    In little space indeed they stand again.
    Yet ere he can free every fettered leg
    From twisted trace or other hind'ring check,
    The Queen herself, leading a jubilant swarm
    Of Amazons, spurs into the ravine
    And severs thus his only path to safety.

ANTILOCHUS.   Ye gods!

CAPTAIN. She stops—dust billowing up and round her there—

In mid-career her charger's flight, and looks,
Her dazzling face thrown back to scan the height,
And measures with her eye the wall of rock.
Her nodding plume, as tho' himself appalled,
Seems to drag back and down her ardent head.
Then suddenly she lays her reins aside,
We see her quickly press her tiny hands,
As though herself now giddy, to her forehead,
O'er which all disarrayed her long locks fall.
Fill'd with dismay at such unwonted sight
Her maidens all press round imploring her
With eager, anxious gestures to hold back.
That one who seems her nearest friend, gently
Encircles her with tender arm; another,
Yet bolder, grasps her charger's hanging rein;
They seek with force to stay her mad resolve.
But she——

DIOMEDE.   What? Does she dare?

ANTILOCHUS.   Tell on!

CAPTAIN.   She does.
Vain their beseeching, vain restraining hands;
With gentle majesty she puts aside
Those who would hold her and begins to trot
Restlessly up and down the sheer-walled cleft,
Seeking if there be nowhere some small path
Will help her longing to those wings it lacks.
And now in furious ardour she begins
To fling herself upon the beetling cliff
Now here, now there, in fierce desire to scale it,
Consumed with senseless hope that thus she may
Seize the rich prey that lies enmesh'd above.
Now she has tested ev'ry crack and cranny
Wash'd by the rains of many a winter storm;
She sees full well the cliff's unclimbable;
And yet, quite reft of judgment, she returns
And starts once more to seek and seek—in vain.
And swings herself indeed, no whit disheartened,
Up on to tracks that ev'n the he-goat shuns,
Swings herself up as much as by the height

Of a great elm. And as she perches there
Upon a jutting block of granite, where
No room would be ev'n for the chamois' hoof,
O'ertower'd on every hand by fearful cliffs,
Not forward and not back daring to move
While with shrill cries her maidens cleave the air,
Sudden to earth she tumbles, rider and steed,
With loosened boulders thund'ring down around,
As though to deepest Tartarus she were bent,
Right to the foot of that sheer cliff again
—And neither breaks her neck nor nothing learns,
But only girds herself again to climb.

ANTILOCHUS. A foaming-jawed hyena! 'Tis no woman!

ODYSSEUS. Automedon, the while?

CAPTAIN.   At last he leaps—
For car and horses now stand in good order
(In all this time Hephaestos could have forged
Almost anew the whole great car of bronze),
He leaps into his place and grasps the reins:
Oh, what relief, what joy to all us Greeks!
But at this moment, as he turns his steeds,
At last the Amazons espy a path
That gently mounts the cliff. They call to her,
Filling the vale with shouts of exultation,
They call the Queen to come, who in her rage
Still hurls herself against the rock's sheer face.
But hearing them she reins her charger back,
Scans for one moment where the path ascends,
Then like a leopard leaping on his prey,
Follows her glance herself. He, great Achilles,
Fled at her coming, ever away from us;
Soon in the valleys he was lost to view,
And what became of him I cannot tell.

ANTILOCHUS. Lost without doubt!

DIOMEDE.   Ah, friends! What should we do?

ODYSSEUS. Why, what our hearts all bid us! Mighty kings,
Up, gird yourselves and wrest him from her grasp.
What though for him we must face wounds and death,

I'll face th' Atrides' wrath when he is safe.

ODYSSEUS, DIOMEDE, ANTILOCHUS, *off*.

SCENE 3

The CAPTAIN. A BAND OF GREEKS, *who have been mounting a small eminence*

A MYRMIDON, *looking out over the countryside*.
Look! Look! Do you not see? Above that ridge
A head appearing, plumed and helmeted?
And now the neck—the massive neck beneath?
The shoulders now, the arms, in flashing steel?
Now! Now!—— The mighty, deep-set chest; oh, see!
Where gleams about his waist the belt of gold!

CAPTAIN. Whose? Whose? By the gods!

MYRMIDON.   Whose? Still in doubt, ye Greeks?
His horses now, their white-starred foreheads—— See!
His chariot's steeds; still but their legs—their hooves
Are hidden by the summit of the ridge.
Ah, now! Clear-cut against the sky behold
The whole equipage, blazing like the sun
That rises jubilant in his early spring.

GREEKS. Triumph! Achilles! Achilles! 'Tis he,
'Tis he! Himself he drives his four-hors'd car.
Rescued! He's safe!

CAPTAIN.   O all ye gods above!
So then be yours the glory!—— Where's Odysseus?
Run, someone, bring the Argive chiefs this news.
A GREEK *goes quickly off*.
Does he head this way, friends?

MYRMIDON.   Oh see! Oh see!

CAPTAIN. What is it? Speak!

MYRMIDON.   Oh, Captain! Past belief!

CAPTAIN. Tell us, then! Speak!

MYRMIDON.   Oh, how he leans far out

Over their flying backs and urges them!
Oh, how he swings the lash around their heads,
And they at the sound—immortal coursers!—they
Devour in thund'ring flight the fleeting ground.
Their throats' hot vapour, streaming out behind,
Seems, by the god of life, to draw the car!
The stag before the hounds is not more swift!
Sight cannot penetrate the whirling wheels
Whose spokes all mingle in a solid disc.

AN AETOLIAN. But, look! Behind him——!

CAPTAIN.   What?

MYRMIDON.   At the mountain's foot——

AETOLIAN. Dust——

MYRMIDON.   Dust, uptowering like a thundercloud
And like the lightning sweeping on——

AETOLIAN.   Ye gods!

MYRMIDON. Penthesilea!

CAPTAIN.   Who?

AETOLIAN.   The Queen herself!
Hard on Achilles' heels with all her band
Of women she comes sweeping o'er the plain.

CAPTAIN. The raging fury!

GREEKS, *calling*.   This way! Here to us!
To us! To us, Achilles! This way, turn!
This way your steeds!

AETOLIAN.   Look, look! How with her thighs
She clips her charger's tiger-striped flanks!
Flat, all her length, upon the mane she stoops
Greedily drinking down the impeding air.
She flies as though sped headlong from the sun;
Numidian arrows are not half so swift.
The rest lag panting far behind, like curs
When once the greyhound girds his strength to run.
Her plume itself can scarcely follow her!

CAPTAIN. And does she gain?

A DOLOPIAN.   She gains!

MYRMIDON.   But not yet near!

DOLOPIAN. She gains! She gains! With ev'ry thund'ring hoof-
    beat
  She swallows down some portion of the space
  That still divides her from great Peleus' son——

MYRMIDON. O all ye gods! Protecting deities!
  Look! Now she is almost as large as he!
  The dust he raises in his headlong flight—
  She breathes it now, borne to her by the wind!
  The charger that she rides, in swift career
  Tears up whole clods of earth that now alight
  Beside him in the body of his car!

AETOLIAN. And now—— Oh, insolence! Nay, madness! Look!
  In wide arc circling off he plays with her.
  But she will take the cord—she'll cut across.
  Look! Look! She intercepts him!

MYRMIDON.   Help! O Zeus!
  Beside him now she rides. Her shadow, see,
  Vast as a giant in the morning sun,
  Now strikes him!

AETOLIAN.   But all unforeseen he wheels——

DOLOPIAN. Wrenches the team and chariot suddenly
  Aside.

AETOLIAN.   To us, to us he flies once more!

MYRMIDON. Oh, he is full of tricks! He cheated her!

DOLOPIAN. But look where she in headlong flight o'ershoots
  The chariot——

MYRMIDON.   Strikes, unseated now, now stumbles——

DOLOPIAN. And falls! She's down!

CAPTAIN.   What?

MYRMIDON.   Down! The Queen herself.
  And over her one of her warrior-maids——

DOLOPIAN. Another now——

MYRMIDON.   A third——

DOLOPIAN.   And yet another——

CAPTAIN. What? Down? They fall?

DOLOPIAN.   They fall——

MYRMIDON.   Captain! They fall,

Like iron molten in the furnace' maw,
All in a heap together, steeds and riders.

CAPTAIN. Might they be all consumed!

DOLOPIAN.   One great dust cloud,
With flashes here and there of arms and armour:
The eye is helpless, strain how it will to see.
A struggling mass of maids—and horses too—
All in a jumbled welter. Chaos' self,
The aboriginal, had more of order.

AETOLIAN. But now—a breeze springs up and clears the dust.
Now one that fell is on her feet again.

DOLOPIAN. Delightful how the heap struggles and heaves!
Now some seek helmets, some their broken spears,
That lie far scattered on the plain.

MYRMIDON.   But look!
Three horses still, and still one rider lies
For dead upon the ground——

CAPTAIN.   Is it the Queen?

AETOLIAN. Penthesilea?

MYRMIDON.   Can it be the Queen?
Ah, no! Would that my eyes saw not so true!
There she stands!

DOLOPIAN.   Where?

CAPTAIN.   Quick, tell us!

MYRMIDON.   There, by Zeus!
Where first she fell, beside that shady oak,
Supports herself upon her horse's neck,
Bareheaded—there's her helmet on the ground—
With feeble hand holds back her tangled hair
And wipes her brow of dust—or is it blood?

DOLOPIAN. By God, 'tis she!

CAPTAIN.   She's indestructible!

AETOLIAN. From such a fall a cat would die; not she!

CAPTAIN. And Peleus' son?

DOLOPIAN.   The gods protect him still.
Three bowshots out, beyond her, he has flown.
She scarce can reach him even with her eyes;

Her thought itself, that longs to catch him, seems
Too faint to leave the refuge of her breast.

MYRMIDON. Triumph! Look there! Odysseus marches forth,
The whole Greek army, flashing back the sun,
Comes marching out from yonder forest's gloom.

CAPTAIN. Odysseus? What! And Diomede as well?
How far is he still distant from their host?

DOLOPIAN. A stone's throw, Captain—hardly that. His team
Is skimming now the ridge above Scamander,
Where all our host is ordered in array.
E'en now he thunders down their ranks——

VOICES, *in the distance.*   Hail! Hail!

DOLOPIAN. They call to him, the Argives——

VOICES.   Hail to thee,
Achilles! Hail, great Peleid, goddess-born!
Hail to thee! Hail!

DOLOPIAN.   Now he has reined his steeds.
Before the Argive princes gathered there,
He reins his steeds. Odysseus steps to greet him.
Down from his car he springs, all grey with dust
Gives to Automedon his reins—now turns—
And they press round him, all the valiant kings.
The Grecian host itself, with jubilant shouts,
Bears him along, close thronging round his knees
The while Automedon with measured step
Leads at their master's side his smoking steeds.
This way they come! The whole triumphal throng
Bears down on us. Hail to thee, child of heaven!
Look all! Oh look this way! Look where he comes!

SCENE 4

Enter ACHILLES, *with* ODYSSEUS, DIOMEDE, ANTILOCHUS *following, and* AUTOMEDON *with the chariot and horses at his side, also the Grecian host.*

ODYSSEUS. Hail, lord of Phthia! With full heart we greet thee!
Thou victor even in the arts of flight!

By Jupiter! When thus behind thy back
Thy spirit's superior power can bring about
Such headlong ruin for thy tender foe,
What then will happen when at last she stands
At bay before thy dreadful countenance?

ACHILLES, *holds his helmet in his hand and wipes the sweat
from his brow. Two* GREEKS, *unknown to him, take one of
his arms and begin to bandage it.*
What's this? What are you doing?

ANTILOCHUS.   Thou art victor
In such a contest of o'erleaping speed,
As never yet unleashèd thunderstorms,
Sweeping resistless over heaven's vault,
Themselves have shown to the astonished world.
Nay, by the Fates! What tho' with grinding wheel
I had crashed through the wonted ruts of life
And heaped upon my hollow breast all sins,
Ev'ry iniquity of Priam's burg,
Had I thy wingèd car, I'd 'scape remorse.

ACHILLES, *to the two* GREEKS, *whose activity seems to annoy
him.* Fools!

A GREEK PRINCE.   Who?

ACHILLES.   Why bother me?

FIRST GREEK.   Keep still! You're bleeding!

ACHILLES.   I know that!

SECOND GREEK.   Keep still, then!

FIRST GREEK.   Let us bandage you!

SECOND GREEK. We're nearly finished——

DIOMEDE.   Here at first 'twas said
The forced withdrawal of my troops had caused
Thee thus to flee; occupied as I was
Here with Odysseus and Antilochus,
Who had brought messages from Agamemnon,
I was not present when this thing befell.
Yet all that I have seen convinces me
That thy so masterly retreat was not constrained
But of free choice. One might indeed suppose
That with the crack of dawn, when we were girding

Our harness on against the day's alarms,
Already thou had'st marked that lucky stone
O'er which the Queen should stumble and crash to earth:
With such sure course, by the eternal gods,
Didst thou entice her to this very stone.

ODYSSEUS. But now, great Phthian hero, you will oblige,
Unless you have in mind some better scheme,
By falling back with us to the Greek camp.
The sons of Atreus bid us all withdraw.
Feigning retreat we are to be the bait
Which shall entice her to Scamander's banks,
Where, falling on her unawares, the King
Will seek to engage her in a general broil.
By Zeus the Thund'rer! There, there or nowhere
Thou 'lt cool the heat that tingles in thy blood
And makes thee insatiate as a yearling buck:
And to this task I wish thee good success.
For to me too she's hateful even to death,
A Fury ranging over all these plains
And crossing all our work. Gladly I'd see,
I do confess, the mark of thy mail'd heel
Scarring the tender roses of her flesh.

ACHILLES, *his eye falling on his horses.* They sweat.

ANTILOCHUS. Who?

AUTOMEDON, *feeling their necks with his hand.*
Ay, like lead.

ACHILLES. Good. Take them off
And, when the air has cooled them thoroughly,
Wash their deep chests, their thighs, and hocks with wine.

AUTOMEDON. The wine will soon be here.

DIOMEDE. My excellent friend,
We fight at senseless odds against them here.
The hills are covered, far as sight can reach,
With rank on serried rank of women in arms;
Locusts that settle on the ripened crop
Fall not so thick nor half so numerous.
Was ever battle won just as we plan?
Who besides thee in all the host can boast
He has so much as seen the centaur Queen?

Vainly, in armour crusted o'er with gold,
We thrust ourselves before her, with loud blare
Of trumpets making known our princely state:
She will not budge from out the rearward ranks.
And if from far off, blown upon the wind,
We hear the silver fluting of her voice,
We first must hack through riffraff soldiery,
Who guard her like ten thousand hounds of hell,
A path of doubtful outcome, void of honour.

ACHILLES, *looking into the distance.* Is she still there?

DIOMEDE.   Whom do you mean?

ANTILOCHUS.   The Queen?

CAPTAIN. They cannot see! These plumes!—— Out of the way!

THE GREEK, *who is binding* ACHILLES' *arm.*
Wait! Just one moment!

A GREEK PRINCE.   Yes! Look! There she is!

DIOMEDE.   Where? Show me!

GREEK PRINCE.   By the oak there, where she fell.
Once more the wanton plume waves from her head.
Her late misfortune seems forgotten——

FIRST GREEK.   There!

SECOND GREEK. Now you can use your arm any way you like.

FIRST GREEK. There, off you go!

   The GREEKS *tie one last knot and drop his arm.*

ODYSSEUS.   Achilles! Did you hear
The arguments we put forward?

ACHILLES.   The arguments?
Not one. What was it? What do you want?

ODYSSEUS.   What want?
Extraordinary! We told you of the orders
From the Atridae. Agamemnon bids
Us straight withdraw into the Grecian camp.
He sent Antilochus—look on him here!—
To bring this fiat of the supreme command.
This is the stratagem—to entice the Queen
With all her Amazons to the plains of Troy,
Where she, caught between two such hosts in arms,

Confined, press'd, squeez'd from every side at once
Must show us clearly if she is our friend;
And we, at least, choose she which side she will,
Will no more be in doubt what's to be done.
I know, Achilles, I can trust your sense
To follow the wisdom of these clear commands.
For madness were it, sheerest lunacy,
When the war calls us urgently to Troy,
To let these warrior-maids embroil us here,
Before we know what thing they want of us,
—If indeed there is anything they want.

ACHILLES, *as he puts on his helmet again.*

Fight then like eunuchs, if it pleases you.
A man I feel myself and to these women,
Though alone of all the host, I'll stand my ground.
Whether you all here, under cooling pines,
Range round them from afar, full of impotent lust,
Shunning the bed of battle in which they sport,
All's one to me; by heav'n you have my blessing,
If you would creep away to Troy again.
What that divine maid wants of me, I know it:
Love's messengers she sends, wings tipp'd with steel,
That bear me all her wishes through the air
And whisper in my ear with death's soft voice.
I never yet was coy with any girl.
You know yourselves, since first my beard began
To show, gladly I've stood at each one's service.
And if from this one I have still refrained,
By Zeus! there's but one cause: I've not yet found
That bush-girt spot where, as her heart desires,
Unhindered I can enjoy her, bedding her
On the hard pillows of our mailèd suits.
In short, go off. I'll follow you to Troy;
I'll soon have had my way with her. But though
I had to woo her many long months through—
Ay, years—I will not guide my chariot there
Back to my friends, I swear 't by Zeus himself,
Nor once again see Ilium's tower'd heights,
Until I first have had my sport with her,
And then, her brow adorned with bleeding gashes,

Shall drag her by the feet behind my car.
Follow me!

Enter a GREEK.

THE GREEK.   Penthesilea seeks thee, Prince.

ACHILLES. And I her. Is she mounted once again?

THE GREEK. Not yet. She comes afoot with lofty grace.
But at her side her charger proudly steps.

ACHILLES. 'Tis good so. Get me too a horse, my friends!
And you, my trusty Myrmidons, follow me all!

ANTILOCHUS. This is stark madness!

ODYSSEUS.   Well, you try to move him
With all your orator's skill, Antilochus!

ANTILOCHUS. We must seize him by force——

DIOMEDE.   Too late! He's gone!

ODYSSEUS. Curse on these women and their crazy war!
All off.

SCENE 5

Enter PENTHESILEA, PROTHOE, MEROE, ASTERIA, *and* AMAZON
SOLDIERY.

AMAZONS. Hail to thee, victorious! Unconquerable!
Queen of the Feast of Roses! Hail! All hail!

PENTHESILEA. Silence! No Rose Feast yet! No victory!
Once more the battle calls me to the field.
That young, defiant war-god—I will tame him.
My friends, ten thousand suns melted in one
Vast heat-ball seem not half so bright to me,
So glorious, as victory over him.

PROTHOE. Dearest, I beg thee——

PENTHESILEA.   Leave me, Prothoe!
Thou'st heard my will. Much sooner couldst thou stem
The torrent leaping down the mountainside,
Than rule the thund'rous ruin of my soul.
I long to see him grov'lling at my feet,

This haughty man, who in this glorious
And gentle field of arms, as no man yet,
Sows strange confusion in my warlike heart.
Is that the conquering Queen, the fearful one,
Proud leader of the warrior Amazons,
Whose form's reflected in his burnished steel,
When I approach him? Oh, can that be she?
Do I not feel—ah! too accursèd I—
While all around the Argive army flees,
When I look on this man, on him alone,
That I am smitten, lamed in my inmost being,
Conquered and overcome—I! Only I!
Where can this passion which thus tramples me,
Harbour in me, who have no breast for love?
Into the battle will I fling myself;
There with his haughty smile he waits me, there
I'll see him at my feet or no more live!

PROTHOE. Will you not lay your head a little while—
My Queen! My dearest!—here upon my heart?
That fall—that blow that shook thy tender breast,
It has enflamed thy blood, confused thy mind.
See how thou tremblest—all thy delicate limbs.
We all implore thee make no rash decision
Until thy mind returns in clear, full strength.
Come rest—refresh thyself here in my arms.

PENTHESILEA. Why? What has happened? What have I been
        saying?
Have I?—— What have I?——

PROTHOE.   For a victory.
That tempts thy fancy as a passing whim
Wilt thou begin again the chance of battle?
Because one wish, I know not what, lies still
Unsatisfied within thy heart, wilt thou
Like a spoil'd child thus wanton cast away
The gain that crowns with joy thy people's prayers?

PENTHESILEA. Hark ye! Accursèd be this day's success!
Ah, see how even my friends, my dearest friends,
League themselves with this fickle fate to-day,
To hurt, frustrate, and thwart me every way!
Where'er my itching hand stirs but to snatch

Renown that thunders by in pelting haste,
And seize him by his flowing yellow locks,
There interposes still some mocking power——
And still my heart is hatred and defiance!
Begone!

PROTHOE, *to herself.* Ye heavenly powers of good protect her!

PENTHESILEA. Am I so selfish? Is it *my* desires
Alone that call me back into the field?
Is it not my people, threatened by the fate
That even in the maniac flush of victory
With audible wingbeat hastens from afar?
What is achieved, that we to evening prayer
Should go, as though the long day's work were done?
'Tis true, the crop is reaped, tied well in sheaves,
Aye, stacked in fat abundance in the barns,
That bursting tower to heaven. Yet balefully
The livid storm cloud overshadows it,
Poised with its levin from on high to strike
These captive youths that you have taken in fight.
You'll never lead them to the fragrant vales
Of our homeland, crown'd all with flowers, with music
Joyous of cymbals and of shrilling pipes.
Lurking in ambush, crafty, insatiate,
I see him everywhere—Achilles, ready to spring
Upon your happy train and scatter it.
He'll follow you and all your captive band
Right to the circling walls of Themiscyra.
Aye, in the holy temple of Artemis
He'll tear from off their limbs the tender chains,
Plaited of roses, and will load our own
With harsh shackles of stithy-forgèd brass.
Should I—'twere madness but to think of it—
Cease now to dog him? I who still for five
Long days of toil and sweat have sought his fall?
Now, when the lightest breath of Fortune's wind
Will shake him like a ripe pomegranate down
To lie vanquished beneath my horse's hoof?
What! Am I not so greatly to complete
What is so fair begun? May I not seize
The laurel wreath that flutters o'er my head?

Not lead, as once I swore, the daughters of Mars
Triumphant to the very top of bliss?
If not, if not—— Then let Mars' pyramid
Crash upon me and them in ruin down!
Cursed be the heart that knows not wise restraint!

PROTHOE. Dread lady! In thine eye is awful fire
To me unknowable, and awful thoughts,
Dark as though children of eternal Night,
Do turn and jostle in my fearful breast.
The hostile band thy mind so strangely fears,
Has fled before thee like the winnow'd chaff;
Hardly one spear can anywhere be seen.
And for Achilles—as our army lies,
He is cut off, he cannot reach Scamander.
But tempt him not again; avoid his sight.
His only thought will be, I promise thee,
To throw himself behind the Grecian wall.
I, only I, will guard the army's rear;
I swear to thee by Zeus, no prisoner,
No one, shall he snatch from thee! Not a glint
Of arms of his, though distant many miles,
Shall fright the host, nor far-off hoof beats' sound,
Borne on the wind, trouble thy maidens' joy.
My head be warranty to thee for this!

PENTHESILEA, *turning suddenly to* ASTERIA.
Can this thing be, Asteria? Speak!

ASTERIA. My Queen——

PENTHESILEA. Can I, as Prothoe demands, lead back
The army thus to Themiscyra?

ASTERIA. Queen!—
Forgive, dread lady, if in my poor sight—

PENTHESILEA. Speak boldly out, I say.

PROTHOE, *timidly*. If you would call
To council all Princesses and enquire
Of them——

PENTHESILEA. Her counsel will I have, no other!
What am I since these few hours past, by heaven!
Pause in which she controls herself.

Asteria, can I lead back the host?
Speak out, can I yet lead it to our home?

ASTERIA. With your good leave, dread lady, I must own
Astonishment consumes me at the sight
That here has met my unbelieving eyes.
With all my people I left the Caucasus,
Thou knowest, one day behind the eager host;
Nor could I catch them in their swift career,
So recklessly they sped, like a torrent in spate.
Not till this day had just begun to dawn
Did we ride in, ready to join the fight;
And then with joyful shout from myriad throats
I hear the news: the victory is won,
The war is over, all our needs fulfilled.
Glad, I assure thee, that the people's prayer
Without my help has been so quickly granted.
I order everything against return;
Yet curious still to see the captive band
Of heroes, booty of our valiant arms,
I find a handful of slaves, hang-dog, cringing,
The very dregs of all the Argive host,
Picked up by our baggage train on some foray
And carried home on shields they'd thrown away.
Before the lordly walls of Troy still stands
The whole Hellenic host; there's Agamemnon,
There's Menelaus, Ajax, Palamede;
Odysseus, Diomede, Antilochus——
They still are free to taunt thee to thy face.
Aye, and that youth, son of the strange sea-nymph,
Dares to oppose thee still, o'erweening man.
His foot he will—declares it openly—
His foot he'll set upon thy queenly neck.
Great daughter of Ares, canst thou ask me still
If we may yet return in triumph home?

PROTHOE, *passionately*.

To the Queen's sword, base woman, heroes have fall'n
As brave and noble ev'ry whit——

PENTHESILEA.   Silence!
Hateful one! She—Asteria—feels as I:

There is but one here worthy of my sword,
And he still strides the field, defiant, free!

PROTHOE. My Queen! Surely thou wilt not let thyself
By passion——

PENTHESILEA.   Viper! Bind thy venom'd tongue!
Out of my sight—or feel thy Queen's full wrath!
Begone!

PROTHOE.   Then I will dare my Queen's full wrath!
Much rather will I never see thy face
Again, than at this moment basely stand
In treacherous silence, worse than flattery.
Thou art not fit, thus all aflame, consumed
With amorous fire, to lead the virgins' war;
As little fit as is the lion to face
The hunter's spear when he has drunk too deep
Of poison craftily set out for him.
Achilles?—— Ah! In this unhappy state,
By all the gods, him thou wilt never win;
Much rather ere the day is done, I tell thee,
Thou'lt lose us in thy madness all these youths
Whom in hard fight we won, the cherished prize
Of infinite toils and dangers palpable.

PENTHESILEA. Now this is past believing strange! What makes
You suddenly so chicken-hearted?

PROTHOE.   Me?

PENTHESILEA. Tell me! Who is your prisoner?

PROTHOE.   Lykaon,
The young prince of the Arcadian host. I think
You saw him yesterday.

PENTHESILEA.   Ah, yes! 'Twas he
That stood with drooping plume and trembling glance
When I surveyed the captives?

PROTHOE.   Trembling! He!
He stood as resolute as e'er Achilles!
My sure-sped arrows crippled him and there
He sank before me; proudly I will lead
Lykaon, proud as any, at the Feast
Of roses to the holy temple's shrine.

PENTHESILEA. In truth? See, at the thought she's all aflame.
Good, then. Thou shalt not lose him. Be content!
Bring him before us from the band of captives,
Lykaon, the Arcadian, bring him here!
Take him, thou too unwarlike virgin, then!
Flee with him lest thou lose him here, flee far,
Far from the din of battle, hide yourselves
In thickets deep of fragrant-smelling elder,
In the wild mountains' steepest-sided glen
Where nightingales pour forth their amorous notes
And celebrate it now, thou wanton girl,
That rite thy heart can not await in patience.
But from our countenance be banishèd
And from our capital forever. All
Thy comfort be thy lover and his kisses
When all—when fame, when honour, country, love,
Thy Queen, aye, and thy friend are lost to thee.
Go, spare me now—go, not a word to me!—
The pain to look upon thee more!

MEROE.　　　　　　　　　　　　Oh, Queen!

ANOTHER PRINCESS, *from among her followers.*
Oh! What a word of doom!

PENTHESILEA.　　　　　　　　Silence, I say!
My vengeance falls on whoso speaks for her!

AN AMAZON, *entering.* Most gracious Queen, Achilles comes.

PENTHESILEA.　　　　　　　　　　He comes!
Up then, my virgins, up! Once more to the fight!
Bring me the spear that deals the mortallest wounds,
The sword that strikes most like the thunderbolt!
This bliss, ye gods, oh, grant it me to-day——
To smite with blade invincible this one
So hot-pursuèd youth down to the dust.
All other joy that to my life is fated,
I do renounce it here, grant me but this.
Asteria! You will lead out the companies.
Keep the Greek host engaged and see to it
The general broil thwart not my special aim.
Not one of you, no matter who she be,
May strike Achilles! She shall taste the sharp,

Swift shaft of death, who touches but his head—
Nay, but one lock—with overweening hand.
'Tis I alone know how to fell this man.
These mailèd arms, dear friends, shall draw him down
(Since thus in suits of mail it must be done!)
Into the tenderest of love's embraces
And press him all unscath'd against my breast.
Grow up to meet his fall, ye flowers of spring,
That none of his dear limbs take injury.
My own heart's blood rather than his, I'd spill.
No more will I now rest, till I have hailed
Him down out of the sky, like a gay bird,
Bright-feathered; yet when once he lies before me
With broken wing, but still with ev'ry speck
Of shimmering purple dust unblemished, then,
Then, ye virgins, then may all the gods
Sweep down from heav'n to celebrate our triumph.
Then homeward wends the joyous march, and I,
Queen of the Feast of Roses to you all!
And now——

As she goes off, she sees PROTHOE *weeping and turns, distressed. Then suddenly, falling upon her neck——*

        My Prothoe! My heart's own sister!
Wilt follow me?

PROTHOE.   Into death and beyond!
Could I without thee meet the Blessèd Ones?

PENTHESILEA. Ah, noble heart, nobler than all! Thou wilt?
Come, then, we'll fight and conquer side by side.
We two or none, and our watchword shall be:
Roses to crown our heroes' temples, or
For ours the cypress!
Exeunt omnes.

SCENE 6

Enter the HIGH PRIESTESS OF DIANA *with* PRIESTESSES, *followed by a band of young girls with baskets of roses on their heads; also the* PRISONERS *led by armed* AMAZONS.

HIGH PRIESTESS. Now, little ones! My dearest rose-maidens!
Show me the fruit of all this morning's labours.
Here by the rocky stream's crystalline falls,
Shaded by this tall pine, here we are safe.
Pour out your harvest here before my feet.

A GIRL, *emptying her basket on the ground.*
Look, holy mother, this is what I picked!

SECOND GIRL. This apronful is mine!

THIRD GIRL.   And here is mine!

FOURTH GIRL. Look, I have gathered all the wanton spring!
The other girls follow suit.

HIGH PRIESTESS. Such sweet profusion grows not on Hymettus!
In truth a day so rich in every bounty
Never yet dawned, Diana, on thy folk.
The mothers bring me gifts, not less the daughters.
By all this double splendour blinded, I
Know not to which I should give warmer thanks.
But children, tell me! Is this all your store?

FIRST GIRL. More than we have here could we nowhere find.

HIGH PRIESTESS. Then were your mothers more industrious.

SECOND GIRL. Most holy dame, 'tis harder far to win
Roses upon these fields than prisoners.
Though on the hills around the bounteous harvest
Of Argive youths stands rank on rank and waits
Only for reaping by the eager scythe,
Yet in these vales so sparingly, believe me,
And so well-fortified the roses bloom,
That it is lighter work to hew through lances
Than break a way through their entwinèd thorns.
——Look here at these poor fingers, gracious lady!

THIRD GIRL. I ventured on a sharply jutting rock
To pick thee one rose, lovelier than all:
Pale still through the embracing, dark green cup,
A scarcely opened bud its beauty gleamed,
Not yet expanded to the kiss of love.
But still I grasp it—then slip, reel, and fall
Down into the abyss and think myself
Lost to the world of day in death's dark womb.

And yet it brought me luck, for there I found
Such myriad splendour of wanton-blooming roses
As would deck out ten feasts of victory.

FOURTH GIRL. I plucked thee, holy priestess of Diana,
I plucked for thee a rose—one rose—no more.
Yet such a rose it is—look, this one here!—
Fit for the wreath a captive king must wear.
Penthesilea could not wish a fairer
For great Achilles, when she has laid him low.

HIGH PRIESTESS. Ay, *when* she has laid Achilles low, thou
    may'st
Thyself hand her this more than kingly rose.
So keep it safe for her, until she comes.

FIRST GIRL. Another time when all the Amazon host
Marches to war with cymbals and with drums,
We will go too, and not—oh, promise us!—
Only to grace the mothers' victory
With rose-plucking and winding toilsome wreaths!
My arm here—look!—can hurl the javelin,
And from my sling the stone flies swift and true.
Why not? Why not? I am no more a child;
And he for whom these sinews here grow strong
Already he fights boldly in the fray.

HIGH PRIESTESS. Well, is that so? And who should know but
    thou?
Hast thou already chosen the roses for him?
Next spring, when they are all abloom once more,
Thou shalt seek out thy man on the field of battle.
——But come! The exultant mothers bid us haste:
Quick! Lace these roses into wreaths of love!

THE GIRL. Yes, quick to work! How do we best begin?

FIRST GIRL, *to the* SECOND. Come here, Glaucothoe!

THIRD GIRL, *to the* FOURTH.   Come, Charmion!

They sit down in pairs.

FIRST GIRL. We—for Ornythia do we wind this wreath,
Who overcame the nodding-plumed Alcestes.

THIRD GIRL. And we—'tis for Parthenion. Athenaeus
Her prisoner is, he with the Gorgon shield.

HIGH PRIESTESS, *to the armed* AMAZONS.

> Have you no thought to entertain your guests?
> How awkwardly you stand, like senseless logs!
> Is it for me to teach the game of love?
> Will you not even dare a friendly word?
> Not ask what all these battle-weary men
> Perchance desire or need? What wants they have?

FIRST AMAZON. They say they have no needs, most holy dame.

SECOND AMAZON. They're angry with us——

THIRD AMAZON.   When we would be kind,
> Defiantly they turn their backs on us.

HIGH PRIESTESS. Why, silly girls! If they are angry now,
> Speak to them! Make them kind! Why in the fray
> Did you deal down on them such pitiless blows?
> Tell them what pleasures are in store for them;
> Soon their unfriendliness will melt away.

FIRST AMAZON, *to a* PRISONER.

> Thou handsome youth, wilt thou on deep-piled rugs
> Rest thy cramp'd limbs? Shall I make ready a couch—
> For thou seemst weary—of tender flowers of spring
> In the deep shade of yonder dark-leaved laurel?

SECOND AMAZON, *also to a* PRISONER.

> Shall I some fragrant-scented oil of Persia
> Mix with the spring-drawn water, clear and cool,
> To lave the dust from thy hot, aching feet?

THIRD AMAZON. Surely the juice of golden oranges,
> Prepared with love for thee—thou wilt not scorn it?

ALL THREE. Tell us! What can we offer you?

A GREEK.   Nothing!

FIRST AMAZON. Strange-mooded men! What gnaws thus at
>   your hearts?
> Now that our arrows sleep within the quiver,
> How can the sight of us affright you still?
> Thou with the rich-wrought belt, what is it you fear?

THE GREEK, *looking at her keenly.*

> For whom are these wreaths wound? Come, tell me that!

FIRST AMAZON. For whom? For you!

THE GREEK.   For us! Have you no shame,

Inhuman girl? So you would lead us decked
With flowers like bulls of sacrifice to our death?

FIRST AMAZON. Strange misconception! Nay, to Dian's fane,
To her deep-shaded oak grove, where sweet orgies
Without constraint or measure wait on you!

THE GREEK, *in astonishment, under his breath to the* PRISONERS.
Was ever dream so crazed as this reality?

SCENE 7

Enter an AMAZON CAPTAIN.

CAPTAIN. What make you in this place, most reverend dame,
While scarce a stone's throw hence our armèd host
Girds once again its loins for bloody war?

HIGH PRIESTESS. The host! Impossible! Where?——

CAPTAIN.   In yonder vale
Licked out by old Scamander. Wilt thou but hark
To the sweet mountain wind that hither blows,
Full well thou'lt hear our great Queen's thund'ring shout,
The clash of naked steel, neighing of steeds,
With bugles, trumpets, horns, and cymbals' clang—
The iron voice of brazen-armèd war.

A PRIESTESS. Quick! Who will spy from yonder hill?

THE GIRLS.   I! I!

They climb up the hill.

HIGH PRIESTESS. The Queen's voice? Not the Queen's! It can-
not be!
Why—if the battle still must rage—did she
Bid me at once prepare the Feast of Roses?

CAPTAIN. The Feast of Roses!—— Whom did she thus
command?

HIGH PRIESTESS. Me! Me myself!

CAPTAIN.   Where? When?

HIGH PRIESTESS.   A moment since,
I stood within the shadow of yon obelisk
When great Achilles, and she upon his heels,

Swept by me swifter than the wind. I cried:
"What news? What news?" as she flew by, and she:
"To the Feast of Roses! Look! Canst thou not see?"
With that was gone, but, going, call'd to me:
"Let us not lack for flowers, thou holy one!"

FIRST PRIESTESS, *to the girls.*

Can you not see her?

FIRST GIRL, *on the hill.*

         Nothing can we see!
Not even a plume can we distinguish there.
Deep gloom of livid thunderclouds blots out
The whole wide field; nought but the surge
Confused of armèd hosts can we descry,
That seek each other on the field of death.

SECOND PRIESTESS. She fights to cover the army's safe retreat.

FIRST PRIESTESS. It must be so.

CAPTAIN.   She stands, I tell you, arm'd
In matchless mail facing great Peleus' son,
Herself, the Queen, fresh as her Persian steed
That rears on high for very wantonness.
Her lowering eye shoots fire as ne'er before;
She draws the air freely, exultantly,
As though her youthful, warlike bosom now
For the first time drank in the breath of battle.

HIGH PRIESTESS. What—by the gods!—What can her purpose
   be?
What can it be, when all around in thousands
Our prisoners lie thick in every wood?
What can remain that she would win by war?

CAPTAIN. You ask what still remains to win by war?

GIRLS, *on the hill.* Ye gods!

FIRST PRIESTESS.   What is it? Tell! Can you see more?

FIRST GIRL. O reverend ladies! Come yourselves!

SECOND PRIESTESS.   Nay! Tell us!

CAPTAIN. What still remains for her to win by war?

FIRST GIRL. See! See! How from a cleft in the black cloud
   The sun as with a pillar of sheerest light
   Falls on the glorious head of Peleus' son!

HIGH PRIESTESS. On whose?

FIRST GIRL.   On his! On his! Whose else could it be?
Radiant he stands upon the rising ground,
Cased all in steel his steed and he; sapphire
Nor chrysolite cannot throw back such rays!
The earth herself, the gay, flower-sprinkled earth,
Wrapped now in thunder vapours' blackest gloom,
Lies but a dark background, a murky foil,
To make his flashing glory brighter yet!

HIGH PRIESTESS. What should our girls know of this Peleus'
        son?
Does it befit a daughter of Mars, a Queen,
To stake her all in battle on one name?

To an AMAZON.

Run quick, Arsinoe, stand before her face
And tell her in the name of my dread goddess:
Mars has this day appeared unto his brides;
I now demand, on pain of the goddess' wrath,
That she do seemly crown the god and lead him
Back to our home, there straightway make for him
The Feast of Roses in Diana's shrine.

Exit the AMAZON.

Was ever yet such madness heard or seen?

FIRST PRIESTESS. Children! Have you no sight yet of the
        Queen?

FIRST GIRL, *on the hill.*
Yes, there she is! The whole field now is clear.

FIRST PRIESTESS. Where can you see her?

GIRL.   Leading all the host.
See how she dances forth to meet him, all
Flashing in golden armour, breathing war!
Is't not as though, in jealous emulation,
She longed to o'erleap the sun-goddess, who now
Kisses Achilles' youthful locks? Oh, look!
What though she wished to vault into the heav'ns
To match her flaming rival on equal terms,
Her stallion could not better do her wish,
So light, so wingèd is his dancing gait.

HIGH PRIESTESS, *to* CAPTAIN.
    Did not one of her virgins then attempt
    To hold her back, to warn her against this thing?

CAPTAIN. All her great vassals of the royal blood
    Opposed her going; here upon this spot
    Did Prothoe attempt her uttermost.
    Not one of all persuasion's subtlest arts
    Could move her to return to Themiscyra.
    Deaf she appeared, stone deaf to reason's voice.
    The most envenom'd of all love's shafts, they say,
    Has pierced her tender heart to make her mad.

HIGH PRIESTESS. What word is this?

GIRLS, *on the hill.* Oh, see! Oh, now they meet!
    Ye gods! Let not Earth shudder at the shock!
    Now, even now, even as I speak, they crash
    Together like two hurtling stars in heav'n!

HIGH PRIESTESS. The Queen, you say? Impossible, my friend!
    Pierced by love's shaft? How can that be? When? Where?
    She who doth wear the girdle of diamonds?
    The daughter of Mars, who lacks even the breast
    Where Cupid's poison'd shafts may strike and lodge?

CAPTAIN. So it is rumoured in the ranks at least,
    And now from Meroe I learned the same.

HIGH PRIESTESS. 'Tis fearful!

The AMAZON *returns.*

FIRST PRIESTESS.   Well, what tidings? Speak at once!

HIGH PRIESTESS. Did you my bidding? Spoke you with the
    Queen?

AMAZON. Forgive me, holy one, I came too late.
    Ever swarmed round by cheering soldiery,
    Flitting now here, now there, she eluded me.
    But Prothoe I met for one brief space
    And told her all your will: and she replied——
    I know not—in the general turmoil I——
    Mayhap, I heard her not aright.

HIGH PRIESTESS.   Speak out!
    What did she say?

AMAZON.   Silent she sat her steed

And looked, methought her eyes brimming with tears,
After the Queen. I told her then, thou wert
Indignant that the war thus senselessly
Should be prolonged for one man's sake alone.
To which she thus replied: "Go to thy priestess
And bid her fall upon her knees and pray
That this one man may be her prize of battle;
Doomed otherwise are we and she together."

HIGH PRIESTESS. Oh, she runs steeply down to the abyss!
'Tis not to Achilles she will fall, when he
Encounters her, but to this inner foe.
And us she drags to ruin with her down;
The ship I see already cleaving the Hellespont,
That bears us captive, slaves, all gaily decked
With wreaths, in mockery of our hateful fate.

FIRST PRIESTESS. What matter now? Here comes the dreadful
news.

SCENE 8

Enter an AMAZON OFFICER.

OFFICER. Flee! Bring the prisoners away! Oh, flee!
The Argive host e'en now bears down on you.

HIGH PRIESTESS. O all ye gods! What fearful thing has
chanced?

FIRST PRIESTESS. Where is the Queen?

OFFICER.   Fallen in battle! All
The army of the Amazons scattered!

HIGH PRIESTESS. Thou art mad! What word hath passed thy
wanton lips?

FIRST PRIESTESS, *to the armed* GUARD.
Lead off the prisoners!

HIGH PRIESTESS.   Tell us! Where? When?

OFFICER. Hear then in brief the whole disastrous tale!
Achilles and the Queen, with lances couched,
Rush to th' encounter, like two thunderbolts

That crash together in the vaults of space.
The lances, weaker than their breasts, are splintered.
He, Peleus' son, still stands; Penthesilea—
She sinks, o'erwhelmed by night, down from her horse.
And as she now, his vengeance' helpless prey,
Writhes in the dust before him, who could doubt
That he will send her straight to the nether world?
Yet, pale himself, he stands moved by strange thoughts,
Most like a shade of Orcus; then exclaims:
"Oh, what a look came from those dying eyes!"
Impetuous down he swings him from his steed,
And while her virgins stand, transfixed with horror,
Remembering too well the Queen's own word,
That none should raise her sword against that man,
Boldly goes to her where she lies, bends down
And calls to her "Penthesilea!" then
Raises her up and holds her in his arms,
Curses the deed that he has done and so,
Lamenting still, calls back her erring spirit.

HIGH PRIESTESS. He—— What? Himself?

OFFICER.   "Leave her, thou impious man!"
The whole host thunders. "Death be his reward,"
Cries Prothoe, "if he'll not budge! Then send
The keenest shaft to find its mark in him!"
And with her stallion forcing him to yield,
Snatches the lifeless Queen from his arms; who then
—Oh, pitiful return to misery!—wakes
And is led off with shattered breast, gasping
For breath, her hair in shameful disarray,
That in the rearmost ranks she may recover.
But he, strange man, incalculable—a god
Has suddenly transmuted that fierce heart
Within the brazen-girdled breast with love—
He cries: "Wait, wait, good friends! I come in peace.
Never again shall war divide our nations!"
And casts his sword away, his shield away,
Strips all his harness from his body and limbs
And follows—with clubs we could have felled him, nay,
With our bare hands, had we not been forbid—
Follows the Queen undaunted through our ranks,

As though he knew already, mad as he is,
His life was sacred, safe from all our shafts.

HIGH PRIESTESS. Who gave this worse than senseless order?

OFFICER.   Who?
The Queen! Who else?

HIGH PRIESTESS.   It is unspeakable!

FIRST PRIESTESS. Oh, see! She comes with feeble, tottering
    steps,
Leaning on Prothoe! Oh, pitiful sight!

SECOND PRIESTESS. Ye gods in heav'n! Must I have eyes to see?

SCENE 9

Enter PENTHESILEA, *pale, with dishevelled hair, scarcely
able to walk, supported by* PROTHOE *and* MEROE; *behind her*
AMAZONS.

PENTHESILEA, *in a feeble voice.*
Set all the dogs upon him! Whip the elephants
With blazing faggots that they trample and crush him!
Drive over him with our steel-scythèd cars!
Mow down his sumptuous limbs and mangle them!

PROTHOE. Dearest! We all implore thee——!

MEROE.   Hear us!

PROTHOE.   He,
He himself, Achilles follows hard behind thee;
Oh, flee, if life is anyway dear to thee!

PENTHESILEA. So crush and bruise this breast!—— How could
    he do it?
Oh, Prothoe! It is as wanton-cruel
As though I were to rive the innocent lyre
That hangs in the night breeze, whispering my name.
At the bear's feet I would cower, nestling close,
Would stroke and fondle the blotch'd panther, who
Approached me with such feelings as I him.

MEROE. Wilt thou not move from here?

PROTHOE.   Wilt thou not flee?

MEROE. Come! Save thyself!

PROTHOE.　　　　　　　　That thing unspeakable,
Must it be done here before all our eyes?

PENTHESILEA. Is mine the fault that I must woo him thus,
Here on the field of war must force his love?
What is it I long for, when I strike at him?
Is it to send him headlong to the shades?
I long—ye gods above! I only long—
To this warm breast I long to draw him close!

PROTHOE. She wanders!

HIGH PRIESTESS.　　　　Hapless girl!

PROTHOE.　　　　　　　　　Her wits are strayed.

HIGH PRIESTESS. She cannot think of aught but him.

PROTHOE.　　　　　　　　　　　　The fall—
Woe's me!—the fall has robbed her of all sense!

PENTHESILEA, *with forced calm.*
Good then. Be it as you wish. I will be calm.
This heart—— Since it must be, I will command it
And do with grace what hard compulsion bids.
Oh, you are right! Why should I like a child
Break with our ancient gods, because one wish,
A passing whim's denied me? Come away.
This happiness—it would have been most pleasant.
But if it will not come to me, I'll not
Storm heaven to get it; rather let it go.
Help me away from here. Get me a horse.
Then I will lead you all back to your home.

PROTHOE. Thrice blessèd, noble lady, be this word
So queenly spoken from thy queenly heart.
Come! All is ready for our flight.

PENTHESILEA, *catching sight of the rose-wreaths in the children's hands: in sudden anger.* How now!
Who gave command to start the rose-plucking?

FIRST GIRL. Dost thou still ask? Hast quite forgot? Who else
But only——

PENTHESILEA.　　　But who?

HIGH PRIESTESS.　　　　　　Thyself didst give command

That we should celebrate the longed-for rites.
From thine own lips I had it. Hast thou forgot?

PENTHESILEA. Curses upon this beastly, wanton haste!
Curses on her that thinks but of the orgies
While war still rages, reeking of death and blood!
A curse on lusts that in my Amazons'
Chaste hearts like unleashed dogs do howl and quite
O'erwhelm the trumpet's brazen-throated voice
And all the leaders' cries of shrill command.
Victory—is that yet won, that you should thus
In fiendish mockery pluck triumphal garlands?
Away with them!
She slashes the wreaths to pieces.

FIRST GIRL.   My Queen! What hast thou done?

SECOND GIRL, *collecting the scattered roses.*
In all the valleys round for mile on mile
The spring has not a rose——

PENTHESILEA.   Would God the spring
Should winter and die! Would God this planet Earth
Lay plucked and broken like these roses here!
Would I could tear apart the coronet
Of the circling globes as now this wreath of flowers!
——O Aphrodite!

HIGH PRIESTESS.   Hideous, hideous fate!

FIRST PRIESTESS. Oh! She is lost!

SECOND PRIESTESS.   Into the pit of hell
Her soul is cast, a plaything there for Furies!

A PRIESTESS, *on the hill.*
Ho, virgins! Save yourselves! The son of Peleus
Swiftly approaches scarce a bowshot off.

PROTHOE. Nay, then, I beg thee, I beseech thee: come!

PENTHESILEA. Oh, I am weary! Deadly, deadly tired!
Sits down.

PROTHOE. My Queen! This is stark madness!

PENTHESILEA.   Flee, if you wish!

PROTHOE. Thou wilt——?

MEROE.   Sit here?

PROTHOE. Thou wilt——?

PENTHESILEA. I will sit here.

PROTHOE. 'Tis madness!

PENTHESILEA. I am too weak to stand, I tell you.
Must I break all my bones? Let me alone.

PROTHOE. Most wretched of all women! Achilles comes
Now scarce a bowshot off!

PENTHESILEA. Good. Let him come.
Oh, let him plant his mail'd foot on my neck—
I have deserved no better. Why are these cheeks
In youthful loveliness still loath to mingle
With mud, the primal matter, from which they sprang?
Let him defile this body of mine, now full
Of pulsing life, drag me behind his car,
Shamefully cast me on the open field,
Give me to dogs and to the filthy clan
Of vultures to be mangled and devoured.
Much better dust than thus a woman scorned!

PROTHOE. Oh, Queen!

PENTHESILEA, *tearing the necklace from her neck.*
Off with these thrice-damned gewgaws! Off!

PROTHOE. Oh, gods above! Is that the calm command
Thy lips did but now promise? Calm thyself!

PENTHESILEA. From the head too—nodding follies! I curse
you all,
More impotent even than arrow or blooming cheeks!
That hand I curse that decked me for the fight
This day, and that deceiving serpent-word
That told me I should conquer. Accursed! Accursed!
Oh, how they stood around me with their mirrors—
Flatt'rers!—on either hand and praised the form
Divine of my smooth limbs, moulded in steel!
Pestilence smite you with your tricks of hell!

GREEKS, *off.* Go on, Achilles! Don't lose heart, man! Here,
This way she went. She can't be far off now.

PRIESTESS, *on the hill.*
O Artemis! Queen, fly for thy life! Or else
It is too late!

PROTHOE.   Sweet cousin! Dearest heart!
Wilt thou in sooth not flee?

PENTHESILEA *leans weeping against a tree.*

                    Then, as thou wilt!
If thou canst not, wilt not—good! Dry thy eyes.
I'll stay beside thee. What's not possible,
What lies not in the precinct of thy will,
What thou *canst* not achieve: the gods forbid
That I should ask it of thee. Leave us, friends.
Go; get you back to our dear native plains.
Go—do not wait! The Queen and I stay here!

HIGH PRIESTESS. What, wretched girl! You aid her in this
    madness?

MEROE. You say she *cannot* move from here?

HIGH PRIESTESS.   Cannot!
Though nothing holds her, no fate binds her here,
Only her infatuate heart!

PROTHOE.   That is her fate!
You'd say steel fetters are unbreakable,
Would you not? I say: she *could* break them, perchance,
But never this feeling which you treat so lightly.
What darkly stirs within her, who can say?
A riddle is every heart's deep-flowing tide.
She longed to seize life's highest prize; almost
She touched it, grasped it. Now her hand will not
Be used to take some other, lesser thing.
Come, wait the end here leaning on my breast.
What is it? Wherefore weeping?

PENTHESILEA.   Pain, oh, pain!

PROTHOE. Where?

PENTHESILEA.   Here.

PROTHOE.   How can I help——?

PENTHESILEA.   No! Nothing, nothing!

PROTHOE. Now calm thyself. Soon it will all be over.

HIGH PRIESTESS, *aside.* Nay, this is madness!

PROTHOE, *aside to her.*   Not a word, I beg!

PENTHESILEA. If 'twere my will to flee—if I did flee—
How might I calm myself? Tell me.

PROTHOE.   You'd go to Pharsos.
There you would find the host, now scattered wide,
Drawn all together; thither I bade them go.
There you would rest, there you would tend your wounds;
And with the next day's light, if so it pleased,
You would renew the virgins' holy war.

PENTHESILEA. If it were possible——! If I had the power——!
The utmost have I done that human strength
Is able—I have tried the impossible—
I have staked all upon one throw—all that I have.
The fateful die is cast—it lies before me:
And I must understand—that I have lost.

PROTHOE. Not so, my dearest heart! It is not so.
Surely you do not so contemn your strength.
That prize for which you strive—is it worth so little
That you should think, too arrogant, all had been done
That could be done—that it was worth no more?
What! Is this string of pearls, so white, so red,
That falls here from thy throat, the only wealth
That thy rich soul can summon to its aid?
So much of which thou'st never thought, could still
Be done to gain thy end, wert thou in Pharsos.
But now, 'tis true, almost it is too late.

PENTHESILEA, with an uneasy gesture.
If I were swift—— Oh, it will make me mad!
Where stands the sun?

PROTHOE.   There, straight above thy head.
This day, before night falls, thou couldst be there.
A treaty we could make, unknown to the Greeks,
With Priam's stronghold; all unnoticed then
We'd reach the sea-shore, where the Greek fleet lies.
At midnight, on a signal, all their vessels
Flame skywards, the camp is stormed, the Argive host,
Crushed in from every side by two such foes,
Torn into shreds, dissolved, tossed far and wide,
Pursued, tracked down, then seized and garlanded
Each lusty youth—we've but to take our pick!

What bliss! What heavenly bliss, if this could be!
I'd ask no rest could I but fight beside thee,
Nor shun the sun's fierce heat. Untiring still,
I would consume my latest ounce of strength,
Until at last my sister had her wish
And Peleus' son, the prize of infinite toils,
Sank at her feet—her spoil, her prisoner!

PENTHESILEA, *who has all this time been looking fixedly at the sun.*

That I could cleave the air with rushing pinions
Far-spreading——!

PROTHOE.   What?

MEROE.   What does she say?

PROTHOE.   My Queen!
What is it you see?

MEROE.   What do you gaze upon?

PROTHOE. Dearest, tell me!

PENTHESILEA.   Too high! I know, too high!
Far off, in flame-rings unapproachable,
He circles sporting round my longing heart.

PROTHOE. Who, dearest Queen? Who sports with thee?

PENTHESILEA.   It is well.
——How do we go?

She collects herself and stands up.

MEROE.   Have you decided then?

PROTHOE. Will you get up? Well, then, my Queen, be strong,
A giant in thy strength! Nor never sink,
Not though all Orcus weigh thee to the ground.
Stand, stand now firm; firm as the arch must stand,
Because each stone longs but to crash to earth.
Present thy head, the keystone of thy self,
To God's lightnings and call to him: "Here! Strike!"
Ay! let him split thee to the very ground,
But never waver in thyself again
As long as any grain of stone and mortar
Still hold together in thy breast. Now come.
Come. Give thy hand.

PENTHESILEA.   Is this the way?—— Or that?

PROTHOE. Either the rocky ground there, which is safer,
Or here the easier valley.

PENTHESILEA.   The rocky ground!
By so much am I nearer him then. Follow me!

PROTHOE. Whom, dearest lady?

PENTHESILEA.   Lend me your arm, my friends.

PROTHOE. As soon as thou hast topp'd that hillock there,
Thou art in safety.

MEROE.   Come now.

PENTHESILEA, *suddenly stopping as she is crossing a bridge.*
                    Listen, though:
One thing is still to do before I go.

PROTHOE. To do still?

MEROE.   What is that?

PROTHOE.   Oh, hapless woman!

PENTHESILEA. One thing still, friends; for I were mad,
That you must grant yourselves, did I not try
Everything possible to gain my end.

PROTHOE, *in great annoyance.*
Would that the earth should open and swallow us!
No hope now of escape!

PENTHESILEA, *startled.* What? What's the matter?
Have I offended her? Friends! Tell me how.

HIGH PRIESTESS. Thou think'st——?

MEROE.   Here on this very spot thou wilt——?

PENTHESILEA. Nothing, my friends, nothing to make her
        angry!
Just to pile Ida on to Ossa, then
Quietly take my place upon the top.

HIGH PRIESTESS. Pile Ida on to——?

MEROE.   Ida on to Ossa?

PROTHOE, *turning away.* Oh, all you gods, protect her!

HIGH PRIESTESS.   Lost forever!

MEROE, *timidly.* This is a task for giants, Queen, not men.

PENTHESILEA. Well! What of that? In what do they excel me?

MEROE. In what excel thee!

PROTHOE.   O gods!

HIGH PRIESTESS.   But even then——?

MEROE. Granted thou hadst accomplished this, what then?

PROTHOE. Ay, granted that, what would'st thou——?

PENTHESILEA.   Foolish child!
By his gold-flaming locks I'd draw him down,
Down, down to me——

PROTHOE.   Whom?

PENTHESILEA.   Whom but Helios,
As he sweeps by me in his fiery car?
The PRINCESSES *look at each other in speechless horror.*

HIGH PRIESTESS. Bear her away by force!

PENTHESILEA *looks down into the stream.*
                    Oh, foolish me!
Why, there he is below me! Take me! I come——!
She is about to throw herself into the stream; PROTHOE *and*
MEROE *catch her as she falls.*

PROTHOE. O wretched, wretched woman!

MEROE.   Lifeless, see!
Limp as a garment, in our arms she falls.

PRIESTESS, *on the hill.*
Achilles is upon you! All in vain
The virgins' phalanx strives to hold him off!

AN AMAZON. Save her, ye gods! Protect our Virgin Queen
From desecrating hands!

HIGH PRIESTESS, *to the* PRIESTESSES.
                    Come hence! Away!
We may not stay amid the clash of war.
Exeunt HIGH PRIESTESS, PRIESTESSES, *and* GIRLS.

SCENE 10

Enter a troop of AMAZONS *with bows in their hands.*

FIRST AMAZON, *calling into the wings.* Back, impious man!

SECOND AMAZON.   He does not hear us call.

THIRD AMAZON. Princesses, if we may not shoot at him,
 There is no way to check his mad career!

SECOND AMAZON. What can we do? Say, Prothoe!

PROTHOE, *busy with the* QUEEN. Let fly
 Ten thousand arrows at him!

MEROE, *to the* ATTENDANTS. Bring us water!

PROTHOE. But still be careful that no wound is deadly!

MEROE. Bring me a helmet full of water!

A PRINCESS, *bringing water.* Here!

THIRD AMAZON, *to* PROTHOE.
 You need not fear. We'll keep you safe!

FIRST AMAZON, *to the rest.* Stand here!
 We'll graze his cheeks and singe his golden hair;
 So let him taste the transient kiss of death.
 They make ready their bows.

SCENE 11

Enter ACHILLES, *without helmet or weapons, some* GREEKS
following.

ACHILLES. Whom would you welcome with these shafts, dear
 girls?
 Surely not my all unprotected breast?
 Should I tear wide this silken shirt as well,
 That you could see how innocent beats my heart?

FIRST AMAZON. Ay, if you will!

SECOND AMAZON. There is no need!

THIRD AMAZON. Shoot now!
 The arrow there, just where he holds his hand!

FIRST AMAZON. That it may pierce his heart and bear it
 onwards
 In flight, like a dead leaf——!

MEROE. Shoot!
 They shoot over his head.

ACHILLES. Foolish children!

With your sweet eyes you hit more certainly.
By all the gods, in very sooth and sadness,
I feel your darts deep in my innermost breast.
Disarmed in every sense, defenceless, here
Before your delicate feet I lay myself.

FIFTH AMAZON, *pierced by a spear from behind the scenes.*
Ye gods above!

Falls.

SIXTH AMAZON, *also smitten.* Alas!

Falls.

SEVENTH AMAZON, *also smitten.* Diana help me!

Falls.

FIRST AMAZON. Oh, fearful man! } *Together.*
MEROE, *busy with the* QUEEN.
      Ah, thrice-unhappy girl!

SECOND AMAZON   And calls himself disarmed! }
PROTHOE, *also busy with the* QUEEN.   Oh! She is dead!

THIRD AMAZON. We stand here while his people
    slaughter us! }
MEROE.   On every hand our virgins are cut down!
  What can we do?

FIRST AMAZON.   Bring out the scythèd car!

SECOND AMAZON. Set all the dogs upon him!

THIRD AMAZON.   Bury him! Crush him
  With huge stones flung from towering elephants!

A PRINCESS, *suddenly leaving the* QUEEN.
  It must be! I will see what a shot can do!

Unslings her bow and strings it.

ACHILLES, *turning from one* AMAZON *to another.*
  How should I credit it? So sweet, so silvery,
  Your voices still belie these ruthless words.
  Thou, blue-eyed beauty, sure it is not thou
  That would unleash the dogs on me to tear me?
  Nor thou whose glory is thy silk-soft locks?
  Think! If unchained upon your hasty word
  With fearful howl these savage beasts sprang on me,
  With your own bodies you would interpose

'Twixt them and me, to save this heart, this stout
Man's heart, that glows with love for none but you!

FIRST AMAZON. Unbridled insolence!

SECOND AMAZON.   Hark how he boasts!

FIRST AMAZON. He thinks with flattering words to lull——

THIRD AMAZON, *calling the first under her breath.* Oterpe!

FIRST AMAZON, *turning round.*
Ah, look! 'Tis she who never yet has missed!
Open your ranks a little!

FIFTH AMAZON.   For what purpose?

FOURTH AMAZON. No questions! You will see!

FIRST AMAZON.   Here! Take this arrow!

PRINCESS, *setting the arrow to the string.*
I will transfix his thighs and cripple him.

ACHILLES, *to a* GREEK *at his side, whose bow is at the ready.*
Shoot her!

PRINCESS.   Ye gods above!
She falls.

FIRST AMAZON.   Oh, dreadful man!

SECOND AMAZON. 'Tis she who's hit and falls!

THIRD AMAZON.   The gods protect us!
Another band of Greeks bears down on us.

SCENE 12

Enter DIOMEDE *with the* AETOLIANS *on one side, soon fol-*
lowed by ODYSSEUS *with the army on the same side as*
ACHILLES.

DIOMEDE. This way, my stout Aetolians! Follow me!
This way!
He leads them over the bridge.

PROTHOE.   O Artemis! Now save us all,
Else are we quite destroyed!
With the help of some AMAZONS *she carries the* QUEEN *to*
the front of the stage.

AMAZONS, *in confusion.*   We are surrounded!
  We are cut off! We are all prisoners!
  Run! Get away while there is time!

DIOMEDE, *to* PROTHOE.   Now yield!

MEROE, *to the fleeing* AMAZONS.
  What! Are you mad? Will you not stand and fight?
  Prothoe! Look!

PROTHOE, *still with the* QUEEN.
               Go after them! Rally them!
  And when thou canst, come back and rescue us!

  The AMAZONS *flee in different directions.* MEROE *follows.*

ACHILLES. Now where is she? Where shines that lovely head?

A GREEK. There!

ACHILLES.   Diomede shall have ten kingly crowns.

DIOMEDE, *to* PROTHOE.
  Once more I call on you to yield!

PROTHOE.   To him
  Who won her, not to thee, I yield. To thee?
  She is Achilles' prize, belongs to him alone.

DIOMEDE, *to his men.* Then cut her down!

AN AETOLIAN.   Come on!

ACHILLES.   He dies this instant
  Who dares to lay a finger on the Queen!
  Mine is she! Out of here! Take yourselves off!

DIOMEDE. Oho! She's thine? Well, by Zeus' inky locks!
  Upon what reason? With what right, may I ask?

ACHILLES. For two good reasons—this right one and this left!

  To PROTHOE.

  Give her!

PROTHOE.   Here, take! In thy big heart she's safe.

ACHILLES, *taking the* QUEEN *in his arms.* Safe, safe!

  To DIOMEDE.

          Go now and smite the fleeing women.
  I must stay here a moment. Do not stay!
  For my sake, go. Do not oppose me! Hell
  Itself I'd challenge for her, much more thee!

He lays her reclining against the root of an oak.

DIOMEDE. Well, then! Follow me!

ODYSSEUS, *passing across the stage with the army.*
        Good luck, Achilles! Good luck!
Shall I send thy thund'ring war-car to thee there?

ACHILLES, *bent over the* QUEEN. There is no need. Not now.

ODYSSEUS.   Good! As thou wilt.
All follow me! Before these women can rally!

ODYSSEUS *and* DIOMEDE *with the army off.*

SCENE 13

PENTHESILEA, PROTHOE, ACHILLES. GREEKS *and*
AMAZONS *in attendance*

ACHILLES, *unbuckling the* QUEEN's *armour.* No breath of life!

PROTHOE.   Oh, may she nevermore
Look on the pallid light of this drear day!
I fear, I fear that she must still awaken.

ACHILLES. Where did I wound her?

PROTHOE.   From that blow, which split
Her breast, she by main force of will did rally.
Thus far we led her, weak and tottering still,
And were about to climb with her this rocky slope,
But pain o'ercame her, whether of her body
So wounded, or of her bruisèd heart: she could not
Abide the thought that thou hadst overcome her.
Her stumbling foot refused its service; vague,
Meaningless babblings passed her anguished lips,
And once again she sank into my arms.

ACHILLES. She stirred!—— Did you not see?

PROTHOE.   Ye gods above!
Has she not yet drunk all her bitter cup?
Look, look! Oh, piteous sight!

ACHILLES.   I feel her breath.

PROTHOE. Great son of Peleus! If thou canst know pity,

If any tender feeling stirs thy breast,
If it is not thy will to slay her nor to entoil
Her trembling senses in the web of madness,
Then grant me this one boon!

ACHILLES.   Say quickly!

PROTHOE. Leave her! Go off! Noblest of men, go off!
Stand not before her face when she awakes.
Remove from here thy attendant company,
And ere to-morrow's sun cast his fresh light
On the far mountain's misty top, let no one
Greet her with that fell word, more bitter than death:
That she is prisoner to Peleus' son.

ACHILLES. So! Does she hate me?

PROTHOE.   Ask not, generous man!
When she returns now to the light with joy
And delicate hope, let not her vanquisher
Be her first sight, killing both hope and joy.
How much is hidden in a woman's breast
It is not meet should see the light of day.
If she at last, since Fate has so ordained,
Must give thee hateful greeting as thy prisoner,
At least do not demand it, that I beg,
Until her spirit is strong to bear such grief.

ACHILLES. My will is, I would have thee know, to do
To her as I did do to Priam's son.

PROTHOE. Oh, fearful man! Not that!

ACHILLES.   Does she fear this?

PROTHOE. Thou wilt accomplish on her nameless shames?
This lovely body in the bloom of youth,
Decked out with beauties as a child with flowers,
Shamefully, like a rotting corpse thou wilt——?

ACHILLES. Say to her that I love her.

PROTHOE.   How? Thou lov'st——?

ACHILLES. How, by the gods above? As men love women;
Chastely—and yet with longing; in innocence—
And yet not loath to rob her of her own.
It is my will to take her for my Queen.

PROTHOE. O blissful words! Say them—say them once more!
　It is thy will?

ACHILLES. 　　　　　　Now may I stay?

PROTHOE. 　　　　　　　　　　Oh, stay,
　Thou godlike man! Let me but kiss thy feet!
　Now, if thou wert not here, I would go seek thee,
　Even beyond the Pillars of Hercules!
　But see! Her eyes are opening——

ACHILLES. 　　　　　　　　　　She moves.

PROTHOE. Now is the time! Withdraw, you there; and thou
　Hide quickly from her sight behind that oak!

ACHILLES, to MYRMIDONS.

　Move off, my friends! Away from here!

ACHILLES' attendants off.

PROTHOE. 　　　　　　　　　Hide well!
　And do not show thyself, I beg, until
　Thou hear'st me call. Achilles! Dost thou promise?
　I cannot tell how her poor mind will be.

ACHILLES. I will obey.

PROTHOE. 　　　　　You may watch us unseen.

SCENE 14

PENTHESILEA, PROTHOE, ACHILLES. Attendant AMAZONS

PROTHOE. Penthesilea! What! Still lost in dreams?
　In what far paradise does thy swift spirit
　Still wheel and hover on its restless wings,
　Leaving its proper seat in strange disgust?
　While Fortune, like a young and lusty prince,
　Enters thy breast and, all amazed to find
　The lovely dwelling-place quite tenantless,
　Turns on his heel and makes again to bend
　His fleeting steps to heaven whence he came.
　Fond girl! Wilt thou not bind the sweet intruder?
　Come, raise thyself and lean on me!

PENTHESILEA.   Where am I?

PROTHOE. Dost thou not know the voice of thy own sister?
This rocky slope, this narrow bridge, these wide
And fertile-teeming plains—do you not know them?
Look, here thy maidens all who wait upon thee:
As though before the gates of some brighter world
They stand and bid thee welcome. Dearest heart,
Wherefore that sigh? What dost thou fear?

PENTHESILEA.   Oh, Prothoe!
I dreamed, I dreamed—ah, what a fearful dream!
How sweet it is, sweet even to tears, to feel
This anguished heart, deadened with pain's excess,
Beat against thy strong heart, now I awake.
I dreamed that in the fiercest clash of war,
Smitten by Achilles' lance, I crash'd to the ground
And loud around me rang my brazen arms,
While Earth herself resounded to my fall.
And while the army in confusion flees—
I still with limbs entangled helpless there—
He has leapt down from off his charger, springs
With triumphant strides towards me, stoops
And seizes me, half swooning as I am,
Raises me up in his strong arms and holds me:
Vainly I seek to find and draw my dagger:
His prisoner I, and with fierce, mocking laughter
He bears me off by force to his hateful tents.

PROTHOE. Ah no, dear Queen! Not that! Not mocking laughter.
His noble generous heart could never mock thee.
If it indeed should hap, what thy dream told,
Truly that were for thee a blissful hour:
I doubt not, in the dust, upon his knees
Before thee as thy slave thou'dst see Achilles.

PENTHESILEA. Accursèd I, if that should ever be!
Accursèd, should I yield my maidenhead
To any man not prisoner of my sword!

PROTHOE. Calm thyself, dearest lady!

PENTHESILEA.   Calm! Why calm?

PROTHOE. Dost thou not lie here safe upon my bosom?
Whatever fate hang poised above thy head,

We will endure together: calm thyself.

PENTHESILEA. But I was calm, my Prothoe, as the sea
That lies landlocked between craggy shores; not one
Feeling that roused a ripple on my heart.
But now this "Calm thyself!" suddenly whips
The unsheltered oceans of my mind to fierce turmoil.
What has befall'n that I must needs be calm?
You stand and look so strangely, so uneasy,
And throw such fearful glances, by the gods,
Behind me there, as though some dreadful thing
With wild, contorted face stood threatening me.
I told thee, it was but a dream, it is not——
Or is it? What? Oh, tell me! Is it real?
Where's Meroe? And Megaris?

She looks behind her and sees ACHILLES.

Oh, horrible!
Most dreaded to my eyes! He stands behind me.
But now my hand is free——

She draws her dagger.

PROTHOE. Stop, senseless girl!

PENTHESILEA. Shameless! Betrayer! Would you thwart me still?

PROTHOE. Achilles! You can save her!

PENTHESILEA. Are you mad?
His only thought to trample me to dust.

PROTHOE. Trample thee? Never!

PENTHESILEA. Away! Leave me, I say!

PROTHOE. But do but look at him, impetuous girl!
Does he not stand unarmed, defenceless there?

PENTHESILEA. Unarmed?

PROTHOE. Why, yes! And ready, if thou wilt,
To have thee chain him with these wreaths of love.

PENTHESILEA. It cannot be!

PROTHOE. Achilles! Speak thyself!

PENTHESILEA. My prisoner he?

PROTHOE. Why, yes! Why, yes! What else?

ACHILLES, *who has come forward.*

In every way that's fair, thy prisoner I!
My only will to flutter out my life
In the soft durance of thy heavenly eyes.

PENTHESILEA *buries her face in her hands.*

PROTHOE. So now, you have heard him say himself 'tis so.
At your encounter he too crashed to earth;
And while you lay lifeless upon the ground
He was disarmed—is't not so?

ACHILLES.   Yes, disarmed.
And then led captive here before thy feet.

He falls on one knee before her.

PENTHESILEA, *after a short pause.*

Welcome—fair greeting then—fresh sweetness of life,
Thou lovely god with the bright cheeks of youth!
And oh, my heart, be rid of that stored blood
That, waiting on his coming, stagnant lies
Oppressive in the chambers of my breast.
You messengers of pleasure, eager-wing'd,
Sap of my youth, life's liquor, stir yourselves,
Flood through my veins, leap, shout for lusty joy,
And let the empurpled banner, steeped in gules,
Flaunt from the imperial watch-tower of my cheeks.
Achilles' self, the goddess-born, is mine!

She rises.

PROTHOE. My dearest Queen, be moderate in thy joy!

PENTHESILEA, *stepping forward.*

Come, then, you victory-crownèd virgins, come,
You daughters of Mars, from head to foot still thick
Encrusted with the blood-caked dust of battle,
Come, leading each by the hand that Argive youth
That she has vanquished on the field of war.
You younger maids draw near that keep the roses;
You have not wreaths enough to deck each brow?
Out then and seek o'er all the fields! And if
The niggard spring refuse me roses, breathe,
Breathe on the plain and it will burgeon for me!
Diana's priestesses! Take up your office,
That wide the thund'ring portals of her house,
Light-radiant, with heady incense sweet,

May open to me like the gates of heaven.
First now the ox, well fattened, short of horn,
Here to the altar; thus the axe strikes home,
Fells him without a sound, and all the vast
And holy building trembles at his fall.
You temple serving-women, strong of limb,
The blood! The blood! Where are you?— Quick! To work!
Wash clean of blood the marble pavement, spread
The fragrance of burned Persian unguents here.
And all you fluttering kirtles, kilt you high!
You golden goblets, overflow with wine!
Bugles, shrill out! Horns, blare your resonant thunder!
Let heaven's firm-planted vault reverberate
To our melodious peals of heady joy!—
Oh, Prothoe! Help me give rein to this
Fierce ecstasy of bliss! Invent, discover,
How I may celebrate a festival
More heavenly than heav'n's own joyous pomps—
The wedding-feast of the dread brides of war,
The seed of Inachus, daughters of Mars!

PROTHOE, *with suppressed emotion.*

I see joy is no less thy bane than sorrow;
No matter which, it straight will make you mad.
You think yourself, fond fool, in Themiscyra.
Oh! When you thus break bounds and range at large,
I am sore tempted to pronounce that word
That lames your wing and tumbles you to earth.
Poor self-deceived, look round thee, where thou art?
Where is the host? The priestesses? Thy friends?
Asteria? Meroe? Megaris? Where are they?

PENTHESILEA, *on her breast.*

Not harsh, my Prothoe! Let my poor heart
Like a dirt-dabbled, happy child, sink deep
One wondrous moment in the stream of joy.
With every splash in those exultant waves
A stain is washed from my sad, sinful breast.
They flee at last, the dread Eumenides;
I feel the approach of godlike presences
And I would join my voice to their happy choir.
Ne'er was I half so ripe for death as now.

Yet one thing before all: I am forgiven?

PROTHOE. My Queen and lady!

PENTHESILEA.   Good! I know, I know!
Thou hast the nobler part of our kindred blood.
They say misfortune purifies the soul,
But I, my love, have never found it so.
Bitterness still, rage against gods and men,
Unseeing passion, are its fruits in me.
With strange perversity I then have hated
On others' faces every mark of joy;
The blithe child playing in its mother's lap
Seemed but conspired to mock my sullen grief.
But now how gladly would I see each thing
Content and happy round about! Dear friend,
Man can be great in grief, ay, even a hero,
But only in happiness is he a god.
But now, much is to do. Without delay
The host shall make all ready for the march.
Soon as the companies both man and beast
Are rested, with the prisoners the whole
Breaks camp and moves to our far native vales——
Where is Lykaon?

PROTHOE.   Who?

PENTHESILEA, *with tender reproach*.   You ask me, who?
That fair Arcadian, of heroic form,
Whom thy sword won thee. Why is he not here?

PROTHOE, *embarrassed*.

My Queen, he lies with all the captive Greeks,
There in the woods, close guarded like the rest.
I pray you grant, as ancient law demands,
That I not see him till the city is reached.

PENTHESILEA. Call him before me! Close guarded in the
        woods!
Here at my Prothoe's feet is his right place.
Dearest, let him be called, I beg of you!
You stand so blighting there as frost in May,
Congealing all my springs of vernal joy.

PROTHOE, *aside*.

Unhappy girl!—— Good, then! Go one of you

And do what you have heard the Queen command.

She signs to an AMAZON *who exit.*

PENTHESILEA. Now, who will fetch the rose-girls to me here?

She catches sight of roses on the ground.

Look! Here are blossoms—— Ah! So sweet to smell!
Here on the ground——

She passes her hand over her brow.

Oh! My evil dream!

To PROTHOE.

Was not the Priestess of Diana here?

PROTHOE. I do not think so, gracious Queen. Mayhap——

PENTHESILEA. But how do the roses come here?

PROTHOE, *quickly.*   Ah! I know.
The girls, when they were searching all the plain
For roses, left one basket here forgotten.
Now this is a most lucky accident!
Look, I will wind thee from these scented blooms
A wreath to honour Achilles. Shall I do it?

She sits down against the oak.

PENTHESILEA. Thou dearest! Kindest! Now you touch my heart!
Good, then. These hundred-petalled buds I'll wind for thee
To be thy wreath of victory for Lykaon.

She too gathers up some roses and sits down by PROTHOE.

Music, my friends, music! I am not calm.
Let your clear song sound out and bring me peace!

A VIRGIN. What should we sing?

ANOTHER.   The triumph song?

PENTHESILEA.   The Hymn.

VIRGIN. So be it! (Deluded still!) Sing, then, and play!

CHOIR OF VIRGINS, *with music.*

Ares withdraws!
See how his gleaming white team,
Trailing vapour to Orcus, sweeps afar!
The loathly goddesses open, the Eumenides,
Then shut to the portals once again behind him.

A VIRGIN. Hymen! Why tarriest thou?
  Kindle the torch-flame and light us! Light us!
  Hymen! Why tarriest thou?

CHOIR. Ares withdraws!
  See how his gleaming white team,
  Trailing vapour to Orcus, sweeps afar!
  The loathly goddesses open, the Eumenides,
  Then shut to the portals once again behind him.

ACHILLES, *moves stealthily up to* PROTHOE *during the singing.*
  Where does this lead me? Speak! I will be told!

PROTHOE. Patience one moment more, great-hearted man.
  I beg you—patience. Then you shall have your will.

  When the wreaths are made, PENTHESILEA *and* PROTHOE *exchange wreaths, embrace each other, and examine them. The music ends. The* AMAZON *returns.*

PENTHESILEA. Well, did you do it?

AMAZON.   Lykaon, gracious Queen,
  The young Arcadian prince, will soon be here.

SCENE 15

PENTHESILEA. Come now, my own Achilles, goddess-born.
  Come, lay thee at my feet. Nay, closer yet!
  No shame nor coyness! Sure, thou dost not fear me?
  Nor hate me neither?

ACHILLES, *at her feet.*   As flowers the spring sunshine!

PENTHESILEA. Then thou canst look on me now as thy sun.
  Diana, gracious lady! See, he is
  Wounded!

ACHILLES.   Grazed by an arrow, that is all.

PENTHESILEA, *taking the wreaths.*
  I pray thee, son of Peleus, never think
  That I did ever wish to take thy life.
  'Tis true, when this arm smote thee, it was bliss;
  But when thus smitten thou didst fall, my heart
  Envied the dust that then was pressed beneath thee.

ACHILLES. Nay, if you love me, do not speak of it.
　　You see, 'tis healing.

PENTHESILEA.　　　　　　Then I am forgiven?

ACHILLES. With all my heart!

PENTHESILEA.　　　　　　　Good. Now I would be taught
　　What wiles the Queen of Love must use, when she
　　Would bind with silken chains the shag-maned lion.

ACHILLES. With her soft hand she strokes his horrid cheeks;
　　Then he is still.

PENTHESILEA.　　　　'Tis well. Then thou wilt not
　　Move more than does the tender turtle-dove
　　When round her neck her mistress lays soft cords.
　　For know, sweet youth, the emotions of this breast
　　Play round thee still like soft caressing hands.
　　She lays garlands round him.

ACHILLES. Who art thou, strange and wondrous woman?

PENTHESILEA.　　　　　　　　　　　So!——
　　I said keep still! Soon I will tell thee all.
　　But first thou must be bound, thus lightly bound,
　　With roses round thy head and round thy throat
　　—Then down around thy arms, thy hands, thy feet,
　　Thence back up to thy head—— Now, it is finished.
　　What do you breathe so?

ACHILLES.　　　　　　Scent of thy warm lips.

PENTHESILEA, *straightening herself a little.*
　　It is the roses. Their scent fills the air.

ACHILLES. Would I might taste those roses where they grow.

PENTHESILEA. At the appointed time my love shall pluck them.
　　She sets one last wreath on his head and lets go of him.
　　So it is finished! See, my Prothoe!
　　Suffused with delicate rose, is he not handsome?
　　The Day new-sprung, I swear it, when from the hills
　　The light-foot Hours come leading him along—
　　His swift feet shedding pearls and diamonds—
　　Looks not more gentle nor more tenderly.
　　Would you not say his eye held back a tear?

In sooth, one well could doubt, when he looks so,
That it is he.

PROTHOE.   Who, sister?

PENTHESILEA.   Who? Achilles!
That man that slew old Priam's greatest son
Before the walls of Troy—— Say! Was it thou?
And didst thou truly, thou, with these thy hands
Pierce his fleet ankles, then behind thy car
Drag him headlong around his native city?
Speak! What's the matter? Why art thou so moved?

ACHILLES. I am that man.

PENTHESILEA, *looking at him sharply.* He says 'tis he.

PROTHOE.   My Queen,
Here by his fine-wrought armour thou canst know him.

PENTHESILEA. How?

PROTHOE.   This is that famed harness—Nay, look close—
That Thetis, his dread mother, suppliant,
Begged of divine Hephaestus, lord of fire.

PENTHESILEA. So, then, I seal thee with this kiss, of all
Mankind the most rebellious, mine! 'Tis I
Who am thy mistress, youthful war-god thou!
Should any ask thee of the people, name my name.

ACHILLES. O thou, who with soft, heavenly radiance,
As though the realms of light had oped their doors,
Descendest on me, strange beyond wit: who art thou?
How do I name thee, when my own soul asks,
In sudden rapture who her mistress is?

PENTHESILEA. When thy soul asks, then name these features.
     That
Be all the name of me dwells in thy mind.
This golden ring indeed I give to thee,
Whose marks are surety to thee I am I;
Show it to any, all will know it mine.
Rings may be lost, a name may be forgotten.
My name forgot, this ring quite lost, couldst thou
Still find my living image in thy heart?
Canst thou, eyes closed, create it in thy mind?

ACHILLES. Clear, true it stands, as graved in diamond.

PENTHESILEA. I am the Queen of all the Amazons;
  My race claims Ares as its first begetter;
  Otrere was my noble mother; me,
  My warlike people calls: Penthesilea.

ACHILLES. Penthesilea.

PENTHESILEA.   Thus I said to thee.

ACHILLES. Dying, my swan shall sing: Penthesilea.

PENTHESILEA. Thou hast thy liberty. Through all the host
  Freely, where'er it pleases, thou may'st walk.
  Quite other chains, more delicate than flowers,
  As brass unbreakable I mean to wind
  About thy heart and bind thee fast to me.
  But till they, link on link, are hammered out
  In passion's heat and adamantine forged,
  No more destructible by time or chance,
  Thou wilt return of right to me again,
  To me, my friend, no other; for 'tis I
  Will serve thee in thy every need or wish.
  Tell me, wilt thou return?

ACHILLES.   As do young stallions
  To that sweet-scented manger where they feed.

PENTHESILEA. Good. I shall trust thy word. Now we begin
  The long march back to our city, Themiscyra.
  Take from my stables what horse suits thy whim.
  Thou shalt have purple tents to dwell in; nor
  Shall slaves to serve thee as befits and do
  Thy royal will in everything be lacking.
  But since upon the march I shall be bound
  By cares of leadership, thou wilt consort
  Still with the other Argive prisoners.
  At home in Themiscyra, not till then,
  Shall I be free to give thee all my heart.

ACHILLES. So it shall be.

PENTHESILEA, *to* PROTHOE.   But tell me now, dear friend,
  Where can thy young Arcadian be?

PROTHOE.   My Queen—!

PENTHESILEA. I would so gladly see thee set the wreath
  Upon his head, my Prothoe.

PROTHOE. He will
Soon come. Indeed, he shall not lose his wreath.

PENTHESILEA, *preparing to rise*.
Good, then. A thousand duties call me, friend.
So let me go.

ACHILLES. What!

PENTHESILEA. Let me rise, I say.

ACHILLES. Thou wilt be gone? Wilt leave me here? Though
still
Thou hast not satisfied my longing breast's
Untaught surmise and baffled questioning?

PENTHESILEA. In Themiscyra, friend.

ACHILLES. No, here, my Queen!

PENTHESILEA. In Themiscyra, friend, in Themiscyra!
Let me go!

PROTHOE, *restraining her, troubled*.
Why? What wilt thou do, dear lady?

PENTHESILEA. Strange question! I must order the companies,
Consult with Meroe and Megaris.
By heaven, have I nought else to do but chatter?

PROTHOE. The army still pursues the fleeing Greeks.
Leave Meroe, who leads the van, that work.
You still have need of rest. Soon as the foe,
Both horse and foot, is back behind Scamander
Shall the victorious host parade before you.

PENTHESILEA, *considering*.
Ah! Here, where I am standing? Is that sure?

PROTHOE. Certain. I promise it.

PENTHESILEA, *to* ACHILLES. Well, then, be brief.

ACHILLES. What is the cause, thou strange and wondrous
woman,
That, Pallas-like, queen of a host in arms,
Thou fling'st thyself, all unprovoked, a bolt
From heaven, into our quarrel here with Troy?
What urges thee, in steel caparisoned,
Full of insensate rage, most like a Fury,
To fall thus headlong on the tribes of Argos?

Thou who dost need but to reveal thy sweet
Person in quiet loveliness and straight
All men will fall before thee worshipping!

PENTHESILEA. Son of the dread sea-goddess! Not for me
The common arts of gentler womanhood!
When to the games the lusty youths rejoicing
Throng to make trial of each other's strength,
I may not, as do your maids, choose my love
And draw him to me with shy downward eyes
Or with bright wanton nosegay, here or here;
I may not in the dark-leaved orange grove,
Where nightingales throb out the forenoon's heat,
Sink on his breast and tell him it is he.
No, on the bloody field of war must I go seek him,
That youth my heart has chosen for its own,
And clip him to me with harsh arms of brass,
Whom rather I would press to this soft breast.

ACHILLES. But whence can spring, how ancient is that law,
Unwomanly, forgive me, nay, unnatural,
A custom strange to all the tribes of men?

PENTHESILEA. From the remotest urn of things revered,
O youth, down from remotest peaks of time,
Unknown, untrodden, wrapped eternally
In divine mystery as in a cloud.
The ban was laid by word of our first mothers,
And we are dumb before it, son of Thetis,
As thou before thy first forefathers' words.

ACHILLES. Speak plainer.

PENTHESILEA.   Be it so, then! Hearken well.
In that far land where the Amazons now dwell,
Lived once, obedient to the gods, a tribe
Of Scythians, warlike, subject to no lord,
Not different from other tribes of men.
For centuries past counting they had called
The high, flower-cradled Caucasus their own;
At whose foot Vexoris, the Ethiop king,
Appearing suddenly, slew all the men
Who stood in arms against him, thence unhindered
Poured through the valleys, slaughtering every male,

Old men and boys, where'er his sword might find them,
Earth's splendour with that race was blotted out.
The victors then, brazen barbarians,
Took to themselves our huts, dwelt in them, fed
Their hateful bodies from our fields' fat crops,
And, that our cup of shame might quite o'erflow,
Forced on our women vile embrace of love.
They tore us, still lamenting our dead menfolk,
From those sad graves into their loathsome beds.

ACHILLES. Crushing in sooth, Queen, was that fate to which
Your woman's nation owes its timely birth.

PENTHESILEA. Yet man rebels, shaking his shoulders free
Of all that gyves his heart beyond endurance;
Ills must be moderate, or he'll not bear them.
Long nights on end, in deepest secrecy,
The women lay in Ares' house and wept,
Graving with passionate prayer the altar steps.
Their beds, by ruffian force defiled, began
To fill with daggers needle-sharp, rough-forged
In the hearth's homely flame from ornaments,
From bodkins, rings, and brooches: only still
They waited on the nuptials of King Vexoris
With Tanais, their Queen, to kiss with these
Keen love-tokens their ravishers' swart breasts.
And when the wedding hour was now at hand,
Into his heart the Queen drove home her blade,
Mars in his stead fulfilled the solemn rite,
And all that race of murderers with knives
In that one night was tickled to the shades.

ACHILLES. Ay! Women's vengeance! I can well believe it!

PENTHESILEA. And now in open folk-moot was decreed:
Free as the wind that sweeps the unsheltered fallow
Are women who have wrought so great a deed,
And to the male no more subservient.
A nation has arisen, a nation of women,
Bound to no overlord, in which no voice
Of arrogant, o'erweening man is heard;
A folk that gives itself its own just laws,
Obeys its own decrees, and can defend

Itself from foes; and Tanais is its Queen.
That man whose eye but looks upon this people
Shall straightway close his eye forever; where
A boy is the sad fruit of that forced mating,
No room for pity! He must straight below,
Down to the shades to meet his savage sire.
Thereon the house of Ares straight was thronged
With folk close-packed, to crown great Tanais
Queen, paramount defender of the state.
But just as she, at that most solemn moment,
Mounted the altar steps, to grasp the bow—
The mighty, golden bow of the Scythian realm,
Which none but kings till then had borne—and take it
From the rich-robed high priestess' hand, sudden
An awful voice was heard uttering these words:
"'Twill but invite menfolk to mockery,
A nation such as this, and 'twill succomb
To the first onset of its warlike neighbours;
For never can weak women, hampered still
By the full-swelling bosom, learn to use
The taut bow's deadly swiftness, as can men!"
One moment long the Queen stood, pondering
What good might spring from counsel of the god.
But as base fear began to sweep the people,
She tore away her own right breast, baptising
Thus all these women who would wield the bow
—Herself, ere she had finished, swooned away—
The Amazons, that is: the breastless ones!
This done, the crown was set upon her head.

ACHILLES. Why then, by God! She had no need of breasts!
She could have been as well a queen of men,
And from my heart I bow in reverence to her.

PENTHESILEA. My friend, upon this deed was utter stillness;
No word, no sound was heard, save that the bow
Fell whirring from the bloodless, lifeless hands
Of the high priestess to the temple floor.
It fell, the mighty golden bow of our race,
Then rang aloud three times from the marble step
With bell-like drone and settled slowly down
And lay mute at her feet, silent as death.

ACHILLES. You women do not follow her, I hope,
In this example?

PENTHESILEA.   Not? Indeed we do!
Maybe not quite so eagerly as she.

ACHILLES, *astonished*. What? Then it is——? Impossible!

PENTHESILEA.   What, then?

ACHILLES. The monstrous rumour then is true indeed?
And all these lovely forms, that stand around thee
In youthful bloom, the pride of womanhood,
Each one decked out with charms, a holy altar
Before which we must bow the knee for love—
Are barbarously, inhumanly, deformed——?

PENTHESILEA. Was that indeed unknown to thee?

ACHILLES, *hiding his face on her breast*.

                          My Queen!
The seat of all youth's tenderest, sweetest feelings
Thus criminally, thus wantonly——

PENTHESILEA.   Fear not!
Here in this left breast they have taken refuge
And are, by that much, nearer to my heart.
Not one shalt thou find lacking, friend, in me.

ACHILLES. In sooth, a dream that's dreamed at grey of dawn
Seems truer far than does this here and now.
But now, proceed.

PENTHESILEA.   What?

ACHILLES.   There is more to come.
For this too daring-proud nation of women
That without help of men arose, how still
Can it without men's help renew itself?
Does old Deucalion from time to time
Toss you a rock or two from his magic store?

PENTHESILEA. Whenever, following yearly reckonings,
The Queen thinks fit to replace whate'er the state
Has lost through death, she calls the blossoming prime
Of all the women——

Stops short and looks at him.

                  Why do you smile?

ACHILLES.   Who? I?

PENTHESILEA. Did you not smile? It seemed so.

ACHILLES.   For thy beauty
My thoughts had strayed. Forgive me. I was wond'ring
If thou wert not come down to me from the moon.

PENTHESILEA, *after a pause.*
Whenever, following yearly reckonings,
The Queen thinks fit to replace whate'er the state
Has lost by death, she calls the blossoming prime
Of all the women from her whole realm together
To Themiscyra. There, in Diana's temple,
She prays for all: that their young wombs may teem
With the sweet fruit of Ares' chaste embrace.
This festival of gentle hope we call
The Feast of Flowering Virgins, and we wait
Until the mantling snow's breathed all to shreds
And spring has pressed his kiss on Earth's cold breast.
The Queen's prayer made, Diana's holy priestess
Passes into the temple of great Mars
And there, prone on the altar steps, she lays
The mothers' wish before the all-seeing god.
The god, then, if he inclines to hear her prayer
—For often he'll not have it: niggardly
Of sustenance are these our snow-capped hills—
The god makes known to us through his high priestess
A people chaste and lordly which shall do
Instead of him the service we have asked.
This people's name and habitation known,
A surging joy runs throughout city and land.
As Brides of Mars we greet the warrior-virgins,
Who from their mothers' hands receive their weapons,
Short sword and arrows; and their youthful limbs,
Joyously waited on by busy hands,
Are quickly cased in brazen wedding garb.
The day is set for their glad journeying;
Faint bugle calls are heard, whispered commands;
The bands of girls swing themselves into the saddle;
Noiseless and stealthy, as though woollen shod,
Under the moon they ride through valley and woodland

To the far burg where lies that chosen folk.
The land once reached, we halt upon its frontier,
Two days of rest for weary man and beast,
Then, like the fiery hurricano's blast,
We sweep into the forest of their menfolk,
Snatch up the ripest of the fallen fruit—
Seeds that are scattered from the thrashing tree-tops—
And bear them with us to our native plains.
Here we conduct them in Diana's temple
Through many a solemn rite, of which the name
Alone is known to me—the Feast of Roses:
Forbidden is it—death is his reward
Who dares approach, except the Brides of Mars.
The seed is sown, and when the crop is up,
We heap on them full measure of glorious gifts;
On steeds richly caparisoned we send
Them home. The Feast of Fruitful Mothers this,
In sooth a festival of little joy.
Ah, son of Thetis! Many a tear is shed,
And many a heart, fast gripped by dreary grief,
Must ask itself: is Tanais the Great
For every binding word so praiseworthy?
What do you muse on?

ACHILLES.   I?

PENTHESILEA.   Who else?

ACHILLES.   My love!
On more than I can yet find words to utter—
And shall I in like manner be dismissed?

PENTHESILEA. I do not know, dear. Do not ask me!

ACHILLES.   Strange!

He falls into thought.

But there is one thing I must understand.

PENTHESILEA. Willingly, friend. Speak freely.

ACHILLES.   Tell me why
Thy hot pursuit was aimed only on me?
Was I then known to thee?

PENTHESILEA.   Ay, that thou wast!

ACHILLES. But how?

PENTHESILEA.   If thou'lt not smile at my foolishness——?

ACHILLES, *smiling.* I know not—thou must promise too.

PENTHESILEA.   Well, then,
I'll tell thee. Already I had seen the feast,
The happy Feast of Roses, twenty times
And three; but always only from afar
Had heard the glad outcry where from the grove
Of holy oaks the temple towers, when Mars
Upon Otrere's, my dear mother's, death
Chose me to be his bride. For you must know,
It is not right that they of the royal blood,
Princesses of our house, of their mere will
Should join the Feast of Flowering Virgins; Mars,
Should he desire, calls them with circumstance,
Worthily, by the mouth of his high priestess.
My dying mother, ashen-pale, lay there—
I held her in my arms—when from the god
They brought to me his solemn salutation
And called on me forthwith to move on Troy,
Thence to conduct him wreathed, in triumph, home.
Now it so happed that never yet was named
To do the god's work any race more welcome
To the Brides of Mars than these Troy-girdling Greeks.
The streets were filled with noise of jubilation;
In every market-place the songs were heard
That tell the tale of that war's giant deeds:
Of Paris' apple and the Rape of Helen,
Of Atreus' sons, stout leaders of the host,
Briseïs, cause of strife, the ships in flames,
And then Patroclus' death, and with what pomp
Thou didst avenge and celebrate his end:
Those deeds and many others then were sung.
But I, consumed with grief and quenchless tears,
Heard but with half an ear the solemn message
Which the god sent me as my mother died.
"Oh, let me stay beside thee, Mother!" I cried.
"Use it once more, thy royal dignity,
—For the last time—and bid these women go."
But she, a queen to her last breath, who long

Had wished to see me in the field—for still
Without heir of the blood she left the throne,
Prey to the wanton greed of ambitious kindred—
She said to me: "Go, child! The god has called thee.
Thou wilt bring back the son of Peleus crowned:
Be thou a mother, proud and glad as I——"
Then gently pressed my hand and left me weeping.

PROTHOE. So then she named him by his name to thee?

PENTHESILEA. She named him, Prothoe. Why should she not,
Mother and daughter speaking privily?

ACHILLES. But why? What cause? Does the law then forbid?

PENTHESILEA. It is not fitting that a daughter of Mars
Should seek her opponent; she must be content
To take whome'er the god sends her in battle.
But it is well if she with eager spirit
Fights only where the noblest foemen stand.
Is that not so?

PROTHOE.   So is it.

ACHILLES.   Well——?

PENTHESILEA.   I wept,
Long, long I wept, a whole grief-laden month,
At my dear mother's grave, neglecting still
The crown that lay beside me masterless,
Until at length the oft-repeated cry
Of the people, who, eager for joyful war,
Impatient, lay encamped around my palace,
Dragged me by force to mount the throne. I came,
Still bowed by grief, with inward-warring heart,
To the temple of Mars; the bow—they gave it me,
The twanging bow of all the Amazons.
And as I took it in my hand I felt
My mother all about me; nought was holier
To me than to make good her dying will.
Then, having strewn upon her bier the sweetest,
Most heaven-scented flowers, I straight struck out
With all the puissance of the Amazons
For Ilium's towers—less honouring in that
Ares, the god of war, by whom I was elect,
Than that dear shade—my mother's, great Otrere's.

ACHILLES. Grief for the dead one moment sapped the fire
  That else runs coursing through thy youthful breast.

PENTHESILEA. I loved her.

ACHILLES.   Good. And then?

PENTHESILEA.   As day by day
  Nearer I drew to old Scamander's stream,
  And every vale around through which I swept
  Echoed the clash of battle before Troy,
  So did my grief abate, and my wide soul
  Drank in the universe of joyful war.
  To myself I said: if they should all together,
  The mighty moments of the daedal past,
  Return for me, if all the company
  Of heroes, whom the songs of minstrels sing,
  Should step down from the stars, I should not find
  Not one more excellent, to crown with roses,
  Than that man whom my mother chose for me—
  So dear, so wild, so sweet, so terrible—
  The slayer of Hector! O thou son of Peleus!
  Ever my single thought when I awoke,
  Ever my dream in sleep wast thou! The world
  Lay stretched before me like a patterned web,
  And in each glorious, wide-gaping mesh
  One of thy deeds with craftman's skill enwoven;
  Upon my heart, as on silk white and fine,
  I burned each deed with colours steeped in flame.
  Now I beheld thee smite him to the earth,
  Though still he fled thee, there before Priam's towers,
  Or now, enflamed in lust of victory,
  Thou did'st turn back to look upon his head,
  Bloody and battered by the ungentle ground.
  Or then 'twas Priam, suppliant in thy tent—
  And I wept scalding tears of joy to think
  That some emotion yet, thou pitiless man,
  Could penetrate and stir thy flinty bosom.

ACHILLES. My dearest Queen!

PENTHESILEA.   But, oh, that moment, when
  With these my eyes, I saw thee—thee thyself!
  There in Scamander's vale thou didst appear,

Ringed round by all Achaea's mightiest—
Wan luminaries before the day-star paling.
Not otherwise would it have seemed to me
If he himself with his snow-gleaming team
Had thundered down upon me from Olympus,
Ares, the god of war, to greet his bride.
Blinded I stood long time, when thou wast gone,
By that swift apparition, as when at night
The lightning plunges down before the wanderer
Or heaven's groaning doors, all radiance,
Open before the soul—and close again.
I knew at once—how should I not, Achilles?—
Whence came the flooding turmoil in my breast:
The god of love had overtaken me.
Of two things then I swore that one should be:
Either to win thee or to perish here.
And now of these the sweeter is my lot——
What is the matter?

Clash of arms is heard far off.

PROTHOE.   Achilles! Listen to me!
You must declare yourself at once to her.

PENTHESILEA, *leaping up.* The Achaeans come! Your weapons!

ACHILLES.   Nay, sit still!
For sure, it is a band of prisoners.

PENTHESILEA. Of prisoners?

PROTHOE, *aside to* ACHILLES. I tell you, 'tis Odysseus!
Your friends, hard pressed by Meroe, fall back.

ACHILLES, *into his beard.* God smite them all to stone!

PENTHESILEA.   What is the matter?

ACHILLES, *with forced cheerfulness.*
Queen! Thou shalt bear me soon the god of Earth!
Prometheus shall arise from his hard bed
And loud proclaim to all the tribes of men:
This is a man, pure image of my thought!
But not to Themiscyra will I go;
No, thou shalt follow me to fertile Phthia:
For when I have wound up the clue of war,
In triumph I shall take thee home and set thee

—Ah, too great bliss!—beside me on the throne.
Clash of arms continues.

PENTHESILEA. What? How? What does he mean?

AMAZONS. Oh, all ye gods!

PROTHOE. Achilles! Wilt thou——?

PENTHESILEA. What? What is the matter?

ACHILLES. Nothing, my Queen! Nothing! No need to fear.
Thou seest, time forces us, and thou must hear
What fate the assembled gods have doomed for thee.
'Tis true, by Love's dominion I am thine,
And never shall I cast these happy bonds.
But by decree of arms thou art my prize:
Before me in the dust thou didst sink down,
Not I before thee, when there we met in battle.

PENTHESILEA, *starting back.* Oh, horrible!

ACHILLES. Not so, I beg, beloved!
Not Cronos' son can alter what is done.
Master thyself and hear unflinching still
The messenger who there draws near with some
Ill-ominous word, I doubt not, for my ear.
To thee—this understand!—he brings thee nought.
Thy fate is fixed forever—locked and sealed.
Thou art my prisoner; a hound of hell
Would guard thee less implacably than I.

PENTHESILEA. Thy prisoner, I?

PROTHOE. Queen! It is even so!

PENTHESILEA, *raising her hands.*
Eternal gods in heaven! You hear my cry!

SCENE 16

Enter a CAPTAIN, *also* ACHILLES' *attendants with his arms.*

ACHILLES. What news do you bring?

CAPTAIN. You must retire, Achilles.
The chance of war, with veering April face,
Once more calls out our foes to victory;

Their headlong thrust's aimed at this very spot,
Their savage warcry still: Penthesilea.

ACHILLES *stands up and tears off the wreaths.*

Bring me my weapons! The horses! Bring the horses!
By God! My brazen car shall mow them down!

PENTHESILEA, *with trembling lip.*

Oh! See him now, so terrible! So changed!

ACHILLES, *raging.* Are they far off?

CAPTAIN.   Not far! Here in the valley
Easily can be seen their golden crescent.

ACHILLES, *doing on his armour.* Get her away!

A GREEK.   Whither?

ACHILLES.   To the Argive camp.
I will be with you in a little space.

THE GREEK, *to* PENTHESILEA. Stand up!

PROTHOE.   Oh, my revered, my well-loved Queen!

PENTHESILEA, *beside herself.*

Hast thou no bolt for me, great son of Cronos?

SCENE 17

Enter ODYSSEUS *and* DIOMEDE *with the* GREEK ARMY.

DIOMEDE, *passing across the stage.*

Away! Away from here, my friend! Away!
The last way out—the last that still lies open—
Even while we talk, those women are cutting it!
Away!

Off.

ODYSSEUS.   Bear off this queen from here, Achaeans.

ACHILLES, *to the* CAPTAIN.

Alexis! Be so good, my friend. Help her.

THE GREEK, *to the* CAPTAIN. She will not move.

ACHILLES, *to the* GREEKS *attendant on him.*

                    My shield, ho! Where's my lance?

Commandingly to PENTHESILEA, *who is resisting.*

Penthesilea!

PENTHESILEA. Oh, great son of Peleus!
Thou wilt not follow me to Themiscyra?
Nor to that temple wilt thou not follow me,
That towers far off above the oak-grove's crowns?
Come to me; there is more that I would tell.

ACHILLES, *now in full armour, goes up to her and gives her his hand.* My Queen!—— To Phthia!

PENTHESILEA.   Oh! To Themiscyra!
My friend! my friend! We must to Themiscyra,
Where Dian's temple thrusts above the oaks!
Aye, though the Blest Abodes were there in Phthia,
Yet, yet, my friend, we must to Themiscyra,
Where Dian's temple thrusts above the tops!

ACHILLES, *taking her up.*
It cannot be. You must forgive me, dearest.
Just such a temple will I build in Phthia.

SCENE 18

Enter MEROE *and* ASTERIA *with the* AMAZON ARMY.

MEROE. Strike him down!

ACHILLES, *lets the* QUEEN *go and turns.*
                    What! Do they ride upon the storm?

THE AMAZONS, *thrusting themselves between* PENTHESILEA *and* ACHILLES. Set the Queen free!

ACHILLES.   Never! By this right hand!
He tries to drag the QUEEN *off.*

PENTHESILEA, *pulling him to her.*
Thou wilt not follow me? Wilt not?

ODYSSEUS.   Away!
Thy stubborn folly will undo us all!
He drags ACHILLES *off.* GREEKS *exeunt.*

SCENE 19

Enter the HIGH PRIESTESS OF DIANA *with the* PRIESTESSES.

THE AMAZONS. Triumph! Triumph! Triumph! Our Queen is
    saved!

PENTHESILEA, *after a pause.*

Accursèd be this shameful cry of triumph!
Accursèd every tongue that utters it,
Accurs'd the servile air on which it swims!
Was I not his by every use of chivalry,
By fairest chance of war his lawful prize?
When man on man makes war—not on the wolf
Or ravening tiger but on his own kind—
Show me the law—I say, show me!—which then
Permits the prisoner who has yielded him
To be set free again from his captor's bonds.
Oh! Son of Peleus!

THE AMAZONS.   What are these words of madness?

MEROE. Most reverend Priestess of Diana, hear!
    Stand not aloof, I beg thee——

ASTERIA.   She is wroth,
    Because we set her free from shameful bonds.

THE HIGH PRIESTESS, *stepping forward out of the crowd of
    women.*

In sooth, worthily hast thou set, O Queen,
I must confess, with these abusive words,
The crown of shame upon this day's doings.
'Tis not alone that thou with scant respect
For custom thus must pick and choose thy foe;
Nor that, rather than hurl him in the dust,
Thyself dost fall, too weak; nor yet that thou,
In thanks for this, dost crown him here with roses.
Thou dost revile as well thy loyal folk
That breaks thy shameful chains, dost turn away
And call the man that topped thee back again.
'Tis well then, daughter of Tanais, 'tis well—

It was an error, nothing more, for which
Too hasty deed I humbly beg forgiveness.
The blood then spilt for thee—we could have spared it;
And all our prisoners, lost for thy sake,
With all my soul I would we had them still.
Here in the people's name I do release thee;
The world is open to thee. Go thy way!
With fluttering kirtle thou canst now pursue
Him who has made thee captive and canst give him
Those chains, by us hewn through, to weld again:
Thy vaunted laws of war demand no less!
Us, gracious Queen, us wilt thou not forbid
Now to break off the war and to begin
At once the long march home to Themiscyra.
For we, at least, we cannot beg those Greeks
Who have escaped to stand and be recaptured;
Cannot as thou, the victor's wreath in hand,
Implore them to fall prostrate at our feet.
Pause.

PENTHESILEA, *reeling.* Prothoe!

PROTHOE.   Dearest sister!

PENTHESILEA.   Oh, do not leave me!

PROTHOE. Never! No, not in death! Why do you tremble?

PENTHESILEA. It is nothing—nothing. Soon I shall be strong.

PROTHOE. A great grief struck thee; show thyself as great.

PENTHESILEA. And they are lost?

PROTHOE.   Who lost, my dearest lady?

PENTHESILEA. That glorious company whom we had reaped—
All lost through me?

PROTHOE.   It is no matter. Soon
Thou shalt win others in another war.

PENTHESILEA, *on* PROTHOE'S *bosom.* Oh, never!

PROTHOE.   How, my Queen?

PENTHESILEA.   Oh, never! Never!
No! I must bury me in endless night!

SCENE 20

Enter a HERALD.

MEROE. A herald comes, my Queen.

ASTERIA.   What is thy will?

PENTHESILEA, *with faint joy.*

'Tis from Achilles!—— Ah, what shall I hear?
No, Prothoe, bid him go.

PROTHOE, *to the* HERALD.   What is thy message?

HERALD. Most mighty Queen! Achilles sends me to thee,
Son of the dread reed-wreathèd Nereid,
And bids me, as his mouth, thus to declare:
Since thou dost lust to carry him away,
Thy prisoner, to thy far native fields,
And he on his side lusts no whit the less
To bear thee to the wide plains of his home;
Thee now he challengeth once more to stand
And face him in the field in mortal combat.
Thus shall the sword, Fate's iron tongue, decide,
Here in the watchful presence of the gods,
Which of you twain is worthier, thou or he,
By their revered, inexorable doom
To lick the dust before his foeman's feet.
Hast thou the heart to trip this measure with him?

PENTHESILEA, *with a momentary pallor.*

Thy tongue be sundered by the levin-bolt,
Glib recreant, before thou speak again!
More welcome to my ear the granite block
That hurtles from the towering crag and leaps,
Striking and bounding, into unfathomed depths.

To PROTHOE.

Thou must repeat it to me word for word.

PROTHOE, *trembling.*

The son of Peleus, so it seems, has sent
Him here to call thee again into the field.
Refuse him out of hand with brief: I will not!

PENTHESILEA. It is impossible!

PROTHOE. What, then, my Queen?

PENTHESILEA. He challenges me—he—to mortal combat?

PROTHOE. I'll tell him thou wilt not and bid him go.

PENTHESILEA. He challenges me—he—to mortal combat?

PROTHOE. Ay, lady, as I said, he'll fight with thee.

PENTHESILEA. He, he, who knows I am too weak by far,
He sends this challenge, Prothoe, to me?
My faithful breast here moves him not a whit
Till he has crushed and split it with his spear?
Did all I whispered to him touch his ear
Only with the empty music of the voice?
Has he forgot the temple midst the oaks?
Was it a block of stone my hand did crown?

PROTHOE. Forget the unfeeling man.

PENTHESILEA, *with burning indignation.* Then be it so!
Now I do feel the strength to stand against him:
Now he shall down and grovel in the dust,
Though Lapiths—ay, though giants fight to save him!

PROTHOE. Belovèd Queen!

MEROE. Hast thou bethought thee well?

PENTHESILEA, *interrupting her.*
You shall have all the prisoners again!

THE HERALD. Thou wilt in combat——?

PENTHESILEA. Fear not! I will meet him!
Ay, me he shall encounter; all the gods
—And Furies too—I do call down to witness.
Thunder.

HIGH PRIESTESS. If my hard words have stung thee, Penthesilea,
Thou wilt not cause me pain——

PENTHESILEA, *suppressing tears.* Nay, holy dame!
Not vainly, be assured, were those words spoken.

MEROE, *to the* PRIESTESS.
Use thy dread office, name, and dignity.

HIGH PRIESTESS. Didst thou not hear his anger?

PENTHESILEA.   Him and all
His thunders down upon my head I call!

FIRST OFFICER, *in agitation.* Princesses all!——

SECOND OFFICER.   It may not be!

THIRD OFFICER.   Impossible!

PENTHESILEA, *in wild ecstasy.*
To me, Ananké! Keeper of the hounds!

FIRST OFFICER. We are dispersed, are weary!

SECOND OFFICER.   Our ranks are thinned!

PENTHESILEA. Thou, Thyrroe—the elephants!

PROTHOE.   My Queen!
With dogs and elephants it is thy will——?

PENTHESILEA. And you, scythed chariots of glinting steel,
You that endow war's harvest festival,
Come, ghastly row on row of reapers, come!
And you that thresh the crop of human corn,
Trampling to nothingness both stalk and grain,
Thronged squadrons, range your ranks about me now!
Thou beauteous horror of war, hear me who call!
Grim-visaged, fell destroyer, come! Oh, come!
*She seizes the great bow of the Amazons from the hand of
an attendant.*
Enter AMAZONS *with hunting dogs on leashes. Later ele-
phants, flaming torches, scythed chariots, etc.*

PROTHOE. Oh, my illustrious Queen! Hear me! Hear me!

PENTHESILEA, *turning to the dogs.*
Up, Tigris, up! I need thee. Up, Leoné!
Up thou, Melampus, shaggy-maned and savage!
Up, Aclé, bane of the mountain fox! Up, Sphinx!
Alektor too, that runs the doe to ground.
Up, Oxus, many a boar has felt thy fangs,
And thou whom the lion daunts not, Hyrcaon!
Loud thunder.

PROTHOE. She is beside herself!

FIRST OFFICER.   Nay! She is mad!

PENTHESILEA *kneels with every sign of madness while the dogs
set up a fearful howling.*

Thee, Ares, I invoke, thou terrible one!
Thee, awful founder of our house, I call!
Oh! Swiftly send me down thy brazen car
In which the walls of cities and the gates
Thou crushest, all-destroyer, and the ranks
Of men, in blocked phalanx, dost trample down.
Oh! Swiftly send me down thy brazen car
That I may set my foot within its shell,
Seize up the reins and, sweeping o'er the fields,
Fall like a thunder-bolt from clouds of wrath
Upon the head of yonder impious Greek!
She rises.

FIRST OFFICER. Princesses!

SECOND OFFICER.　　　　Up! Prevent her! She is mad!

PROTHOE. Hear me, great Queen, I beg!

PENTHESILEA, *drawing the bow.* Ah! Here is sport!
Now I can see if my shaft still flies true.
She aims at PROTHOE.

PROTHOE, *dropping to the ground.* Ye gods!

A PRIESTESS, *quickly moving behind* PENTHESILEA.
　　　　　　Achilles calls!

A SECOND, *doing the same.*　　　The son of Peleus!

A THIRD. Here, here behind thee!

PENTHESILEA, *turning.*　　　Where?

FIRST PRIESTESS.　　　　Was it not he?

PENTHESILEA. No, no! The Furies are not yet assembled.
Follow me, Ananké! Follow me, my friends!
Exit with the bulk of the army amid violent claps of thunder.

MEROE, *raising* PROTHOE. O fearful fate!

ASTERIA.　　　　Go after her! Prevent her!

HIGH PRIESTESS, *deathly pale.*
Eternal gods! What doom hangs over us?
Exeunt omnes.

SCENE 21

Enter ACHILLES *and* DIOMEDE. *Later* ODYSSEUS *and finally the* HERALD.

ACHILLES. Listen, Diomede! Be a good comrade now,
Don't say a word to that old Puritan,
Sour-faced Odysseus, of what I'm going to tell you;
I hate it worse than plague—it makes me sick—
When he puts on that smug, censorious face.

DIOMEDE. Did you in truth send her the herald, Achilles?
Did you in truth?

ACHILLES.   Now listen, friend, one word:
—But you keep quiet, do you understand?
No comment! Not a word!—This wondrous woman,
Half Fury, half goddess, she loves me; I—
What care I for the Grecian women? I swear,
By Hades! By the Styx!—I love her too!

DIOMEDE. What?

ACHILLES.   Yes. But still a whim, to her most holy,
Commands that I fall vanquished by her sword.
That must come first; then love's work can begin.
So then I sent her——

DIOMEDE.   Madman!

ACHILLES.   He'll not listen!
What he has never seen, in all the world,
In all his life, with those blue eyes of his,
That he'll not grasp—he cannot—even in thought.

DIOMEDE. Then you——? You mean——? You will—?

ACHILLES, *after a pause*.   What will I do?
What is this monstrous thing that I will do?

DIOMEDE. You mean, you've challenged her to mortal combat,
Simply that she——?

ACHILLES.   Now by cloud-shaking Zeus!
She will not harm me, I tell you! Sooner far
Would her mailed arm mangle her own fair bosom

And cry: "Triumph!" when her heart's blood spurts forth,
Than it would rage against me! A month, no more,
I will do service to her hot desires,
A month, or maybe two, not longer: surely
In that time all your old, sea-chafèd isthmus
Will not crumble and melt away! Thereafter,
As from her own red lips I know, I am free—
Free as the roe upon the heath. If she
Will follow me then, it were bliss pure and boundless,
If I could set her on my fathers' throne.

Enter ODYSSEUS.

DIOMEDE. Odysseus! Here a moment!

ODYSSEUS.   How now, Achilles?
You have challenged the Queen into the field.
Will you, all wearied as the companies are,
Stake all once more upon the chance of war?

DIOMEDE. There'll be no chance of war, no fighting, friend;
He will surrender himself her prisoner.

ODYSSEUS. What?

ACHILLES, *flushing violently.*

          Take your face away, for God's sake, man!

ODYSSEUS. He will——?

DIOMEDE.   Just so. Hack pieces off her helmet
Like a gladiator, look ghastly and rage,
Rattle upon his shield until sparks fly—
Then mutely lay him, her devoted slave,
Down in the dust before her little feet.

ODYSSEUS. Is this man raving mad, great son of Peleus?
Did you not hear what he——?

ACHILLES, *controlling himself.* I pray you, friend,
Let it not curl, that upper lip—not curl!
It makes me mad to see it, by the gods,
A twitching madness even to my fist.

ODYSSEUS, *enraged.*
Now by Cocytus' flaming waves! I will
Be told whether my ears hear right or no!
You will now, son of Tydeus, be so good
And swear upon your oath that what I ask

Is so; I must and shall have certainty!
He will surrender himself her prisoner?

DIOMEDE. Even so!

ODYSSEUS.   Will follow her to Themiscyra?

DIOMEDE. That too.

ODYSSEUS.   And all this war for Helen's sake
Before Troy citadel, he will like a toy
In his infatuation cast away
Because some brighter plaything steals his fancy?

DIOMEDE. By Jupiter, 'tis so!

ODYSSEUS, *folding his arms*. I may not credit it.

ACHILLES. He speaks of the citadel of Troy.

ODYSSEUS.   What?

ACHILLES.   What?

ODYSSEUS. Did you not say something?

ACHILLES.   I?

ODYSSEUS.   You!

ACHILLES.   I said:
He speaks of the citadel of Troy.

ODYSSEUS.   Why, yes!
Rage in my heart, I asked if it were true
That all this war for Helen's sake before
Troy town were sheer forgot like a dream at dawn.

ACHILLES, *stepping up to him*.
Son of Laertes! If the towers of Ilium
Should sink from sight—you follow?—so that a lake,
A blue lake, lay where once those towers had been,
And hoary fisherfolk by the moon's pale light
Made fast their skiffs to those drowned weathercocks;
If a huge pike should rule in Priam's palace,
Or in fair Helen's bed a pair of otters
Or stinking water rats should breed and litter
It were to me no less than it is now.

ODYSSEUS. By the Styx, friend Diomede! It is no jest!

ACHILLES. By the Styx! By the marsh of Lerna! Ay, by Hades!
By all that's on the earth or under it

Or in some third abode: it is no jest!
It is my will to see Diana's temple.

ODYSSEUS, *aside to* DIOMEDE.

See that he does not leave this spot, my friend—
If you will be so good.

DIOMEDE.   If I——! Why, surely!
Yourself be but so good and lend me your arms.

Enter the HERALD.

ACHILLES. Ah! Will she fight? What news, friend? Will she
     fight?

HERALD. Ay, she will fight; already she comes on.
But 'tis with dogs and elephants she comes
And a whole savage host on horseback: what
Their part in this single combat is yet dark.

ACHILLES. This is her tribute paid to custom. Come!
Oh, she is full of tricks, by all the gods!
——You say, with dogs?

HERALD.   Yes.

ACHILLES.   And with elephants?

HERALD. Right terrible to see, great son of Peleus!
Were it her intent to fall on Agamemnon
In the walled camp before Troy, she could not come
In darker nor more awful panoply.

ACHILLES, *to himself.*

Sure they will feed from your hand. Come, follow me!
Oh! They are tame as she.

Exit with his attendants.

DIOMEDE.   Nay! He is mad!

ODYSSEUS. Come, we must seize and bind him! Up, you Greeks!

DIOMEDE. Here come the Amazons! We must away!

Exeunt omnes.

SCENE 22

Enter the HIGH PRIESTESS, *pale and anxious, and several other* PRIESTESSES *and* AMAZONS.

HIGH PRIESTESS. Bring binding cords, you women!

FIRST PRIESTESS.   What has happened?

HIGH PRIESTESS. Drag her to the ground! Overpower her!
    Bind her fast!

AN AMAZON. Do you mean the Queen?

HIGH PRIESTESS.   That lewd she-dog I mean!
    No more can she be held by human hands.

THE AMAZONS. Most reverend mother, you seem all distraught.

HIGH PRIESTESS. Three of her maids she trampled underfoot
    Whom we had sent to halt her; Meroe,
    For that she threw herself upon her knees
    Imploring her with every sweet endearment,
    She set the dogs on her and chased her away.
    And me—as I approached her still far off,
    Stooping straightway, darting hate-laden glances
    Upon me, she from the ground with both hands tore
    A mighty stone—that moment was my last
    But I withdrew among the common folk.

FIRST PRIESTESS. 'Tis fearful!

SECOND PRIESTESS.   Horrible it is to hear!

HIGH PRIESTESS. And now with maniac tread among her hounds
    With foam-flecked lip she goes and calls them sisters,
    Who howl and howl; most like a Maenad she,
    Dancing across the fields, her bow in hand,
    She urges on the pack that pants for blood
    Around her, bidding them seize the fairest prey
    That ever, so she tells them, ranged the earth.

AMAZONS. Gods of the dark! What fearful punishment!

HIGH PRIESTESS. Therefore with cords, you daughters of Ares,
        quickly
    There where the ways meet, there lay snares for her,

Covered with leaves, before her hurrying feet,
And drag her down; when she is tripped and stumbles,
Hold her and bind her like a rabid dog.
When she is bound, we then shall bear her home
And see if some way she may yet be saved.

THE AMAZON HOST, *off*.
Triumph! Triumph! Triumph! Achilles falls!
Captive the hero! Soon victorious
The Queen shall wreathe his yellow head with roses!
Pause.

HIGH PRIESTESS, *her voice half stifled with joy.*
Did I hear aright?

PRIESTESSES *and* AMAZONS. Oh! all the gods be praised!

HIGH PRIESTESS. Was this in truth the exultant shout of joy?

FIRST PRIESTESS. The cry of victory, most holy dame.
A sound more blessèd never did I hear.

HIGH PRIESTESS. You maidens, who will bring me news?

SECOND PRIESTESS. Terpé!
Quick! Tell us what you see from yonder hill?

AN AMAZON, *who has mounted the hill, horror-struck.*
You grim and ghastly gods of nether hell!
Be witness to my words—— Oh, fearful spectacle!

HIGH PRIESTESS. How now! How now! Has she beheld Medusa?

PRIESTESSES. What do you see? Speak! Speak!

AMAZON. Penthesilea—
Grovelling she couches by her grizzly hounds,
She whom a woman's womb did bear, and rends—
His limbs she rends and mangles into shreds!

HIGH PRIESTESS. Oh horror! Horror!

ALL. Deed unspeakable!

AMAZON. See where it comes, bleached o'er with death's own
hue,
The word that solves for us the gruesome riddle.
She descends from the hill.

SCENE 23

Enter MEROE.

MEROE. O you, Diana's holy priestesses,
  And you, Ares' chaste daughters, hear me speak:
  I am the Afric Gorgon and to stone—
  Behold!—Your bodies' warmth I freeze at once.

HIGH PRIESTESS. Oh, ghastly sight! Say what befell.

MEROE.   You know,
  She moved to meet that youth whom she so loves,
  —She who from this time forth no name can name—
  In the confusion of her youthful senses
  Arming with all the horrid terrors of war
  Her hot desire to seize and to possess him.
  Ringed round with howling hounds and elephants
  She strode before, the great bow in her hand:
  War that rages among the citizens,
  Fell form that drips with brothers' blood, when he
  Stalks through the land with giant strides of woe,
  Swinging the torch of death o'er blossoming cities,
  He looks not half so terrible as she.
  Achilles, so 'tis said in all the host,
  Had challenged her only that he—poor fool!—
  Of his free will might yield to her in combat:
  For he too—oh, all-powerful are the gods!—
  He loved her too, stirred strangely by her youth,
  And wished to follow her to Dian's temple:
  He now approaches, dreaming of sweet delights,
  And comes alone, his friends left far behind.
  But now, as she with such heaped horror bears
  Rumbling upon him, who half playfully
  Is armed but with a spear and thinks no danger,
  Sudden he stops, turning his slender neck,
  Listens, then flees in horror, stops, then flees,
  Like a young roe that in the rocky gorge
  Hears from afar the shag-maned lion's roar.

He calls, "Odysseus!" but fear bates his voice;
Casts anxious eyes behind and calls, "Diomede!"
And still has hope to flee back to his friends
And stands, seeing his road already cut,
And throws his hands aloft and stoops and creeps
Into a pine tree's shelter—ah, poor wretch!—
That hangs heavy, drooping its branches down.
The Queen, meanwhile, unfaltering nears apace
—The dogs hard on her heels—and spies afar
With hunter's glance scanning the woods and hills;
And just as he, parting the close-grown boughs,
Is fain to sink a suppliant at her feet,
"His antlers still betray the stag!" she cries
And straight, with strength of madness born, she draws
The mighty bow till the ends touch and kiss
And raises up the bow and aims and shoots,
Driving the arrow through his throat. He falls;
The folk gives forth a barbarous shout of triumph.
But he still lives, most miserable of men;
The jutting shaft deep buried in his throat,
He staggers gasping to his feet, stumbles
Full length, is up again and seeks to flee.
But quick "On him!" she calls, "Tigris! On him, Leoné!
Dirké! Melampus! Sphinx! On him! Hyrcaon!"
And flings herself—herself with the whole pack!—
Upon him and by his helmet's plume, a bitch
In company of dogs—one grips his breast,
Another's jaws close on his neck—drags him
To earth, that far around the ground re-echoes.
He, writhing in a pool of his own gore,
Touches her delicate cheek and calls to her:
"Penthesilea! What dost thou? My belovèd!
Is this the Feast of Roses thou didst promise?"
But she—the lioness had been moved to hear,
Who ravening stalks over the barren snow,
And hideous howls, seeking some hapless prey—
She strikes, first tearing his armour from his limbs,
Strikes deep her teeth into his snowy breast,
She and the dogs in ghastly rivalry,
Oxus and Dirké rending his right flank,

And with them she his left; as I appeared,
Black blood was dripping from her mouth and hands.
Pause of horror.

If ye have heard my words, O women, speak
And give some sign that ye still live and breathe.
Pause.

FIRST PRIESTESS, *weeping on the breast of the* SECOND.
Oh, such a virgin, Hermia! So modest!
So deft in all the arts of women's hands!
So lovely when she danced or when she sang!
So full of wisdom, dignity, and grace!

HIGH PRIESTESS. Her never did Otrere bear! The Gorgon
There in the palace whelped such monstrous brood!

FIRST PRIESTESS, *continuing.*
The nightingale that dwells around Diana's
High temple might have been her gentle mother.
Rocked in the topmost branches she would sit,
Fluting and warbling, warbling and fluting still
The breathless long night through, that afar the wand'rer
Hearkened and in his heart strange longing stirred.
The mottled worm that sported in the dust
Before her delicate feet, she would not crush;
She would recall the shaft ere it could pierce
The savage wild boar's shoulder, and his eye,
Glazing in death, could drag her to her knees
Before him, melted quite in soft remorse.
Pause.

MEROE. And now she stands there mute, hedged round with
            horror,
Beside his corpse. The dogs snuff at her hands
While she stares stony out, her face an empty page
—The bow still laid triumphant on her shoulder—
Out into the infinite in awful silence.
We with our hair on end fearfully ask her:
What she has done? No answer. Does she know us?
No word. Will she go with us? Silent still.
I could endure no more and fled to you.

SCENE 24

Enter PENTHESILEA, *the body of* ACHILLES *covered with a red pall.* PROTHOE *and others.*

FIRST AMAZON. Look, look, my friends! See where she comes apace
Crowned all with nettles—oh, unhappy sight!—
That she has worked into the wreath of thorns.
This her victorious laurel! Now she walks
Behind his body, gaily, with bow on shoulder,
As though her mortal foe lay slaughtered there.

SECOND PRIESTESS. Her hands! Look at her hands——!

FIRST PRIESTESS.   Oh! Turn away!

PROTHOE, *sinking on the* HIGH PRIESTESS' *breast.*
My mother!—— Oh!

HIGH PRIESTESS, *in horror.* Diana be my witness!
Not mine the blame for this most cruel deed!

FIRST AMAZON. Straight before the High Priestess now she stands.

SECOND AMAZON. She makes a sign.

HIGH PRIESTESS.   Avaunt, thou ghastly creature!
Thou denizen of hell! Avaunt, I say!
Take this my veil, take it and cover her!

She tears off her own veil and throws it in PENTHESILEA'S *face.*

FIRST AMAZON. A walking corpse, no more! Still quite unmoved——

SECOND AMAZON. Still she makes signs——

THIRD AMAZON.   She points and points again——

FIRST AMAZON. Points always down, to the High Priestess' feet.

SECOND AMAZON. Look, look!

HIGH PRIESTESS.   What do you want of me? Begone!
Go to the ravens, shade! Go, fade away!
That look will shrivel up my whole heart's peace.

FIRST AMAZON. Ah! Now she is understood——

SECOND AMAZON. Now she is calm.

FIRST AMAZON. Achilles—that was it!—he must be placed
Before the feet of great Diana's priestess.

THIRD AMAZON. But why before the priestess' feet? Why there?

FOURTH AMAZON. What can her meaning be?

HIGH PRIESTESS. What means this, pray?
Why should the body stand before me here?
Let mountains cover it, trackless, snow-crowned,
Ay, and the memory of thy deed as well!
Did I, thou—woman no more, how should I name thee?—
Did I with inhuman tongue demand this murder?
If a gentle rebuke from the kind mouth of love
Can cause such monstrous deeds, then must we hope
The Furies for their part will teach us kindliness!

FIRST AMAZON. Relentless still she gazes at the Priestess.

SECOND AMAZON. Straight in her face——

THIRD AMAZON. Unwavering, unwinking,
As though she wished to look her through and through.

HIGH PRIESTESS. Come, Prothoe, I beg you, come, dear girl.
I cannot bear the sight; lead her away.

PROTHOE, *weeping.* Oh, misery!

HIGH PRIESTESS. Be strong!

PROTHOE. The deed she did
Is far too horrible; leave me alone.

HIGH PRIESTESS. Command thyself!—— And yet her mother was
fair.
Come, offer her assistance; lead her off.

PROTHOE. I will not ever look on her again!

SECOND AMAZON. That slim arrow—look how she ponders it——

FIRST AMAZON. Turns it this way and that——

THIRD AMAZON. Intently scans it!

FIRST PRIESTESS. It seems that is the shaft with which she
felled him?

FIRST AMAZON. Ay, so it is.

SECOND AMAZON. Now she cleans it of blood,
Busily wiping off each tiniest stain.

THIRD AMAZON. What might her thoughts be now?

SECOND AMAZON.   And now the feathers
—She dries them, smooths them, gently teases them
With delicate grace—now each lies properly.
Oh, what a sight!

THIRD AMAZON.   Tell us, is that her custom?

FIRST AMAZON. Does she always do so?

FIRST PRIESTESS.   Arrows and bow
She keeps with her own hand in proper order.

SECOND PRIESTESS. The bow was holy to her, no doubt of that.

SECOND AMAZON. And now she takes the quiver from her
        shoulder
And sets the arrow back where it belongs.

THIRD AMAZON. Now she is finished——

SECOND AMAZON.   Now the job is done——

FIRST PRIESTESS. And now once more she looks into the world.

SEVERAL WOMEN. Oh, wretched, wretched sight! Oh, dreary
        waste,
Barren as desert sands where no grass grows!
Gay gardens which the lava flow has wasted,
Seethed in the earth's dark womb and belched afar
O'er all the blossoming paradise of her heart—
More pleasant these to look on than her face.

PENTHESILEA *shudders violently and lets the bow fall.*

HIGH PRIESTESS. What? What? Oh, dreadful!

PROTHOE, *startled.*   Now what will she do?

FIRST AMAZON. Down to the earth she lets the great bow
        plunge.

SECOND AMAZON. See how it falters——

FOURTH AMAZON.   Sways and clanging falls——

SECOND AMAZON. Writhes once more on the ground——

THIRD AMAZON.   And dies at last,
As it was born at first to Tanais.
        Pause.

HIGH PRIESTESS, *turning suddenly to her.*
Great Queen and lady! Oh, forgive, I pray!
Diana is full well content with thee.

I see thou hast atoned; her wrath is turned.
The mighty founder of our women's realm,
Tanais' self, I cannot well deny,
She did not wield the bow more worthily.

FIRST AMAZON. She is silent——

SECOND AMAZON.   Her eyes are wet——

THIRD AMAZON.   She lifts her hand,
All bloody still. What will she do?—— Oh, see!

SECOND AMAZON. Heartrending sight, wounding more keen
   than knives!

FIRST AMAZON. She wipes away a tear.

HIGH PRIESTESS, *sinking on* PROTHOE's *breast.* O Artemis!
Oh, what a tear!

FIRST PRIESTESS.   Ay, such a tear, most reverend,
As creeps into the bosoms of men and there
Wildly jangles the fire-bells of the heart
And cries "Havoc!" that all the teeming crowd,
Fickle and light to move, comes welling forth
Out of our eyes and, gathering then in lakes,
Weeps for the pitiless ruin of a soul.

HIGH PRIESTESS, *bitterly.*
Well, then—— If Prothoe will not help the Queen,
She must soon perish here in her distress.

PROTHOE, *after signs of a violent inner struggle, goes up to her
   and speaks in a voice still broken by sobs.*
Will you not rest awhile, my dearest Queen?
Will you not lean against my faithful breast?
This dreadful day has seen you oft in battle
And brought you sufferings manifold; from these
Come, seek repose upon my faithful breast!

PENTHESILEA *looks around as though seeking a seat.*

PROTHOE. Quick! Bring a seat! You see it is her wish.

The AMAZONS *roll along a rock for her.* PENTHESILEA *sits
   down supported by* PROTHOE. PROTHOE *sits too.*

PROTHOE. Surely you know me, sister-heart?

PENTHESILEA *looks at her; her face brightens a little.*

PROTHOE.   I am
Prothoe, who loves you dearly.

PENTHESILEA *gently strokes her cheek.*

PROTHOE.   Oh, dear heart!
Before whom my heart falls on its knees to worship,
How thou dost move me!
She kisses the QUEEN's *hand.*

                        Sure, thou art very weary?
No need to guess what thou hast been at. Ah, well!
Vict'ry cannot always be cleanly won.
The signs of his trade ever become the master.
But now—would it not be well to clean thyself,
Thy face and hands? Shall I get water for thee?
My dearest Queen!

PENTHESILEA *looks down at herself and nods.*

PROTHOE.   Good, then. It is her will.
She signs to the AMAZONS, *who go to fetch water.*
And gently thou shalt lie on cool, soft rugs
And win repose from thy too hard day-labour.

FIRST PRIESTESS. Be careful! If you sprinkle her with water,
She will remember.

HIGH PRIESTESS.   Surely. 'Tis my hope.

PROTHOE. Thy hope, most holy one? For me, I fear it.

HIGH PRIESTESS, *seeming to consider two courses.*
But why? Wherefore? That way is too much danger,
Unless indeed the body of Achilles——

PENTHESILEA *flashes a terrible glance at the* HIGH PRIESTESS.

PROTHOE. Oh, silence!

HIGH PRIESTESS.   Nothing, my Queen! Nothing, nothing!
All shall remain as thou wilt—nothing be changed.

PROTHOE. Take off your laurel-crown, so full of thorns;
We all do know you were victorious.
Undo this button here—now you can breathe.
And look!—— A wound, a deep gash! Ah, poor dear!
You have not spared yourself, indeed you have not,
And so 'tis just that you should triumph now.
Oh, Artemis!

Two AMAZONS *bring a great shallow marble basin, filled with water.*

PROTHOE.   Here! Set the basin down.
Now, shall I sprinkle water on your head?
You'll not be startled? Why, what are you doing?

PENTHESILEA *drops from her seat on to her knees before the basin and drenches her head with water.*

PROTHOE. Why, look at that! You are right strong again!
That makes you feel better?

PENTHESILEA *looks around her.*   Oh, Prothoe!

Again drenches herself with water.

MEROE, *joyfully.* She speaks!

HIGH PRIESTESS.   Now all the gods be praised!

PROTHOE.   Good, good!

MEROE. So she is given back to us!

PROTHOE.   Wonderful!
Right under water with your head, dear! There!
There! And again! Again! Like a young swan!

MEROE. The darling!

FIRST PRIESTESS.   Look how she hangs her pretty head!

MEROE. And how she lets the water trickle down.

PROTHOE. Now—are you done?

PENTHESILEA.   Wonderful! Wonderful!

PROTHOE. Then we must put you back on to your seat.
Quick, let me have your veils, you priestesses,
That I may dry her dripping locks with them.
Here, Phania, yours! And Terpé's. Help me, sisters!
We'll cover all her head and neck with them.
That's right! And now we set you back on your seat.

She covers the QUEEN, *lifts her on to the seat, and draws her close to her breast.*

PENTHESILEA. I feel—— Oh!——

PROTHOE.   Better, dear?

PENTHESILEA.   Blissfully well!

PROTHOE. My sister-heart! Sweet darling! Dearest mine!

PENTHESILEA. Oh, tell me! Am I in Elysium?

Art thou one of those ever-youthful nymphs,
That seemly wait upon our heavenly Queen,
When she steps down to the crystalline pool
While the hushed oak-leaves whispering hold their breath?
Dost thou but counterfeit, to give me joy,
My Prothoe's loved features? Tell! Oh, tell!

PROTHOE. No, dearest Queen! No, no! It is not so.
I am indeed thy Prothoe, who hold
Thee here embraced, and what thy eyes behold,
It is the world, our transient, brittle world,
On which the gods look down but from afar.

PENTHESILEA. Good, good. That too is good. It is no matter.

PROTHOE. What, dearest lady?

PENTHESILEA.   I am well pleased, I say.

PROTHOE. My love, explain thyself. We cannot guess——

PENTHESILEA. I am glad that I still am. Now let me be.
Pause.

MEROE. Strange, strange!

HIGH PRIESTESS.   A change most unaccountable!

MEROE. If it were possible to make her tell——

PROTHOE. What was it stirred in thee this strange belief
That thou didst walk already with the shades?

PENTHESILEA, *after a pause, in a sort of ecstasy.*
I am so happy, sister! More than happy!
Quite ripe for death, Goddess, I feel myself.
'Tis true, I do not know all that befell,
And yet I could believe and, trusting, die,
That I had overcome and won Achilles.

PROTHOE, *aside to the* HIGH PRIESTESS.
Quick now, take off the body!

PENTHESILEA, *sitting up eagerly.* Prothoe!
Whom do you speak with?

PROTHOE, *as the bearers still hesitate.* Quickly! Go!

PENTHESILEA.   Diana!
Great goddess! Is it true?

PROTHOE.   What true, my dear one?
Stand close together! So!

She signs to the PRIESTESSES *to hide the body which is being picked up.*

PENTHESILEA, *her hands before her face, joyfully.*

Oh, all ye gods!

Oh, give me courage now to look around!

PROTHOE. Why, Queen! What do you think? What can you hope?

PENTHESILEA, *looking round.* Dearest! You play with me.

PROTHOE.   No, no, by Zeus!

I do not play with thee!

PENTHESILEA, *with rising impatience.* Most holy dames!
Do me the pleasure! Stand apart!

HIGH PRIESTESS, *pressing close together with the other women.*

My Queen!

PENTHESILEA, *rising.* Diana! Wherefore should I not? Diana!
Once—once already he stood close behind me.

MEROE. Oh, look! How horror creeps upon her!

PENTHESILEA, *to the* AMAZONS, *who are carrying the body.*

Hold!

What is it you carry? I must know it! Stop!

She thrusts the women aside and pushes her way to the body.

PROTHOE. Oh, Queen! My Queen! No further! Look no further!

PENTHESILEA. Is it he, my maidens? He?

ONE BEARER, *as the body is set down.* Who is that he?

PENTHESILEA. 'Tis not impossible; I see that now.
A swallow's wing now—that I might have crippled
And it might still be healed and fly again;
The stag I lure into my park with arrows.
But greased and treacherous is the marksman's art;
Our master shot into the heart of happiness
Envious and tricksy gods turn all awry.
What? Was my blow too deadly? Is it he?

PROTHOE. Oh, by the awful powers that rule Olympus,
Ask not——!

PENTHESILEA.   Stand back, I say! E'en though his wound
Gape at me like the frantic jaws of hell:

Yet I will see him!

She draws back the pall.

Oh, monstrous women! Who has done this thing?

PROTHOE. Can *you* ask that?

PENTHESILEA.   O Artemis! Holy Queen!
Now is the end come for thy child!

HIGH PRIESTESS. She falls to the ground!

PROTHOE.   Ye gods in heaven above!
Why didst not let her be, as I counselled?
Much better had it been for thee, poor soul!
To wander still in the mind's dim eclipse,
Forever and forever, than to see
Once more the dreadful light of this sad day.
Hear me, belovèd sister!

HIGH PRIESTESS.   Hear, my Queen!

MEROE. We all—all thy people—do share thy pain.

HIGH PRIESTESS. Raise thyself up!

PENTHESILEA, *half rising.* Ah, all these bleeding roses!
Ah, this red wreath of gashes round his head
Whose buds, scattering scent—fresh scent of graves—
Go down to make a festival for worms!

PROTHOE, *tenderly.* And yet it was her love that wreathed him
          thus.

MEROE. Ay, all too firm——!

PROTHOE.   With thorns among the roses,
So eager was she it should be forever!

HIGH PRIESTESS. Get thee away!

PENTHESILEA.   But one thing I must know:
Who was my rival in such godless love?
I do not ask who struck him down while yet
He lived; I swear by our eternal gods
He shall go from me free—no bird more free.
But who thus slew the slain—that would I know;
On that thou must give answer, Prothoe.

PROTHOE. What, gracious lady?

PENTHESILEA.   Understand me well!
I will not know who thus from out his breast

Stole the sweet spark of life; I will not know it
—Because I will not; so my whimsy jumps.
He is forgiven; free he is to flee.
But who to do this robbery could shun
Thus cruelly the open door and must
Through every snow-white alabaster wall
Break in upon this temple; who could thus
Horribly mar this youth, the high gods' image,
That life no more disputes with foul corruption
Which shall be lord; who thus hath done to him
That Pity hath no tears for him, and Love
—Love the immortal, now a harlot grown—
Faithless must turn away from him in death:
Whoe'er he be, my vengeance smites him. Speak!

PROTHOE, *to* HIGH PRIESTESS.

What answer can we give to such delusion?

PENTHESILEA. What? Must I wait to hear?

MEROE.   O most dread Queen!
If it can bring thee ease in thy distress,
Thy vengeance fall on which of us thou wilt;
Here we all stand, each glad to be thy victim.

PENTHESILEA. Mark me! They'll say that it was I who did it!

HIGH PRIESTESS, *timidly,*

Who else, unhappy girl, but only——

PENTHESILEA.   Thou
Black queen of hell in borrowed robes of light!
To my face thou darest——?

HIGH PRIESTESS.   Artemis be my witness!
And all this company that here surrounds thee
—They must confirm my words! It was thy arrow
That smote him first—ah, had it been but that!
But thou, in the wild turmoil of thy rage,
Didst throw thyself, as he sank to the ground,
With all thy dogs upon him and didst sink—
Oh, my faint lip rebels!—It will not utter
What thou hast done. Ask not! Come, we must go!

PENTHESILEA. My Prothoe must say if this is true.

PROTHOE. My Queen and lady! Do not ask me that!

PENTHESILEA. What? I? I did——? With all my dogs about me?
  With these my tiny hands they say I could——?
  And this too gentle mouth, so soft for love——?
  Made for quite other service than to tear——!
  These two, for sport helping each other on,
  Mouth now and hand, now hand, now mouth again——?

PROTHOE. O Queen! No more!

HIGH PRIESTESS.   I cry woe! Woe upon thee!

PENTHESILEA. Nay, look! Of that you never can persuade me.
  Not though 'twere graved in flame upon the night,
  Not though the vast voice of the storm should cry it,
  Even so to both I still would cry: Ye lie!

MEROE. Let this faith stand, unshakable as the hills;
  Not we who will do aught to make it totter.

PENTHESILEA. How came it he would not defend his life?

HIGH PRIESTESS. He loved thee still, oh, hapless girl! He came
  To give himself to thee, thy prisoner.
  That his intent when he did challenge thee!
  He came to thee, dreaming sweet dreams of peace,
  Eager to follow thee to Dian's temple.
  But thou——

PENTHESILEA. Was it so?

HIGH PRIESTESS.   Didst smite him.

PENTHESILEA.   And then tore him?

PROTHOE. Oh, do not ask me, Queen!

PENTHESILEA.   Or was it not so?

MEROE. She is fearful!

PENTHESILEA.   I did kiss him dead?

FIRST PRIESTESS.   O Heavens!

PENTHESILEA. Surely I kissed him? Or did I tear him? Speak!

HIGH PRIESTESS. Woe! Woe upon thee! Hide thyself!
  Eternal darkness cover thee from sight!

PENTHESILEA. So—it was a mistake. Kissing—biting—
  Where is the difference? When we truly love
  It's easy to do one when we mean the other.

MEROE. Help her, ye gods!

PROTHOE, *taking her arm.* Away now! Come!

PENTHESILEA. Nay! Leave me!

She disengages herself and falls on her knees before the body.

Poor man, of all men poorest, you forgive me?
It was a slip—believe me!—the wrong word——
I must control my too impetuous lips.
But now I tell you clearly what I meant:
This, my belovèd, this—and nothing more.

She kisses him.

HIGH PRIESTESS. Get her away!

MEROE. She must not stay here longer.

PENTHESILEA. How many a girl, her soft arms fast entwined
About her man's neck, says that she loves him so
Beyond words she could eat him up for love.
And then, poor fool, when she would prove her words,
Sated she is of him—sated almost to loathing.
Now, my belovèd, that was not my way.
Why, look: when my soft arms were round thy neck,
I did it word for word; it was no pretending.
I was not quite so mad as they would have it.

MEROE. Oh, monstrous and more monstrous! What a word!

HIGH PRIESTESS. Lay hold of her! Bring her away!

PROTHOE. My Queen!

PENTHESILEA *allows* PROTHOE *to help her up.*

Good, good! Look I am here.

HIGH PRIESTESS. You will go with us?

PENTHESILEA. With you? No!
Go back to Themiscyra and be happy,
If you are able—
My Prothoe above all—
All of you——
And—now a word in secret, none must hear:
Tanais' ashes, scatter them to the winds!

PROTHOE. And thou? What wilt thou do, my sister-heart?

PENTHESILEA. I?

PROTHOE. Thou!

PENTHESILEA.   Look, I will tell you, Prothoe:
I do renounce the law that binds us women
And I will follow him, this youth.

PROTHOE. My Queen, what do you mean?

HIGH PRIESTESS.   Unhappy girl!

PROTHOE. You will——?

HIGH PRIESTESS.   You mean——?

PENTHESILEA.   What? Why, of course!

MEROE.   Oh, heaven!

PROTHOE. One word then, sister-heart, here in your ear——

PROTHOE tries to take her dagger from her.

PENTHESILEA. What then? What do you seek there in my belt?
Oh, that! Wait, wait! I had not guessed your thought—
Here is the dagger.

She takes the dagger from her belt and gives it to PROTHOE.

Will you have the arrows?

She takes the quiver from her shoulder.

The whole quiver—look, how I pour it out.

She pours all the arrows on the ground.

'Tis true, in one way it would be very sweet——

She picks up one or two of them.

For this one—was it not? Or was it this one?
Yes, this one! Right! But never mind! Take them!
Take all these shafts and keep them.

She gathers up the whole bundle and gives it to PROTHOE.

PROTHOE.   Give me them.

PENTHESILEA. For now I will step down into my breast
As into a mine and there will dig a lump
Of cold ore, an emotion that will kill.
This ore I temper in the fires of woe
To hardest steel; then steep it through and through
In the hot, biting venom of remorse;
Carry it then to Hope's eternal anvil
And sharpen it and point it to a dagger;
Now to this dagger do I give my breast:
So! So! So! So! Once more! Now, it is good.

She falls and dies.

PROTHOE, *lifting the* QUEEN. She's dead!

MEROE.   Ay, she has followed him.

PROTHOE.   'Tis well!
For here there was no place for her abiding.
She lays her back on the ground.

HIGH PRIESTESS. A brittle thing, ye gods, is humankind!
She that lies broken here, a few hours since
Swept proudly on her course among the peaks.

PROTHOE. Her blooming was too proud and glorious!
Vainly the gale will shake the withered oak,
But with a crash he flings the living down,
Grasping with ruffian hands her copious locks.

THE PRINCE OF HOMBURG

A PLAY

Heinrich von Kleist

(1811)

English Version by James Kirkup

CHARACTERS

FRIEDRICH WILHELM, *Elector of Brandenburg*

HIS WIFE

PRINCESS NATALIA OF ORANGE, *his niece, colonel-in-chief of a regiment of dragoons*

FIELD-MARSHAL DÖRFLING

PRINCE FRIEDRICH ARTHUR OF HOMBURG, *colonel of cavalry*

COLONEL KOTTWITZ, *of the regiment of the Princess of Orange*

HENNINGS
TRUCHSS ⎱ *colonels in the infantry*

COUNT HOHENZOLLERN, *of the Elector's suite*

GOLTZ

COUNT GEORG VON SPARREN

STRANZ ⎱ *captains of the horse*

SIEGFRIED VON MÖRNER

COUNT REUSS

AN OFFICER OF THE GUARD

OFFICERS. CORPORALS *and* CAVALRYMEN. COURTIERS. LADIES OF THE COURT. PAGES. GUARDS. SERVANTS. TOWNSPEOPLE

The year is 1675.

ACT I

SCENE 1

Fehrbellin: a garden in the old French style. In the back-ground, a castle with a balustraded slope leading down from it. It is night. Early summer.

The PRINCE OF HOMBURG is lying on a garden seat, his shirt open at the neck, half-waking, half-sleeping; the seat is under an oak tree. He is plaiting himself a wreath.

The ELECTOR, HIS WIFE, the PRINCESS NATALIA OF ORANGE, the COUNT OF HOHENZOLLERN, GOLTZ, captain of the horse, and others steal quietly out of the castle and look down upon the PRINCE from the balustrade. There are PAGES carrying lighted torches.

HOHENZOLLERN. There he lies, our brave cousin, the noble
　　　　Prince of Homburg!
Here to our headquarters at Fehrbellin he has returned at
　　　　last.
For the past three days, leading his troops of horse,
He has most keenly harried the routed Swedish squadrons.
You, sire, gave orders that he was to pause no more
Than three hours here, time for him to get his breath again
And for his men to provide themselves with fresh supplies.
Then he was to take up his position on the heights of
　　　　Hackelberg,
And launch a brisk attack upon the Swedish general
　　　　Wrangel
Who now is attempting to make a stand along the Rhyn.

ELECTOR. That is so.

HOHENZOLLERN. Well, sire, the Prince has let it be known to
　　　　his commanders
That on the stroke of ten, according to our plan,

They will set out from here;
He himself was to snatch brief rest for his weary limbs
In order to prepare himself for the encounter
That is to start as soon as it is light.

ELECTOR. So I was given to understand. Well, then——?

HOHENZOLLERN. The hour has struck. The cavalry
Are in the saddle, and their horses
Paw the ground below the ramparts.
They are all ready, all but one. And that
Is their leader, the noble Prince of Homburg!
We have sought for him with lights and lanterns,
And where do we find him?

He takes a torch from a PAGE.

Here, as dreamy
As a sleep-walker.
Though you, sire, would never countenance
Our warnings on this subject,
The summer moonlight has bewitched him,
And led him to this secluded garden-seat,
Where, as if he were dreaming, he weaves himself
The imagined symbol of his own immortal fame:
The glorious wreath of triumph and renown!

ELECTOR. What? No!

HOHENZOLLERN. These are the facts. Look,
You can see him lying there!

ELECTOR. Is he asleep? It can't be!

HOHENZOLLERN. Fast asleep. You need only call his name,
And you will see him suddenly collapse!

A silence.

ELECTOR'S WIFE. The young man is not well, I'm sure.

NATALIA. He needs a doctor.

ELECTOR'S WIFE. He needs our compassion.

To HOHENZOLLERN.

This is no time for easy jests.

HOHENZOLLERN, *handing back the torch.* Have no fear, ladies.
He is in perfect health, or I'm a dead man!
The Swedes will feel the power of his arm

To-morrow in the field!
Believe me, ladies, what you see is nothing more
Than a passing abstraction of the mind.

ELECTOR. Indeed! I thought we were living in a fairy-tale!
Come, friends, follow me,
And let us observe a little closer
This strange indisposition.

They proceed down the slope.

COURTIER, *to* PAGES. Hold back there with the torches!

HOHENZOLLERN. No, let them come too!
The whole town could go up in flames,
And his mind would have no more heed of it
Than of the diamond that sparkles on his finger.

They gather round the PRINCE: *torches flare.*

ELECTOR, *bending over him.* What kind of wreath is he
making?
A wreath of willow leaves?

HOHENZOLLERN. Hah! A wreath of willow? No, my lord,
It is a laurel wreath he winds,
Such as he has seen in the portraits of the heroes
That hang in the Armoury in Berlin.

ELECTOR. Where did he find a laurel bush,
Here in the sandy soil of Brandenburg?

HOHENZOLLERN. The gods alone can tell us that!

COURTIER. Sir, the gardeners here
Cultivate in the French gardens
Some queer foreign plants.

ELECTOR. By heaven, how strange it is! And yet,
I think I understand
The fire that slumbers in this young fool's breast.

HOHENZOLLERN. The fire of to-morrow's battle, I'll be bound,
sire.
He's dreaming now of heaven-gazing astronomers
Who weave to-night's great stars for him
Into a victor's crown.

The PRINCE *gazes on the wreath.*

COURTIER. Look, now he's finished it.

HOHENZOLLERN. Oh, what a thousand pities
  That there's no mirror here!
  Then he would go to it, as vain as any girl,
  And try his wreath on this way, that way,
  As if it were a new hat covered with flowers.

ELECTOR. By Jupiter, but I must see
  How far he'll go in this bedevilment.

The ELECTOR *takes the wreath from the* PRINCE, *who looks at him in sudden confusion. The* ELECTOR *twists his golden chain about the wreath and gives it to* NATALIA. *The* PRINCE *jumps up. The* ELECTOR *steps away and walks slowly backwards, with* NATALIA *holding the wreath aloft. The* PRINCE, *with outstretched arms, follows after her.*

PRINCE, *whispering.* Natalia! My love! My bride!

ELECTOR. Quickly, now! Away!

HOHENZOLLERN. What does the fool say?

COURTIER. What was that he whispered to her?

They all begin ascending the slope.

PRINCE. Frederick! My lord! My father!

HOHENZOLLERN. What devil's got into him?

ELECTOR, *still moving backwards.* Open the door for me!

PRINCE. Oh, my mother!

HOHENZOLLERN. Why, he's mad! Mad!

ELECTOR'S WIFE. Whom does he call mother?

PRINCE, *snatching at the wreath.* Oh, my dearest one!
  Why do you turn away from me? Natalia!

He seizes the PRINCESS' *glove.*

HOHENZOLLERN. What was that?

COURTIER. The wreath?

NATALIA. No.

HOHENZOLLERN, *opening the door.* Quick, come in, sire!
  Let the whole scene suddenly vanish from his sight!

ELECTOR. Back! Back into the darkness, Frederick, Prince of
      Homburg!
  Back into the dark and nothingness!
  If you will grace us with your presence,

We shall meet again upon the field of battle.
Victory cannot be won by dreams!
*They all suddenly go inside. The door shuts with a great
rattle of chains. A silence.*

SCENE 2

The PRINCE *stands for a moment dumbfounded outside the
door, then, his hand holding the glove against his forehead, slowly descends the slope. When he reaches the bottom, he turns round and gazes at the door again.*

SCENE 3

HOHENZOLLERN *returns through a gate set in the wall under
the slope. He is followed by a* PAGE.

PAGE, *softly.* Sir! My lord! A word! I beg of you, my lord——

HOHENZOLLERN, *testily.* Quiet, you little monkey! Well, what
    is it?

PAGE. I have been sent to you my lord—I——

HOHENZOLLERN. You'll wake him with your chattering. Well,
    what's the matter?

PAGE. Sir, I am sent to you by the Elector.
    His Highness begs you, when the Prince awakes,
    Not to breathe a word about the little trick
    He played on him just now.

HOHENZOLLERN. He might have known I wouldn't do that.
    Be off with you now and chatter yourself to sleep
    In some convenient tree! Hop!
    The PAGE *off.*

SCENE 4

HOHENZOLLERN *and the* PRINCE

HOHENZOLLERN, *placing himself some distance behind the* PRINCE, *who is still gazing up at the door.* Arthur!

The PRINCE *collapses.*

So! A bullet couldn't have done better
Or hit more truly at the very brain.

He goes closer to him.

Now I'm curious to know
What sort of tale he will concoct
To explain away his sleeping here.

He leans over him.

Arthur! Hey, what the devil's the matter with you?
What do you think you're doing here,
Alone, and in the middle of the night?

PRINCE. What is it, my dear?

HOHENZOLLERN. Well, damn me, I must tell him!
The cavalry that is under *your* command
Departed over an hour ago, and you
Lie here in the garden, sound asleep.

PRINCE. What cavalry?

HOHENZOLLERN. The Mamelukes! By thunder,
As true as I stand here, he doesn't know
That he's a colonel in the cavalry of Brandenburg!

PRINCE, *jumping up.* Quick! My helmet! My armour!

HOHENZOLLERN, *ironical.* Now, where would *they* be?

PRINCE. Over there, Heinrich, to the right,
There, on the stool!

HOHENZOLLERN. Where? What stool?

PRINCE. But I'm sure—I *think* I put them there,
On the stool.

HOHENZOLLERN. Then go and take them off the stool!

PRINCE. Whose glove is this?

He stares at the glove in his hand.

HOHENZOLLERN. How should *I* know?

To himself.

Confound it!
He's stolen one of the Princess' gloves;
No one noticed it!

Suddenly sharper.

Come on now! Let's be off!
What are you waiting for? Come on!

PRINCE, *throwing the glove away.* Yes, I'm coming!
Hey, Franz, you rascal, where are you?
You were supposed to wake me up!

HOHENZOLLERN, *staring at him.* He's stark, staring mad!

PRINCE. To tell the truth, dear Heinrich,
I hardly know yet where I am.

HOHENZOLLERN. You're in Fehrbellin, you dreamy dunder-
head!
In one of the garden walks that lie
At the rear of the castle.

PRINCE. Darkness, cover my confusion!
The moonlight must have bewitched me once again!

Pulling himself together.

Forgive me! Now I know what it was.
Yesterday, you remember, it was so hot,
I felt it would be too warm to lie in bed to-night.
Half-dead with weariness, I crept
Into the cool of this great garden.
The night, like an Egyptian bride, all stars,
So soft, so warm and heavy with the scent of flowers,
Seemed to be waiting here
For me, her bridegroom,
And slowly drew me down into her arms.
What's the time?

HOHENZOLLERN. Half past eleven.

PRINCE. And the squadrons have set out?

HOHENZOLLERN. Upon the stroke of ten, according to plan. By now
The regiment of the Princess Natalia of Orange
Will have led them to the heights of Hackelberg,
Where in the morning they are to cover
The infantry's secret advance on Wrangel.

PRINCE. No matter! They have as their leader
Good old Kottwitz, who grasps thoroughly
The purpose of this manoeuvre.
In any case, I should have had to come back here
To headquarters, and at two o'clock in the morning, to receive
My final instructions from Field-marshal Dörfling.
So it was better, after all, that I should have stayed on here.
Come, let us go! What does the Elector know of this?

HOHENZOLLERN. Huh! He's long since in his bed and fast asleep.

They are about to go. The PRINCE *stops, turns, and picks up the glove.*

PRINCE. What peculiar dream was it I dreamed?
It seemed to me as if a royal castle,
All glittering with gold and silver, suddenly
Opened its doors to me.
And down its marble-balustraded slope
Descended towards me, like a ring of dancers,
All those who are nearest to my heart;
The Elector, and his lady, and—the third one—
What was her name?

HOHENZOLLERN. Who was it?

PRINCE, *pensive.* The one I am always thinking of.
There *is* only one.

HOHENZOLLERN. Baroness Platen?

PRINCE. Dear Heinrich, how could you——

HOHENZOLLERN. La Ramin?

PRINCE. No, friend, that's not——

HOHENZOLLERN. Mademoiselle Bork? Or the Winterfeld?

PRINCE. No, no! Where are your eyes?
You cannot see the pearl for the ring that is only its setting.

HOHENZOLLERN. Devil take it! Explain yourself, man!
Which lady do you mean?

PRINCE. No matter. No, no matter.
Since I awoke, her name
Has slipped my memory.
But—it is no matter, it does not concern——

HOHENZOLLERN. Good. Well, go on with the dream.

PRINCE. All right, but
You mustn't interrupt me!
The Elector, his forehead high as Zeus upon Olympus,
Is holding a wreath of laurel in his hand.
He comes right up to me.
My heart beats faster.
He winds his golden chain about the wreath,
And, so that she may lay it on my head,
He hands it to—— Oh, dear one!

HOHENZOLLERN. Damn it all, to whom?

PRINCE. Oh, my dear friend!

HOHENZOLLERN. Well, come on, tell me!

PRINCE. To—— Oh, it must have been Baroness Platen.

HOHENZOLLERN. She's away in Prussia now.

PRINCE. Baroness Platen. Really, it *must* have been her.
Or else la Ramin.

HOHENZOLLERN. Eugh! La Ramin! That one with the red hair?
You're sure it wasn't la Platen, the one
With those sly little violet eyes? Eh?
We know she pleases you.

PRINCE. *She* pleases me.

HOHENZOLLERN. Well, anyhow, you say she—this woman—
Held out the wreath to you?

PRINCE. She holds it high, like the goddess of Fame herself,
In perfect hands.
I see her lift the wreath, on which the golden chain is
      glittering,
As if she desires to lay its crown upon a hero's head.
And I, with inexpressible emotion,
Reach out my hands to grasp it:
I feel I should cast myself down before her.

And then, as the scent of flowers hanging in a valley
Is suddenly by fresh winds utterly dispersed,
So suddenly the faces round me vanish,
Vanish up the long and marble-balustraded slope,
On which I climb, trying to follow them: the path
Seems to stretch out infinitely to the doors of heaven.
I run from side to side and try to capture
One face out of all those loved ones.
But in vain! The castle door is opened wide,
A blaze of lightning flashes out, and then
The door swings to, with a heavy thunder-brattle.
Now all that remains to me of that sweet vision
Is a glove torn roughly from her in my dazed pursuit.
And, now I am awake again, O ye almighty gods, it is
A glove I hold here in my hand!

HOHENZOLLERN. And now you think this glove belongs to *her?*

PRINCE. To whom?

HOHENZOLLERN. Why, to la Platen.

PRINCE. Yes. La Platen. Really. Or—to la Ramin.

HOHENZOLLERN, *laughing.*
You're a great joker, you and your visions!
Who knows? Perhaps this glove is just
The fragrant memory of some
Idyllic dalliance with a real shepherdess?
The memory of an hour when
You didn't sleep?

PRINCE. What! Me? By my one and only love——

HOHENZOLLERN. Get along with you! For all I care,
It could be la Platen or la Ramin
Or anyone you care to mention.
On Sunday there is a post to Prussia.
You can write and ask your beauty
If she has lost, by any chance, a glove.
Away! It's nearly midnight.

PRINCE, *dreamily, to himself.* You are right. Let's to bed.
But there is one thing more:
Is the Elector's wife still here,
And is her niece still with her,

The charming Princess of Orange,
Who arrived some days ago at Fehrbellin?

HOHENZOLLERN. Why do you ask me that?
I really believe, the fool——

PRINCE. Why?—— Oh,
I was ordered to place at their disposal
An escort of thirty men to lead them
Out of the theatre of war,
And as you know
I was to put Captain Ramin in charge of them.

HOHENZOLLERN. They must have long since left.
They are surely already on the way; if not, then
On the point of departure.
Ramin waited the entire evening at the gate,
Ready to leave at any moment.
But let us be off. It is midnight now,
And before the battle starts
I too should like to rest awhile.

Midnight striking as they go.

SCENE 5

The ELECTOR'S WIFE *and* PRINCESS NATALIA *in travelling
clothes, led by a* COURTIER, *come in and sit down at the side
of the stage.* LADIES OF THE COURT. *Then the* ELECTOR,
FIELD-MARSHAL DÖRFLING, *the* PRINCE OF HOMBURG *with the
glove tucked into his collar,* HOHENZOLLERN, TRUCHSS, COLO-
NEL HENNINGS, CAPTAIN GOLTZ, *and several other* GENERALS,
COLONELS, *and* OFFICERS.

ELECTOR. What was that firing? Is it Götz?

DÖRFLING. It is Colonel Götz, sire,
Who left yesterday with the advance party.
He has already sent an officer
To set your mind at rest about the issue of the engagement:
There was a Swedish outpost, sire, a thousand strong,
That had stormed the lower slopes of Hackelberg,
But Götz has got the situation in the mountains well in hand,

And tells me that you may consider
His forward position well established.

ELECTOR, *to* OFFICERS. Gentlemen, Field-marshal Dörfling here
Is familiar with the plan of battle I have made.
I pray you, write it down upon your tablets.

The OFFICERS *gather on the other side of the stage round
the* FIELD-MARSHAL *and prepare to write.*

ELECTOR, *turning to the* COURTIER. Has Captain Ramin come
with the coach?

COURTIER. He'll be here in a moment, sire.
The horses will soon be harnessed.

ELECTOR, *sitting on a stool behind* HIS WIFE *and the* PRINCESS.
Captain Ramin shall conduct my dear Elsa,
And thirty stout horsemen shall accompany him.
You are to go to Castle Kalkhuhn, the residence of
My chancellor, near Havelberg, beyond the river Havel,
Where no Swede now dare let himself be seen.

ELECTOR'S WIFE. Is the ferry running again?

ELECTOR. Across the Havel? Everything is under our control.
In any case, it will be daylight when you get there.
A silence.

Natalia, dear child, why are you so silent?
What is wrong with my girl?

NATALIA. Dear Uncle, I am afraid.

ELECTOR. And yet my little one has nothing to be afraid of.
She was no safer in her mother's arms.
A silence.

ELECTOR'S WIFE. When, do you think, shall we see each other
again?

ELECTOR. When God has sent me victory,
As I do not doubt He will.
Perhaps in the course of the next few days.

PAGES *come and serve the* LADIES *with refreshments.*
DÖRFLING *is busy dictating. The* PRINCE OF HOMBURG,
tablets and pencil in hand, is staring at the LADIES.

DÖRFLING. Gentlemen, the plan of battle which His Highness
has devised

Aims to separate the retreating Swedish troops
From the bridgehead covering their rear across the Rhyn.
Our aim is to destroy them. Utterly destroy them.
Colonel Hennings!

HENNINGS. Here!

He writes.

DÖRFLING. Who, according to our leader's plan, commands
  to-day
The right wing of the infantry battalions,
Shall endeavour, creeping through what cover he can find,
To circumvent the enemy's left wing.
Then he shall move in resolutely,
Cutting off the enemy line of retreat towards the bridges,
And, together with Baron Truchss——
Baron Truchss!

TRUCHSS. Here!

He writes.

DÖRFLING. Who meanwhile will have taken up positions
With his artillery upon the heights——

TRUCHSS, *writing.* "With his artillery upon the heights——"

DÖRFLING. Have you got that?

He goes on.

Will seek to drive the Swedish forces
Into the marshy region behind their right-hand wing.

Enter a GUARD.

GUARD. Madame, the coach is waiting.

The LADIES *rise.*

DÖRFLING. The Prince of Homburg——

ELECTOR. Is Captain Ramin ready?

GUARD. In the saddle, sire, waiting at the main gate.

The ELECTOR, HIS WIFE, *and* NATALIA *take leave of one
another.*

TRUCHSS, *writing.* "Into the marshy region behind their right
  wing——"

DÖRFLING. The Prince of Homburg—— Where *is* the Prince of
  Homburg?

HOHENZOLLERN, *whispering.* Arthur!

PRINCE, *starting.* Here!

HOHENZOLLERN. What's the matter with you?

PRINCE. What are my marshal's orders?

He is blushing: fiddles with pencil and parchment and forces himself to write.

DÖRFLING. The Prince of Homburg, to whom
His Highness has once more entrusted,
As at Rathenow, the glorious command of all
The cavalry of Brandenburg——

He breaks off.

By which we mean to imply no derogation
To Colonel Kottwitz, who will be at hand
To give advice and his most valuable assistance——

Half aloud to CAPTAIN GOLTZ.

Is the colonel here?

GOLTZ. No, sir, he has sent me in his place
To receive his instructions from you.

The PRINCE *is again looking towards the* LADIES.

DÖRFLING. Will establish his position in the plain
Close by the village of Hackelwitz,
Opposite the enemy's right wing,
But out of the range of his cannon.

GOLTZ, *writing.* "But out of the range of his cannon——"

The ELECTOR'S WIFE *is tying a scarf round the* PRINCESS' *neck. The* PRINCESS, *about to draw on a glove, is looking about her, as if seeking for something.*

ELECTOR. What are you looking for, my dear?

ELECTOR'S WIFE. Have you lost something?

NATALIA. I don't know, Aunt. My glove——

They all look about them.

ELECTOR, *to the* COURT LADIES.

Dear ladies, would you be so kind,
And give yourselves the trouble of helping us?

ELECTOR'S WIFE. You've got it in your hand, child.

NATALIA. That's for the right hand. But where's the other?

ELECTOR. Perhaps you have left it in your apartments?

NATALIA. Dear Bork, *would* you mind——?

   COURT LADY *off.*

ELECTOR, *calling after her.* Make haste!

PRINCE, *to himself.* By all the powers above!

   He takes the glove from his collar.

DÖRFLING, *consulting the parchment in his hand.*

   But out of the range of their cannon.

   Continuing.

   His Highness the Prince shall then——

PRINCE. She's looking for the glove.

   He looks at the glove in his hand and at the PRINCESS.

DÖRFLING. In accordance with our commander's express desires——

GOLTZ, *writing.* "In accordance with our commander's express desires."

DÖRFLING. However the tide of battle turn, the Prince

   Shall remain in the position that has been assigned to him——

PRINCE. Now! I must find out if this is it!

   He lets his handkerchief fall and with it the glove: he picks up the handkerchief but leaves the glove lying where everyone may see it.

DÖRFLING, *surprised.* What is His Highness the Prince of Homburg doing?

HOHENZOLLERN, *whispering.* Arthur!

PRINCE. Here!

HOHENZOLLERN. This is beyond a joke.

PRINCE. At your service, sir.

   He again takes up pencil and parchment tablet. The FIELD-MARSHAL *looks at him for a moment undecided. There is a silence.*

GOLTZ, *writing.* "Shall remain in the position that has been assigned to him——"

DÖRFLING, *continuing.* Until the moment when,

   Driven back by Hennings and by Truchss——

PRINCE, *whispering to* GOLTZ. Who? What?

> *Looking at* GOLTZ' *notes.*

My dear Goltz! Who? *Me?*

GOLTZ. Yes, you! Who else would it be?

PRINCE. I shall—remain in the position——

GOLTZ. That's right.

DÖRFLING. Well, now, are you with us, sir?

PRINCE. I shall remain in the position that has been
Assigned to me——

> *He writes.*

DÖRFLING. Until the moment when,
Driven back by Hennings and by Truchss——

> *He breaks off.*

The enemy's left wing, routed and dispersed,
Is forced upon its right-hand flank,
And all the Swedish battalions in disorder
Flounder in the marshes that are riddled
With bogs and pits and ditches. Death-traps.
There, gentlemen, we shall annihilate them.

ELECTOR. Pages, ho! Bring lights! Dear ladies,
Take my arm!

> *They make to go.*

DÖRFLING. "Then he shall command his trumpeters to sound
their fanfares."

ELECTOR'S WIFE, *as some of the* OFFICERS *salute her.*
Gentlemen,
Au revoir. Do not let us disturb you.

> *Here* DÖRFLING *also salutes her and* PRINCESS.

ELECTOR, *stopping short.* Why, here is the Princess' glove!
Quick, pick it up!

COURTIER. Where?

ELECTOR. Right in front of our dear cousin, the Prince.

PRINCE. Right in front of *me?* Why! Is it yours?

> *He picks it up and brings it to* PRINCESS.

NATALIA. Thank you, noble Prince.

PRINCE, *bewildered.* Is it—yours?

NATALIA. It is mine, indeed, the one I was looking for.

She takes it and puts it on.

ELECTOR'S WIFE, *to* PRINCE, *as she departs.* Farewell! Farewell!
Good luck, and God be with you!
Well, then, till we meet again! Let it be soon,
And let it be a joyful meeting!

The ELECTOR *leaves with* LADIES, *followed by* LADIES OF
THE COURT, GUARDS, *and* PAGES.

PRINCE *stands thunderstruck for a moment, then strides back
triumphantly to the group of* OFFICERS.

Then he shall command his trumpeters to sound their
fanfares!

He pretends to be writing.

DÖRFLING, *consulting his parchment.* Then he shall command
his trumpeters to sound their fanfares—— But
First, lest some misunderstanding
Cause him to attack before the appointed time——

He breaks off.

GOLTZ, *writing.* "Some misunderstanding cause him to attack
Before the appointed time——"

PRINCE, *greatly agitated, whispering to* HOHENZOLLERN.
Heinrich!

HOHENZOLLERN. *Now* what is it? What's the matter with you?

PRINCE. But—— Didn't you *see?*

HOHENZOLLERN. I saw nothing. Be quiet, now, or you'll be done
for.

DÖRFLING, *continuing.* The Prince will send him a staff-officer
Who shall convey to him—now mark this well—
The express order to attack the enemy.
Until that moment, he shall not
Command his trumpeters to sound their fanfares.

The PRINCE *stands dreaming.*

Have you got that?

GOLTZ, *writing.* "Until that moment, he shall not
Command his trumpeters to sound their fanfares——"

DÖRFLING, *raising his voice.* Your Highness,
Have you noted what I said?

PRINCE. Sir?

DÖRFLING. Have you got it written down?

PRINCE. About—the fanfares?

HOHENZOLLERN, *in an irritated whisper.*
Fanfares! Fanfares! Devil take you!
"Until that moment, he shall not——"

GOLTZ, *as* HOHENZOLLERN. "Lest some misunderstanding——"

PRINCE, *interrupting.*
Yes, yes! I've got it! "Until then, he shall not——"
And then, "he shall command his trumpeters to sound their
    fanfares!"

He writes. A silence.

DÖRFLING. Baron Goltz, please make a note
That, if it is at all possible, I should like
To speak personally to Colonel Kottwitz
Before the encounter.

GOLTZ, *meaningfully.* I shall see to the matter.
You may depend on me, sir.

A silence. Enter the ELECTOR.

ELECTOR. Well, now, gentlemen, the sky is lightening.
Have you taken good note of everything?

DÖRFLING. It is done, Your Highness. The plan of your
    campaign
Has been communicated most precisely to your generals.

ELECTOR, *taking up his hat and gloves and cloak.*
Prince Frederick of Homburg, sir,
Allow me to recommend to you
The virtues of calmness, coolness in action.
You know that you already
Have thrown away two victories along the Rhine;
Keep a firm hand on yourself, cousin,
And do not deprive me of a third to-day.
For upon the day's victorious issue
Depend my honour, my country, and my title.

To OFFICERS.

Gentlemen, follow me. Hey, Franz!

A SQUIRE. Here, sire!

ELECTOR. Quickly now, lead out my battle horse, the white
one!
I must be on the field before the rising of the sun!
He departs, followed by GENERALS, COLONELS, *and* OFFICERS.

SCENE 6

PRINCE, *alone, coming forward.* And now, Fortune,
You whose veils the winds of chance
Are filling like a lifted sail,
Come, and move beside me!
This night, dear, terrible goddess,
I felt you lightly touch my brow.
Out of the fullness of the starry night
You cast a token of your favours to me,
And I seized it as you wandered smiling by.
To-day I shall seek you out, you daughter of the gods,
And grasp you to my breast upon the field of battle
Till you spill out all your riches round my feet.
Yes, Fortune! Though you were bound by chains of iron
To all the triumphal chariots of Sweden,
This day I shall possess you utterly,
Possess you, Fortune, and never let you go!
He strides swiftly away.

ACT II

SCENE 1

The battlefield at Fehrbellin

KOTTWITZ, HOHENZOLLERN, GOLTZ, *and others leading the cavalry.*

KOTTWITZ, *off.* Cavalry, halt here, and dismount!

HOHENZOLLERN AND GOLTZ. Halt, men! Halt!

As they are entering.

KOTTWITZ, *off.* Somebody help me down!

HOHENZOLLERN AND GOLTZ. Hold on! We're coming!

They go off again.

KOTTWITZ, *off.*

I thank you, gentlemen. Ouf! A plague on my old bones!
May you both, when you get to my age,
Be blessed with sons who'll do the same for you!

He enters, followed by HOHENZOLLERN, GOLTZ *and other* OFFICERS.

Yes, as long as I'm in the saddle, I'm a boy again.
But when the time comes to dismount,
I feel the soul's being torn out of my body.

He looks round him.

Where is His Highness, the Prince, our leader?

HOHENZOLLERN. The Prince will be back here soon.

KOTTWITZ. Where is he?

HOHENZOLLERN. He went back to the village that we passed
Just now, on our left, hidden in trees.
But he will be returning instantly.

AN OFFICER. Is it true that he fell from his horse during
The hours of darkness?

HOHENZOLLERN. I believe so, yes.

KOTTWITZ. He had a fall?

HOHENZOLLERN, *turning back to him.* Nothing serious!
  His horse shied at a windmill.

OFFICER. The black horse?

HOHENZOLLERN. Yes. Fortunately, he rolled from the saddle as
  The horse fell down, and got away with a scratch.
  Nothing worth speaking about.

KOTTWITZ, *ascending a slight eminence.*
  Ah! What a sweet morning!
  A day created by the Lord of life
  For gentler things than fighting!
  The sun's rose opens and shimmers through the clouds,
  And the heart, rejoicing in the freshly scented air,
  Soars up to heaven with the leaping lark!

GOLTZ. Did you find Field-marshal Dörfling, sir?

KOTTWITZ. Er—— No, damn it. What does His Excellency
    think I am?
  An arrow? An eagle? A flash of thought?
  He's had me running everywhere about the battlefield:
  I've been to the forward party at the top of Hackelberg,
  And right to the bottom again to visit the rear.
  I met everybody but the Marshal. So
  I went back to my own men.

GOLTZ. He will be very sorry to have missed you. It seems
  He had something of importance to tell you.

OFFICER. Here comes the Prince.

SCENE 2

The PRINCE *enters, a bandage round his temples.*

KOTTWITZ. A right hearty welcome to Your Highness! Now
  I want you to see how I've disposed, in your absence,
  Our cavalry in this hollow down below.
  I think you will approve what I have done.

PRINCE. Good morning, Kottwitz! Good morning, friends!
Kottwitz,
  You know I approve of everything you do!

HOHENZOLLERN. What were you doing, Arthur, down in the
  village?
  You're looking so serious!

PRINCE. I—I went to the chapel
  Whose golden spire glints above the trees.
  They were ringing the bells for prayer as we passed by;
  I wanted to go and kneel a moment at the altar.

KOTTWITZ. That shows a rare devoutness in a young man and
  a soldier.
  A task that is begun with prayer
  Will find itself crowned with happiness, success, and victory!

PRINCE. There was something I wanted to ask you, Heinrich——

  He draws HOHENZOLLERN *aside a little.*

  What were the instructions Dörfling gave me
  Last night at the general staff headquarters meeting?

HOHENZOLLERN. You weren't paying attention. I could see
  that.

PRINCE. My attention was—divided. I don't know what it was.
  Writing to dictation always confuses me.

HOHENZOLLERN. This time, fortunately, he didn't tell you
  Anything of much importance.
  Hennings and Truchss, who command the infantry,
  Are to lead the attack,
  And your assignment is as follows:
  You stay here in the valley with the cavalry,
  Ready to move in the moment you are given
  The signal to charge against the enemy.

PRINCE, *after a silence, in which he resumes his reverie.*
  What a wondrous thing!

HOHENZOLLERN. What do you mean, Arthur?

  He looks at the PRINCE. *Sound of cannon.*

KOTTWITZ. Ho, there, men! Into your saddles!
  That was Hennings! The battle has started!

They all climb the eminence.

PRINCE. *Who* is it?

HOHENZOLLERN. Colonel Hennings, Arthur,
Who has brought his men secretly round to Wrangel's rear.
Come up; you can see everything from here.

GOLTZ, *from the top of the hill.* See how vigorously he deploys
His companies along the Rhine!

PRINCE, *shading his eyes with his hand.* Is that Hennings
Over there, on our right flank?

FIRST OFFICER. Yes, Your Highness.

PRINCE. How the devil has that come about?
Yesterday he was on the left.

Distant cannon-fire.

KOTTWITZ. By thunder, look! Wrangel is turning
All his twelve cannon upon Hennings' men.

FIRST OFFICER. The Swedes have good entrenchments,
I will say that for them!

SECOND OFFICER. The devil they have! They've got their out-
works piled
Nearly as high as the church spire!

Firing close by.

GOLTZ. That'll be Truchss!

PRINCE. Truchss?

KOTTWITZ. Yes, it'll be Truchss, making a frontal attack
To come to the relief of Hennings.

PRINCE. But why is he in the centre?

Loud firing.

GOLTZ. Look! I think they've set fire to the village!

THIRD OFFICER. It's burning, now, all right!

FIRST OFFICER. It's burning! It's burning!
The flames are leaping from the tower!

GOLTZ. Ha! The Swedes are sending out messengers!

SECOND OFFICER. Their lines are breaking! They're on the
march!

KOTTWITZ. Where?

FIRST OFFICER. On their right flank!

THIRD OFFICER. That's right! The columns are moving. Three
    regiments.
They look as if they want to strengthen the left flank.

SECOND OFFICER. Upon my oath! And they're bringing their
    cavalry forward
To cover the advance of the right flank!

HOHENZOLLERN, *laughing*. Ha, ha! They'll soon quit the field
    again
When they see us laid in ambush up here!
Musketry fire.

KOTTWITZ. Look, men! Look!

SECOND OFFICER. Hark!

FIRST OFFICER. Musket fire!

THIRD OFFICER. They're fighting now in front of the trenches.

GOLTZ. By God! I've never in all my life
Heard such a thunderous din!

HOHENZOLLERN. Shoot! Shoot! Split the ground wide open!
You'll dig your own grave if you do!
A silence. Then distant shouts of victory.

FIRST OFFICER. By the great god of victory!
Wrangel's turning tail!

HOHENZOLLERN. No, it can't be!

GOLTZ. By heaven, boys! Watch their left flank!
They're pulling out of the trenches,
And taking their cannon with them!

ALL. We've won! Victory! We've won! Won!

PRINCE, *striding down from hill*. Into the saddle, Kottwitz!
Come on and follow me!

KOTTWITZ. Wait, gentlemen, be calm!

PRINCE. To horse! Sound the trumpets! Fanfares! Follow me!

KOTTWITZ. I say, wait!

PRINCE, *passionately*. Damnation take you! Hell and
    damnation!

KOTTWITZ. His Royal Highness the Elector made it clear
That we should wait upon *his* order to attack.
Goltz, read the instructions to this gentleman.

PRINCE. Wait upon *his* order! Oh, Kottwitz! Is your steed
　　Afraid to take the jump? Wait upon *his* order!
　　Can't you hear the order sounding here—in the heart?

KOTTWITZ. What order?

HOHENZOLLERN, *to* PRINCE. I beg of you——

KOTTWITZ. In my heart? My *heart*——?

HOHENZOLLERN. Be reasonable, Arthur!

GOLTZ. Listen to me, Colonel——

KOTTWITZ, *indignant*.

　　Oho! So that's the way you want it, my young fellow!
　　Let me tell you, sir, I could ride you,
　　You and your black beauty, to a standstill!
　　Forward, gentlemen, forward! Trumpeters, the fanfares!

GOLTZ, *to* KOTTWITZ. Not that, Colonel! You mustn't! No! No!

SECOND OFFICER. Hennings hasn't reached the river yet.

FIRST OFFICER. Take his sword away!

PRINCE. My sword? From me?

　　He shoves the OFFICER *away.*

　　You impertinent oaf! Do you not know
　　How an officer of Brandenburg behaves?
　　I'll have *your* sword!
　　And the scabbard with it!

　　He tears off the OFFICER'S *sword, scabbard, and belt.*

FIRST OFFICER. Your Highness, such an action, by——

PRINCE, *striding up to him*. Hold your tongue!

HOHENZOLLERN, *to the* OFFICER. Be quiet! Are you out of your
　　mind?

PRINCE, *to an* ORDERLY. Orderly!

　　He hands over the sword.

　　Take him to headquarters.
　　Keep him under close arrest.

　　To KOTTWITZ *and the other* OFFICERS.

　　Now, gentlemen, these are *my* orders!
　　Whoever will not follow me
　　Is a coward and a traitor!
　　Is there anyone here who will not follow me?

A silence.

Speak!

KOTTWITZ. You've already heard my answer.
Why do you carry on like this?

HOHENZOLLERN, *conciliatory*. We just wanted to let you know
Our own opinion.

KOTTWITZ. I'm with you. But upon your own head be it!

PRINCE, *calmer*. On my own head be it! Follow me, gentlemen!
They all exeunt.

SCENE 3

A room in a village. A COURTIER, *booted and spurred, enters. A* PEASANT *and* HIS WIFE *are sitting working at a table.*

COURTIER. Greetings, good people! Have you any room for
     guests?

PEASANT. Oh yes, we'll make room.

HIS WIFE. Who are they?

COURTIER. Our illustrious sovereign lady, and no other!
A wheel came off her carriage just outside the village,
And, as we have heard that victory has been won,
We do not need to travel any further.

BOTH, *rising*. What! Victory! Have we won? Merciful God!

COURTIER. Did you not know?
The Swedish forces are well and truly vanquished,
If not for good, at least for this campaign.
And Brandenburg is safe from fire and sword once more.
But look: here comes Her Highness now.

SCENE 4

Enter the ELECTOR'S WIFE, *pale and distraught.* PRINCESS
NATALIA *and several* LADIES OF THE COURT *follow her.*

ELECTOR'S WIFE, *in the doorway.*

Mademoiselle Bork! Winterfeld!
Come, give me your arms!

NATALIA. My dearest!

COURT LADIES. She's so pale! She's faint!

They support her.

ELECTOR'S WIFE. Lead me to a chair. I must sit down.
Dead, did he say? Dead?

NATALIA. Oh, my dearest, dearest one!

ELECTOR'S WIFE. Call the bringer of this tragic news.
I shall speak to him myself.

SCENE 5

Enter CAPTAIN VON MÖRNER, *wounded, and led by two*
CAVALRYMEN.

ELECTOR'S WIFE. What do you bring me,
Bearer of dread tidings?
Tell me the worst. What is it?

MÖRNER. Alas, dear lady, what these two eyes,
To their eternal sorrow, had never wished to see.

ELECTOR'S WIFE. What?

MÖRNER. The Elector is—no more.

NATALIA. Oh, heaven, what dreadful blow is this you send us?

She covers her face.

ELECTOR'S WIFE. Tell me how he met his death.
And, as the lightning-stroke that fells the wanderer
For one last instant illuminates his blazing world,
So let your message strike my brain.
And when you have spoken,
Let darkness sweep its final curtains down upon my sinking
head!

MÖRNER, *goes up to her, accompanied by his two* CAVALRY-
MEN.
Madame, the Prince of Homburg charged
On Wrangel in the plain as soon as the enemy,
Beset by Truchss, began to waver and withdraw.

Already through the first two Swedish lines
The Prince had cut his way with all his cavalry:
But then they found themselves attacked
By so murderous a rain of fire, that their ranks
Were beaten down like corn beneath a tempest.
The Prince then called a halt within the shelter of
The hill and tried to reassemble his depleted ranks.

NATALIA. My dearest! Be brave!

ELECTOR'S WIFE. Leave me alone! Go on!

MÖRNER. At that moment, we saw emerging from the dust of
    battle
Our noble sovereign, riding with the standard-bearers
Right at the front of Truchss' forces:
How straight and splendidly he rode, the sun
Illuminating him, and the white horse he rode upon
As if it were the very path of victory they trod!
At this great spectacle we were perturbed,
And grouped ourselves again, though sore beset,
In the cover of a hill, and from there
Beheld him entering the dreadful furnace of the fight.
Then, suddenly, both horse and rider
Fell to the dust. Two standard-bearers
Fell beside him and covered our great leader with
Their spreading flags.

NATALIA. Oh, dear lady!

FIRST LADY. O God in heaven!

ELECTOR'S WIFE. Go on! On!

MÖRNER. This terrible sight
Struck anguish to the Prince's heart.
Like the wild bear, goaded by fury and revenge,
He urged us after him,
And broke through the last enemy defences.
The trenches and the walls of earth
Are overwhelmed at one fell swoop,
The adversary overthrown and routed,
Scattered and destroyed, his cannon, flags,
Wagons, drums, and standards—all are seized—
The Swedes' entire equipment captured.
And if the Rhyn itself

Had not saved some from massacre,
Not one of the enemy had been left alive
To sit by his fireside and tell his children:
"I was at Fehrbellin and saw the hero fall."

ELECTOR'S WIFE. Your victory, sir, is bought too dearly.
I do not care for victories at such a cost.
I would rather have back
The price you paid to win it.
She falls into a dead faint.

FIRST LADY. O God in heaven! Help us! Help our lady!
She has lost her senses. Oh!

NATALIA *is weeping.*

SCENE 6

Enter the PRINCE OF HOMBURG.

PRINCE. Oh, my dearest Natalia!
He holds his hand to his heart with emotion.

NATALIA. So it is true?

PRINCE. If only I might answer "No" to that!
If only, with the blood of this still-faithful heart,
I could restore his own to life again!

NATALIA, *drying her tears.* Have they found the body?

PRINCE. Alas! Until this moment I have been concerned en-
    tirely
With vengeance: how could I undertake the task?
But I have sent a full detachment of my men
To seek his body on the field of death:
He will be brought back here by nightfall.

NATALIA. Who is there now to stand against the Swedes
In this unhappy war? Who in the world is there
To shield us from our enemies
Who now have robbed us of his fortune and his fame?

PRINCE, *taking her hand.* I, lady, shall defend your cause!
I shall be the guardian angel with the flaming sword
Defending the approaches to your desolated throne!

It was the Elector's dearest wish to see
That Brandenburg was freed before the year was out:
Allow me, lady,
To be the executor of that last wish!

NATALIA. My dear, devoted cousin!

She withdraws her hand.

PRINCE, *breaking off a moment.* Oh, Natalia, have you thought
What is to become of you now?

NATALIA. What is there left for me,
Now that this thunderstroke has opened up
A chasm at my feet?
My beloved mother and my father, lie
In their vaulted tombs in Amsterdam.
Dordrecht, my inheritance, is devastated,
Now an ashen ruin.
Hounded by the armies of the tyrant Spain,
My cousin Maurits, Prince of Orange,
Despairs of saving either his own children or
Our royal house. And now
My last support is taken from me: my fortune,
Always a fragile plant, must wither utterly and die.
Now for a second time, I am an orphan.

PRINCE, *putting an arm round her waist.* Oh, my dear friend!
If this hour of sorrow were not sacred to
The memory of the dead, then I would say to you:
Cast your tendrils round the bastion of my soldier's breast,
And feel the heart that now for years has quickened only
At the scent that only your sweet flowers breathe!

NATALIA. My dear, good cousin!

PRINCE. Will you? Will you?

NATALIA. But what if I should grow,
Not only on the bark of this great trunk,
But to its very heart?

She leans against his breast.

PRINCE. If only—— If only——

NATALIA. We must go.

PRINCE, *holding her.* It is the heart that matters,
The heart, Natalia, the inmost heart!

He kisses her; she tears herself away.

O God, if only he were here
To see this union of our souls!
If only we might look at him and say,
"Father, give us your blessing!"

He covers his face with his hands: NATALIA *returns to the* ELECTOR'S WIFE.

SCENE 7

A CAVALRY SERGEANT *hurries on.*

SERGEANT. Your Highness, I hardly dare reveal to you
The rumour that is put about!
The Elector is alive!

PRINCE. Alive?

SERGEANT. Let heaven be my witness!
Count Sparren has this moment brought the news.

NATALIA. Oh, lady, have you heard?

She rushes to ELECTOR'S WIFE *and embraces her.*

PRINCE. Who is the messenger?

SERGEANT. Count von Sparren, sir,
Who with his own eyes has seen our leader
Safe and sound in Hackelwitz with Truchss' army!

PRINCE. Quick! Go and bring him here!

SCENE 8

The cavalry SERGEANT *brings on* COUNT VON SPARREN.

ELECTOR'S WIFE. Ah! Let me not be cast down twice in the
          abyss!

NATALIA. No, no, you will not be!

ELECTOR'S WIFE. Is Frederick alive?

NATALIA, *raising her and holding her with both hands.*
Yes, you can be joyful once again!

SERGEANT. Here is the officer.

They come forward.

PRINCE. Count von Sparren, sir!
Is it true that you have seen our illustrious leader
Safe and sound with Truchss in Hackelwitz?

SPARREN. Yes, Your Highness, in the chapel courtyard,
Where he was giving orders to his staff
Concerning the burial of the dead.

COURT LADIES. Oh, heaven! Tears of joy!

They embrace each other.

ELECTOR'S WIFE. Oh, Natalia! Natalia!

NATALIA. Oh, such happiness
Is almost too great to bear!

They embrace.

PRINCE. But did I not see, from the forefront of the cavalry,
His white horse, hit by cannon-shot,
Fall with him to the dust?

SPARREN. The white horse fell indeed, and its rider too.
But the rider, Your Highness, was not our leader!

PRINCE. Not our leader? Then how——

NATALIA. Oh, wonderful! Oh!

She stands beside ELECTOR'S WIFE.

PRINCE. Speak! Each word you utter
Hangs on my mind as heavily as gold!

SPARREN. Then prepare yourselves to listen to
The most moving thing you ever heard!
Deaf to all warnings for his safety, our sovereign
Persisted in riding his dazzling white charger, which
Froben, his equerry, bought for him in England.
As in every encounter, our Elector once again
Was the target of our enemy's concerted fire.
The riders who escorted him could barely come
Within a hundred paces of their master,
So dense a hail of bullets, deadly shot, and splintering
     grenades
Surrounded and swept around him like a fiery flood,
While every soldier left alive unwillingly

Sought refuge on its stormy banks.
He alone, like an intrepid swimmer breasting the inferno's
    blazing tide,
And boldly waving signs of reassurance to his men,
Pressed slowly upwards to the very source
From which the cataract of molten fire sprang!

PRINCE. Yes, by heaven! It was a terrifying sight!

SPARREN. Then Froben, one of the few of all those valiant men
Who was able to follow closely on his leader, said to me:
"Cursed be the day when I paid good red gold
For that white horse our brave Elector rides!
Now would I give twice what I paid that day
If it could have a grey coat, or a brown!"
Full of a tremulous concern,
He rides up to our sovereign and cries:
"Your Highness, your horse is getting out of hand.
Allow me to take charge of him a while!"
With these words, he jumps down from his sorrel
And takes our sovereign's charger by the bridle.
Our leader then dismounts and smiles, then answers:
"The defect that you have noticed, my old man,
Is hardly one that could be cured by daylight.
I beg of you, take him away behind the hill,
Where our foe will not observe him 'getting out of hand.'"
Then he mounts the sorrel that Froben rode
And gallops off to where his duty lies.
But scarcely is Froben in the white horse's saddle,
Than a murderous rain of shot from a redoubt
Brings down his charger, and Froben falls,
A sacrifice to his fidelity.
He did not rise again.

A short silence.

PRINCE. His courage had the best reward.
If I had ten lives to lose,
I could not use them better than his one!

NATALIA. Brave Froben!

ELECTOR'S WIFE. What a hero!

NATALIA. A less noble death than his
Would still be worthy of our tears!

They weep.

PRINCE. Enough! Now to the matter in hand. Where is
The Elector? Has he set up his headquarters in Hackelwitz?

SPARREN. I should have told you and I beg forgiveness.
His Highness has departed for Berlin;
His generals are requested to join him there.

PRINCE. Berlin! Is the campaign at an end?

SPARREN. Really, I am astonished that you do not know of
this.
Count Horn, the Swedish general,
Presented his proposals for an armistice with Sweden,
Which was signed at our headquarters
Almost immediately afterwards.
In fact, if I have understood aright
Field-marshal Dörfling, Sweden has begun negotiations
For a general peace which may soon be a reality.

ELECTOR'S WIFE. Oh, happy day!

She rises.

My husband safe, and peace at last!

PRINCE. Come. Let us journey to Berlin without delay
And join him there. Madame, may I ask you for a seat
In your conveyance that I may more swiftly reach
The capital?

ELECTOR'S WIFE. You are welcome, and with all my heart,
To ride with us.

PRINCE, *sitting down to write.*
I must send first a note to Kottwitz,
And in a moment I shall be with you.

He hands the note to the CAVALRY SERGEANT. *Then he turns
again to the* ELECTOR'S WIFE *and lays his arm round*
NATALIA.

Besides, I should like to take advantage of this journey
To make of you, with all due modesty, a personal request——

NATALIA. Bork! Quick, my scarf, if you please!

ELECTOR'S WIFE. A request? From you?

COURT LADY. You have the scarf already round your neck, my
lady!

PRINCE. Well? Can you not guess?

ELECTOR'S WIFE. No. Nothing!

PRINCE. What? Not the slightest inkling?

ELECTOR'S WIFE. It doesn't matter. To-day there is no one in
the world
I would say "No" to, whatever he asked me.
And to you, the victor in battle, least of all.
Come! We must away!

PRINCE. Madame! Do you realize what you have said?
Am I to understand your answer will be "Yes?"

ELECTOR'S WIFE. It's time to go. We can talk further in the
coach.
Come, Prince, give me your arm!

PRINCE. O, great Caesar! Now I climb the ladder
That will lead me to your star!

He leads the LADIES *off; the rest follow.*

SCENE 9

*Berlin. The pleasure-garden of the old palace. In the back-
ground stands the palace chapel, with a flight of steps. Bells
ringing. The chapel is brightly lit. We see* FROBEN's *body
borne on and placed on a splendid catafalque. The* ELEC-
TOR, FIELD-MARSHAL DÖRFLING, COLONEL HENNINGS, COUNT
TRUCHSS, *and several other* COLONELS *and* OFFICERS *enter.
A number of* OFFICERS *carrying dispatches enter to them.
In the church and on the castle square there are people of
all ages and of both sexes.*

ELECTOR. Whoever it was that led the cavalry charges
On the day of the battle and made them advance
Without awaiting my express command,
Compelling the enemy to retreat before
Colonel Hennings could destroy the bridges,
He, I proclaim, is to be put to death!
He shall be court-martialled.
So it was not the Prince of Homburg who led the cavalry?

TRUCHSS. No, he was not, sire.

ELECTOR. Who informs me so?

TRUCHSS. The cavalry officers can reassure you on that point.
They told me before the engagement had begun
That the Prince had had a fall;
He was gravely wounded in the head and thighs.
They saw his wounds being dressed inside a church.

ELECTOR. Well, anyhow, this has been a brilliant victory.
To-morrow I shall give thanks to God for it
Before His holy altar. But were this victory
Ten times greater, it would not excuse
Him by whose fault it chanced to come my way.
More battles than just this one I must fight,
And I demand obedience to the law.
Whoever led the cavalry into that battle
Will answer for his insubordination with his head!
He shall be court-martialled, sentenced, executed.
Come, gentlemen, let us go and pray.

SCENE 10

Enter the PRINCE OF HOMBURG, *carrying three Swedish
standards,* COLONEL KOTTWITZ *with two,* COUNT HOHEN-
ZOLLERN, GOLTZ, *and* REUSS, *each with one flag, followed
by several other* OFFICERS, CORPORALS, *and* CAVALRYMEN
with flags, drums, and standards.

DÖRFLING, *as soon as he sees the* PRINCE.
The Prince of Homburg!
Truchss! What does this mean?

ELECTOR. How did you find your way here, Prince?
Where have you come from?

PRINCE. From Fehrbellin, Your Highness.
I bring you these trophies of victory!

He lays his three standards before the ELECTOR: OFFICERS,
CORPORALS, *and* CAVALRYMEN *do likewise.*

ELECTOR, *taken aback.* You are wounded, so I heard, and
            gravely too?
Did you not say so, Baron Truchss?

PRINCE, *gaily*. Not I!

TRUCHSS. I don't understand!

PRINCE. My horse fell with me before the fight began,
But I received only the merest scratch.
The field surgeon bound it up for me,
But it was really nothing.

ELECTOR. So it was you who led the cavalry?

PRINCE, *staring at him*. Of course! Is it me you ask?
Are these trophies not sufficient proof, sire?

ELECTOR. Take off his sword. He is under arrest.

DÖRFLING, *shocked*. What? Who?

ELECTOR, *walking over the flags*.
Kottwitz, my hearty greetings!

TRUCHSS. Damnation!

KOTTWITZ. By heaven, I don't rightly know——

ELECTOR. What do you say?
Looking keenly at him.
Look what a harvest our victory has reaped!
This flag belonged to the Swedish guard,
Did it not?
He takes up a flag, holds it out and examines it.

KOTTWITZ. Sire?

DÖRFLING. Highness?

ELECTOR. To be sure it did! It's from the times
Of King Gustavus Adolphus!
Read me the inscription.

KOTTWITZ. I think it's——

DÖRFLING. *Per aspera ad astra*, it says.

ELECTOR. That could not be said
Of the engagement at Fehrbellin.
A silence.

KOTTWITZ, *embarrassed*. Your Highness, a word——

ELECTOR. What is it? Take all these flags
And all these drums and standards
And hang them from the pillars of the chapel:

They will look well to-morrow
At our victory thanksgiving.

The ELECTOR *turns to his* COURTIERS, *takes the dispatches,*
opens, and reads them.

KOTTWITZ, *aside.* By thunder, he's going a bit too far!

After some hesitation, he takes up his two flags; the others
follow suit. Finally, when only the PRINCE's *three flags are*
left, KOTTWITZ *takes these also, so that he is carrying five*
flags.

AN OFFICER, *going up to the* PRINCE.
Prince, your sword, if you please!

HOHENZOLLERN, *with a flag, going to* PRINCE's *side.*
Arthur! Keep calm!

PRINCE. Is this a dream? Do I wake or sleep?
Is this me? Am I still in my right mind?

GOLTZ. Prince, I advise you to give him your sword.
And keep silent.

PRINCE. A prisoner?

HOHENZOLLERN. That is so.

GOLTZ. Under close arrest.

PRINCE. May one ask why?

HOHENZOLLERN, *firmly.* Not now.
We warned you. You engaged the enemy too soon.
The order was, not to move from your position
Until the signal.

PRINCE. Help me, friends! Help me! I'm going mad!

GOLTZ. Be quiet!

PRINCE. Well? Was it the troops of Brandenburg
That were defeated? Was it?

HOHENZOLLERN, *stamping his foot.* That's nothing to do with it!
Orders are to be obeyed!

PRINCE, *bitterly.* Ah!

HOHENZOLLERN, *leaving him.* Don't worry! You won't lose your
          head.

GOLTZ, *likewise.* He'll probably release you in the morning.

The ELECTOR *folds his dispatches and comes back to join his* OFFICERS.

PRINCE, *after he has unbuckled his sword.*

It seems my cousin Frederick will play the part of Brutus
And sees himself in some official portrait sitting
In a lofty seat, wearing the imperial toga,
The articles of war held in a magisterial hand,
While in the foreground lie the flags of Sweden.
Ha! He will not find in me a faithful son
Who will adore him even as the axe descends!
I am a Brandenburger, heart and soul:
Generosity, forgiveness—these are the virtues I
Was bred to honour.
And when he comes to me and tries to ape
Some antique Roman with a language
Dead as the ancient history in which his obstinacy lies
        embalmed,
I feel for him only pity and dismay!

He gives the sword to the OFFICER *and goes.*

ELECTOR. Take him to the headquarters at Fehrbellin
And convoke the military court
That will pass judgement on him.

He goes off into the chapel. He is followed by the flag-bearers. While he is kneeling in prayer with his suite at FROBEN's *bier, the flags are hung from the pillars of the chapel. A funeral march.*

ACT III

SCENE 1

The PRINCE's *prison at Fehrbellin. In the background, two* CAVALRYMEN *mounting guard over the* PRINCE. *Enter* HOHENZOLLERN.

PRINCE. Is it you, Heinrich? Welcome!
I am free at last?

HOHENZOLLERN, *astonished.* God be praised!

PRINCE. What do you say?

HOHENZOLLERN. Free? Has he sent you back your sword?

PRINCE. No.

HOHENZOLLERN. Nothing?

PRINCE. No.

HOHENZOLLERN. Then how can you be free?

A silence.

PRINCE. I thought you had brought me—my release.
It doesn't matter.

HOHENZOLLERN. I don't know anything.

PRINCE. Oh, it doesn't matter! It doesn't matter, do you hear?
He'll be sending someone else.

He carries two chairs forward.

Sit down! Now, tell me, what's the news?
Has the Elector returned from Berlin?

HOHENZOLLERN, *absent-mindedly.* He has. Yesterday evening.

PRINCE. And I suppose the victory thanksgiving ceremony
Was performed in the desired way?
Was the Elector present in the chapel?

HOHENZOLLERN. Yes, with his wife and Natalia.
The chapel was most gloriously illuminated.
During the *Te Deum* we could hear

Prodigious salvos being fired on the castle square.
The Swedish flags and standards
Hung swaying like solemn trophies from all the pillars.
And on our sovereign's express command
Your name was given from the pulpit as
That of the victor of Fehrbellin.

PRINCE. So I have heard. Now, what else? What's on your
   mind?
Your countenance, dear friend, is far from gay!

HOHENZOLLERN. Have you spoken to anyone?

PRINCE. To Goltz. Not here, but at the castle,
Where I was subjected to interrogation.

A silence.

HOHENZOLLERN, *anxiously.* Arthur, what do you think of your
   position,
After this sudden change of fortune?

PRINCE. What do I think? I think the same as you and Goltz;
The same as the military court.
The Elector has performed his duty, as required.
Now he will listen to the promptings of his heart.
Oh, he'll put a serious visage on and say:
"You disobeyed me!" Perhaps let fall a word or two
Like execution, death, imprisonment.
"But now I give you back your freedom!" he will say,
And round the scabbard that contained the sword of victory
Perhaps he'll tie the ribbon of an order,
Or some decoration—— Though if he doesn't, well,
No matter. I don't deserve all that.

HOHENZOLLERN. Oh, Arthur!

He stops short.

PRINCE. Well?

HOHENZOLLERN. Are you so sure still of all this?

PRINCE. I should think so! He is fond of me, I know,
As if I were his son: since my earliest days
He has given me a thousand proofs of it.
Why do you look so doubtful?
Did he not seem always to rejoice,
Almost as much as I did, at my growing fame?

Do I not owe everything to him?
And now, after having raised me with his own
Devoted hands, you think he'll trample down into the dust
So ruthlessly his favourite plant
Merely because it put out rather too
Abundantly and hastily its buds and flowers?
His greatest foe could not convince me of it;
Much less can you, who know and cherish him.

HOHENZOLLERN, *grave*. You have stood court-martial, Arthur,
And you still believe all this?

PRINCE. Yes! Because I have stood court-martial
I still believe! By heaven!
No tribunal goes as far as they have gone
Unless their intention is to pardon me!
It was precisely there, at the bar of justice,
That I regained my confidence again.
Was it, after all, such a terrible offence?
One punishable by—death? Was it?
To advance two minutes earlier than I should have,
In order to make the Swedish forces bite the dust?
What other criminal offence have I committed?
I have nothing on my conscience.
How could he possibly have set me up before
That court of heartless judges, that like owls
Sat there and hooted their funereal notes at me?
How could he do it, if he did not intend
To step among them, like a god from the machine,
At the last moment and reprieve me with a joking word?
No, friend, he piles upon my head these clouds and mid-
   night shadows
Only to be able to disperse their darkness for me like a rising
   sun:
It's a caprice, a royal one. I do not grudge him that!

HOHENZOLLERN. All the same, your sentence has been passed.

PRINCE. So I hear: the death sentence, I believe.

HOHENZOLLERN, *astounded*. You knew?

PRINCE. Goltz, who was present at the verdict of the court,
   Acquainted me with their decision.

HOHENZOLLERN. But, heavens above, man! Aren't you—— Don't
    you——

PRINCE. Not in the slightest.

HOHENZOLLERN. But you're mad!
    On what do you base this calm assurance?

PRINCE. On—a feeling I have about him.

    He stands up.

    I beg of you, leave me alone!
    Why should I plague myself with useless doubts?

    He reflects a moment, then sits down again. A silence.

    The court-martial *had* to pass a sentence of death:
    That was according to the laws by which it acts.
    But rather than let such a judgement be fulfilled,
    Rather than let a faithful and devoted servant
    Be delivered up to execution, Frederick would tear
    His own heart from his breast and pour out
    His life-blood drop by drop upon the ground.

HOHENZOLLERN. Arthur, I'm telling you that——

PRINCE, *moodily.* Oh, not again, dear Heinrich!

HOHENZOLLERN. The Field-marshal——

PRINCE. No! Don't tell me!

HOHENZOLLERN. Just one word, Arthur!
    If this means nothing to you,
    Then I'll say no more.

PRINCE, *turns back to him.* Didn't you hear me say
    I know it all? Oh, well, what is it?

HOHENZOLLERN. Field-marshal Dörfling has just taken
    The death-warrant to the castle;
    The Elector, instead of exercising the prerogative of mercy,
    Wished to append his signature.

PRINCE. Well, what of that?

HOHENZOLLERN, *aghast.* What of that?

PRINCE. His signature, did you say?

HOHENZOLLERN. I can assure you, on my word of honour.

PRINCE. On the death-warrant?—— No! Perhaps on some
    report——

HOHENZOLLERN. It was the death-warrant.

PRINCE. Who told you this?

HOHENZOLLERN. Field-marshal Dörfling himself.

PRINCE. When?

HOHENZOLLERN. Just now.

PRINCE. When he came back from seeing the Elector?

HOHENZOLLERN. As he was coming down the stairway from
The Elector's private rooms.
He must have seen my thunderstruck expression,
For he added: "Everything is not yet lost.
There's still another day——"
But his grim white lips belied his words,
Which should have been: "There is no hope."

PRINCE, *jumping up*. He couldn't—— No! He couldn't dream
Of imposing such a monstrous penalty!
Would he, because of the almost undetectable
Flaw in the diamond of victory that I presented to him,
Would he tread the victor in the dust?
That would be a deed so infamous,
The worst excesses of the Dey of Tunis would appear
As harmless as a children's game beside it.
The luxurious monster Sardanapalus
Would seem like a rosy cherub borne on silvery wings;
Oh, such a deed would set
The whole tyrannous troop of Roman emperors,
Like innocent babes expired at their mothers' breasts,
At God's right hand!

HOHENZOLLERN, *also jumping up*. Arthur, you must realize——

PRINCE. And the Field-marshal held his tongue?

HOHENZOLLERN. What could he say?

PRINCE. Oh, God, I was so full of hope!

HOHENZOLLERN. Could you perhaps, unconsciously or not,
Have committed some folly that offended him?

PRINCE. Never!

HOHENZOLLERN. Try to remember.

PRINCE. Never, I tell you!

The very shadow that he cast was sacred to me.

HOHENZOLLERN. Arthur, do not be angry with me, if I doubt
  your words.
It is said that the Swedish envoy, Count Horn,
Has come to negotiate the marriage of
Princess Natalia of Orange with his master,
King Carolus Gustavus,
And that the Elector has been bitterly offended
By something that his wife revealed to him:
The Princess has already set her heart on someone.
Have you had anything to do with this?

PRINCE. Why?

HOHENZOLLERN. Have you?

PRINCE. My friend, I have. Now all is clear to me.
The proposal sets the seal upon my luckless fate.
It is I who am the cause of her refusal,
For she is betrothed to me.

HOHENZOLLERN. You idiot! What were you thinking of?
How often have I warned you?

PRINCE. Oh, friend, help me, save me!
I am lost! I am lost!

HOHENZOLLERN. How can we get you out of this?
Would you like to speak to the Elector's wife?

PRINCE. Guard!

GUARD. Sir!

PRINCE. Bring me your captain.
  He hastily takes a cloak from the wall and puts on a feath-
  ered hat which is lying on the table.

HOHENZOLLERN, *helping him.* With a little ingenuity,
This interview can save your life.
If the Elector can make a suitable
Peace-settlement with the King of Sweden,
His heart, I am certain, will be reconciled to you,
And in another hour or two you will be free.

The CAPTAIN *comes on.*

PRINCE, *to the* CAPTAIN.
Stranz, you are the captain of the guard.
Will you allow me to absent myself from here awhile?
It is an urgent, personal affair.

STRANZ. Your Highness, I have no authority over you.
You are free to go wherever you please.
Those are the orders I was given.

PRINCE. Strange! So I am not a prisoner?

STRANZ. You are a prisoner upon parole.
Your word, Prince, is security enough.

PRINCE, *going.* I see! Very well. It doesn't matter. Come!
    Farewell!

HOHENZOLLERN. The fetters follow in the prince's trail.

PRINCE. I am going only to the castle
And will very shortly be returned.

Exeunt omnes.

The apartments of the ELECTOR'S WIFE. *She comes in with*
NATALIA.

ELECTOR'S WIFE. Come, Natalia. Now is your chance.
Count Horn and the Swedish delegation
Have just left the castle.
I can see a light burning in your uncle's rooms.
Go and see him, speak to him,
And try to save your prince.

They are about to go.

SCENE 4

A COURT LADY *enters.*

LADY. Your Highness, the Prince of Homburg waits outside!
 I could hardly believe my eyes!

ELECTOR'S WIFE. It can't be!

NATALIA. The Prince himself?

ELECTOR'S WIFE. He's still under arrest?

LADY. He's waiting. He seems perplexed. He hasn't even
 Taken off his cloak and hat. He says he must
 Speak to you.

ELECTOR'S WIFE, *displeased.* How thoughtless! To betray his
 word!

NATALIA. Perhaps he has an explanation——

ELECTOR'S WIFE, *after reflection.* Let him come in.
 She sits down.

SCENE 5

Enter the PRINCE OF HOMBURG.

PRINCE. Oh, my lady!
 He falls on his knees before her.

ELECTOR'S WIFE. Prince, what are you doing here?

PRINCE. Oh, let me lie here at your feet!

ELECTOR'S WIFE, *with controlled emotion.*
 You are a prisoner, sir,
 And yet you break your word and come to me!
 Why do you add another error to the first?

PRINCE, *insistently.* Do you realize what has happened to me?

ELECTOR'S WIFE. Indeed, I know it all.
 But what can I, a powerless woman, do for you?

PRINCE. Oh, lady, you would not speak to me like this

If you could feel the cold of death
I carry round me everywhere!
To me, these ladies here around you,
The Princess, you yourself, and all still left alive
Appear endowed with saving grace from heaven,
And with heaven's strength!
The most lowly mortal is to me
A god! Oh! I could hang myself upon the neck
Of your most humble stableman,
Imploring him to save me. Save me!
On the whole of God's wide earth,
Only I am helpless, abandoned, and can do
Nothing, nothing.

ELECTOR'S WIFE. You are not yourself. What has happened?

PRINCE. Ah! I have seen my grave, my dark hole in the cold
  ground!
As I was coming here, I saw it in the torch-light,
The tomb that to-morrow morning shall receive
This body. Look, lady, these eyes:
They want to cover them with heavy darkness;
This breast: they want to shatter it with lead!
Upon the market square, the windows are already taken
That will look down upon my sandy stage
And on my final scene.
And I, who now, from life's most lofty peak,
Still gaze upon the future, as if it were a legendary land,
Shall lie to-morrow rotting between two narrow boards,
With at my head a stone, to tell you who I—*was!*

The PRINCESS, *who until now has been standing, leaning on
the shoulders of her* COURT LADIES, *collapses with her head
upon a table and weeps.*

ELECTOR'S WIFE. My son! If such is the will of heaven,
You must face your destiny with courage and with calm!

PRINCE. Oh, God's earth, dear mother, is so fair!
I implore you, do not go before the fatal hour strikes
And leave me all alone to enter those black shades!
If I have been in error, let him punish me,
But must it be the bullets of a firing-squad?
Let him reduce me to the ranks, dismiss me from the army,

And take my honours all away, if such must be the law!
Oh, God in heaven,
Since I have seen my grave, I only want to live,
And honour and dishonour are alike to me!

ELECTOR'S WIFE. Stand up, my son, stand up! Why do you
    talk like this?
You are distracted. Compose yourself!

PRINCE. No, lady, until you swear to me
That you will cast yourself before him
And beg him for my life!
Your childhood friend, my mother, when she was dying,
Gave me into your care and said:
"Love him like a son when I shall be no more!"
And you knelt by her bed and wept
And kissed her hand and said:
"It shall be as if I had myself conceived
And borne him."
Now I remind you of that promise.
Go, as if you had yourself conceived
And borne me, and say to him:
"I beg for mercy, mercy for my son! Let him go free!"
And then come back to me and tell me: "You are free!"

ELECTOR'S WIFE, *weeping.*

My dear son, I have already done so.
I pleaded with him, but in vain.

PRINCE. Every claim to happiness I now abjure!
Don't forget to tell him also
That I no longer wish to take Natalia in marriage!
Every spark of feeling for her now has vanished from my
    heart.
She is free again, free as the wild deer in the heathered
    hills,
Utterly free, as if I never had existed.
Now she is free to marry whom she will or whom she must.
And if it be the King of Sweden, Carolus Gustavus,
She has my warm felicitations.
I only want to go back to my own estate.
There I shall build, pull down, and build again,
And sow my fields, and reap them till the sweat

Pours down my breast, and labour hard,
As if for wife and child: but I shall be alone there.
And when I have reaped, then I shall sow again,
Turning calmly in the year's great circle, that is life's
Until, at close of day, life sinks and dies.

ELECTOR'S WIFE. Come, my son! Go back to prison.
I shall intercede for you again, but not before
You have returned to prison.

The PRINCE *rises. He speaks to* NATALIA.

PRINCE. My poor child, you are weeping! The sun to-day
Is lighting all your hopes the way to death?
I shall always be, I know, your first,
But not, I hope, your only love, although
Your pure face tells me, clear as day,
That you will never give your heart to any other man.
What comfort could I bring you, I, most wretched of all
     mortal souls?
Go, and spend your days within a cloister by the Rhine,
Or find in the mountains a young boy with golden locks
Like mine, and teach him how to call you "Mother."
Then, when he has grown to manhood, you will show him
How they close the eyelids of the dead.
That is the only happiness now left to you!

NATALIA, *bravely, putting her hand in his and rising.*
Go, my hero, return to your prison cell
And, on the way, look calmly, deep into
The grave that has been opened to receive you.
It is no more terrible and no wider
Than the grave that always waited for you on the field of
     battle!
I shall be true to you, even in death,
If death it be. Meanwhile, I shall go and speak
To my uncle and try to find the words to save you:
Perhaps I shall be lucky and, if I touch his heart,
I shall deliver you from all your troubles.

PRINCE, *looking at her enraptured, folding his hands in prayer.*
Lady, if at your shoulders you had two great wings,
I should take you for an angel and this room for heaven!
Oh, heaven! Did I hear aright? That *you* will speak for *me?*

Where did you find this quiverful of words,
That now you dare to speak to the Elector?
Can you aim so true, so high, so far?
Ah, how sweet it is, the sudden ray of hope!

NATALIA. God will put the arrows in my hands,
And, with His grace, they shall reach their mark!
But if the Elector cannot change
The sentence of the court—well, then,
You, the hero, shall submit to death as only heroes can!
And you, who in life so often triumphed on the field,
Will triumph even more in this, your final fight!

ELECTOR'S WIFE. Away! Time flies, and every moment now is
    precious!

PRINCE. Now may all the saints of paradise protect you.
Farewell! Farewell! And whatever be the outcome,
Let me know the answer soon! Oh, let it be—success!

They all leave.

ACT IV

SCENE 1

In the ELECTOR's *apartments. The* ELECTOR *is standing holding some papers at a lamplit table.* NATALIA *comes through the centre door and kneels, though at some distance away from him. A silence.*

NATALIA. My noble uncle, Frederick of Brandenburg!

ELECTOR, *laying papers aside.* Natalia!

He tries to raise her.

NATALIA. No! No!

ELECTOR. What is it, my child?

NATALIA. I cast myself down before you, as is fitting
For a suppliant. I come, sire,
To implore your mercy for our cousin Homburg.
Not for my own sake do I wish him to be spared:
No, though I love him and do not conceal my love,
Not for my own sake do I come;
He may take whatever wife he pleases.
What I want, sire, is that he
Should simply be allowed to live,
That he should be left to live upon the earth,
Independent, free, and unrestrained,
As I would wish a flower to live,
Whose singularity and beauty pleased me.
This I would ask of you, my sovereign and my friend,
And know that you will lend an ear to my request.

ELECTOR, *raising her.* My little daughter! How could you ask
    such things?
Do you know what crime it is your cousin Homburg has
    committed?

NATALIA. Oh, my dear uncle!

ELECTOR. Well? Has he not done wrong?

NATALIA. Wrong? Oh, that fault, how innocently he committed it!
Could those clear blue eyes, that pale blond head
Belong to one who willingly would make the least false step?
A little fault it was, that should have been forgiven
Even before he had the time to say: "Forgive me!"
You cannot trample this bright flower in the dust!
Rather, for his poor dead mother's sake,
You must press him to your heart and say:
"Come, be sad no more,
You are as dear to me as life itself!"
Was it not eagerness to add more glory to your name
That, in the heat of battle, tempted him to break
The letter, not the spirit, of the law?
And, oh! When his youthful rashness fired him to break it,
Did he not thrust with manly ardour at the dragon's head?
The reward of victory is not the grave!
To crown the victor, then to execute him!
History does not require such a gesture,
For it would be a gesture so beyond all common use,
That it might easily be taken as inhuman, sire.
And heaven knows, there is no gentler man on earth than
you.

ELECTOR. My sweet Natalia! If I were some fearful tyrant,
Your words—I feel it in my heart—
Would have moved my iron will to fresh compassion.
But tell me this: how can my duty allow me to reverse
The verdict that a solemn court has passed?
What would be the consequences of a deed like that?

NATALIA. For whom? For you?

ELECTOR. No, child, I am not thinking of myself,
But of my country.

NATALIA. Oh, sire! Is there nothing more? Your country!
Your country is not going to be ruined
Because you showed some human mercy!
You have known only the discipline of camp and battlefield.
To countermand the verdict of a military court
Is to you an act of insubordination and disorder.
The rules of war and of a soldier's life

Must be obeyed, I know. How much more
The rules of real, human love must be obeyed!
The heart has its rules and reasons too.
The country that you have fought for and created
Stands secure and firm, sire, as a rock.
It would need quite other, wilder tempests now to over-
    throw it
Than this one small capitulation that I ask of you.
I see your country growing to a glorious future,
More splendid and more beautiful each day in your de-
    scendants' hands,
With towers and pinnacles and castles rich in legend,
To be the joy of friends and the terror of your enemies.
But such a glittering future will not come
From this cold, barren will,
That in my uncle's glowing autumn, now at peace,
Will turn to chilling winter all
The springing summer of our cousin Homburg's blood!

ELECTOR. Does our cousin Homburg think as you?

NATALIA. My cousin?

ELECTOR. Does he think that in our land of Brandenburg
It matters little whether law or anarchy is master?

NATALIA. Oh, he is young yet——

ELECTOR. Well?

NATALIA. Oh, my dear uncle,
I have no answer but my tears.

ELECTOR, *moved*. But why, my child? What is the matter?

NATALIA. He thinks of only one thing: to be saved!
He only sees the pointing barrels of the firing-team,
The rifles laid to their steady shoulders,
So terrible a sight, it drives all thoughts out of his mind
But one: and that is, how to keep alive.
The whole of Brandenburg might be destroyed,
And he would notice nothing.
See what you have done to this great hero's heart!
She turns away, weeping.

ELECTOR, *utterly astonished*. No! Natalia! It can't be possible!
Does he—does he beg for mercy?

NATALIA. Oh, why did you ever condemn him to——

ELECTOR. Answer me! Does he ask for mercy? God in heaven,
What has happened to him? Why are you weeping?
Did you speak to him? Tell me! Did you speak to him?

NATALIA, *leaning on his breast.*
Yes, a while ago, in my aunt's apartments,
Where he came to see us under cover of the dusk,
In a dark mantle, with his hat down on his eyes,
Embarrassed, furtive, and distracted,
His natural grace and dignity all overthrown,
A lamentable, pitiable sight!
Never should I have dreamed that he,
A man whom history has called a hero,
Could have fallen quite so far!
It is only a woman you see here,
One who is frightened by the merest worm:
But if death suddenly appeared before me
Wearing its most terrifying mask,
It would not find me so deprived of will,
So weak, so crushed, so utterly unlike a hero!
Oh, how meaningless is human grandeur!

ELECTOR. Come, now, dear child! By heaven, courage!
He is free!

NATALIA. Free, Your Highness?

ELECTOR. I have pardoned him! I shall draft at once
The order for his release.

NATALIA. Oh, my dearest uncle! Is it really true?

ELECTOR. I give my word.

NATALIA. You've really pardoned him? He will not be executed?

ELECTOR. I promise you. How could I resist
The arguments of such a warrior?
You know that in my heart of hearts
I have a great respect for his opinion.
If he can show the sentence we have passed on him to be
In any way unjust, I shall reverse it.
He brings her a chair.
Sit down here a moment.

He goes to his table, sits, and writes.

NATALIA, *aside.* Heart, why do you beat so hard
Against the walls of this weak house?

ELECTOR, *writing.* Is the Prince still in the castle?

NATALIA. No. He returned to the prison.

ELECTOR *finishes and seals the letter and turns with it in his
hand towards the* PRINCESS.

ELECTOR. So my little daughter was in tears!
Could I, whose every care it is to make her happy,
Cloud the heaven of her candid eyes?

He puts his arm round her.

Will you take the letter to him?

NATALIA. To the prison?

ELECTOR *gives her the letter.* And why not? Ho, guards!

Enter GUARDS.

Have the coach brought to the door! The Princess
Is paying a visit to Colonel von Homburg!

Exeunt GUARDS.

Then he can thank you for his life.

He embraces her.

My dear child! Do you forgive me?

NATALIA, *after a silence.*
Sire, what it was that moved your heart to clemency
I do not know and do not ask.
One thing I know—I feel it in my soul—
You would not play a trick on me.
Whatever the contents of this letter,
I believe that they may save him
And I thank you for your tenderness.

She kisses his hand.

ELECTOR. Be sure of that, my dear, and set your heart at rest.
Our cousin Homburg's fate
Depends now only on himself.

They go.

SCENE 2

The PRINCESS NATALIA's *apartments.* NATALIA,
two COURT LADIES, *and the* COUNT REUSS

NATALIA. What is this you bring me, Count Reuss?
Is it from my regiment? Is it important?
Can it not wait until the morning?

REUSS *hands her the letter.* It is from Colonel Kottwitz, Your
Highness.

NATALIA. Quick! What does he say?

She opens it.

REUSS. It is a request, both boldly phrased, as you will see,
And yet respectful, to His Highness the Elector,
Drafted in favour of the Prince of Homburg.

NATALIA, *reading.* "Humble supplication . . .
From the regiment of the Princess of Orange. . . ."

Pause.

Who wrote this request?

REUSS. As you might guess from that untutored script,
Colonel Kottwitz wrote it.
His noble name stands at the top.

NATALIA. And what are these thirty or so signatures below it?

REUSS. The names of the officers, Your Highness,
In precedence of rank.

NATALIA. And why was it to me that the request was sent?

REUSS. Your Highness, we would very respectfully ask of you
If, as our colonel-in-chief, you would place your name
At the head of all the rest;
A space has been left, as you can see.

A pause.

NATALIA. Count Reuss, I think this is unnecessary now.
I have just heard that the Prince
Is likely to be pardoned by His Highness.

REUSS, *joyful*. Oh! Is it true?

NATALIA. In any case, as this statement, skilfully used,
Will certainly help to turn the scales,
And my uncle may even find it welcome
In the last analysis,
I agree to your proposal and will sign my name.
She goes to table, as if to write.

REUSS. We shall be most grateful for your help.
A pause.

NATALIA, *turning back to him*. I can find here only
My own regiment, Count!
Where are the Bomsdorf Cuirassiers,
And the Götz and Anhalt-Pless Dragoons?

REUSS. Your Highness, it is not because their hearts
Are less warmly disposed towards the Prince than ours.
It was rather unfortunate for our petition
That Kottwitz is encamped at Arnstein,
Away from all the other regiments
Which are quartered here at Fehrbellin.
And there were no facilities
For sending our petition out to every regiment.

NATALIA. All the same, I feel it takes away from
The value of your intervention.
Are you quite certain, Count,
That if you could contact the officers in Fehrbellin
They would lend their support to our petition?

REUSS. I can answer for their undivided loyalty
To us and to the Prince's cause.
Not only the cavalry would pledge themselves;
I'm sure the entire army of Brandenburg
Would gladly sign their names.

NATALIA, *after a silence*. Why do you not send officers
As delegates to all the regiments in town?

REUSS. The colonel has refused permission.
He did not wish, he said, to undertake
Anything that might be called sedition.

NATALIA. What a curious hero! Both brave and timorous!
But fortunately the Elector, I remember now,

Charged me, as he was so preoccupied,
With sending orders out to Kottwitz,
Whose present quarters are too cramped,
To install himself at Fehrbellin.
I'll do it now.

She sits down and writes.

REUSS. Ah, Your Highness, what an admirable decision!
Nothing could be more favourable to our cause.

NATALIA, *writing.* Use the occasion to the best advantage,
Count!

She seals the letter and stands again.

Meanwhile—you understand!—this letter
Will remain in your portfolio; you will not go with it
To Arnstein to deliver it to Kottwitz
Before I give you my express commission!

She hands the letter to him.

GUARD, *entering.* Your Highness, at the master's orders
The coach is waiting for you in the courtyard.

NATALIA. Bring it to the door! I'm coming now.

A pause, during which she goes to the table and thoughtfully draws on her gloves.

Count Reuss, will you accompany me
On my visit to the Prince of Homburg?
I wish to speak to him.
There is a seat for you inside my coach.

REUSS. Your Highness, it is a great honour——

He offers her his arm.

NATALIA, *to* COURT LADIES. Follow us, my friends.

To REUSS.

Perhaps, sir,
This visit will have some bearing on
My instructions for you regarding the letter.

Exeunt.

SCENE 3

HOMBURG *in prison. He hangs his hat on the wall and drops dispiritedly on a cushion on the ground.*

PRINCE. "Life," says the dervish, "is a journey, and a short
  one."
  How true! The furthest we ever get
  Is five or six feet above the earth,
  And the same distance underneath it!

Lying almost full-length.

  Well, now I'm halfway between the two! One day
  A man can bear his head up proudly on his shoulders;
  The next it's hanging low with fear;
  And the next day it's lying at his feet.
  Ah, well, they say the sun shines up there too
  And over brighter fields than we have here.
  I believe that's true: a pity that the eye should rot
  Before it can glimpse those wonders——

SCENE 4

Enter PRINCESS NATALIA, *led by* COUNT REUSS, *captain of the horse, and followed by* COURT LADIES. *An* ATTENDANT *goes before them with a torch.*

ATTENDANT. Her Royal Highness, the Princess Natalia of
  Orange!

PRINCE *jumps up.* Natalia!

NATALIA, *whispering to* REUSS. Leave us alone a moment!

  REUSS *and* ATTENDANT *off.*

PRINCE. My dearest Princess!

NATALIA. My dearest cousin!

PRINCE. Well, what is the news? How do I stand?

NATALIA. Good news, Prince. All is well. As I had guessed,

You have been pardoned, you are free; here is a letter
From the Elector, confirming it.

PRINCE. It can't be possible! Oh no! It must be a dream——

NATALIA. Read the letter. You'll see it's no dream.

PRINCE, *reading.* "Your Highness, the Prince of Homburg,
When I consigned you, on account of your premature
    attack,
To prison, I believed I was doing my duty.
And I counted on your recognition of this fact.
But if you are of the opinion
That I have done you an injustice,
Then will you kindly send me word—
A single line will do—
And at once I shall restore to you
Your sword and your command."

NATALIA *grows pale. A silence. The* PRINCE *gives her a
questioning look.*

NATALIA, *with a look of sudden joy.* There, you see!
A line, that's all he wants!
Oh, my dear friend, you are free!

She presses his hand.

PRINCE. My angel!

NATALIA. Oh, happy, happy moment! Look,
Here is the pen. Take it and write!

PRINCE. What signature is this?

NATALIA. That is "F", his sign for Frederick.
That is how he always signs himself.
Oh, Bork! You must be happy for me!
You must be happy too!
Oh, I knew his kindness is as infinite as the sea.
Bring a chair for His Highness, he must write at once!

PRINCE. He says: If I am of the opinion——

NATALIA, *interrupting.* Of course! Hurry, now. Sit down.
I shall dictate your reply to you.

She sets a chair for him.

PRINCE. I'll just read the letter over once again.

NATALIA, *snatching the letter from him.*

What good will that do?
Did you not see, in the courtyard of the church,
The grave yawn up to you with open jaws?
Time is short. Sit down and write!

PRINCE, *smiling.* Really you're acting now as if the grave
Were set to pounce upon me like a panther.

He sits down and takes up the pen. She turns away to weep.

NATALIA. Now write, if you do not want to make me angry
with you!

The PRINCE *rings for a* SERVANT, *who enters.*

PRINCE. Paper and ink! Some sealing-wax! A seal!

The SERVANT, *after having brought these things, goes off
again. The* PRINCE *writes. Silence. He tears up the letter he
has started and throws it under the table.*

A bad beginning.

He takes another sheet of paper.

NATALIA *picks up the letter.* Why? What did you say?
But that is very good! That's excellent!

PRINCE, *muttering.* Pooh! It might have been written by a
cobbler,
Not by a Prince. I must turn it more gracefully.

A silence. He tries to snatch the ELECTOR's *letter again,
which* NATALIA *still holds in her hand.*

What did he really say in the letter?

NATALIA, *refusing to give it to him.* Nothing! Nothing at all!

PRINCE, *insisting.* Give it to me!

NATALIA. But you've read it!

PRINCE, *tearing it from her grasp.* What if I have?
I must see what terms to use in my reply.

He opens the letter and reads it again.

NATALIA, *aside.* Oh, God! Now all is lost again!

PRINCE, *perplexed.* Look here! How very curious!
Did you miss this part?

NATALIA. No. Which part?

PRINCE. He leaves the decision to myself!

NATALIA. Oh, that! Yes, he does.

PRINCE. How noble of him, and how dignified!
    That is the way a great man should behave!

NATALIA. Oh, his generosity is boundless!
    Now, do as he asks you and write
    One line in answer! You see,
    It is only the outward form that must be
    Complied with. As soon as he has just that one line from
        you,
    Then everything will go quite smoothly!

PRINCE, *putting the letter aside*. No, my dear Natalia,
    I must think over it until to-morrow.

NATALIA. But—— I cannot understand you!
    What does it mean, this change?
    Why? What is the use of waiting?

PRINCE, *rising abruptly*. I beg of you, do not ask me.
    You haven't seen the implications of his letter!
    "If I am of the opinion that he has done me an injustice!"
    Well, that is one thing I cannot write to him,
    And if you force me now to send an answer,
    By heaven, it will be: "Your Highness, *you* are in the right!"
    He sits down again by the table and reads the letter.

NATALIA, *deathly pale*. You lunatic! What do you say?
    She bends over him.

PRINCE, *taking her hand*. One moment! Wait—— I think I've
      got it!

NATALIA. What?

PRINCE. I know now how I should reply.

NATALIA, *sadly*. Homburg!

PRINCE, *taking up the pen*. I'm listening. What is it?

NATALIA. My dearest Prince! I can only praise
    The generous impulse of your heart.
    But let me tell you this:
    The regiment already has been chosen
    Whose firing-team will pay its last respects to you
    To-morrow morning. A salvo of musket-shot
    Will greet you as you stand upon the mound of earth
    That will be shovelled over you when you are lying
    In the grave it came from.

If your noble conscience now forbids you
To protest against the sentence and to annul it
By writing as his letter asks you to,
Then I can assure you that, as things stand now,
He will consider it his duty to be more than human
And to-morrow morning he will have his orders mercilessly
    carried out!

PRINCE. It doesn't matter any more.

NATALIA. Doesn't matter——?

PRINCE. Let him do as he likes.
I know now that I am doing as I should.

NATALIA, *horror-stricken, approaching him.* You monster!
Have you written it——?

PRINCE. "Signed, Homburg. Fehrbellin, the twelfth——"
There! It's finished!
He puts letter in envelope and seals it.
Ho, there, Franz!

NATALIA. Oh, God in heaven!

PRINCE, *rising, to* FRANZ *who enters.*
Take this letter to His Highness, the Elector.
Exit FRANZ.

I will not appear despicable and weak
Before a man who treats me with such great nobility!
Guilt lies heavily upon my heart,
And I cannot hide it. If his pardon must depend
Only upon my own impertinent objections,
Then I do not merit and do not want forgiveness!

NATALIA, *embracing him.* Oh, let me kiss you!
And if the bullets were to lay you low
This instant, I should still be unable to contain my love!
I would rejoice as well as weep for you,
And cry, for all to hear, "I love you!"
But—if you insist upon the right
To follow the dictates of your heart,
Then I must too!
Count Reuss!

ATTENDANT *opens the door: the* COUNT *enters.*

REUSS. Your Highness!

NATALIA. Now go, and take your letter!
　Go to Arnstein, and to Colonel Kottwitz!
　His Highness the Elector's orders are:
　The regiment must come at once to Fehrbellin!
　I shall wait on its arrival
　Here, at midnight!
　They all leave.

ACT V

SCENE 1

A room in the castle at Fehrbellin. The ELECTOR, *in a night robe, comes out of an adjoining room, followed by* TRUCHSS, HOHENZOLLERN, *and* GOLTZ. PAGES *with lighted torches.*

ELECTOR. Kottwitz? With the regiment of Princess Natalia?
Here in Fehrbellin?

TRUCHSS, *opening a window.* Yes, your noble Highness!
Look, you can see them there,
Drawn up before the castle!

ELECTOR. Well? Will someone give me an explanation?
Who gave orders for the regiment to come to Fehrbellin?

HOHENZOLLERN. Sire, I do not know.

ELECTOR. The orders I gave them were
That they take up quarters in the town of Arnstein!
Go and find Kottwitz! Bring him here!

GOLTZ. Sire, he will presently be here.

ELECTOR. Where is he?

GOLTZ. At the Town Hall, so I hear,
Where the entire general staff is gathered.

ELECTOR. But why?

HOHENZOLLERN. I do not know.

TRUCHSS. Sire, would you allow us for a while
To absent ourselves and join them there?

ELECTOR. In the Town Hall?

HOHENZOLLERN. In the council-chamber of the chiefs of staff.
We gave our word that we would join them there.

ELECTOR, *after a brief hesitation.* You may go.

GOLTZ. Come, then, gentlemen!

The OFFICERS *depart.*

SCENE 2

ELECTOR. Strange! If I were the Dey of Tunis,
I should sound the alarm at such a mysterious conspiracy.
The streets would be strewn with the bodies of my
        janizaries,
And at the doors of my seraglio
I should deploy a ring of cannon!
But as it is old Hans Kottwitz I must deal with,
A native of Preignitz too, who plays the rebel pasha,
I must handle him as it befits
A Brandenburger and a gentleman:
I'll take hold of one of those rare silver locks
He still has on his trusty head
And lead him by it quietly,
Together with his twelve great squadrons,
Back to Arnstein, to his headquarters.
But quietly. Why should I rouse the sleeping town?

*He turns again for a moment to the window, then goes back
to his table and rings. Two* SERVANTS.

You, go down into the streets,
Pretend to be a curious stranger,
And find out all you can!

SERVANT. Yes, Your Highness!

He goes.

ELECTOR, *to the other.* You, go and find my uniform and wig
And bring them here!

The SERVANT *brings them in. The* ELECTOR *puts them on,
with his princely regalia.*

SCENE 3

FIELD-MARSHAL DÖRFLING *enters.*

DÖRFLING. Sire! The army has rebelled!

ELECTOR, *still busy dressing.* Calm, Dörfling! Keep calm.
You know how I detest it when
People enter my apartments unannounced!
What do you want?

DÖRFLING. Forgive me, Your Highness! It is an occurrence
Of particular gravity has brought me here
So unceremoniously.
Colonel Kottwitz without authority has brought
His regiment here; about a hundred officers
Are gathered round him in the Hall of the Knights.
They are circulating a petition
That sets your authority in question.

ELECTOR. I know already. What else can it be
But an intervention in favour of the Prince
Whom the military court condemned to death?

DÖRFLING. Precisely.

ELECTOR. Well, my heart is with them in their cause.

DÖRFLING. But they must be mad! It is said
They want to present their petition to you
In the castle and without delay!
And, should you persevere—Your Highness,
I can hardly say it!—should you persevere
In your unrelenting attitude, they plan
To liberate the Prince by force of arms!

ELECTOR, *fierce.* Who told you that?

DÖRFLING. Who? Why, the Countess von Retzoff,
The cousin of my wife, whom you may trust.
Last evening she visited her uncle's, the magistrate
Von Retzoff's house, where officers
Were quite openly expressing these ideas.

ELECTOR. If it had been a man who told you that,

I might have believed it.
I've only to show myself outside the prison
To scare away those prating heroes from the Prince.

DÖRFLING. Sire, I beseech you, if it is your will
Eventually to free the Prince and pardon him,
Do it now, before some disagreeable circumstance arises!
Every army loves, as you must know, a hero.
Let not this fire that glows in every soldier's breast
Become an unholy and destructive conflagration!
Kottwitz and his supporters still do not know
That I am faithful to you and have warned you of their
  plans.
Send, sire, before it is too late,
His sword back to the Prince, for he has earned it.
History will remember it as a most generous deed
And she will have one sorry deed the less to reckon with!

ELECTOR. First I must consult the Prince, His Highness,
Who as you know was not imprisoned arbitrarily,
And cannot arbitrarily be freed.
But I shall speak to these gentlemen, when they arrive.

DÖRFLING, *aside*. Damnation take it!
He is armoured against every attack!

SCENE 4

Two GUARDS *enter; one is carrying a letter.*

FIRST GUARD. Your Highness! Colonels Kottwitz, Hennings,
  Truchss, and others respectfully request an audience!

ELECTOR, *to the other* GUARD, *taking the letter from him.*
  Is it from
  The Prince of Homburg?

SECOND GUARD. Yes, Your Highness.

ELECTOR. Who gave it you?

SECOND GUARD. The sentinel who guards the outer door,
  To whom it was handed by the Prince's orderly.

  The ELECTOR *sits at the table and reads; after he has read
  the letter, he turns and calls a* PAGE.

ELECTOR. Bring me the Prince's death-warrant!
And also the safe-conduct for Count von Horn,
The Swedish envoy.

PAGE *off.*

To the FIRST GUARD.

Bring in Colonel Kottwitz and his followers!

SCENE 5

COLONELS KOTTWITZ *and* HENNINGS, COUNTS TRUCHSS, HOHEN-
ZOLLERN, *and* SPARREN, COUNT REUSS, CAPTAINS GOLTZ *and*
STRANZ *and other* COLONELS *and* OFFICERS *enter.*

KOTTWITZ, *presenting the petition.* My noble sovereign, sire,
Allow me to present to you, with all respect,
And in the name of the entire army, this petition.

ELECTOR. Kottwitz, before I will take it, you must tell me,
Who gave you orders to come to Fehrbellin?

KOTTWITZ, *surprised.* With the dragoons?

ELECTOR. Yes, with the regiment.
I had assigned you to quarters in Arnstein.

KOTTWITZ. Sire, it was on your orders I came here.

ELECTOR. Indeed? Show me the order.

KOTTWITZ. Here it is, Your Highness.

ELECTOR, *reading.* "Natalia. Fehrbellin.
On the orders of my noble uncle,
Prince Friedrich Wilhelm,
Elector of Brandenburg——"

KOTTWITZ. By thunder, sire, I hope
You knew about this order?

ELECTOR. No, no, you see. . . .
Who was it who brought the order to you?

KOTTWITZ. Count Reuss!

ELECTOR, *after a short pause.*
Well, Kottwitz, you are thrice welcome,
And, after all, your arrival is most opportune.

Colonel Homburg having been condemned to death,
The twelve squadrons under your command are chosen
To pay him the last respects to-morrow, at dawn.

KOTTWITZ, *horrified.* Sire!

ELECTOR, *giving back the order.* Is your regiment still standing
In front of the castle, Colonel,
In the cold and foggy air of night?

KOTTWITZ. I'm sorry, it was so dark, sire——

ELECTOR. Why have you not dismissed them?

KOTTWITZ. Your Highness, I *have* dismissed them.
They have been quartered on the town,
As you commanded.

ELECTOR, *turning towards the window.*
What? A few moments ago——
Well! You've soon found stabling for your horses, Colonel.
That is all to the good! I congratulate you! Now!
What brings you here? What news have you got for me?

KOTTWITZ. Sire, this petition from your faithful army.

ELECTOR. Give it here!

KOTTWITZ. But what you have just said—— Your words
Have overthrown my hopes completely!

ELECTOR. What words have cast away can be retrieved by
words.
Reading.
"Petition to His Highness, the Elector of Brandenburg,
Imploring the supreme favour of mercy for
Our beloved general, now most grievously incarcerated,
Prince Friedrich Arthur von Hessen-Homburg."
To the assembled OFFICERS.
Gentlemen, that is a noble name!
It is not unworthy of your universal approbation.
He looks at the petition again.
Who is the author of this plea?

KOTTWITZ. It is I.

ELECTOR. Is the Prince acquainted with the contents?

KOTTWITZ. Not in the slightest! It is we alone

Who have conceived and drafted it.

ELECTOR. I request your patience for a moment.

He goes to the table and reads through the petition. A long pause.

Hm! Curious!—— So, Kottwitz, you old warrior,
You take the Prince's defence upon your shoulders?
You approve his action in attacking Wrangel
Before the sign was given?

KOTTWITZ. Yes, Your Highness. Kottwitz approves his action.

ELECTOR. You were of quite a different opinion
Upon the field of battle.

KOTTWITZ. I had not summed up the situation well enough.
I should have accepted with greater readiness
The Prince's decision, for he is a great tactician.
The Swedes were wavering on their left flank,
But their right flank was sending out
Fresh reinforcements. If he had waited, sire,
For your command, they would have captured our redoubts
And victory would never have been ours.

ELECTOR. Yes. You like to fancy it was so.
But I had despatched Hennings, as you know,
To cut off the retreat to the Swedish bridge-heads
Which covered Wrangel's rear-guard.
If you cavalry officers had respected my orders,
Hennings would successfully have brought off his ma-
   noeuvre.
In two hours he could have seized the bridges,
Set them on fire, positioned himself along the Rhine,
And Wrangel would have been annihilated, root and
   branch,
Lost in the marshes and the hidden swamps.

KOTTWITZ. Only a bungling novice, sire, not a soldier like
   yourself,
Would want to snatch at Fate's most glorious wreath!
Until to-day, you always took whatever Fate might offer,
However small a triumph it might be.
The dragon that was bleeding Brandenburg to death
Was routed: for one day, was that not enough?

What if he lies a week or so and licks his wounds
Until they heal again? We know now how to conquer him,
And are full of eagerness to take him on again!
Let us get hand to hand again with Wrangel,
And by thunder we'll have him pushed back to the Baltic!

ELECTOR. You old fool, what right have you to hope for that,
When any hot-head takes it upon himself
To jump upon my chariot of war and seize the reins?
Do you believe that disobedience will always be
Crowned with a laurel wreath by smiling Fortune?
I do not relish victory that, out of the blue,
Falls into my lap, a sport of chance!
I will uphold the law, the goddess
To whom I owe my life, my throne, my crown,
And who conceived for me a race of triumphs!

KOTTWITZ. Sire. The supreme, the very highest law
That can govern such a noble heart as yours
Is not a law that can be taken at the letter of your will.
It is your country, and it is your crown.
It is the wearer of that crown—yourself.
What does it signify for men like you, a rule
Which says that an enemy cannot be conquered
Unless he lies before you in the dust, with all his flags?
The only and the highest rule is conquest!
Will you brandish in your fist like a living sword
The army burning with desire to serve you,
Or let it hang, a lifeless blade,
Upon your golden girdle?
A poor fool it must have been, deprived of sense and feeling,
Who framed those rules! And it is a bad,
Short-sighted policy that, because a human instinct
Once proved fatal, determines to forget
The score of times when only instinct,
And obedience to instinct, saved the day!
And on the field of battle, do you think
I'd shed my blood for honour or for gold?
God forfend! My blood's too precious for such small rewards!
No! My best, my happiest reward, the one I always hope
    to win

And work for freely, independently, and owing
No account of it to any man—that is to serve
The greater glory and the majesty of Brandenburg, defend
The fame and honour of your own immortal name!
That is the reward for which I sell my heart!
Grant that for this unbidden victory now
You doom the Prince of Homburg,
And if I, to-morrow, wandering like a shepherd
Through the woods and mountains with my squadrons,
By chance encounter opportunities for victory,
By God! I should be a miserable coward if
I did not act with vigour, as our Prince once did,
And snatch another triumph for the fame of Brandenburg!
If you then came to me, Your Highness,
With your rule-book in your hand, and said:
"Kottwitz, you have forfeited your head!"
Why, then, I'd up and answer: I know, sire;
Take it; here it is; for when I swore the oath
That bound me, head and hand to you and to your crown,
My heart and soul were in it, and my head as well,
And I would deny you nothing that belongs to you!

ELECTOR. I cannot hold my own against you,
You brave and wonderful old soldier!
Your words have pierced my heart with crafty oratory;
My heart, which, as you know, is full of love for you.
But I must call an advocate, one
Who can plead my cause far better than myself!

He rings for a SERVANT, *who enters.*

The Prince of Homburg! Have him brought here from
The prison!

The SERVANT *goes.*

He will teach you, Kottwitz, I assure you,
What obedience and discipline should be!
He has, at any rate, sent me a letter here
That reads quite differently from
The subtle disquisitions upon freedom
That you have served up to me here to-day
As if I were a new boy in the bottom class
At some pretentious military college!

He returns to his desk and reads the letter.

KOTTWITZ, *astounded.* Who? What?

HENNINGS. The Prince himself?

TRUCHSS. It can't be!

Rather ill at ease, the OFFICERS *talk together.*

ELECTOR. From whom is this other letter?

HOHENZOLLERN. From me, sire.

ELECTOR, *reading.* "Proof that his Highness the Elector
Was himself responsible for the Prince's act——"
Now, by heaven, that's going a bit too far!
Do you mean to say you throw the whole responsibility
For the Prince's error on myself, Hohenzollen?

HOHENZOLLERN. I do, sire.

ELECTOR. By Jupiter! Will wonders never cease?
One man explains to me he isn't guilty:
The other that *I'm* guilty!
I must confess I am curious to see how you will state your
case.

HOHENZOLLERN. If you will be so good, sire, and recollect that
night
In which we found the Prince asleep upon a seat
In the garden underneath an oak, you will remember
He was holding in his hand a laurel wreath and seemed
To be dreaming of the victory on the coming day.
You, sire, desiring to sound the deepest motives of his heart,
Removed the garland from his hands and wound
Your golden chain about it. You were smiling.
Then you gave the wreath, entwined with gold,
To the lady who is your noble niece.
At such a heavenly sight, the Prince
Rises in confusion, for he longs to take
So dear an object from such lovely hands.
But then, you swiftly move away from him,
Drawing the Princess backwards with you;
The door opens to receive you;
The lovely maiden and the gold-hung laurel wreath
Vanish.

And he, alone, and bearing in his hand a glove
That comes from he knows not what fair hand,
Remains behind at midnight in the garden
Of the moonlit castle.

ELECTOR. What glove?

HOHENZOLLERN. Sire, let me finish!
The whole thing was just a game; but to him,
I later learnt, it meant much more.
For, when I crept towards him and, as if by chance,
Through one of the garden's lower gates
And woke him, and brought him to his senses once again,
The memory caused a flood of joy to fill his being.
You cannot, sire, imagine anything more touching!
He related the whole event, down to the smallest detail,
As if it were a dream that he remembered.
And so vividly did he imagine he had dreamed
That the conviction grew in him
That heaven had given him a sign which meant
That everything—the maiden, the wreath, the golden chain—
Would be accorded him by God upon the day of battle.

ELECTOR. Hm! How strange! But what about the glove?

HOHENZOLLERN. This fragment of his dream, the one reality
        remaining from his vision,
Both destroys and strengthens his belief.
At first he looks upon it with wide-open eyes.
The glove is white: it would appear
It comes from a lady's hand—yet
As he has encountered no one in the moonlit garden
From whom he could have taken it,
He puts it from his mind, forgets what he cannot under-
        stand,
And tucks it absent-mindedly into the collar of his coat.

ELECTOR. Well? What then?

HOHENZOLLERN. Then he enters the castle, taking his notebooks
And his pencil, to concentrate most seriously upon
The marshal's orders, which he is to note
For reference on the field of battle.
Your own lady, sire, and the Princess, dressed for travelling,
Happen to be waiting also in the hall.

Who can imagine the immeasurable astonishment
That seized him when he saw
That the glove out of his dream
Was the one the Princess sought!
Time and again the marshal called him to attention:
"The Prince of Homburg!" "What are your orders, sir?"
Is all he can reply, trying to collect his wits.
He was so ringed with wonders,
A thunderbolt could have fallen, and——

He stops.

ELECTOR. Was it the Princess' glove?

HOHENZOLLERN. He stands like a stone, his pencil frozen in his
    hand.
And yet he is alive, a living statue!
But all feeling is extinguished in him
By so many marvels all at once.
Only in the morning, when
The sound of the cannon brings him to his senses,
He turns to me, and asks:
"Heinrich, what was it Marshal Dörfling said to me
Yesterday, concerning the order of battle?"

DÖRFLING. Sire, I can vouch for Hohenzollern's words.
The Prince, I recollect,
Paid no attention to whatever I was saying.
I'd often known him to be rather cloudy-headed,
But never before that day
Have I seen him in a fit of such intense abstraction.

ELECTOR. Well, now, if I have understood you both aright,
This is the crowning proof of Homburg's innocence.
If I had not played my little game on this young dreamer,
I should not have anything to reproach him with to-day?
He wouldn't have been distracted at the meeting
Nor disobedient on the field of battle?
Eh? Well? Isn't that your meaning, gentlemen?

HOHENZOLLERN. Sire, I leave you to draw your own con-
    clusions.

ELECTOR. Then you are either an idiot or a silly fool!
If you had not called me down into the garden,
Then, as my curiosity would not have been aroused,

I should not have played my harmless game upon this
    dreamer.
And so I feel quite able to declare
That the one responsible for Homburg's error
Was not me—but you yourself!
Oh! What Delphic oracles I have for officers!

HOHENZOLLERN. Sire, I can say no more. But I am sure
My words have left their mark within your heart!

SCENE 6

Enter an OFFICER.

OFFICER. Your Highness, the Prince of Homburg will presently
    appear!

ELECTOR. Good. Bring him here.

OFFICER. Sire, a moment's grace.
As he was passing by the chapel
He asked the gatekeeper to admit him to the graveyard.

ELECTOR. The graveyard?

OFFICER. Yes, Your Highness.

ELECTOR. Why?

OFFICER. To tell you the truth, sire, I hardly know.
It seems, he wanted to see the tomb
To which your sentence has condemned him.

The OFFICERS *gather together and talk.*

ELECTOR. Very well! As soon as he comes, let him in.

He goes back to the papers on his desk.

TRUCHSS. Here he comes now, with the officers of the guard.

SCENE 7

Enter the PRINCE OF HOMBURG: OFFICERS *of the guard.*

ELECTOR. My dear young Prince,
　I have summoned you here to come to my rescue!
　Colonel Kottwitz has presented me
　With this petition in your favour,
　Signed by a hundred noble names:
　The army, it appears, demands your release
　And disapproves the sentence of the court.
　Read it and see for yourself!
　　He gives HOMBURG *the petition.*

PRINCE *gives it a brief glance, then turns to address the circle
　of* OFFICERS.
　Kottwitz, give me your hand, old friend!
　What you have done for me is more
　Than I deserved from you,
　Whom I so cavalierly treated in the field!
　And now, go back, as swiftly as you came,
　To Arnstein and do not grieve for me.
　I have thought it over well and have decided
　To accept the punishment to which I was condemned.
　　He gives the petition back to KOTTWITZ.

KOTTWITZ. No, you can never——

HOHENZOLLERN. Does he *want* to die?

TRUCHSS. He cannot and he shall not die.

SEVERAL OFFICERS, *coming towards the* PRINCE.
　Your Highness! We beg of you! Prince! Listen to us!

PRINCE. No. I have made my decision. It is unalterable.
　I wish to glorify the sacred laws of war
　That I, in view of the entire army, scorned and violated.
　It is a freely-given and a willing death.
　Oh, my brothers-in-arms, what is a victory worth
　That I perhaps might gain against the Swedish general
　Beside the victory we shall gloriously win to-morrow

Over the most pernicious enemies we know,
The enemies within ourselves: defiance, arrogance?
A triumph over Wrangel is a paltry thing.
As for the foreign foes who would subdue us to their yoke,
Whether I live or die, you know they cannot win,
And that the sons of Brandenburg
Will walk in freedom on their native earth.
For it is theirs, and all the splendour of its plains
Belongs to them alone!

KOTTWITZ. My dear Prince! Friend or son? What shall I call
 you?

TRUCHSS. Dear God in heaven!

KOTTWITZ. Let me kiss your hand!

They all crowd round him.

PRINCE, *turning away from them to address the* ELECTOR.
My sovereign, you whom I used to call—
For once I had the right, now cast away—
By the gentler name of father, I cast myself
Before you, and my heart
Is full to overflowing!
Forgive me, if on the morning of decision
I served you with too-impetuous eagerness:
My death will help to wash away my sin.
My heart now is reconciled and full of ease:
It accepts the justice of your will.
But comfort it by saying that your own great heart
Is free from anger too! And let it grant me,
In my hour of death, one more request!

ELECTOR. Speak, hero! Tell me your desire.
I give you my soldier's word:
Your wish, whatever it is, shall be respected.

PRINCE. Sire, do not purchase with your niece's hand
The peace that you must win from Sweden.
Dismiss from your camp the go-between
Who made you such an ignominious proposal!
Give him his answer in a round of shot!

ELECTOR *kisses* HOMBURG's *forehead.*
It shall be done, my son. With this last kiss,

I give you my promise.
Why should there be another sacrifice
To war's misfortunes?
May every word that you have spoken be the seed
Of new and greater victories for Brandenburg,
And be the death of Sweden!
"She is affianced to the Prince of Homburg," I shall tell him.
Victor of Fehrbellin, who gave his life for victory!
His spirit will defend her on the field of battle,
For he is dead but marches on forever with the foremost
    flags!

He embraces the PRINCE, *and raises him.*

PRINCE. Now you have given back my life to me!
I pray that every triumph, every blessing
May now fall upon your hero's head in gay profusion!
Go, my sovereign lord, do battle!
Vanquish the globe itself, if it defy you,
For it is your duty and your right!

ELECTOR. Guards, accompany His Highness back to prison!

SCENE 8

NATALIA *and the* ELECTOR'S WIFE *appear at the door, followed by* COURT LADIES.

NATALIA. No! Do not speak to me of what is fitting:
What, in this hour of peril, is
More fitting than my love for him?
Oh, my dear, unhappy friend!

PRINCE, *brusquely.* Let me go!

TRUCHSS. Never, Prince! Never!

Several OFFICERS *bar his way.*

PRINCE. Take me away!

HOHENZOLLERN, *to* ELECTOR. Your Highness, if your heart——

PRINCE, *tearing himself away from them.* You tyrants!
Would you have them drag me to the place of execution
Bound hand and foot with chains?

Let me away! I have settled my account with life.
He goes with GUARDS.

NATALIA. Oh, Earth, receive me!
Why should I look upon the sun again?
She weeps on the bosom of her aunt.

SCENE 9

DÖRFLING. God and creation! Must it come to this?
The ELECTOR *is speaking aside to an* OFFICER.

KOTTWITZ, *coldly.* My lord, after what has happened,
Are we released now from to-morrow's——

ELECTOR. No! I shall discharge you when the time has come.
*He looks at him a moment. Then he takes the papers that
the* PAGE *brought in and turns away from the table towards
the* FIELD-MARSHAL.

Here is the safe-conduct for Count Horn!
This would be the Prince's wish, that I am bound to honour:
In three days' time, we declare war again!
A silence. He casts a glance at the death-warrant.

Gentlemen, I lay the decision in your hands.
The Prince of Homburg, during the past year,
Has, through his thoughtlessness and disobedience,
Cost me two of my most brilliant victories.
He also spoilt a third for me.
Now he's a graduate in the school of war,
Can you entrust yourselves to him again? A fourth time?

KOTTWITZ *and* TRUCHSS, *together.* Your Highness means—— Do
we understand——

ELECTOR. Can you? Can you?

KOTTWITZ. Sire, by the living God,
You could be standing in peril of your life
On the very edge of some steep precipice,
He wouldn't lift a finger now to save you
Or ever draw his sword again without your full permission!

ELECTOR, *tearing up the death-warrant.*
  Come, then, my friends,
  Follow me to the garden.
  They all depart.

SCENE 10

The setting is as in Act I. It is night again. The PRINCE *is
led, a bandage round his eyes, through the lower garden
gate by* CAPTAIN REUSS. OFFICERS OF THE GUARD. *In the distance, the muted drums of a funeral march.*

PRINCE. Now, Immortality, you are entirely mine!
  You shine, with the radiance of a thousand suns,
  Through my eyes' dark bandages into my very soul!
  My arms feel like a pair of slowly spreading wings
  That bear my spirit through the quiet lofts of air;
  And as a ship whose sail fills with the evening wind
  Sees the lighted harbour sink along the rising waves,
  So, like the happy shore, my dying life
  Drowns slowly in the dusk of death:
  Now I can distinguish only forms and colours,
  And under my weightless feet
  Drift only clouds and those ethereal vapours
  That are the mists of time.
He sits down on the garden-seat beneath the oak. CAPTAIN
STRANZ *draws away from him and gazes up towards the
top of the slope.*

PRINCE. Ah! How sweet the midnight violet smells!
  Did you not notice how it smells?
STRANZ comes back again.

STRANZ. They are gillyflowers and pinks.

PRINCE. Gillyflowers? How do they come to be here?

STRANZ. I don't know. It seems a maiden
  Planted them here.
  Would you like one?

PRINCE. Thank you. When I go home
  I'll put it in water.

SCENE 11

Enter the ELECTOR, *with the laurel wreath, round which the golden chain is hung;* HIS WIFE, PRINCESS NATALIA, FIELD-MARSHAL DÖRFLING, COLONELS KOTTWITZ, HOHENZOLLERN, GOLTZ, *etc.* LADIES OF THE COURT, OFFICERS *and* PAGES *bearing torches appear on the balustraded slope.* HOHENZOLLERN *comes with a handkerchief, which he waves at* CAPTAIN STRANZ, *who then leaves the* PRINCE *and goes to speak to the* GUARDS *in the background.*

PRINCE. Dear Stranz, what is all this light?

STRANZ, *returning to him.* Prince, would you kindly rise?

PRINCE. What is it now?

STRANZ. Nothing you need be afraid of!
I want only to unbind your eyes.

PRINCE. So the hour of my deliverance has come at last?

STRANZ. Yes! Look now and live!

The ELECTOR *gives the wreath, on which the golden chain is shining, to the* PRINCESS, *takes her by the hand, and leads her down the slope, followed by all* LADIES *and* GENTLEMEN. *Surrounded by* TORCH-BEARERS, *the* PRINCESS *goes up to the* PRINCE, *who stares at her astounded, lays the wreath on his head, the chain round his neck, and presses his hand to her heart. The* PRINCE *falls unconscious.*

NATALIA. Look! His waking has killed him with happiness!

HOHENZOLLERN, *lifting him up.* Help me! Help!

ELECTOR. Let the thunder of the royal cannon wake him!

Cannon are fired. A triumphal march. The castle is illuminated in every window.

KOTTWITZ. Hail! Hail to the Prince of Homburg!

OFFICERS. Hail! Hail! Hail!

ALL. Hail to the victor of Fehrbellin!

A moment's silence.

PRINCE. Tell me: is this a dream?

KOTTWITZ. A dream: what else?

OFFICERS. To horse! Away!

TRUCHSS. Into battle!

DÖRFLING. To victory! To victory!

ALL. Death to all the enemies of Brandenburg!

THREE NOTES

1

The Goethe, Schiller, and Kleist plays that have been included in English-language anthologies between 1900 and 1950 are listed in *Index to Plays in Collections* by John H. Ottemiller (New York: The Scarecrow Press, Third Edition, 1957) with the exception of an abridged version of *The Broken Pitcher* in Winifred Katzin's *Short Plays from Twelve Countries* (London, Harrap, 1937). Collected editions of Goethe and Schiller were issued in Bohn's Standard Library over a century ago and remained in print for some decades. Details on these and related items can be found in the standard bibliography of the field: *A Critical Bibliography of German Literature in English Translation, 1481–1927*, by B. Q. Morgan, Second Edition, 1938, (Stanford, California: Stanford University Press, 1938). *Käthchen of Heilbronn* appears in *Fiction and Fantasy of German Romance,* ed. Pierce and Schreiber (New York: Oxford University Press, 1927). *The Feud of the Schroffensteins* appears in the periodical *Poet Lore,* Volume 25. A complete translation of *The Broken Pitcher* was published by the University of North Carolina Press in 1961. Translations of *The Prince of Homburg* have been recently issued by both the Liberal Arts Press and Barron's Educational Series.

Perhaps the most serviceable books in English concerning our three German playwrights (*as* playwrights) are: Ronald Peacock's *Goethe's Major Plays* (New York: Hill and Wang, 1959); F. L. Stahl's *Friedrich Schiller's Drama* (New York: Oxford University Press, 1954); and F. L. Stahl's *Heinrich von Kleist's Dramas* (Oxford: Basil Blackwell, 1948.). A new edition of Stahl's *Kleist* is promised for 1962: the book is distributed in the United States, at least in theory, by Macmillan. Ronald Peacock's important essay, "Goethe's Version of Poetic Drama," is included in the 1960 edition of his *The*

Poet in the Theatre (New York: Hill and Wang Dramabooks.)

The following works of Schiller are currently published in paper back by the Frederick Ungar Publishing Company of New York: *Friedrich Schiller, an Anthology for Our Time; Don Carlos; Mary Stuart* and *The Maid of Orleans; Wallenstein.* Readers interested in the further resources of the paper back field should consult the latest edition of *Paperbound Books in Print* (New York: R. R. Bowker Company); it is issued quarterly. One item of special interest: Goethe's *Urfaust* has at last been published in English—in Barron's Educational Series.

2

The principles governing translations issued under my editorship were briefly suggested in the note, "Adaptation vs. Translation" in *The Modern Theatre,* Volumes 1 and 2. As in the earlier series, each translator has been given his head: one is allowed to say, "I can get my effects without departing an inch from the original," another to claim the right to make such departures as he considers necessary. This is not a matter only of the translator's temperament and abilities. Different materials demand different treatment. I applaud, for example, Mr. Hamburger's utter fidelity to Goethe's text while appreciating Mr. Kirkup's assumption that a like fidelity to Schiller could only produce a tiresome piece of English. That is partly because Schiller is not so great a writer: reverences is due only to supreme genius. But it is partly also that the English language cannot be used in Schiller's way. We have to be much more sparing in our use of declamatory rhetoric or we become either funny or dull. (The French had Corneille; the Germans, Schiller; we had only *The Conquest of Granada* and *Cato* and *Virginius.*) One should not pass from the realization that the adequate translation of literature is impossible to the conclusion that plodding literalness is the least of the possible evils. Schiller cannot be translated in his totality. But more of him comes through in such a free treatment as Mr.

Kirkup's than in any of those line-by-line deflations of his genius which purport to be faithful renderings.

In short, the Schiller texts in the present book stand a little apart from the Goethe and Kleist. Mr. Kirkup's *Don Carlos* is Schiller recreated by a man of 1958. The Mellish-Bentley *Mary Stuart* is different again. Joseph Mellish, an Englishman resident in Jena, was a personal friend of both Goethe and Schiller and is often mentioned in their mutual correspondence. The translation which Schiller commissioned from Mellish before *Mary Stuart* had even been published in German is the basis of the present text. I thought there was something to be gained by the use of the English of 1800 and I knew I couldn't attempt such English myself—except a few words at a time—without courting disaster. As Mellish achieved one of the best versions of Schiller ever made, there was, in any case, no reason not to enlist his services. On the other hand, what even his rendering loses of Schiller's rhythm and glamour makes his script seem long. And seeming long (as against great length *per se*) is a fault. Nor was it to be corrected by ommissions. Even after large cuts were made, the play seemed long. Even short passages from it seemed long! This was due to a manner of saying things which we aptly call long-winded. Everyone took many, many words to get out the simplest thought. It was necessary, not merely to omit certain sentences and speeches, but to compress the sentences and speeches that remained. Necessarily, the task entailed some new writing. The curious are invited to consult Mellish's original effort which was in print throughout most of the nineteenth century.

By offering less of Schiller than Mellish did, I hope to be offering more.

3

It has been objected that Mr. Kirkup's brilliant stage version of *Don Carlos* shortens excessively two of the key scenes. Two "missing passages" of some importance are reprinted here from the old Bohn edition. The first would follow "Freedom of

thought/ Is what our people need" on page 163, above; the
other would follow "Yes. Yes. Go on." on page 193, above.

(a)

Posa casts himself at the King's feet.

KING, *surprised, turns away his face, then again looks towards
the Marquis.* Enthusiast most strange! arise; but I——

MARQUIS. Look round on all the glorious face of nature,
On freedom it is founded—see how rich,
Through freedom it has grown. The great Creator
Bestows upon the worm its drop of dew,
And gives free will a triumph in abodes
Where lone corruption reigns. See your creation,
How small, how poor! The rustling of a leaf
Alarms the mighty lord of Christendom.
Each virtue makes you quake with fear. While he
Not to disturb fair freedom's blest appearance,
Permits the frightful ravages of evil
To waste his fair domains. The great Creator
We see not—he conceals himself within
His own eternal laws. The sceptic sees
Their operation but beholds not Him.
"Wherefore a God?" he cries, "the world itself
Suffices for itself!" And Christian prayer
Ne'er praised him more than doth this blasphemy.

KING. And will you undertake to raise up this
Exalted standard of weak human nature
In my dominions?

MARQUIS.   You can do it, sire.
Who else? Devote to your own people's bliss
The kingly power, which has too long enriched
The greatness of the throne alone. Restore
The prostrate dignity of human nature,
And let the subject be, what once he was,
The end and object of the monarch's care,
Bound by no duty save a brother's love.
And when mankind is to itself restored,
Roused to a sense of its own innate worth,

When freedom's lofty virtues proudly flourish——
Then, sire, when you have made your own wide realms
The happiest in the world, it then may be
Your duty to subdue the universe.

KING. I've heard you to the end. Far differently
I find, than in the minds of other men,
The world exists in yours.

(b)

MARQUIS.   To this point
I'm guiltless. But the unaccustomed beams
Of royal favour dazzled me. The rumour,
As I had well foreseen, soon reached thine ears,
But by false delicacy basely bribed,
And blinded by my vain desire to end
My enterprise alone, I kept concealed
From friendship's ear my hazardous design.
This was my fatal error; here I failed.
I know it. My self-confidence was madness.
Pardon that confidence. 'Twas founded, Carlos,
Upon our friendship's everlasting base.

At two points I have brought this last speech closer to the
German original.

E.B.
1962